MW01031231

Expert Python Programming
Second Edition

Become an ace Python programmer by learning best coding practices and advance-level concepts with Python 3.5

Michał Jaworski

Tarek Ziadé

BIRMINGHAM - MUMBAI

Expert Python Programming
Second Edition

Copyright © 2016 Packt Publishing

All rights reserved. No part of this book may be reproduced, stored in a retrieval system, or transmitted in any form or by any means, without the prior written permission of the publisher, except in the case of brief quotations embedded in critical articles or reviews.

Every effort has been made in the preparation of this book to ensure the accuracy of the information presented. However, the information contained in this book is sold without warranty, either express or implied. Neither the authors, nor Packt Publishing, and its dealers and distributors will be held liable for any damages caused or alleged to be caused directly or indirectly by this book.

Packt Publishing has endeavored to provide trademark information about all of the companies and products mentioned in this book by the appropriate use of capitals. However, Packt Publishing cannot guarantee the accuracy of this information.

First published: September 2008

Second edition: May 2016

Production reference: 1160516

Published by Packt Publishing Ltd.
Livery Place
35 Livery Street
Birmingham B3 2PB, UK.

ISBN 978-1-78588-685-0

www.packtpub.com

Credits

Authors
Michał Jaworski
Tarek Ziadé

Reviewer
Facundo Batista

Commissioning Editor
Kunal Parikh

Acquisition Editor
Meeta Rajani

Technical Editor
Pankaj Kadam

Copy Editor
Laxmi Subramanian

Proofreader
Safis Editing

Indexer
Rekha Nair

Graphics
Jason Monteiro

Production Coordinator
Aparna Bhagat

Cover Work
Aparna Bhagat

About the Authors

Michał Jaworski has 7 years of experience in Python. He is also the creator of graceful, which is a REST framework built on top of falcon. He has been in various roles at different companies: from an ordinary full-stack developer through software architect to VP of engineering in a fast-paced start-up company. He is currently a lead backend engineer in TV Store team at Opera Software. He is highly experienced in designing high-performance distributed services. He is also an active contributor to some of the popular Python open source projects.

Tarek Ziadé is an engineering manager at Mozilla, working with a team specialized in building web services in Python at scale for Firefox. He's contributed to the Python packaging effort and has worked with a lot of different Python web frameworks since Zope in the early days.

Tarek has also created Afpy, the French Python User Group, and has written two books on Python in French. He has delivered numerous talks and tutorials in French at international events such as Solutions Linux, PyCon, OSCON, and EuroPython.

About the Reviewer

Facundo Batista is a specialist in the Python programming language, with more than 15 years of experience with it. He is a core developer of the language, and a member by merit of the Python Software Foundation. He also received the 2009 Community Service Award for organizing PyCon Argentina and the Argentinian Python community as well as contributions to the standard library and work in translating the Python documentation.

He delivers talks in the main Python conferences in Argentina and other countries (The United States and Europe). In general, he has strong distributed collaborative experience from being involved in FLOSS development and working with people around the globe for more than 10 years.

He worked as a telecommunication engineer at Telefónica Móviles and Ericsson, and as a Python expert at Cyclelogic (developer in chief) and Canonical (senior software developer, his current position).

He also loves playing tennis, and is a father of two wonderful children.

www.PacktPub.com

eBooks, discount offers, and more

Did you know that Packt offers eBook versions of every book published, with PDF and ePub files available? You can upgrade to the eBook version at www.PacktPub.com and as a print book customer, you are entitled to a discount on the eBook copy. Get in touch with us at customercare@packtpub.com for more details.

At www.PacktPub.com, you can also read a collection of free technical articles, sign up for a range of free newsletters and receive exclusive discounts and offers on Packt books and eBooks.

https://www2.packtpub.com/books/subscription/packtlib

Do you need instant solutions to your IT questions? PacktLib is Packt's online digital book library. Here, you can search, access, and read Packt's entire library of books.

Why subscribe?

- Fully searchable across every book published by Packt
- Copy and paste, print, and bookmark content
- On demand and accessible via a web browser

Table of Contents

Preface

Python rocks!

From the earliest version in the late 1980s to the current version, it has evolved with the same philosophy: providing a multiparadigm programming language with readability and productivity in mind.

People used to see Python as yet another scripting language and wouldn't feel right about using it to build large systems. However, over the years and thanks to some pioneer companies, it became obvious that Python could be used to build almost any kind of system.

In fact, many developers that come from another language are charmed by Python and make it their language of choice.

This is something you are probably aware of if you have bought this book, so there's no need to convince you about the merits of the language any further.

This book is written to express many years of experience of building all kinds of applications with Python, from small system scripts done in a couple of hours to very large applications written by dozens of developers over several years.

It describes the best practices used by developers when working with Python.

This book covers some topics that do not focus on the language itself but rather on the tools and techniques used to work with it.

In other words, this book describes how an advanced Python developer works every day.

What this book covers

Chapter 1, Current Status of Python, showcases the current state of the Python language and its community. It shows how Python is constantly changing, why it is changing, and also why these facts are important for anyone who wants to call themselves a Python professional. This chapter also features the most popular and canonical ways of working in Python—popular productivity tools and conventions that are de facto standards now.

Chapter 2, Syntax Best Practices – below the Class Level, presents iterators, generators, descriptors, and so on, in an advanced way. It also covers useful notes about Python idioms and internal CPython types implementations with their computational complexities as a rationale for showcased idioms.

Chapter 3, Syntax Best Practices – above the Class Level, explains syntax best practices, but focuses above the class level. It covers more advanced object-oriented concepts and mechanisms available in Python. This knowledge is required in order to understand the last section of the chapter, which presents different approaches to metaprogramming in Python.

Chapter 4, Choosing Good Names, involves choosing good names. It is an extension to PEP 8 with naming best practices, but also gives tips on designing good APIs.

Chapter 5, Writing a Package, explains how to create the Python package and which tools to use in order to properly distribute it on the official Python Package Index or any other package repository. Information about packages is supplemented with a brief review of the tools that allow you to create standalone executables from Python sources.

Chapter 6, Deploying Code, aims mostly at Python web developers and backend engineers, because it deals with code deployments. It explains how Python applications should be built in order to be easily deployed to remote servers and what tools you can use in order to automate that process. This chapter dovetails with *Chapter 5, Writing a Package*, because it shows how packages and private package repositories can be used to streamline your application deployments.

Chapter 7, Python Extensions in Other Languages, explains why writing C extensions for Python might be a good solution sometimes. It also shows that it is not as hard as it seems to be as long as the proper tools are used.

Chapter 8, Managing Code, gives some insight into how a project code base can be managed and explains how to set up various continuous development processes.

Chapter 9, Documenting Your Project, covers documentation and provides tips on technical writing and how Python projects should be documented.

Chapter 10, Test-Driven Development, explains the basic principles of test-driven development and the tools that can be used in this development methodology.

Chapter 11, Optimization – General Principles and Profiling Techniques, explains optimization. It provides profiling techniques and an optimization strategy guideline.

Chapter 12, Optimization – Some Powerful Techniques, extends *Chapter 11, Optimization – General Principles and Profiling Techniques*, by providing some common solutions to the performance problems that are often found in Python programs.

Chapter 13, Concurrency, introduces the vast topic of concurrency in Python. It explains what concurrency is, when it might be necessary to write concurrent applications, and what are the main approaches to concurrency for Python programmers.

Chapter 14, Useful Design Patterns, concludes the book with a set of useful design patterns and example implementations in Python.

What you need for this book

This book is written for developers who work under any operating system for which Python 3 is available.

This is not a book for beginners, so I assume you have Python installed in your environment or know how to install it. Anyway, this book takes into account the fact that not everyone needs to be fully aware of the latest Python features or officially recommended tools. This is why the first chapter provides a recap of common utilities (such as virtual environments and pip) that are now considered standard tools of professional Python developers.

Who this book is for

This book is written for Python developers who wish to go further in mastering Python. And by developers I mean mostly professionals, so programmers who write software in Python for a living. This is because it focuses mostly on tools and practices that are crucial for creating performant, reliable, and maintainable software in Python.

It does not mean that hobbyists won't find anything interesting. This book should be great for anyone who is interested in learning advance-level concepts with Python. Anyone who has basic Python skills should be able to follow the content of the book, although it might require some additional effort from less experienced programmers. It should also be a good introduction to Python 3.5 for those who are still a bit behind and continue to use Python in version 2.7 or older.

Finally, the groups that should benefit most from reading this book are web developers and backend engineers. This is because of two topics featured in here that are especially important in their areas of work: reliable code deployments and concurrency.

Conventions

In this book, you will find a number of text styles that distinguish between different kinds of information. Here are some examples of these styles and an explanation of their meaning.

Code words in text, database table names, folder names, filenames, file extensions, pathnames, dummy URLs, user input, and Twitter handles are shown as follows: "Use the `str.encode(encoding, errors)` method, which encodes the string using a registered codec for encoding."

A block of code is set as follows:

```
[print("hello world")
print "goodbye python2"
```

When we wish to draw your attention to a particular part of a code block, the relevant lines or items are set in bold:

```
cdef long long fibonacci_cc(unsigned int n) nogil:
    if n < 2:
        return n
    else:
        return fibonacci_cc(n - 1) + fibonacci_cc(n - 2)
```

Any command-line input or output is written as follows:

```
$ pip show pip
---
Metadata-Version: 2.0
Name: pip
Version: 7.1.2
Summary: The PyPA recommended tool for installing Python packages.
Home-page: https://pip.pypa.io/
Author: The pip developers
Author-email: python-virtualenv@groups.google.com
```

```
License: MIT
Location: /usr/lib/python2.7/site-packages
Requires:
```

New terms and **important words** are shown in bold. Words that you see on the screen, for example, in menus or dialog boxes, appear in the text like this: "Clicking the **Next** button moves you to the next screen."

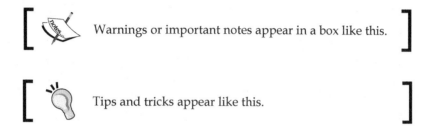

Warnings or important notes appear in a box like this.

Tips and tricks appear like this.

Reader feedback

Feedback from our readers is always welcome. Let us know what you think about this book—what you liked or disliked. Reader feedback is important for us as it helps us develop titles that you will really get the most out of.

To send us general feedback, simply e-mail feedback@packtpub.com, and mention the book's title in the subject of your message.

If there is a topic that you have expertise in and you are interested in either writing or contributing to a book, see our author guide at www.packtpub.com/authors.

Customer support

Now that you are the proud owner of a Packt book, we have a number of things to help you to get the most from your purchase.

Downloading the example code

You can download the example code files for this book from your account at http://www.packtpub.com. If you purchased this book elsewhere, you can visit http://www.packtpub.com/support and register to have the files e-mailed directly to you.

You can download the code files by following these steps:

1. Log in or register to our website using your e-mail address and password.
2. Hover the mouse pointer on the **SUPPORT** tab at the top.
3. Click on **Code Downloads & Errata**.
4. Enter the name of the book in the **Search** box.
5. Select the book for which you're looking to download the code files.
6. Choose from the drop-down menu where you purchased this book from.
7. Click on **Code Download**.

You can also download the code files by clicking on the **Code Files** button on the book's webpage at the Packt Publishing website. This page can be accessed by entering the book's name in the **Search** box. Please note that you need to be logged in to your Packt account.

Once the file is downloaded, please make sure that you unzip or extract the folder using the latest version of:

- WinRAR / 7-Zip for Windows
- Zipeg / iZip / UnRarX for Mac
- 7-Zip / PeaZip for Linux

The code bundle for the book is also hosted on GitHub at `https://github.com/PacktPublishing/Expert-Python-Programming_Second-Edition`. We also have other code bundles from our rich catalog of books and videos available at `https://github.com/PacktPublishing/`. Check them out!

Errata

Although we have taken every care to ensure the accuracy of our content, mistakes do happen. If you find a mistake in one of our books—maybe a mistake in the text or the code—we would be grateful if you could report this to us. By doing so, you can save other readers from frustration and help us improve subsequent versions of this book. If you find any errata, please report them by visiting `http://www.packtpub.com/submit-errata`, selecting your book, clicking on the **Errata Submission Form** link, and entering the details of your errata. Once your errata are verified, your submission will be accepted and the errata will be uploaded to our website or added to any list of existing errata under the Errata section of that title.

To view the previously submitted errata, go to `https://www.packtpub.com/books/content/support` and enter the name of the book in the search field. The required information will appear under the **Errata** section.

Piracy

Piracy of copyrighted material on the Internet is an ongoing problem across all media. At Packt, we take the protection of our copyright and licenses very seriously. If you come across any illegal copies of our works in any form on the Internet, please provide us with the location address or website name immediately so that we can pursue a remedy.

Please contact us at copyright@packtpub.com with a link to the suspected pirated material.

We appreciate your help in protecting our authors and our ability to bring you valuable content.

Questions

If you have a problem with any aspect of this book, you can contact us at questions@packtpub.com, and we will do our best to address the problem.

1
Current Status of Python

Python is good for developers.

No matter what operating system you or your customers are running, it will work. Unless you are coding platform-specific things, or using a platform-specific library, you can work on Linux and deploy on other systems, for example. However, that's not uncommon anymore (Ruby, Java, and many other languages work in the same way). Combined with the other qualities that we will discover throughout this book, Python becomes a smart choice for a company's primary development language.

This book is focused on the latest version of Python, 3.5, and all code examples are written in this version of the language unless another version is explicitly mentioned. Because this release is not yet widely used, this chapter contains some description of the current *status quo* of Python 3 to introduce readers to it, as well as some introductory information on modern approaches to development in Python. This chapter covers the following topics:

- How to maintain compatibility between Python 2 and Python 3
- How to approach the problem of environment isolation both on application and operating system level for the purpose of development
- How to enhance the Python prompt
- How to install packages using pip

A book always starts with some appetizers. So, if you are already familiar with Python (especially with the latest 3.x branch) and know how to properly isolate environments for development purposes, you can skip the first two sections of this chapter and just read the other sections quickly. They describe some tools and resources that are not essential but can highly improve productivity in Python. Be sure to read the section on application-level environment isolation and pip, though, as their installation is mandatory for the rest of the book.

Where are we now and where we are going?

Python history starts somewhere in the late 1980s, but its 1.0 release date was in the year 1994, so it is not a very young language. There could be a whole timeline of major Python releases mentioned here, but what really matters is a single date: December 3, 2008 – the release date of Python 3.0.

At the time of writing, seven years have passed since the first Python 3 release. It is also four years since the creation of PEP 404 — the official document that "un-released" Python 2.8 and officially closed the 2.x branch. Although a lot of time has passed, there is a specific dichotomy in the Python community — while the language develops very fast, there is a large group of its users that do not want to move forward with it.

Why and how does Python change?

The answer is simple — Python changes because there is such a need. The competition does not sleep. Every few months a new language pops out out of nowhere claiming to solve problems of all its predecessors. Most projects like these lose developers' attention very quickly and their popularity is driven by a sudden hype.

Anyway, this is a sign of some bigger issue. People design new languages because they find the existing ones unsuitable for solving their problems in the best ways possible. It would be silly not to recognize such a need. Also, more and more wide spread usage of Python shows that it could, and should, be improved in many places.

Lots of improvements in Python are often driven by the needs of particular fields where it is used. The most significant one is web development, which necessitated improvements to deal with concurrency in Python.

Some changes are just caused by the age and maturity of the Python project. Throughout the years, it has collected some of the clutter in the form of de-organized and redundant standard library modules or some bad design decisions. First, the Python 3 release aimed to bring major clean-up and refreshment to the language, but time showed that this plan backfired a bit. For a long time, it was treated by many developers only like curiosity, but, hopefully, this is changing.

Getting up to date with changes – PEP documents

The Python community has a well-established way of dealing with changes. While speculative Python language ideas are mostly discussed on specific mailing lists (`python-ideas@python.org`), nothing major ever gets changed without the existence of a new document called a PEP. A **PEP** is a **Python Enhancement Proposal**. It is a paper written that proposes a change on Python, and is a starting point for the community to discuss it. The whole purpose, format, and workflow around these documents is also standardized in the form of a Python Enhancement Proposal— precisely, PEP 1 document (`http://www.python.org/dev/peps/pep-0001`).

PEP documents are very important for Python and depending on the topic, they serve different purposes:

- **Informing**: They summarize the information needed by core Python developers and notify about Python release schedules
- **Standardizing**: They provide code style, documentation, or other guidelines
- **Designing**: They describe the proposed features

A list of all the proposed PEPs is available as in a document—PEP 0 (`https://www.python.org/dev/peps/`). Since they are easily accessible in one place and the actual URL is also very easy to guess, they are usually referred to by the number in the book.

Those who are wondering what the direction is in which the Python language is heading but do not have time to track a discussion on Python mailing lists, the PEP 0 document can be a great source of information. It shows which documents have already been accepted but are not yet implemented and also which are still under consideration.

PEPs also serve additional purposes. Very often, people ask questions like:

- Why does feature A work that way?
- Why does Python not have feature B?

In most such cases, the extensive answer is available in specific PEP documents where such a feature has already been mentioned. There are a lot of PEP documents describing Python language features that were proposed but not accepted. These documents are left as a historical reference.

Python 3 adoption at the time of writing this book

So, is Python 3, thanks to new exciting features, well adopted among its community? Sadly, not yet. The popular page Python 3 Wall of Superpowers (`https://python3wos.appspot.com`) that tracks the compatibility of most popular packages with the Python 3 branch was, until not so long ago, named Python 3 Wall of Shame. This situation is changing and the table of listed packages on the mentioned page is slowly turning "more green" with every month. Still, this does not mean that all teams building their applications will shortly use only Python 3. When all popular packages are available on Python 3, the popular excuse — the packages that we use are not ported yet — will no longer be valid.

The main reason for such a situation is that porting the existing application from Python 2 to Python 3 is always a challenge. There are tools like 2to3 that can perform automated code translation but they do not ensure that the result will be 100% correct. Also, such translated code may not perform as well as in its original form without manual adjustments. The moving of existing complex code bases to Python 3 might involve tremendous effort and cost that some organizations may not be able to afford. Still such costs can be split in time. Some good software architecture design methodologies, such as service-oriented architecture or microservices, can help to achieve this goal gradually. New project components (services or microservices) can be written using the new technology and existing ones can be ported one at a time.

In the long run, moving to Python 3 can only have beneficial effects on a project. According to PEP-404, there won't be a 2.8 release in the 2.x branch of Python anymore. Also, there may be a time in the future when all major projects such as Django, Flask, and numpy will drop any 2.x compatibility and will only be available on Python 3.

My personal opinion on this topic can be considered controversial. I think that the best incentive for the community would be to completely drop Python 2 support when creating new packages. This, of course, greatly limits the reach of such software but it may be the only way to change the way of thinking of those who insist on sticking to Python 2.x.

The main differences between Python 3 and Python 2

It has already been said that Python 3 breaks backwards compatibility with Python 2. Still, it is not a complete redesign. Also, it does not mean that every Python module written for a 2.x release will stop working under Python 3. It is possible to write completely cross-compatible code that will run on both major releases without additional tools or techniques, but usually it is possible only for simple applications.

Why should I care?

Despite my personal opinion on Python 2 compatibility, exposed earlier in this chapter, it is impossible to simply forget about it right at this time. There are still some useful packages (such as fabric, mentioned in *Chapter 6, Deploying the Code*) that are really worth using but are not likely to be ported in the very near future.

Also, sometimes we may be constrained by the organization we work in. The existing legacy code may be so complex that porting it is not economically feasible. So, even if we decide to move on and live only in the Python 3 world from now on, it will be impossible to completely live without Python 2 for some time.

Nowadays, it is very hard to name oneself a professional developer without giving something back to the community, so helping the open source developers in adding Python 3 compatibility to the existing packages is a good way to pay off the "moral debt" incurred by using them. This, of course, cannot be done without knowing the differences between Python 2 and Python 3. By the way, this is also a great exercise for those new in Python 3.

The main syntax differences and common pitfalls

The Python documentation is the best reference for differences between every release. Anyway, for readers' convenience, this section summarizes the most important ones. This does not change the fact that the documentation is mandatory reading for those not familiar with Python 3 yet (see `https://docs.python.org/3.0/whatsnew/3.0.html`).

The breaking changes introduced by Python 3 can generally be divided into a few groups:

- Syntax changes, wherein some syntax elements were removed/changed and other elements were added
- Changes in the standard library
- Changes in datatypes and collections

Syntax changes

Syntax changes that make it difficult for the existing code to run are the easiest to spot—they will cause the code to not run at all. The Python 3 code that features new syntax elements will fail to run on Python 2 and vice versa. The elements that are removed will make Python 2 code visibly incompatible with Python 3. The running code that has such issues will immediately cause the interpreter to fail raising a SyntaxError exception. Here is an example of the broken script that has exactly two statements, of which none will be executed due to the syntax error:

```
print("hello world")
print "goodbye python2"
```

Its actual result when run on Python 3 is as follows:

```
$ python3 script.py
  File "script.py", line 2
    print "goodbye python2"
                          ^
SyntaxError: Missing parentheses in call to 'print'
```

The list of such differences is a bit long and, from time to time, any new Python 3.x release may add new elements of syntax that will raise such errors on earlier releases of Python (even on the same 3.x branch). The most important of them are covered in *Chapter 2, Syntax Best Practices – below the Class Level*, and *Chapter 3, Syntax Best Practices – above the Class Level*, so there is no need to list all of them here.

The list of things dropped or changed from Python 2.7 is shorter, so here are the most important ones:

- print is no longer a statement but a function instead, so the parenthesis is now obligatory.
- Catching exceptions changed from except exc, var to except exc as var.
- The <> comparison operator has been removed in favor of !=.

- `from module import *` (https://docs.python.org/3.0/reference/ simple_stmts.html#import) is now allowed only on a module level, no longer inside the functions.

- `from .[module] import name` is now the only accepted syntax for relative imports. All imports not starting with the dot character are interpreted as absolute imports.

- The `sort()` function and the list's `sorted()` method no longer accept the `cmp` argument. The `key` argument should be used instead.

- Division expressions on integers such as 1/2 return floats. The truncating behavior is achieved through the `//` operator like `1//2`. The good thing is that this can be used with floats too, so `5.0//2.0 == 2.0`.

Changes in the standard library

Breaking changes in the standard library are the second easiest to catch after syntax changes. Each subsequent version of Python adds, deprecates, improves, or completely removes standard library modules. Such a process was regular also in the older versions of Python (1.x and 2.x), so it does not come as a shock in Python 3. In most cases, depending on the module that was removed or reorganized (like `urlparse` being moved to `urllib.parse`), it will raise exceptions on the import time just after it was interpreted. This makes such issues so easy to catch. Anyway, in order to be sure that all such issues are covered, the full test code coverage is essential. In some cases (for example, when using lazily loaded modules), the issues that are usually noticed on import time will not appear before some modules are used in code as function calls. This is why, it is so important to make sure that every line of code is actually executed during tests suite.

Lazily loaded modules

A lazily loaded module is a module that is not loaded on import time. In Python, `import` statements can be included inside of functions so import will happen on a function call and not on import time. In some cases, such loading of modules may be a reasonable choice but in most cases, it is a workaround for poorly designed module structures (for example, to avoid circular imports) and should be generally avoided. For sure, there is no justifiable reason to lazily load standard library modules.

Changes in datatypes and collections

Changes in how Python represents datatypes and collections require the most effort when the developer tries to maintain compatibility or simply port existing code to Python 3. While incompatible syntax or standard library changes are easily noticeable and the most easy to fix, changes in collections and types are either nonobvious or require a lot of repetitive work. A list of such changes is long and, again, official documentation is the best reference.

Still, this section must cover the change in how string literals are treated in Python 3 because it seems to be the most controversial and discussed change in Python 3, despite being a very good thing that now makes things more explicit.

All string literals are now Unicode and `bytes` literals require a b or B prefix. For Python 3.0 and 3.1 using u prefix (like `u"foo"`) was dropped and will raise a syntax error. Dropping that prefix was the main reason for all controversies. It made really hard to create code that was compatible in different branches of Python—version 2.x relied on this prefix in order to create Unicode literals. This prefix was brought back in Python 3.3 to ease the integration process, although without any syntactic meaning.

The popular tools and techniques used for maintaining cross-version compatibility

Maintaining compatibility between versions of Python is a challenge. It may add a lot of additional work depending on the size of the project but is definitely doable and worth doing. For packages that are meant to be reused in many environments, it is an absolute must have. Open source packages without well-defined and tested compatibility bounds are very unlikely to become popular, but also, closed third-party code that never leaves the company network can greatly benefit from being tested in different environments.

It should be noted here that while this part focuses mainly on compatibility between various versions of Python, these approaches apply for maintaining compatibility with external dependencies like different package versions, binary libraries, systems, or external services.

The whole process can be divided into three main areas, ordered by importance:

- Defining and documenting target compatibility bounds and how they will be managed
- Testing in every environment and with every dependency version declared as compatible
- Implementing actual compatibility code

Declaration of what is considered compatible is the most important part of the whole process because it gives the users of the code (developers) the ability to have expectations and make assumptions on how it works and how it can change in the future. Our code can be used as a dependency in different projects that may also strive to manage compatibility, so the ability to reason how it behaves is crucial.

While this book tries to always give a few choices rather than to give an absolute recommendation on specific options, here is one of the few exceptions. The best way so far to define how compatibility may change in the future is by the proper approach to versioning numbers using *Semantic Versioning* (`http://semver.org/`), or shortly, semver. It describes a broadly accepted standard for marking the scope of change in code by the version specifier consisting only of three numbers. It also gives some advice on how to handle deprecation policies. Here is an excerpt from its summary:

Given a version number `MAJOR.MINOR.PATCH`, increment:

- A `MAJOR` version when you make incompatible API changes
- A `MINOR` version when you add functionality in a backwards-compatible manner
- A `PATCH` version when you make backwards-compatible bug fixes

Additional labels for pre-release and build metadata are available as extensions to the `MAJOR.MINOR.PATCH` format.

When it comes to testing, the sad truth is that to be sure that code is compatible with every declared dependency version and in every environment (here, the Python version), it must be tested in every combination of these. This, of course, may not be possible when the project has a lot of dependencies because the number of combinations grows rapidly with every new dependency in a version. So, typically some trade off needs to be made so that running full compatibility tests does not take ages. A selection of tools that help testing in so-called matrixes is presented in *Chapter 10, Test-Driven Development*, that discusses testing in general.

The benefit of using projects that follow semver is that usually what needs to be tested are only major releases because minor and patch releases are guaranteed not to include backwards incompatible changes. This is only true if such projects can be trusted not to break such a contract. Unfortunately, mistakes happen to everyone and backward incompatible changes happen in a lot of projects, even on patch versions. Still, since semver declares strict compatibility on minor and patch version changes, breaking it is considered a bug, so it may be fixed in patch release.

Implementation of the compatibility layer is last and also least important if bounds of that compatibility are well-defined and rigorously tested. Still there are some tools and techniques that every programmer interested in such a topic should know.

The most basic is Python's `__future__` module. It ports back some features from newer Python releases back into the older ones and takes the form of import statement:

```
from __future__ import <feature>
```

Features provided by `future` statements are syntax-related elements that cannot be easily handled by different means. This statement affects only the module where it was used. Here is an example of Python 2.7 interactive session that brings Unicode literals from Python 3.0:

```
Python 2.7.10 (default, May 23 2015, 09:40:32) [MSC v.1500 32 bit
(Intel)] on win32
Type "help", "copyright", "credits" or "license" for more
information.
>>> type("foo")  # old literals
<type 'str'>
>>> from __future__ import unicode_literals
>>> type("foo")  # now is unicode
<type 'unicode'>
```

Here is a list of all the available `__future__` statement options that developers concerned with 2/3 compatibility should know:

- `division`: This adds a Python 3 division operator (PEP 238)
- `absolute_import`: This makes every form of `import` statement not starting with a dot character interpreted as an absolute import (PEP 328)
- `print_function`: This changes a `print` statement into a function call, so parentheses around `print` becomes mandatory (PEP 3112)
- `unicode_literals`: This makes every string literal interpreted as Unicode literals (PEP 3112)

A list of the __future__ statement options is very short and it covers only a few syntax features. The other things that have changed like the metaclass syntax (which is an advanced feature covered in *Chapter 3, Syntax Best Practices – above the Class Level*), are a lot harder to maintain. Reliably handling of multiple standard library reorganizations also cannot be solved by future statements. Happily, there are some tools that aim to provide a consistent layer of ready-to-use compatibility. The most commonly known is Six (https://pypi.python.org/pypi/six/) that provides whole common 2/3 compatibility boilerplate as a single module. The other promising but slightly less popular tool is the future module (http://python-future.org/).

In some situations, developers may not want to include additional dependencies in some small packages. A common practice is the additional module that gathers all the compatibility code, usually named compat.py. Here is an example of such a compat module taken from the python-gmaps project (https://github.com/swistakm/python-gmaps):

```
# -*- coding: utf-8 -*-
import sys

if sys.version_info < (3, 0, 0):
    import urlparse  # noqa

    def is_string(s):
        return isinstance(s, basestring)

else:
    from urllib import parse as urlparse  # noqa

    def is_string(s):
        return isinstance(s, str)
```

Such a `compat.py` module is popular even in projects that depends on Six for 2/3 compatibility because it is a very convenient way to store code that handles compatibility with different versions of packages used as dependencies.

> **Downloading the example code**
>
> You can download the example code files for this book from your account at `http://www.packtpub.com`. If you purchased this book elsewhere, you can visit `http://www.packtpub.com/support` and register to have the files e-mailed directly to you.
>
> You can download the code files by following these steps:
>
> - Log in or register to our website using your e-mail address and password.
> - Hover the mouse pointer on the **SUPPORT** tab at the top.
> - Click on **Code Downloads & Errata**.
> - Enter the name of the book in the **Search** box.
> - Select the book for which you're looking to download the code files.
> - Choose from the drop-down menu where you purchased this book from.
> - Click on **Code Download**.
>
>
>
> Once the file is downloaded, please make sure that you unzip or extract the folder using the latest version of:
>
> - WinRAR / 7-Zip for Windows
> - Zipeg / iZip / UnRarX for Mac
> - 7-Zip / PeaZip for Linux
>
> The code bundle for the book is also hosted on GitHub at `https://github.com/PacktPublishing/Expert-Python-Programming_Second-Edition`. We also have other code bundles from our rich catalog of books and videos available at `https://github.com/PacktPublishing/`. Check them out!

Not only CPython

The main Python implementation is written in the C language and is called **CPython**. It is the one that the majority of people refer to when they talk about Python. When the language evolves, the C implementation is changed accordingly. Besides C, Python is available in a few other implementations that are trying to keep up with the mainstream. Most of them are a few milestones behind CPython, but provide a great opportunity to use and promote the language in a specific environment.

Why should I care?

There are plenty of alternative Python implementations available. The Python Wiki page on that topic (`https://wiki.python.org/moin/PythonImplementations`) features more than 20 different language variants, dialects, or implementations of Python interpreter built with something else than C. Some of them implement only a subset of the core language syntax, features, and built-in extensions but there is at least a few that are almost fully compatible with CPython. The most important thing to know is that while some of them are just toy projects or experiments, most of them were created to solve some real problems – problems that were either impossible to solve with CPython or required too much of the developer's effort. Examples of such problems are:

- Running Python code on embedded systems
- Integration with code written for runtime frameworks such as Java or .NET or in different languages
- Running Python code in web browsers

This section provides a short description of subjectively most popular and up-to-date choices that are currently available for Python programmers.

Stackless Python

Stackless Python advertises itself as an enhanced version of Python. Stackless is named so because it avoids depending on the C call stack for its own stack. It is in fact a modified CPython code that also adds some new features that were missing from core Python implementation at the time Stackless was created. The most important of them are microthreads managed by the interpreter as a cheap and lightweight alternative to ordinary threads that must depend on system kernel context switching and tasks scheduling.

The latest available versions are 2.7.9 and 3.3.5 that implement 2.7 and 3.3 versions of Python respectively. All the additional features provided by Stackless are exposed as a framework within this distribution through the built-in `stackless` module.

Stackless isn't the most popular alternative implementation of Python, but it is worth knowing because ideas introduced in it have had a strong impact on the language community. The core switching functionality was extracted from Stackless and published as an independent package named `greenlet`, which is now a basis for many useful libraries and frameworks. Also, most of its features were re-implemented in PyPy—another Python implementation that will be featured later. Refer to `http://stackless.readthedocs.org/`.

Jython

Jython is a Java implementation of the language. It compiles the code into Java byte code, and allows the developers to seamlessly use Java classes within their Python modules. Jython allows people to use Python as the top-level scripting language on complex application systems, for example, J2EE. It also brings Java applications into the Python world. Making Apache Jackrabbit (which is a document repository API based on JCR; see `http://jackrabbit.apache.org`) available in a Python program is a good example of what Jython allows.

The latest available version of Jython is Jython 2.7, and this corresponds to 2.7 version of the language. It is advertised as implementing nearly all of the core Python standard library and uses the same regression test suite. The version of Jython 3.x is under development.

The main differences of Jython as compared to CPython implementation are:

- True Java's garbage collection instead of reference counting
- The lack of **GIL (global interpreter lock)** allows a better utilization of multiple cores in multi-threaded applications

The main weakness of this implementation of the language is the lack of support for C Python Extension APIs, so no Python extensions written in C will work with Jython. This might change in the future because there are plans to support the C Python Extension API in Jython 3.x.

Some Python web frameworks such as Pylons were known to be boosting Jython development to make it available in the Java world. Refer to `http://www.jython.org`.

IronPython

IronPython brings Python into the .NET Framework. The project is supported by Microsoft, where IronPython's lead developers work. It is quite an important implementation for the promotion of a language. Besides Java, the .NET community is one of the biggest developer communities out there. It is also worth noting that Microsoft provides a set of free development tools that turn Visual Studio into full-fledged Python IDE. This is distributed as Visual Studio plugins named **PVTS (Python Tools for Visual Studio)** and is available as open source code on GitHub (`http://microsoft.github.io/PTVS`).

The latest stable release is 2.7.5 and it is compatible with Python 2.7. Similar to Jython, there is some development around Python 3.x implementation, but there is no stable release available yet. Despite the fact that .NET runs primarily on Microsoft Windows, it is possible to run IronPython also on Mac OS X and Linux. This is thanks to Mono, a cross platform, open source .NET implementation.

Main differences or advantages of IronPython as compared to CPython are as follows:

- Similar to Jython, the lack of GIL (global interpreter lock) allows the better utilization of multiple cores in multi-threaded applications
- Code written in C# and other .NET languages can be easily integrated in IronPython and vice versa
- Can be run in all major web browsers through Silverlight

When speaking about weaknesses, IronPython, again, seems very similar to Jython because it does not support the C Python Extension APIs. This is important for developers who would like to use packages such as numpy that are largely based on C extensions. There is a project called ironclad (refer to `https://github.com/IronLanguages/ironclad`) that aims to allow using such extensions seamlessly with IronPython, albeit its last known supported release is 2.6 and development seems to have stopped at this point. Refer to `http://ironpython.net/`.

PyPy

PyPy is probably the most exciting implementation, as its goal is to rewrite Python into Python. In PyPy, the Python interpreter is itself written in Python. We have a C code layer carrying out the nuts-and-bolts work for the CPython implementation of Python. However, in the PyPy implementation, this C code layer is rewritten in pure Python.

This means you can change the interpreter's behavior during execution time and implement code patterns that couldn't be easily done in CPython.

PyPy currently aims to be fully compatible with Python 2.7, while PyPy3 is compatible with Python 3.2.5 version.

In the past, PyPy was interesting mostly for theoretical reasons, and it interested those who enjoyed going deep into the details of the language. It was not generally used in production, but this has changed through the years. Nowadays, many benchmarks show that surprisingly PyPy is often way faster than the CPython implementation. This project has its own benchmarking site that tracks the performance of each version measured using tens of different benchmarks (refer to `http://speed.pypy.org/`). It clearly shows that PyPy with JIT enabled is at least a few times faster than CPython. This and other features of PyPy makes more and more developers decide to switch to PyPy in their production environments.

The main differences of PyPy as compared to the CPython implementation are:

- Garbage collection is used instead of reference counting
- Integrated tracing JIT compiler that allows impressive improvements in performance
- Application-level Stackless features are borrowed from Stackless Python

Like almost every other alternative Python implementation, PyPy lacks the full official support of C Python Extension API. Still it, at least, provides some sort of support for C extensions through its CPyExt subsystem, although it is poorly documented and still not feature complete. Also, there is an ongoing effort within the community in porting NumPy to PyPy because it is the most requested feature. Refer to `http://pypy.org`.

Modern approaches to Python development

A deep understanding of the programming language of choice is the most important thing to harness as an expert. This will always be true for any technology. Still, it is really hard to develop a good software without knowing the common tools and practices within the given language community. Python has no single feature that could not be found in some other language. So, in direct comparison of syntax, expressiveness, or performance, there will always be a solution that is better in one or more fields. But the area in which Python really stands out from the crowd is in the whole ecosystem built around the language. Its community has, for years, polished the standard practices and libraries that help to create more reliable software in a shorter time.

The most obvious and important part of the mentioned ecosystem is a huge collection of free and open source packages that solve a multitude of problems. Writing new software is always an expensive and time-consuming process. Being able to reuse the existing code instead of *reinventing the wheel* greatly reduces the time and costs of development. For some companies, it is the only reason their projects are economically feasible.

Due to this reason, Python developers put a lot of effort on creating tools and standards to work with open source packages created by others. Starting from virtual isolated environments, improved interactive shells and debuggers, to programs that help to discover, search, and analyze the huge collection of packages available on **PyPI (Python Package Index)**.

Application-level isolation of Python environments

Nowadays, a lot of operating systems come with Python as a standard component. Most Linux distributions and Unix-based systems such as FreeBSD, NetBSD, OpenBSD, or OS X come with Python are either installed by default or available through system package repositories. Many of them even use it as part of some core components—Python powers the installers of Ubuntu (Ubiquity), Red Hat Linux (Anaconda), and Fedora (Anaconda again).

Due to this fact, a lot of packages from PyPI are also available as native packages managed by the system's package management tools such as `apt-get` (Debian, Ubuntu), `rpm` (Red Hat Linux), or `emerge` (Gentoo). Although it should be remembered that the list of available libraries is very limited and they are mostly outdated when compared to PyPI. This is the reason why `pip` should always be used to obtain new packages in the latest version as a recommendation of **PyPA (Python Packaging Authority)**. Although it is an independent package starting from version 2.7.9 and 3.4 of CPython, it is bundled with every new release by default. Installing the new package is as simple as this:

```
pip install <package-name>
```

Among other features, `pip` allows forcing specific versions of packages (using the `pip install package-name==version` syntax) and upgrading to the latest version available (using the `--upgrade` switch). The full usage description for most of the command-line tools presented in the book can be easily obtained simply by running the command with the `-h` or `--help` switch, but here is an example session that demonstrates the most commonly used options:

```
$ pip show pip
---
Metadata-Version: 2.0
Name: pip
Version: 7.1.2
Summary: The PyPA recommended tool for installing Python packages.
Home-page: https://pip.pypa.io/
Author: The pip developers
Author-email: python-virtualenv@groups.google.com
License: MIT
Location: /usr/lib/python2.7/site-packages
Requires:


$ pip install 'pip<7.0.0'
Collecting pip<7.0.0
  Downloading pip-6.1.1-py2.py3-none-any.whl (1.1MB)
    100% |████████████████████████████| 1.1MB 242kB/s
Installing collected packages: pip
  Found existing installation: pip 7.1.2
    Uninstalling pip-7.1.2:
      Successfully uninstalled pip-7.1.2
Successfully installed pip-6.1.1
You are using pip version 6.1.1, however version 7.1.2 is available.
You should consider upgrading via the 'pip install --upgrade pip'
command.


$ pip install --upgrade pip
You are using pip version 6.1.1, however version 7.1.2 is available.
You should consider upgrading via the 'pip install --upgrade pip'
command.
```

```
Collecting pip
  Using cached pip-7.1.2-py2.py3-none-any.whl
Installing collected packages: pip
  Found existing installation: pip 6.1.1
    Uninstalling pip-6.1.1:
      Successfully uninstalled pip-6.1.1
Successfully installed pip-7.1.2
```

In some cases, `pip` may not be available by default. From Python 3.4 version onwards (and also Python 2.7.9), it can always be bootstrapped using the `ensurepip` module:

```
$ python -m ensurepip
Ignoring indexes: https://pypi.python.org/simple
Requirement already satisfied (use --upgrade to upgrade): setuptools in /
usr/lib/python2.7/site-packages
Collecting pip
Installing collected packages: pip
Successfully installed pip-6.1.1
```

The most up-to-date information on how to install pip for older Python versions is available on the project's documentation page at `https://pip.pypa.io/en/stable/installing/`.

Why isolation?

`pip` may be used to install system-wide packages. On Unix-based and Linux systems, this will require super user privileges, so the actual invocation will be:

```
sudo pip install <package-name>
```

Note that this is not required on Windows since it does not provide the Python interpreter by default, and Python on Windows is usually installed manually by the user without super user privileges.

Anyway, installing system-wide packages directly from PyPI is not recommended and should be avoided. This may seem like a contradiction with the previous statement that using `pip` is a PyPA recommendation, but there are some serious reasons for that. As explained earlier, Python is very often an important part of many packages available through operating system package repositories and may power a lot of important services. System distribution maintainers put a lot of effort in selecting the correct versions of packages to match various package dependencies. Very often, Python packages that are available from system's package repositories contain custom patches or are kept outdated only to ensure compatibility with some other system components. Forcing an update of such a package using `pip` to a version that breaks some backwards compatibility might break some crucial system services.

Doing such things only on the local computer for development purposes is also not a good excuse. Recklessly using `pip` that way is almost always asking for trouble and will eventually lead to issues that are very hard to debug. This does not mean that installing packages from PyPI globally is a strictly forbidden thing, but it should always be done consciously and while knowing the related risks.

Fortunately, there is an easy solution to this problem—environment isolation. There are various tools that allow the isolation of the Python runtime environment at different levels of system abstraction. The main idea is to isolate project dependencies from packages required by different projects and/or system services. The benefits of this approach are:

- It solves the "Project X depends on version 1.x but Project Y needs 4.x" dilemma. The developer can work on multiple projects with different dependencies that may even collide without the risk of affecting each other.

- The project is no longer constrained by versions of packages that are provided in his system distribution repositories.

- There is no risk of breaking other system services that depend on certain package versions because new package versions are only available inside such an environment.

- A list of packages that are project dependencies can be easily "frozen", so it is very easy to reproduce them.

The easiest and most lightweight approach to isolation is to use application-level virtual environments. They focus only on isolating the Python interpreter and packages available in it. They are very easy to set up and are very often just enough to ensure proper isolation during the development of small projects and packages.

Unfortunately, in some cases, this may not be enough to ensure enough consistency and reproducibility. For such cases, system-level isolation is a good addition to the workflow and some available solutions to that are explained later in this chapter.

Popular solutions

There are several ways to isolate Python at runtime. The simplest and most obvious, although hardest to maintain, is to manually change PATH and PYTHONPATH environment variables and/or move Python binary to a different place to affect the way it discovers available packages and change it to a custom place where we want to store our project's dependencies. Fortunately, there are several tools available that help in maintaining virtual environments and how installed packages are stored in the system. These are mainly: virtualenv, venv, and buildout. What they do under the hood is in fact the same as what we would do manually. The actual strategy depends on the specific tool implementation, but generally, they are more convenient to use and can provide additional benefits.

virtualenv

Virtualenv is by far the most popular tool in this list. Its name simply stands for Virtual Environment. It's not a part of the standard Python distribution, so it needs to be obtained using pip. It is one of the packages that is worth installing system-wide (using sudo on Linux and Unix-based systems).

Once it is installed, a new virtual environment is created using the following command:

```
virtualenv ENV
```

Here, ENV should be replaced by the desired name for the new environment. This will create a new ENV directory in the current working directory path. It will contain a few new directories inside:

- bin/: This is where the new Python executable and scripts/executables provided by other packages are stored.
- lib/ and include/: These directories contain the supporting library files for the new Python inside the virtual environment. The new packages will be installed in ENV/lib/pythonX.Y/site-packages/.

Once the new environment is created, it needs to be activated in the current shell session using Unix's source command:

```
source ENV/bin/activate
```

This changes the state of the current shell sessions by affecting its environment variables. In order to make the user aware that he has activated the virtual environment, it will change the shell prompt by appending the (ENV) string at its beginning. Here is an example session that creates a new environment and activates it to illustrate this:

```
$ virtualenv example
New python executable in example/bin/python
Installing setuptools, pip, wheel...done.
$ source example/bin/activate
(example)$ deactivate
$
```

The important thing to note about virtualenv is that it depends completely on its state stored on a filesystem. It does not provide any additional abilities to track what packages should be installed in it. These virtual environments are not portable and should not be moved to another system/machine. This means that the new virtual environment needs to be created from scratch for each new application deployment. Because of that, there is a good practice used by virtualenv users to store all project dependencies in the requirements.txt file (this is the naming convention), as shown in the following code:

```
# lines followed by hash (#) are treated as a comments

# strict version names are best for reproducibility
eventlet==0.17.4
graceful==0.1.1

# for projects that are well tested with different
# dependency versions the relative version specifiers
# are acceptable too
falcon>=0.3.0,<0.5.0

# packages without versions should be avoided unless
# latest release is always required/desired
pytz
```

With such files, all dependencies can be easily installed using pip because it accepts the requirements file as its output:

```
pip install -r requirements.txt
```

What needs to be remembered is that the requirements file is not always the ideal solution because it does not define the exact list of dependencies, only those that are to be installed. So, the whole project can work without problems in a development environment but will fail to start in others if the requirements file is outdated and does not reflect actual state of environment. There is, of course, the `pip freeze` command that prints all packages in the current environment but it should not be used blindly — it will output everything, even packages that are not used in the project but installed only for testing. The other tool mentioned in the book, `buildout`, addresses this issue, so it may be a better choice for some development teams.

> For Windows users, `virtualenv` under Windows uses a different naming for its internal structure of directories. You need to use `Scripts/`, `Libs/`, and `Include/` instead of `bin/`, `lib/`, `include/`, to better match development conventions on that operating system. The commands used for activating/deactivating the environment are also different; you need to use ENV/Scripts/activate.bat and ENV/Scripts/deactivate.bat instead of using `source` on `activate` and `deactivate` scripts.

venv

Virtual environments shortly became well established and a popular tool within the community. Starting from Python 3.3, creating virtual environments is supported by standard library. The usage is almost the same as with Virtualenv, although command-line options have quite a different naming convention. The new `venv` module provides a `pyvenv` script for creating a new virtual environment:

pyvenv ENV

Here, ENV should be replaced by the desired name for the new environment. Also, new environments can now be created directly from Python code because all functionality is exposed from the built-in `venv` module. The other usage and implementation details, like the structure of the environment directory and activate/deactivate scripts are mostly the same as in Virtualenv, so migration to this solution should be easy and painless.

For developers using newer versions of Python, it is recommended to use `venv` instead of Virtualenv. For Python 3.3, switching to `venv` may require more effort because in this version, it does not install `setuptools` and `pip` by default in the new environment, so the users need to install them manually. Fortunately, it has changed in Python 3.4, and also due to the customizability of `venv`, it is possible to override its behavior. The details are explained in the Python documentation (refer to `https://docs.python.org/3.5/library/venv.html`), but some users might find it too tricky and will stay with Virtualenv for that specific version of Python.

buildout

Buildout is a powerful tool for bootstrapping and the deployment of applications written in Python. Some of its advanced features will also be explained later in the book. For a long time, it was also used as a tool to create isolated Python environments. Because Buildout requires a declarative configuration that must be changed every time there is a change in dependencies, instead of relying on the environment state, these environments were easier to reproduce and manage.

Unfortunately, this has changed. The `buildout` package since version 2.0.0 no longer tries to provide any level of isolation from system Python installation. Isolation handling is left to other tools such as Virtualenv, so it is still possible to have isolated Buildouts, but things become a bit more complicated. A Buildout must be initialized inside an isolated environment in order to be really isolated.

This has a major drawback as compared to the previous versions of Buildout, since it depends on other solutions for isolation. The developer working on this code can no longer be sure whether the dependencies description is complete because some packages can be installed by bypassing the declarative configuration. This issue can of course be solved using proper testing and release procedures, but it adds some more complexity to the whole workflow.

To summarize, Buildout is no longer a solution that provides environment isolation but its declarative configuration can improve maintainability and the reproducibility of virtual environments.

Which one to choose?

There is no best solution that will fit every use case. What is good in one organization may not fit the workflow of other teams. Also, every application has different needs. Small projects can easily depend on sole `virtualenv` or `venv` but bigger ones may require additional help of `buildout` to perform more complex assembly.

What was not described in detail earlier is that previous versions of Buildout (buildout<2.0.0) allowed the assembly of projects in an isolated environment with similar results as provided by Virtualenv. Unfortunately, 1.x branch of this project is no longer maintained, so using it for that purpose is discouraged.

I would recommend to use `venv` module instead of Virtualenv whenever it is possible. So, this should be the default choice for projects targeting Python versions 3.4 and higher. Using `venv` in Python 3.3 may be a little inconvenient due to a lack of built-in support for `setuptools` and `pip`. For projects targeting a wider spectrum of Python run times (including alternative interpreters and 2.x branch), it seems that Virtualenv is the best choice.

System-level environment isolation

In most cases, software implementation can iterate fast because developers reuse a lot of existing components. Don't Repeat Yourself—this is a popular rule and motto of many programmers. Using other packages and modules to include them in the codebase is only a part of that culture. What also can be considered under "reused components" are binary libraries, databases, system services, third-party APIs, and so on. Even whole operating systems should be considered as reused.

Backend services of web-based applications are a great example of how complex such applications can be. The simplest software stack usually consists of a few layers (starting from the lowest):

- A database or other kind of storage
- The application code implemented in Python
- An HTTP server such as Apache or NGINX

Of course such stack can be even simpler but it is very unlikely. In fact, big applications are often so complex that it is hard to distinguish single layers. Big applications can use many different databases, be divided into multiple independent processes, and use many other system services for caching, queuing, logging, service discovery, and so on. Sadly, there are no limits for complexity and it seems that code simply follows the second law of thermodynamics.

What really is important is that not all of the software stack elements can be isolated on the level of Python runtime environment. No matter whether it is an HTTP server such as NGINX or RDBMS such as PostgreSQL, they are usually available in different versions on different systems. Making sure that everyone in a development team uses the same versions of every component is very hard without proper tools. It is theoretically possible that all developers in a team working on a single project will be able to get the same versions of services on their development boxes. But all this effort is futile if they do not use the same operating system as in the production environment. And forcing a programmer to work on something else other than his beloved system of choice is impossible for sure.

The problem lies in the fact that portability is still a big challenge. Not all services will work in exactly the same way in production environments as they do on the developer's machines and that is very unlikely to change. Even Python can behave differently on different systems despite how much work is put in to make it cross-platform. Usually, this is well documented and happens only in places that depend directly on system calls, but relying on the programmer's ability to remember a long list of compatibility quirks is quite an error prone strategy.

A popular solution to this problem is by isolating whole systems as application environments. This is usually achieved by leveraging different types of system virtualization tools. Virtualization, of course, reduces performance, but with modern computers that have hardware support for virtualization, the performance loss is usually negligible. On the other hand, a list of possible gains is very long:

- The development environment can exactly match the system version and services used in production, which helps in solving compatibility issues
- Definitions for system configuration tools such as Puppet, Chef, or Ansible (if used) can be reused for configuration of the development environment
- The newly hired team members can easily hop into the project if the creation of such environments is automated
- The developers can work directly with low system-level features that may not be available on operating systems they use for work, for example, **FUSE** (**File System in User Space**) that is not available in Windows

Virtual development environments using Vagrant

Vagrant currently seems to be the most popular tool that provides a simple and convenient way to create and manage development environments. It is available for Windows, Mac OS, and a few popular Linux distributions (refer to `https://www.vagrantup.com`). It does not have any additional dependencies. Vagrant creates new development environments in the form of virtual machines or containers. The exact implementation depends on a choice of virtualization providers. VirtualBox is the default provider and it is bundled with the Vagrant installer but additional providers are available as well. The most notable choices are VMware, Docker, LXC (Linux Containers), and Hyper-V.

The most important configuration is provided to Vagrant in a single file named `Vagrantfile`. It should be independent for every project. The following are the most important things it provides:

- Choice of virtualization provider
- Box used as a virtual machine image
- Choice of provisioning method
- Shared storage between a VM and a VM's host
- Ports that need to be forwarded between a VM and its host

Syntax language for the `Vagrantfile` is Ruby. The example configuration file provides a good template to start the project and has an excellent documentation, so the knowledge of this language is not required. Template configuration can be created using a single command:

```
vagrant init
```

This will create a new file named `Vagrantfile` in the current working directory. The best place to store this file is usually the root of the related project sources. This file is already a valid configuration that will create a new VM using the default provider and base box image. No provisioning is enabled by default. After the addition of `Vagrantfile`, the new VM is started using:

```
vagrant up
```

The initial start can take a few minutes because the actual box must be downloaded from the Web. There is also some initialization process that may take some time depending on the used provider, box, and system performance every time the already existing VM is brought up. Usually, this takes only a couple of seconds. Once the new Vagrant environment is up and running, developers can connect to SSH using this shorthand:

```
vagrant ssh
```

This can be done anywhere in the project source tree below the location of `Vagrantfile`. For developers' convenience, we will look in the directories above for the configuration file and match it with the related VM instance. Then, it establishes the secure shell connection, so the development environment can be interacted with like any ordinary remote machine. The only difference is that the whole project source tree (root defined as a location of `Vagrantfile`) is available on the VM's filesystem under `/vagrant/`.

Containerization versus virtualization

Containers are an alternative to full machine virtualization. It is a lightweight method of virtualization, where the kernel and operating system allow the running of multiple isolated user space instances. OS is shared between containers and host, so it theoretically requires less overhead than in full virtualization. Such a container contains only application code and its system-level dependencies, but from the perspective of processes running inside, it looks like a completely isolated system environment.

Software containers got their popularity mostly thanks to Docker; that is one of the available implementations. Docker allows to describe its container in the form of a simple text document called `Dockerfile`. Containers from such definitions can be built and stored. It also supports incremental changes, so if new things are added to the container then it does not need to be recreated from scratch.

Different tools such as Docker and Vagrant seem to overlap in features but the main difference between them is the reason why these tools were built. Vagrant, as mentioned earlier, is built primarily as a tool for development. It allows to bootstrap the whole virtual machine with a single command, but does not allow to simply pack it and deploy or release as is. Docker, on the other hand, is built exactly for that — preparing complete containers that can be sent and deployed to production as a whole package. If implemented well, this can greatly improve the process of product deployment. Because of that, using Docker and similar solutions (Rocket, for example) during development makes sense only if it also has to be used in the deployment process on production. Using it only for isolation purposes during development may generate too much overhead and also has a drawback of not being consistent.

Popular productivity tools

A productivity tool is a bit of a vague term. On one hand, almost every open source code package released and available online is a kind of productivity booster — it provides ready-to-use solutions to some problem, so no one needs to spend time on it (ideally speaking). On the other hand, one could say that the whole of Python is about productivity. And both are undoubtedly true. Almost everything in this language and community surrounding it seems to be designed in order to make software development as productive as it is possible.

This creates a positive feedback loop. Since writing code is fun and easy, a lot of programmers spend their free time to create tools that make it even easier and fun. And this fact will be used here as a basis for a very subjective and non-scientific definition of a productivity tool — a piece of software that makes development easier and more fun.

By nature, productivity tools focus mainly on certain elements of the development process such as testing, debugging, and managing packages and are not core parts of products that they help to build. In some cases, they may not even be referred to anywhere in the project's codebase despite being used on a daily basis.

The most important productivity tools, `pip` and `venv`, were already discussed earlier in this chapter. Some of them have packages for specific problems, such as profiling and testing, and have their own chapters in the book. This section is dedicated to other tools that are really worth mentioning, but have no specific chapter in the book where they could be introduced.

Custom Python shells – IPython, bpython, ptpython, and so on

Python programmers spend a lot of time in interactive interpreter sessions. It is very good for testing small code snippets, accessing documentation, or even debugging code at run time. The default interactive Python session is very simple and does not provide many features such as tab completion or code introspection helpers. Fortunately, the default Python shell can be easily extended and customized.

The interactive prompt can be configured with a startup file. When it starts, it looks for the PYTHONSTARTUP environment variable and executes the code in the file pointed to by this variable. Some Linux distributions provide a default startup script, which is generally located in your home directory. It is called .pythonstartup. Tab completion and command history are often provided to enhance the prompt and are based on the readline module. (You need the readline library.)

If you don't have such a file, you can easily create one. Here's an example of the simplest startup file that adds completion with the <Tab> key and history:

```python
# python startup file
import readline
import rlcompleter
import atexit
import os

# tab completion
readline.parse_and_bind('tab: complete')

# history file
histfile = os.path.join(os.environ['HOME'], '.pythonhistory')
try:
    readline.read_history_file(histfile)

except IOError:
    pass

atexit.register(readline.write_history_file, histfile)
del os, histfile, readline, rlcompleter
```

Create this file in your home directory and call it .pythonstartup. Then, add a PYTHONSTARTUP variable in your environment using the path of your file:

Setting up the PYTHONSTARTUP environment variable

If you are running Linux or Mac OS X, the simplest way is to create the startup script in your home folder. Then, link it with a PYTHONSTARTUP environment variable set into the system shell startup script. For example, the Bash and Korn shells use the .profile file, where you can insert a line as follows:

```
export PYTHONSTARTUP=~/.pythonstartup
```

If you are running Windows, it is easy to set a new environment variable as an administrator in the system preferences, and save the script in a common place instead of using a specific user location.

Writing on the PYTHONSTARTUP script may be a good exercise but creating good custom shell all alone is a challenge that only few can find time for. Fortunately, there are a few custom Python shell implementations that immensely improve the experience of interactive sessions in Python.

IPython

IPyhton (http://ipython.scipy.org) provides an extended Python command shell. Among the features provided, the most interesting ones are:

- Dynamic object introspection
- System shell access from the prompt
- Profiling direct support
- Debugging facilities

Now, IPython is a part of the larger project called Jupyter that provides interactive notebooks with live code that can be written in many different languages.

bpython

bpython (http://bpython-interpreter.org/) advertises itself as a fancy interface to the python interpreter. Here are some of the accented on the projects page:

- In-line syntax highlighting
- Readline-like autocomplete with suggestions displayed as you type
- Expected parameter lists for any Python function
- Autoindentation
- Python 3 support

ptpython

ptpython (`https://github.com/jonathanslenders/ptpython/`) is another approach to the topic of advanced Python shells. In this project, core prompt utilities implementation is available as a separate package called `prompt_toolkit` (from the same author). This allows you to easily create various aesthetically pleasing interactive command-line interfaces.

It is often compared to bpython in functionalities but the main difference is that it enables a compatibility mode with IPython and its syntax that enables additional features such as `%pdb`, `%cpaste`, or `%profile`.

Interactive debuggers

Code debugging is an integral element of the software development process. Many programmers can spend most of their life using only extensive logging and `print` statements as their primary debugging tools but most professional developers prefer to rely on some kind of debugger.

Python already ships with a built-in interactive debugger called `pdb` (refer to `https://docs.python.org/3/library/pdb.html`). It can be invoked from the command line on the existing script, so Python will enter post-mortem debugging if the program exits abnormally:

```
python -m pdb script.py
```

Post-mortem debugging, while useful, does not cover every scenario. It is useful only when the application exists with some exception if the bug occurs. In many cases, faulty code just behaves abnormally but does not exit unexpectedly. In such cases, custom breakpoints can be set on a specific line of code using this single-line idiom:

```
import pdb; pdb.set_trace()
```

This will cause the Python interpreter to start the debugger session on this line during run time.

`pdb` is very useful for tracing issues and at first glance, it may look very familiar to the well-known GDB (GNU Debugger). Because Python is a dynamic language, the `pdb` session is very similar to an ordinary interpreter session. This means that the developer is not limited to tracing code execution but can call any code and even perform module imports.

Sadly, because of its roots (bdb), the first experience with pdb can be a bit overwhelming due to the existence of cryptic short letter debugger commands such as h, b, s, n, j, and r. Whenever in doubt, the help pdb command typed during the debugger session will provide extensive usage and additional information.

The debugger session in pdb is also very simple and does not provide additional features like tab completion or code highlighting. Fortunately, there are few packages available on PyPI that provide such features available from alternative Python shells mentioned in the previous section. The most notable examples are:

- ipdb: This is a separate package based on ipython
- ptpdb: This is a separate package based on ptpython
- bpdb: This is bundled with bpython

Useful resources

The Web is full of useful resources for Python developers. The most important and obvious ones were already mentioned earlier but here they are repeated to keep this list consistent:

- Python documentation
- PyPI—Python Package Index
- PEP 0—Index of Python Enhancement Proposals

The other resources such as books and tutorials are useful but often get outdated very fast. What does not get outdated are the resources that are actively curated by the community or released periodically. The two that are mostly worth recommending are:

- Awesome-python (https://github.com/vinta/awesome-python), which includes a curated list of popular packages and frameworks
- Python Weekly (http://www.pythonweekly.com/) is a popular newsletter that delivers to its subscribers dozens of new and interesting Python packages and resources every week

These two resources will provide the reader with tons of additional reading for several months.

Summary

This chapter started with topic differences between Python 2 and 3 with advice on how to deal with the current situation where a big part of its community is torn between two worlds. Then, it came to the modern approaches to Python development that were surprisingly developed mostly due to this unfortunate split between two major versions of the language. These are mostly different solutions to the environment isolation problem. The chapter ended with a short summary of the popular productivity tools as well as popular resources for further reference.

2
Syntax Best Practices – below the Class Level

The ability to write an efficient syntax comes naturally with time. If you take a look back at your first program, you will probably agree with this. The right syntax will appear to your eyes as a good-looking piece of code, and the wrong syntax as something disturbing.

Besides the algorithms that are implemented and the architectural design for your program, taking great care over how it is written weighs heavily on how it will evolve. Many programs are ditched and rewritten from scratch because of their obtuse syntax, unclear APIs, or unconventional standards.

But Python has evolved a lot in the last few years. So, if you were kidnapped for a while by your neighbor (a jealous guy from the local Ruby developers user group) and kept away from the news, you will probably be astonished by its new features. From the earliest version to the current one (3.5 at this time), a lot of enhancements have been made to make the language clearer, cleaner, and easier to write. Python basics have not changed drastically, but the tools to play with them are now a lot more ergonomic.

This chapter presents the most important elements of modern syntax and tips on their usage:

- List comprehensions
- Iterators and generators
- Descriptors and properties
- Decorators
- `with` and `contextlib`

The code performance tips for speed improvement or memory usage are covered in *Chapter 11, Optimization – General Principles and Profiling Techniques*, and *Chapter 12, Optimization – Some Powerful Techniques*.

Python's built-in types

Python provides a great set of datatypes. This is true for both numeric types and also collections. Regarding the numeric types, there is nothing special about their syntax. There are, of course, some differences for defining literals of every type and some (maybe) not well-known details regarding operators, but there aren't a lot of choices left for developers. Things change when it comes to collections and strings. Despite the "there should be only one way to do something" mantra, the Python developer is really left with plenty of choices. Some of the code patterns that seem intuitive and simple to beginners are often considered non-*Pythonic* by experienced programmers because they are either inefficient or simply too verbose.

Such *Pythonic* patterns for solving common problems (by many programmers called idioms) may often seem like only aesthetics. This cannot be more wrong. Most of the idioms are driven by the fact how Python is implemented internally and on how built-in structures and modules work. Knowing more of such details is essential for a good understanding of the language. Also, the community itself is not free from myths and stereotypes about how things in Python work. Only by digging deeper yourself, will you be able to tell which of the popular statements about Python are really true.

Strings and bytes

The topic of strings may provide some confusion for programmers that are used to programming only in Python 2. In Python 3, there is only one datatype capable of storing textual information. It is `str` or, simply, string. It is an immutable sequence that stores Unicode code points. This is the major difference from Python 2, where `str` represents byte strings—something that is now handled by the `bytes` objects (but not exactly in the same way).

Strings in Python are sequences. This single fact should be enough to include them in the section covering other container types, but they differ from other container types in one important detail. Strings have very specific limitations on what type of data they can store, and that is Unicode text.

`bytes` and its mutable alternative (`bytearray`) differs from `str` by allowing only bytes as a sequence value—integers in the range `0 <= x < 256`. This may be confusing at the beginning, since when printed, they may look very similar to strings:

```
>>> print(bytes([102, 111, 111]))
b'foo'
```

The true nature of `bytes` and `bytearray` is revealed when it is converted to another sequence type like `list` or `tuple`:

```
>>> list(b'foo bar')
[102, 111, 111, 32, 98, 97, 114]
>>> tuple(b'foo bar')
(102, 111, 111, 32, 98, 97, 114)
```

A lot of Python 3 controversy was about breaking the backwards compatibility for string literals and how Unicode is dealt with. Starting from Python 3.0, every un-prefixed string literal is Unicode. So, literals enclosed by single quotes (`'`), double quotes (`"`), or groups of three quotes (single or double) without any prefix represent the `str` datatype:

```
>>> type("some string")
<class 'str'>
```

In Python 2, the Unicode literals required the u prefix (like u`"some string"`). This prefix is still allowed for backward compatibility (starting from Python 3.3), but does not hold any syntactic meaning in Python 3.

Bytes literals were already presented in some of the previous examples, but let's explicitly present its syntax for the sake of consistency. Bytes literals are also enclosed by single quotes, double quotes, or triple quotes, but must be preceded by a b or B prefix:

```
>>> type(b"some bytes")
<class 'bytes'>
```

Note that there is no `bytearray` literals in the Python syntax.

Last but not least, Unicode strings contain "abstract" text that is independent from the byte representation. This makes them unable to be saved on the disk or sent over the network without encoding to binary data. There are two ways to encode string objects into byte sequences:

- Using the `str.encode(encoding, errors)` method, which encodes the string using a registered codec for encoding. Codec is specified using the `encoding` argument, and, by default, it is `'utf-8'`. The second errors argument specifies the error handling scheme. It can be `'strict'` (default), `'ignore'`, `'replace'`, `'xmlcharrefreplace'`, or any other registered handler (refer to the built-in `codecs` module documentation).

- Using the `bytes(source, encoding, errors)` constructor, which creates a new bytes sequence. When the source is of the `str` type, then the `encoding` argument is obligatory and it does not have a default value. The usage of the `encoding` and `errors` arguments is the same as for the `str.encode()` method.

Binary data represented by `bytes` can be converted to a string in the analogous ways:

- Using the `bytes.decode(encoding, errors)` method, which decodes the bytes using the codec registered for encoding. The arguments of this method have the same meaning and defaults as the arguments of `str.encode()`.

- Using the `str(source, encoding, error)` constructor, which creates a new string instance. Similar to the `bytes()` constructor, the `encoding` argument in the `str()` call has no default value and must be provided if the bytes sequence is used as a source.

Naming – bytes versus byte string

Due to changes made in Python 3, some people tend to refer to the `bytes` instances as byte strings. This is mostly due to historic reasons—`bytes` in Python 3 is the sequence type that is the closest one to the `str` type from Python 2 (but not the same). Still, the `bytes` instance is a sequence of bytes and also does not need to represent textual data. So, in order to avoid any confusion, it is advisable to always refer to them as either `bytes` or a byte sequence despite their similarities to strings. The concept of strings is reserved for textual data in Python 3 and this is now always `str`.

Implementation details

Python strings are immutable. This is also true to byte sequences. This is an important fact because it has both advantages and disadvantages. It also affects the way strings should be handled in Python efficiently. Thanks to immutability, strings can be used as dictionary keys or `set` collection elements because once initialized, they will never change their value. On the other hand, whenever a modified string is required (even with only tiny modification), a completely new instance needs to be created. Fortunately, `bytearray` as a mutable version of `bytes` does not introduce such an issue. Byte arrays can be modified in-place (without the need of new object creation) through item assignments and can be dynamically resized exactly like lists—using appends, pops, inserts, and so on.

String concatenation

Knowing the fact that Python strings are immutable imposes some problems when multiple string instances need to be joined together. As stated before, concatenating any immutable sequences result in the creation of a new sequence object. Consider that a new string is built by the repeated concatenation of multiple strings, as follows:

```
s = ""
for substring in substrings:
    s += substring
```

This will result in a quadratic runtime cost in the total string length. In other words, it is highly inefficient. For handling such situations, there is the `str.join()` method available. It accepts iterable of strings as the argument and returns a joined string. Because it is the method, the actual idiom uses the empty string literal as a source of method:

```
s = "".join(substrings)
```

The string providing this method will be used as a separator between joined substrings; consider the following example:

```
>>> ','.join(['some', 'comma', 'separated', 'values'])
'some,comma,separated,values'
```

It is worth remembering that just because it is faster (especially for large lists), it does not mean that the `join()` method should be used in every situation where two strings need to be concatenated. Despite being a widely recognized idiom, it does not improve code readability – and readability counts! There are also some situations where `join()` may not perform as well as ordinary concatenation through addition. Here some examples of them:

- If the number of substrings is small and they are not contained already by some iterable—in some cases, an overhead of creating a new sequence just to perform concatenation can overshadow the gain of using `join()`.

- When concatenating short literals, thanks to constant folding in CPython, some complex literals (not only strings) such as `'a' + 'b' + 'c'` to `'abc'` can be translated to a shorter form at compile time. Of course, this is enabled only for constants (literals) that are relatively short.

Ultimately, the best readability of string concatenation if the number of strings is known beforehand is ensured by proper string formatting, by either using the `str.format()` method or the `%` operator. In code sections where the performance is not critical or gain from optimizing string concatenation is very little, string formatting is recommended as the best alternative.

Constant folding and peephole optimizer

CPython uses the peephole optimizer on compiled source code in order to improve performance. This optimizer implements a number of common optimizations directly on Python's byte code. As mentioned, constant folding is one such feature. The resulting constants are limited in length by a hardcoded value. In Python 3.5, it is still invariably equal to 20. Anyway, this particular detail is rather a curiosity than a thing that can be relied on in day-to-day programming. Information of other interesting optimizations performed by peephole optimizer can be found in the `Python/peephole.c` file of Python's source code.

Collections

Python provides a good selection of built-in data collections that allows you to efficiently solve many problems if you choose wisely. Types that you probably already know are those that have dedicated literals:

- Lists
- Tuples
- Dictionaries
- Sets

Python is of course not limited to these four and it extends the list of possible choices through its standard library. In many cases, the solution to a problem may be as simple as making a good choice for data structure. This part of the book aims to ease such a decision by providing deeper insight into the possible options.

Lists and tuples

The two most basic collection types in Python are lists and tuples, and they both represent sequences of objects. The basic difference between them should be obvious for anyone who has spent more than a few hours with Python—lists are dynamic so can change their size, while tuples are immutable (they cannot be modified after they are created).

Tuples, despite having many various optimizations that makes allocation/ deallocation of small objects fast, are the recommended datatype for structures where the position of the element is information by itself. For example, tuple may be a good choice for storing a pair of (x, y) coordinates. Anyway, details regarding tuples are rather uninteresting. The only important thing about them in the scope of this chapter is that `tuple` is **immutable** and thus **hashable**. What this means will be covered later in a *Dictionaries* section. More interesting than tuple is its dynamic counterpart, `list`, how it really works, and how to deal with it efficiently.

Implementation details

Many programmers easily confuse Python's list type with the concept of linked lists found often in standard libraries of other languages such as C, C++, or Java. In fact, CPython lists are not lists at all. In CPython, lists are implemented as variable length arrays. This should also be true for other implementations such as Jython and IronPython, although such implementation details are often not documented in these projects. The reasons for such confusion are clear. This datatype is named **list** and also has an interface that could be expected from any linked list implementation.

Why is it important and what does it mean? Lists are one of the most popular data structures and the way they are used greatly affects every application's performance. Also, CPython is the most popular and used implementation, so knowing its internal implementation details is crucial.

In detail, lists in Python is a contiguous array of references to other objects. The pointer to this array and the length is stored in a lists head structure. This means that every time an item is added or removed, the array of references needs to be resized (reallocated). Fortunately, in Python, these arrays are created with exponential over-allocation, so not every operation requires a resize. This is how the amortized cost of appending and popping elements can be low in terms of complexity. Unfortunately, some other operations that are considered "cheap" in ordinary linked lists have relatively high computational complexity in Python:

- Inserting an item at arbitrary place using the list.insert method — complexity O(n)
- Deleting an item using list.delete or using del — complexity O(n)

Here, n is the length of a list. At least retrieving or setting an element using index is an operation that cost is independent of the list's size. Here is a full table of average time complexities for most of the list operations:

Operation	Complexity
Copy	O(n)
Append	O(1)
Insert	O(n)
Get item	O(1)
Delete item	O(n)
Iteration	O(n)
Get slice of length k	O(k)
Del slice	O(n)
Set slice of length k	O(k+n)

Operation	Complexity
Extend	O(k)
Multiply by *k*	O(nk)
Test existence (`element in list`)	O(n)
`min()`/`max()`	O(n)
Get length	O(1)

For situations where a real linked list is needed (or simply, a data structure that has `appends` and `pop` at each side at O(1) complexity), Python provides `deque` in `collections` built-in module. This is a generalization of stacks and queues and should work fine anywhere where a doubly linked list is required.

List comprehensions

As you probably know, writing a piece of code such as this is painful:

```
>>> evens = []
>>> for i in range(10):
...     if i % 2 == 0:
...         evens.append(i)
...
>>> evens
[0, 2, 4, 6, 8]
```

This may work for C, but it actually makes things slower for Python because:

- It makes the interpreter work on each loop to determine what part of the sequence has to be changed
- It makes you keep a counter to track what element has to be treated
- It requires an additional function lookup to be performed at every iteration because `append()` is a list's method

A list comprehension is the correct answer to this pattern. It uses wired features that automate parts of the previous syntax:

```
>>> [i for i in range(10) if i % 2 == 0]
[0, 2, 4, 6, 8]
```

Besides the fact that this writing is more efficient, it is way shorter and involves fewer elements. In a bigger program, this means fewer bugs and code that is easier to read and understand.

List comprehensions and internal array resize

There is a myth among some Python programmers that the list comprehensions can be a workaround for the fact that the internal array representing the list object must be resized with every few additions. Some say that the array will be allocated once in just the right size. Unfortunately, this isn't true.

The interpreter during evaluation of the comprehension can't know how big the resulting container will be and it can't preallocate the final size of the array for it. Due to this, the internal array is reallocated in the same pattern as it would be in the `for` loop. Still, in many cases, list creation using comprehensions is both cleaner and faster than using ordinary loops.

Other idioms

Another typical example of a Python idiom is the usage of `enumerate`. This built-in function provides a convenient way to get an index when a sequence is used in a loop. Consider the following piece of code as an example:

```
>>> i = 0
>>> for element in ['one', 'two', 'three']:
...     print(i, element)
...     i += 1
...
0 one
1 two
2 three
```

This can be replaced by the following code, which is shorter:

```
>>> for i, element in enumerate(['one', 'two', 'three']):
...     print(i, element)
...
0 one
1 two
2 three
```

When the elements of multiple lists (or any iterables) need to be aggregated in a one-by-one fashion, then the built-in `zip()` function may be used. This is a very common pattern for uniform iteration over two same-sized iterables:

```
>>> for item in zip([1, 2, 3], [4, 5, 6]):
...     print(item)
...
(1, 4)
(2, 5)
(3, 6)
```

Note that the results of `zip()` can be reversed by another `zip()` call:

```
>>> for item in zip(*zip([1, 2, 3], [4, 5, 6])):
...     print(item)
...
(1, 2, 3)
(4, 5, 6)
```

Another popular syntax element is sequence unpacking. It is not limited to lists and tuples and will work with any sequence type (even strings and byte sequences). It allows you to unpack a sequence of elements into another set of variables as long as there are as many variables on the left-hand side of the assignment operator as the number of elements in the sequence:

```
>>> first, second, third = "foo", "bar", 100
>>> first
'foo'
>>> second
'bar'
>>> third
100
```

Unpacking also allows you to capture multiple elements in a single variable using starred expressions as long as it can be interpreted unambiguously. Unpacking can also be performed on nested sequences. This can come in handy especially when iterating on some complex data structures built of sequences. Here are some examples of more complex unpacking:

```
>>> # starred expression to capture rest of the sequence
>>> first, second, *rest = 0, 1, 2, 3
>>> first
```

```
0
>>> second
1
>>> rest
[2, 3]

>>> # starred expression to capture middle of the sequence
>>> first, *inner, last = 0, 1, 2, 3
>>> first
0
>>> inner
[1, 2]
>>> last
3

>>> # nested unpacking
>>> (a, b), (c, d) = (1, 2), (3, 4)
>>> a, b, c, d
(1, 2, 3, 4)
```

Dictionaries

Dictionaries are one of the most versatile data structures in Python. `dict` allows to map a set of unique keys to values as follows:

```
{
    1: ' one',
    2: ' two',
    3: ' three',
}
```

Dictionary literals are a very basic thing and you should already know them. Anyway, Python allows programmers to also create a new dictionary using comprehensions similar to the list comprehensions mentioned earlier. Here is a very simple example:

```
squares = {number: number**2 for number in range(100)}
```

What is important is that the same benefits of using list comprehensions apply to dictionary comprehensions. So, in many cases, they are more efficient, shorter, and cleaner. For more complex code, when many `if` statements or function calls are required to create a dictionary, the simple `for` loop may be a better choice, especially if it improves the readability.

For Python programmers new to Python 3, there is one important note about iterating over dictionary elements. The dictionary methods: `keys()`, `values()`, and `items()` no longer have lists as their return value types. Also, their counterparts `iterkeys()`, `itervalues()`, and `iteritems()` that returned iterators instead are missing in Python 3. Instead, what `keys()`, `values()`, and `items()` return now are view objects:

- `keys()`: This returns the `dict_keys` object that provides a view on all the keys of a dictionary
- `values()`: This returns the `dict_values` object that provides views on all the values of a dictionary
- `items()`: This returns the `dict_items` object providing views on all (`key`, `value`) two tuples of a dictionary

View objects provide a view on the dictionary content in a dynamic way, so every time the dictionary changes, the views will reflect these changes, as shown in this example:

```
>>> words = {'foo': 'bar', 'fizz': 'bazz'}
>>> items = words.items()
>>> words['spam'] = 'eggs'
>>> items
dict_items([('spam', 'eggs'), ('fizz', 'bazz'), ('foo', 'bar')])
```

View objects join the behavior of lists returned by implementation of old methods with iterators returned by their "iter" counterparts. Views do not need to redundantly store all values in memory (like lists do), but still allow getting their length (using `len`) and testing membership (using the `in` clause). Views are, of course, iterable.

The last important thing is that both views returned by the `keys()` and `values()` methods ensure the same order of keys and values. In Python 2, you could not modify the dictionary content between these two calls if you wanted to ensure the same order of retrieved keys and values. `dict_keys` and `dict_values` are now dynamic so even if the content of a dictionary will change between `keys()` and `values()` calls, the order of iteration is consistent between these two views.

Implementation details

CPython uses hash tables with pseudo-random probing as an underlying data structure for dictionaries. It seems like a very deep implementation detail, but it is very unlikely to change in the near future, so it is also a very interesting fact for the programmer.

Due to this implementation detail, only objects that are **hashable** can be used as a dictionary key. An object is hashable if it has a hash value that never changes during its lifetime and can be compared to different objects. Every Python's built-in type that is immutable is also hashable. Mutable types such as list, dictionaries, and sets are not hashable and so they cannot be used as dictionary keys. Protocol that defines if a type is hashable consists of two methods:

- `__hash__`: This provides the hash value (as an integer) that is needed by the internal `dict` implementation. For objects that are instances of user-defined classes, it is derived from their `id()`.

- `__eq__`: This compares if two objects that have the same value. All objects that are instances of user-defined classes compare unequal, by default, except for themselves.

Two objects that are compared equal must have the same hash value. The reverse does not need to be true. This means collisions of hashes are possible — two objects with the same hash may not be equal. It is allowed, and every Python implementation must be able to resolve hash collisions. CPython uses **open addressing** to resolve such collisions (`https://en.wikipedia.org/wiki/Open_addressing`). Still, the probability of collisions greatly affects performance, and if it is high, the dictionary will not benefit from its internal optimizations.

While three basic operations: adding, getting, and deleting an item have an average time complexity equal to O(1), their amortized worst case complexities are a lot higher — O(n), where n is the current dictionary size. Additionally, if user-defined class objects are used as dictionary keys and they are hashed improperly (with a high risk of collisions), then this will have a huge negative impact on the dictionary performance. The full table of CPyhton's time complexities for dictionaries is as follows:

Operation	Average complexity	Amortized worst case complexity
Get item	O(1)	O(n)
Set item	O(1)	O(n)
Delete item	O(1)	O(n)
Copy	O(n)	O(n)
Iteration	O(n)	O(n)

It is also important to know that the *n* number in worst-case complexities for copying and iterating the dictionary is the maximum size that the dictionary ever achieved, rather than the current item count. In other words, iterating over the dictionary that once was huge but has greatly shrunk in time may take a surprisingly long time. So, in some cases, it may be better to create a new dictionary object if it has to be iterated often instead of just removing elements from the previous one.

Weaknesses and alternatives

One of the common pitfalls of using dictionaries is that they do not preserve the order of elements in which new keys were added. In some scenarios, when dictionary keys use consecutive keys whose hashes are also consecutive values (for example, using integers), the resulting order might be the same due to the internal implementation of dictionaries:

```
>>> {number: None for number in range(5)}.keys()
dict_keys([0, 1, 2, 3, 4])
```

Still, using other datatypes which hash differently shows that the order is not preserved. Here is an example in CPython:

```
>>> {str(number): None for number in range(5)}.keys()
dict_keys(['1', '2', '4', '0', '3'])
>>> {str(number): None for number in reversed(range(5))}.keys()
dict_keys(['2', '3', '1', '4', '0'])
```

As shown in the preceding code, the resulting order is both dependent on the hashing of the object and also on the order in which the elements were added. This is not what can be relied on because it can vary with different Python implementations.

Still, in some cases, the developer might need dictionaries that preserve the order of additions. Fortunately, the Python standard library provides an ordered dictionary called `OrderedDict` in the `collections` module. It optionally accepts an iterable as the initialization argument:

```
>>> from collections import OrderedDict
>>> OrderedDict((str(number), None) for number in range(5)).keys()
odict_keys(['0', '1', '2', '3', '4'])
```

It also has some additional features such as popping items from both ends using the `popitem()` method or moving the specified element to one of the ends using the `move_to_end()` method. A full reference on that collection is available in the Python documentation (refer to `https://docs.python.org/3/library/collections.html`).

The other important note is that in very old code bases, `dict` may be used as a primitive set implementation that ensures the uniqueness of elements. While this will give proper results, this should be omitted unless Python versions lower than 2.3 are targeted. Using dictionaries this way is wasteful in terms of resources. Python has a built-in `set` type that serves this purpose. In fact, it has a very similar internal implementation to dictionaries in CPython, but offers some additional features as well as specific set-related optimizations.

Sets

Sets are a very robust data structure that are useful mostly in situations where the order of elements is not as important as their uniqueness and efficiency of testing if an element is contained by a collection. They are very similar to analogous mathematic concepts. Sets are provided as built-in types in two flavors:

- `set()`: This is a mutable, non-ordered, finite collection of unique, immutable (hashable) objects
- `frozenset()`: This is an immutable, hashable, non-ordered collection of unique, immutable (hashable) objects

The immutability of `frozenset()` makes it possible to be used as dictionary keys and also other `set()` and `frozenset()` elements. A plain mutable `set()` cannot be used within another set or frozenset content as this will raise `TypeError`:

```
>>> set([set([1,2,3]), set([2,3,4])])
Traceback (most recent call last):
  File "<stdin>", line 1, in <module>
TypeError: unhashable type: 'set'
```

The following set initializations are completely correct:

```
>>> set([frozenset([1,2,3]), frozenset([2,3,4])])
{frozenset({1, 2, 3}), frozenset({2, 3, 4})}
>>> frozenset([frozenset([1,2,3]), frozenset([2,3,4])])
frozenset({frozenset({1, 2, 3}), frozenset({2, 3, 4})})
```

Mutable sets can be created in three ways:

- Using a `set()` call that accepts optional iterable as the initialization argument, such as `set([0, 1, 2])`
- Using a set comprehension such as `{element for element in range(3)}`
- Using set literals such as `{1, 2, 3}`

Note that using literals and comprehensions for sets requires extra caution because they are very similar in form to dictionary literals and comprehensions. Also, there is no literal for empty set objects—empty curly brackets { } are reserved for empty dictionary literals.

Implementation details

Sets in CPython are very similar to dictionaries. As a matter of fact, they are implemented like dictionaries with dummy values, where only keys are actual collection elements. Also, sets exploit this lack of values in mapping for additional optimizations.

Thanks to this, sets allow very fast additions, deletions, and checking for element existence with the average time complexity equal to O(1). Still, since the implementation of sets in CPython relies on a similar hash table structure, the worst-case complexity for these operations is O(n), where *n* is the current size of a set.

Other implementation details also apply. The item to be included in a set must be hashable, and if instances of user-defined classes in a set are hashed poorly, this will have a negative impact on the performance.

Beyond basic collections – the collections module

Every data structure has its shortcomings. There is no single collection that can suit every problem and four basic types of them (tuple, list, set, and dictionary) is still not a wide range of choices. These are the most basic and important collections that have a dedicated literal syntax. Fortunately, Python provides a lot more options in its standard library through the `collections` built-in module. One of them was already mentioned (`deque`). Here are the most important collections provided by this module:

- `namedtuple()`: This is a factory function for creating tuple subclasses whose indexes can be accessed as named attributes
- `deque`: This is a double-ended queue, list-like generalization of stacks and queues with fast appends and pops on both ends
- `ChainMap`: This is a dictionary-like class to create a single view of multiple mappings
- `Counter`: This is a dictionary subclass for counting hashable objects
- `OrderedDict`: This is a dictionary subclass that preserves the order the entries were added in
- `defaultdict`: This is a dictionary subclass that can supply missing values with a provided default

More details on selected collections from the collections module and some advice on where it is worth using them are provided in *Chapter 12, Optimization – Some Powerful Techniques.*

Advanced syntax

It is hard to objectively tell which element of language syntax is advanced. For the purpose of this chapter on advanced syntax elements, we will consider the elements that do not directly relate to any specific built-in datatypes and which are relatively hard to grasp at the beginning. The most common Python features that may be hard to understand are:

- Iterators
- Generators
- Decorators
- Context managers

Iterators

An **iterator** is nothing more than a container object that implements the iterator protocol. It is based on two methods:

- __next__: This returns the next item of the container
- __iter__: This returns the iterator itself

Iterators can be created from a sequence using the `iter` built-in function. Consider the following example:

```
>>> i = iter('abc')
>>> next(i)
'a'
>>> next(i)
'b'
>>> next(i)
'c'
>>> next(i)
Traceback (most recent call last):
  File "<input>", line 1, in <module>
StopIteration
```

When the sequence is exhausted, a `StopIteration` exception is raised. It makes iterators compatible with loops since they catch this exception to stop cycling. To create a custom iterator, a class with a __next__ method can be written, as long as it provides the special method __iter__ that returns an instance of the iterator:

```
class CountDown:
    def __init__(self, step):
        self.step = step
    def __next__(self):
        """Return the next element."""
        if self.step <= 0:
            raise StopIteration
        self.step -= 1
        return self.step
    def __iter__(self):
        """Return the iterator itself."""
        return self
```

Here is example usage of such iterator:

```
>>> for element in CountDown(4):
...     print(element)
...
3
2
1
0
```

Iterators themselves are a low-level feature and concept, and a program can live without them. But they provide the base for a much more interesting feature, generators.

The yield statement

Generators provide an elegant way to write simple and efficient code for functions that return a sequence of elements. Based on the `yield` statement, they allow you to pause a function and return an intermediate result. The function saves its execution context and can be resumed later, if necessary.

For instance, the Fibonacci series can be written with an iterator (this is the example provided in the PEP about iterators):

```
def fibonacci():
    a, b = 0, 1
    while True:
        yield b
        a, b = b, a + b
```

You can retrieve new values from generators as if it were iterators, so using `next()` function or `for` loops:

```
>>> fib = fibonacci()
>>> next(fib)
1
>>> next(fib)
1
>>> next(fib)
2
>>> [next(fib) for i in range(10)]
[3, 5, 8, 13, 21, 34, 55, 89, 144, 233]
```

This function returns a `generator` object, a special iterator, which knows how to save the execution context. It can be called indefinitely, yielding the next element of the suite each time. The syntax is concise, and the infinite nature of the algorithm does not disturb the readability of the code anymore. It does not have to provide a way to make the function stoppable. In fact, it looks similar to how the series would be designed in pseudocode.

In the community, generators are not used so often because the developers are not used to thinking this way. The developers have been used to working with straight functions for years. Generators should be considered every time you deal with a function that returns a sequence or works in a loop. Returning the elements one at a time can improve the overall performance, when they are passed to another function for further work.

In that case, the resources used to work out one element are most of the time less important than the resources used for the whole process. Therefore, they can be kept low, making the program more efficient. For instance, the Fibonacci sequence is infinite, and yet the generator that generates it does not require an infinite amount of memory to provide the values one at a time. A common use case is to stream data buffers with generators. They can be paused, resumed, and stopped by third-party code that plays over the data, and all the data does not need to be loaded before starting the process.

The `tokenize` module from the standard library, for instance, generates tokens out of a stream of text and returns an `iterator` for each treated line that can be passed along to some processing:

```
>>> import tokenize
>>> reader = open('hello.py').readline
>>> tokens = tokenize.generate_tokens(reader)
>>> next(tokens)
TokenInfo(type=57 (COMMENT), string='# -*- coding: utf-8 -*-', start=(1, 0), end=(1, 23), line='# -*- coding: utf-8 -*-\n')
>>> next(tokens)
TokenInfo(type=58 (NL), string='\n', start=(1, 23), end=(1, 24), line='# -*- coding: utf-8 -*-\n')
>>> next(tokens)
TokenInfo(type=1 (NAME), string='def', start=(2, 0), end=(2, 3), line='def hello_world():\n')
```

Here, we can see that `open` iterates over the lines of the file and `generate_tokens` iterates over them in a pipeline, doing additional work. Generators can also help in breaking the complexity and raising the efficiency of some data transformation algorithms that are based on several suites. Thinking of each suite as an `iterator`, and then combining them into a high-level function is a great way to avoid a big, ugly, and unreadable function. Moreover, this can provide a live feedback to the whole processing chain.

In the following example, each function defines a transformation over a sequence. They are then chained and applied. Each function call processes one element and returns its result:

```
def power(values):
    for value in values:
        print('powering %s' % value)
        yield value
```

```
def adder(values):
    for value in values:
        print('adding to %s' % value)
        if value % 2 == 0:
            yield value + 3
        else:
            yield value + 2
```

Here is the possible result of using these generators together:

```
>>> elements = [1, 4, 7, 9, 12, 19]
>>> results = adder(power(elements))
>>> next(results)
powering 1
adding to 1
3
>>> next(results)
powering 4
adding to 4
7
>>> next(results)
powering 7
adding to 7
9
```

Keep the code simple, not the data

It is better to have a lot of simple iterable functions that work over sequences of values than a complex function that computes the result for entire collection at once.

Another important feature available in Python regarding generators is the ability to interact with the code called with the next function. yield becomes an expression, and a value can be passed along with a new method called send:

```
def psychologist():
    print('Please tell me your problems')
    while True:
        answer = (yield)
        if answer is not None:
            if answer.endswith('?'):
                print("Don't ask yourself too much questions")
            elif 'good' in answer:
```

```
            print("Ahh that's good, go on")
        elif 'bad' in answer:
            print("Don't be so negative")
```

Here is an example session with our `psychologist()` function:

```
>>> free = psychologist()
>>> next(free)
Please tell me your problems
>>> free.send('I feel bad')
Don't be so negative
>>> free.send("Why I shouldn't ?")
Don't ask yourself too much questions
>>> free.send("ok then i should find what is good for me")
Ahh that's good, go on
```

`send` acts like `next`, but makes `yield` return the value passed to it inside of the function definition. The function can, therefore, change its behavior depending on the client code. Two other functions were added to complete this behavior—`throw` and `close`. They raise an error into the generator:

- `throw`: This allows the client code to send any kind of exception to be raised.

- `close`: This acts in the same way, but raises a specific exception, `GeneratorExit`. In that case, the generator function must raise `GeneratorExit` again, or `StopIteration`.

 Generators are the basis of other concepts available in Python—coroutines and asynchronous concurrency, which are covered in *Chapter 13, Concurrency*.

Decorators

Decorators were added in Python to make function and method wrapping (a function that receives a function and returns an enhanced one) easier to read and understand. The original use case was to be able to define the methods as class methods or static methods on the head of their definition. Without the decorator syntax, it would require a rather sparse and repetitive definition:

```
class WithoutDecorators:
    def some_static_method():
        print("this is static method")
    some_static_method = staticmethod(some_static_method)
```

```
    def some_class_method(cls):
        print("this is class method")
    some_class_method = classmethod(some_class_method)
```

If the decorator syntax is used for the same purpose, the code is shorter and easier to understand:

```
class WithDecorators:
    @staticmethod
    def some_static_method():
        print("this is static method")

    @classmethod
    def some_class_method(cls):
        print("this is class method")
```

General syntax and possible implementations

The decorator is generally a named object (`lambda` expressions are not allowed) that accepts a single argument when called (it will be the decorated function) and returns another callable object. "Callable" is used here instead of "function" with premeditation. While decorators are often discussed in the scope of methods and functions, they are not limited to them. In fact, anything that is callable (any object that implements the __call__ method is considered callable), can be used as a decorator and often objects returned by them are not simple functions but more instances of more complex classes implementing their own __call__ method.

The decorator syntax is simply only a syntactic sugar. Consider the following decorator usage:

```
@some_decorator
def decorated_function():
    pass
```

This can always be replaced by an explicit decorator call and function reassignment:

```
def decorated_function():
    pass
decorated_function = some_decorator(decorated_function)
```

However, the latter is less readable and also very hard to understand if multiple decorators are used on a single function.

Decorator does not even need to return a callable!

As a matter of fact, any function can be used as a decorator because Python does not enforce the return type of decorators. So, using some function as a decorator that accepts a single argument but does not return callable, let's say `str`, is completely valid in terms of syntax. This will eventually fail if the user tries to call an object decorated this way. Anyway, this part of decorator syntax creates a field for some interesting experimentation.

As a function

There are many ways to write custom decorators, but the simplest way is to write a function that returns a subfunction that wraps the original function call.

The generic patterns is as follows:

```
def mydecorator(function):
    def wrapped(*args, **kwargs):
        # do some stuff before the original
        # function gets called
        result = function(*args, **kwargs)
        # do some stuff after function call and
        # return the result
        return result
    # return wrapper as a decorated function
    return wrapped
```

As a class

While decorators almost always can be implemented using functions, there are some situations when using user-defined classes is a better option. This is often true when the decorator needs complex parametrization or it depends on a specific state.

The generic pattern for a nonparametrized decorator as a class is as follows:

```
class DecoratorAsClass:
    def __init__(self, function):
        self.function = function

    def __call__(self, *args, **kwargs):
        # do some stuff before the original
        # function gets called
        result = self.function(*args, **kwargs)
        # do some stuff after function call and
        # return the result
        return result
```

Parametrizing decorators

In real code, there is often a need to use decorators that can be parametrized. When the function is used as a decorator, then the solution is simple—a second level of wrapping has to be used. Here is a simple example of the decorator that repeats the execution of a decorated function the specified number of times every time it is called:

```
def repeat(number=3):
    """Cause decorated function to be repeated a number of times.

    Last value of original function call is returned as a result
    :param number: number of repetitions, 3 if not specified
    """
    def actual_decorator(function):
        def wrapper(*args, **kwargs):
            result = None
            for _ in range(number):
                result = function(*args, **kwargs)
            return result
        return wrapper
    return actual_decorator
```

The decorator defined this way can accept parameters:

```
>>> @repeat(2)
... def foo():
...     print("foo")
...
>>> foo()
foo
foo
```

Note that even if the parametrized decorator has default values for its arguments, the parentheses after its name is required. The correct way to use the preceding decorator with default arguments is as follows:

```
>>> @repeat()
... def bar():
...     print("bar")
...
>>> bar()
bar
bar
bar
```

Missing these parentheses will result in the following error when decorated function is called:

```
>>> @repeat
... def bar():
...     pass
...
>>> bar()
Traceback (most recent call last):
  File "<input>", line 1, in <module>
TypeError: actual_decorator() missing 1 required positional
argument: 'function'
```

Introspection preserving decorators

Common pitfalls of using decorators is not preserving function metadata (mostly docstring and original name) when using decorators. All the previous examples have this issue. They created a new function by composition and returned a new object without any respect to the identity of the original one. This makes the debugging of functions decorated that way harder and will also break most of the auto-documentation tools that may be used because the original docstrings and function signatures are no longer accessible.

But let's see this in detail. Assume that we have some dummy decorator that does nothing more than decorating and some other functions decorated with it:

```
def dummy_decorator(function):
    def wrapped(*args, **kwargs):
        """Internal wrapped function documentation."""
        return function(*args, **kwargs)
    return wrapped


@dummy_decorator
def function_with_important_docstring():
    """This is important docstring we do not want to lose."""
```

If we inspect `function_with_important_docstring()` in a Python interactive session, we can notice that it has lost its original name and docstring:

```
>>> function_with_important_docstring.__name__
'wrapped'
>>> function_with_important_docstring.__doc__
'Internal wrapped function documentation.'
```

A proper solution to this problem is to use the built-in `wraps()` decorator provided by the `functools` module:

```python
from functools import wraps


def preserving_decorator(function):
    @wraps(function)
    def wrapped(*args, **kwargs):
        """Internal wrapped function documentation."""
        return function(*args, **kwargs)
    return wrapped


@preserving_decorator
def function_with_important_docstring():
    """This is important docstring we do not want to lose."""
```

With the decorator defined in such a way, the important function metadata is preserved:

```python
>>> function_with_important_docstring.__name__
'function_with_important_docstring.'
>>> function_with_important_docstring.__doc__
'This is important docstring we do not want to lose.'
```

Usage and useful examples

Since decorators are loaded by the interpreter when the module is first read, their usage should be limited to wrappers that can be generically applied. If a decorator is tied to the method's class or to the function's signature it enhances, it should be refactored into a regular callable to avoid complexity. In any case, when the decorators are dealing with APIs, a good practice is to group them in a module that is easy to maintain.

The common patterns for decorators are:

- Argument checking
- Caching
- Proxy
- Context provider

Argument checking

Checking the arguments that a function receives or returns can be useful when it is executed in a specific context. For example, if a function is to be called through XML-RPC, Python will not be able to directly provide its full signature as in the statically-typed languages. This feature is needed to provide introspection capabilities, when the XML-RPC client asks for the function signatures.

The XML-RPC protocol

The XML-RPC protocol is a lightweight **Remote Procedure Call** protocol that uses XML over HTTP to encode its calls. It is often used instead of SOAP for simple client-server exchanges. Unlike SOAP, which provides a page that lists all callable functions (WSDL), XML-RPC does not have a directory of available functions. An extension of the protocol that allows discovering the server API was proposed, and Python's xmlrpc module implements it (refer to https://docs.python.org/3/library/xmlrpc.server.html).

A custom decorator can provide this type of signature. It can also make sure that what goes in and comes out respects the defined signature parameters:

```python
rpc_info = {}


def xmlrpc(in_=(), out=(type(None),)):
    def _xmlrpc(function):
        # registering the signature
        func_name = function.__name__
        rpc_info[func_name] = (in_, out)
        def _check_types(elements, types):
            """Subfunction that checks the types."""
            if len(elements) != len(types):
                raise TypeError('argument count is wrong')
            typed = enumerate(zip(elements, types))
            for index, couple in typed:
                arg, of_the_right_type = couple
                if isinstance(arg, of_the_right_type):
                    continue
                raise TypeError(
                    'arg #%d should be %s' % (index,
                        of_the_right_type))

        # wrapped function
        def __xmlrpc(*args):  # no keywords allowed
```

```
            # checking what goes in
            checkable_args = args[1:]   # removing self
            _check_types(checkable_args, in_)
            # running the function
            res = function(*args)
            # checking what goes out
            if not type(res) in (tuple, list):
                checkable_res = (res,)
            else:
                checkable_res = res
            _check_types(checkable_res, out)

            # the function and the type
            # checking succeeded
            return res
        return __xmlrpc
    return _xmlrpc
```

The decorator registers the function into a global dictionary and keeps a list of the types for its arguments and for the returned values. Note that the example was highly simplified to demonstrate argument-checking decorators.

A usage example is as follows:

```
class RPCView:
    @xmlrpc((int, int))   # two int -> None
    def meth1(self, int1, int2):
        print('received %d and %d' % (int1, int2))

    @xmlrpc((str,), (int,))   # string -> int
    def meth2(self, phrase):
        print('received %s' % phrase)
        return 12
```

When it is read, this class definition populates the rpc_infos dictionary and can be used in a specific environment, where the argument types are checked:

```
>>> rpc_info
{'meth2': ((<class 'str'>,), (<class 'int'>,)), 'meth1': ((<class
'int'>, <class 'int'>), (<class 'NoneType'>,))}
>>> my = RPCView()
>>> my.meth1(1, 2)
received 1 and 2
>>> my.meth2(2)
```

```
Traceback (most recent call last):
  File "<input>", line 1, in <module>
  File "<input>", line 26, in __xmlrpc
  File "<input>", line 20, in _check_types
TypeError: arg #0 should be <class 'str'>
```

Caching

The caching decorator is quite similar to argument checking, but focuses on those functions whose internal state does not affect the output. Each set of arguments can be linked to a unique result. This style of programming is the characteristic of **functional programming** (refer to http://en.wikipedia.org/wiki/Functional_ programming) and can be used when the set of input values is finite.

Therefore, a caching decorator can keep the output together with the arguments that were needed to compute it, and return it directly on subsequent calls. This behavior is called **memoizing** (refer to http://en.wikipedia.org/wiki/Memoizing) and is quite simple to implement as a decorator:

```python
import time
import hashlib
import pickle

cache = {}

def is_obsolete(entry, duration):
    return time.time() - entry['time'] > duration

def compute_key(function, args, kw):
    key = pickle.dumps((function.__name__, args, kw))
    return hashlib.sha1(key).hexdigest()

def memoize(duration=10):
    def _memoize(function):
        def __memoize(*args, **kw):
            key = compute_key(function, args, kw)

            # do we have it already ?
            if (key in cache and
                    not is_obsolete(cache[key], duration)):
                print('we got a winner')
                return cache[key]['value']
```

```
            # computing
            result = function(*args, **kw)
            # storing the result
            cache[key] = {
                'value': result,
                'time': time.time()
            }
            return result
        return __memoize
    return _memoize
```

A SHA hash key is built using the ordered argument values, and the result is stored in a global dictionary. The hash is made using a pickle, which is a bit of a shortcut to freeze the state of all objects passed as arguments, ensuring that all arguments are good candidates. If a thread or a socket is used as an argument, for instance, a PicklingError will occur. (Refer to https://docs.python.org/3/library/pickle.html.) The duration parameter is used to invalidate the cached value when too much time has passed since the last function call.

Here's an example of the usage:

```
>>> @memoize()
... def very_very_very_complex_stuff(a, b):
...     # if your computer gets too hot on this calculation
...     # consider stopping it
...     return a + b
...
>>> very_very_very_complex_stuff(2, 2)
4
>>> very_very_very_complex_stuff(2, 2)
we got a winner
4
>>> @memoize(1) # invalidates the cache after 1 second
... def very_very_very_complex_stuff(a, b):
...     return a + b
...
>>> very_very_very_complex_stuff(2, 2)
4
>>> very_very_very_complex_stuff(2, 2)
we got a winner
```

```
4
>>> cache
{'c2727f43c6e39b3694649ee0883234cf': {'value': 4, 'time':
1199734132.7102251)}
>>> time.sleep(2)
>>> very_very_very_complex_stuff(2, 2)
4
```

Caching expensive functions can dramatically increase the overall performance of a program, but it has to be used with care. The cached value could also be tied to the function itself to manage its scope and life cycle, instead of a centralized dictionary. But in any case, a more efficient decorator would use a specialized cache library based on advanced caching algorithm.

 Chapter 12, Optimization – Some Powerful Techniques, provides detailed information and techniques on caching.

Proxy

Proxy decorators are used to tag and register functions with a global mechanism. For instance, a security layer that protects the access of the code, depending on the current user, can be implemented using a centralized checker with an associated permission required by the callable:

```
class User(object):
    def __init__(self, roles):
        self.roles = roles


class Unauthorized(Exception):
    pass


def protect(role):
    def _protect(function):
        def __protect(*args, **kw):
            user = globals().get('user')
            if user is None or role not in user.roles:
                raise Unauthorized("I won't tell you")
            return function(*args, **kw)
        return __protect
    return _protect
```

This model is often used in Python web frameworks to define the security over publishable classes. For instance, Django provides decorators to secure function access.

Here's an example, where the current user is kept in a global variable. The decorator checks his or her roles when the method is accessed:

```
>>> tarek = User(('admin', 'user'))
>>> bill = User(('user',))
>>> class MySecrets(object):
...     @protect('admin')
...     def waffle_recipe(self):
...         print('use tons of butter!')
...
>>> these_are = MySecrets()
>>> user = tarek
>>> these_are.waffle_recipe()
use tons of butter!
>>> user = bill
>>> these_are.waffle_recipe()
Traceback (most recent call last):
File "<stdin>", line 1, in <module>
File "<stdin>", line 7, in wrap
__main__.Unauthorized: I won't tell you
```

Context provider

A context decorator makes sure that the function can run in the correct context, or run some code before and after the function. In other words, it sets and unsets a specific execution environment. For example, when a data item has to be shared among several threads, a lock has to be used to ensure that it is protected from multiple access. This lock can be coded in a decorator as follows:

```
from threading import RLock
lock = RLock()


def synchronized(function):
    def _synchronized(*args, **kw):
        lock.acquire()
        try:
            return function(*args, **kw)
```

```
        finally:
            lock.release()
    return _synchronized


@synchronized
def thread_safe():  # make sure it locks the resource
    pass
```

Context decorators are more often being replaced by the usage of the context managers (the `with` statement) that are also described later in this chapter.

Context managers – the with statement

The `try...finally` statement is useful to ensure some cleanup code is run even if an error is raised. There are many use cases for this, such as:

- Closing a file
- Releasing a lock
- Making a temporary code patch
- Running protected code in a special environment

The `with` statement factors out these use cases by providing a simple way to wrap a block of code. This allows you to call some code before and after block execution even if this block raises an exception. For example, working with a file is usually done like this:

```
>>> hosts = open('/etc/hosts')
>>> try:
...     for line in hosts:
...         if line.startswith('#'):
...             continue
...         print(line.strip())
... finally:
...     hosts.close()
...
127.0.0.1       localhost
255.255.255.255 broadcasthost
::1             localhost
```

This example is specific to Linux since it reads the host file located in etc, but any text file could have been used here in the same way.

By using the with statement, it can be rewritten like this:

```
>>> with open('/etc/hosts') as hosts:
...     for line in hosts:
...         if line.startswith('#'):
...             continue
...         print(line.strip )
...
127.0.0.1       localhost
255.255.255.255 broadcasthost
::1             localhost
```

In the preceding example, open used as a context manager ensures that the file will be closed after executing the for loop and even if some exception will occur.

Some other items that are compatible with this statement are classes from the threading module:

- threading.Lock
- threading.RLock
- threading.Condition
- threading.Semaphore
- threading.BoundedSemaphore

General syntax and possible implementations

The general syntax for the with statement in the simplest form is:

```
with context_manager:
    # block of code
    ...
```

Additionally, if the context manager provides a context variable, it can be stored locally using the as clause:

```
with context_manager as context:
    # block of code
    ...
```

Note that multiple context managers can be used at once, as follows:

```
with A() as a, B() as b:
    ...
```

This is equivalent to nesting them, as follows:

```
with A() as a:
    with B() as b:
        ...
```

As a class

Any object that implements the **context manager protocol** can be used as a context manager. This protocol consists of two special methods:

- `__enter__(self)`: More on this can be found at https://docs.python.org/3.3/reference/datamodel.html#object.__enter__

- `__exit__(self, exc_type, exc_value, traceback)`: More on this can be found at https://docs.python.org/3.3/reference/datamodel.html#object.__exit__

In short, the execution of the `with` statement proceeds as follows:

1. The `__enter__` method is invoked. Any return value is bound to target the specified as clause.

2. The inner block of code is executed.

3. The `__exit__` method is invoked.

`__exit__` receives three arguments that are filled when an error occurs within the code block. If no error occurs, all three arguments are set to `None`. When an error occurs, `__exit__` should not re-raise it, as this is the responsibility of the caller. It can prevent the exception being raised though, by returning `True`. This is provided to implement some specific use cases, such as the `contextmanager` decorator that we will see in the next section. But for most use cases, the right behavior for this method is to do some cleaning, like what would be done by the `finally` clause; no matter what happens in the block, it does not return anything.

The following is an example of some context manager that implements this protocol to better illustrate how it works:

```
class ContextIllustration:
    def __enter__(self):
        print('entering context')
```

```
def __exit__(self, exc_type, exc_value, traceback):
    print('leaving context')

    if exc_type is None:
        print('with no error')
    else:
        print('with an error (%s)' % exc_value)
```

When run without exceptions raised, the output is as follows:

```
>>> with ContextIllustration():
...     print("inside")
...
entering context
inside
leaving context
with no error
```

When the exception is raised, the output is as follows:

```
>>> with ContextIllustration():
...     raise RuntimeError("raised within 'with'")
...
entering context
leaving context
with an error (raised within 'with')
Traceback (most recent call last):
  File "<input>", line 2, in <module>
RuntimeError: raised within 'with'
```

As a function – the contextlib module

Using classes seems to be the most flexible way to implement any protocol provided in the Python language but may be too much boilerplate for many use cases. A `contextlib` module was added to the standard library to provide helpers to use with context managers. The most useful part of it is the `contextmanager` decorator. It allows you to provide both `__enter__` and `__exit__` parts in a single function, separated by a `yield` statement (note that this makes the function a generator). The previous example written with this decorator would look like the following code:

```
from contextlib import contextmanager

@contextmanager
def context_illustration():
```

```
    print('entering context')

    try:
        yield
    except Exception as e:
        print('leaving context')
        print('with an error (%s)' % e)
        # exception needs to be reraised
        raise
    else:
        print('leaving context')
        print('with no error')
```

If any exception occurs, the function needs to re-raise it in order to pass it along. Note that the `context_illustration` could have some arguments if needed, as long as they are provided in the call. This small helper simplifies the normal class-based context API exactly as generators do with the classed-based iterator API.

The three other helpers provided by this module are:

- `closing(element)`: This returns the context manager that calls the element's close method on exit. This is useful for classes that deal with streams, for instance.

- `supress(*exceptions)`: This suppresses any of the specified exceptions if they occur in the body of the with statement.

- `redirect_stdout(new_target)` and `redirect_stderr(new_target)`: This redirects the `sys.stdout` or `sys.stderr` output of any code within the block to another file of the file-like object.

Other syntax elements you may not know yet

There are some elements of the Python syntax that are not popular and rarely used. It is because they either provide very little gain or their usage is simply hard to memorize. Due to this, many Python programmers (even with years of experience) simply do not know about their existence. The most notable examples of such features are as follows:

- The `for ... else` clause
- Function annotations

The for ... else ... statement

Using the `else` clause after the `for` loop allows you to execute a code of block only if the loop ended "naturally" without terminating with the `break` statement:

```
>>> for number in range(1):
...     break
... else:
...     print("no break")
...
>>>
>>> for number in range(1):
...     pass
... else:
...     print("break")
...
break
```

This comes in handy in some situations because it helps to remove some "sentinel" variables that may be required if the user wants to store information if a `break` occurred. This makes the code cleaner but can confuse programmers not familiar with such syntax. Some say that such meaning of the `else` clause is counterintuitive, but here is an easy tip that helps you to remember how it works—memorize that `else` clause after the `for` loop simply means "no break".

Function annotations

Function annotation is one of the most unique features of Python 3. The official documentation states that *annotations are completely optional metadata information about the types used by user-defined functions*, but in fact, they are not restricted to type hinting, and also there is no single feature in Python and its standard library that leverages such annotations. This is why this feature is unique—it does not have any syntactic meaning. Annotations can simply be defined for a function and can be retrieved in runtime, but that is all. What to do with them is left to the developers.

The general syntax

A slightly modified example from the Python documentation shows best how to define and retrieve function annotations:

```
>>> def f(ham: str, eggs: str = 'eggs') -> str:
...       pass
...
>>> print(f.__annotations__)
{'return': <class 'str'>, 'eggs': <class 'str'>, 'ham': <class 'str'>}
```

As presented, parameter annotations are defined by the expression evaluating to the value of the annotation preceded by a colon. Return annotations are defined by the expression between the colon denoting the end of the def statement and literal -> that follows the parameter list.

Once defined, annotations are available in the __annotations__ attribute of the function object as a dictionary and can be retrieved during application runtime.

The fact that any expression can be used as the annotation and it is located just near the default arguments allows to create some confusing function definitions as follows:

```
>>> def square(number: 0<=3 and 1=0) -> (\
...       +9000): return number**2
>>> square(10)
100
```

However, such usage of annotations serves no other purpose than obfuscation and even without them it is relatively easy to write code that is hard to read and maintain.

The possible uses

While annotations have a great potential, they are not widely used. An article explaining new features added to Python 3 (refer to https://docs.python.org/3/whatsnew/3.0.html) says that the intent of this feature was "to encourage experimentation through metaclasses, decorators, or frameworks". On the other hand, **PEP 3107** that officially proposed function annotations lists the following set of possible use cases:

- Providing typing information
    - Type checking
    - Let IDEs show what types a function expects and returns

- ° Function overloading / generic functions
- ° Foreign-language bridges
- ° Adaptation
- ° Predicate logic functions
- ° Database query mapping
- ° RPC parameter marshaling
- Other information
  - ° Documentation for parameters and return values

Although the function annotations are as old as Python 3, it is still very hard to find any popular and actively maintained package that uses them for something else than type checking. So function annotations are still mostly good only for experimentation and playing — the initial purpose why they were included in initial release of Python 3.

Summary

This chapter covered various best syntax practices that do not directly relate to Python classes and object-oriented programming. The first part of the chapter was dedicated to syntax features around Python sequences and collections, strings and byte-related sequences were also discussed. The rest of the chapter covered independent syntax elements of two groups — those that are relatively hard to understand for beginners (such as iterators, generators, and decorators) and those that are simply less known (the `for...else` clause and function annotations).

3
Syntax Best Practices –
above the Class Level

We will now focus on syntax best practices for classes. It is not intended to cover design patterns here, as they will be discussed in *Chapter 14, Useful Design Patterns*. This chapter gives an overview of the advanced Python syntax to manipulate and enhance the class code.

Object model evolved greatly during history of Python 2. For a long time we lived in a world where two implementations of the object-oriented programming paradigm coexisted in the same language. These two models were simply referred to as *old-style* and *new-style* classes. Python 3 ended this dichotomy and only model known as *new-style* classes is available to the developers. Anyway, it is still important to know how both of them worked in Python 2 because it will help you in porting old code and writing backwards compatible applications. Knowing how the object model changed will also help you in understanding why it is designed that way right now. This is the reason why the following chapter will have a relatively large number of notes about old Python 2 features despite this book targets the latest Python 3 releases.

The following topics will be discussed in this chapter:

- Subclassing built-in types
- Accessing methods from super classes
- Using properties and slots
- Metaprogramming

Subclassing built-in types

Subclassing built-in types in Python is pretty straightforward. A built-in type called `object` is a common ancestor for all built-in types as well as all user-defined classes that have no explicit parent class specified. Thanks to this, every time a class that behaves almost like one of the built-in types needs to be implemented, the best practice is to subtype it.

Now, we will show you the code for a class called `distinctdict`, which uses this technique. It is a subclass of the usual Python `dict` type. This new class behaves in most ways like an ordinary Python `dict`. But instead of allowing multiple keys with the same value, when someone tries to add a new entry with an identical value, it raises a `ValueError` subclass with a help message:

```python
class DistinctError(ValueError):
    """Raised when duplicate value is added to a distinctdict."""


class distinctdict(dict):
    """Dictionary that does not accept duplicate values."""
    def __setitem__(self, key, value):
        if value in self.values():
            if (
                (key in self and self[key] != value) or
                key not in self
            ):
                raise DistinctError(
                    "This value already exists for different key"
                )

        super().__setitem__(key, value)
```

The following is an example of using `distictdict` in interactive session:

```python
>>> my = distinctdict()
>>> my['key'] = 'value'
>>> my['other_key'] = 'value'
Traceback (most recent call last):
  File "<input>", line 1, in <module>
  File "<input>", line 10, in __setitem__
DistinctError: This value already exists for different key
>>> my['other_key'] = 'value2'
>>> my
{'key': 'value', 'other_key': 'value2'}
```

If you take a look at your existing code, you may find a lot of classes that partially implement the built-in types, and could be faster and cleaner as subtypes. The `list` type, for instance, manages the sequences and could be used every time a class works internally with a sequence:

```python
class Folder(list):
    def __init__(self, name):
        self.name = name

    def dir(self, nesting=0):
        offset = "  " * nesting
        print('%s%s/' % (offset, self.name))

        for element in self:
            if hasattr(element, 'dir'):
                element.dir(nesting + 1)
            else:
                print("%s  %s" % (offset, element))
```

Here is an example usage in interactive session:

```python
>>> tree = Folder('project')
>>> tree.append('README.md')
>>> tree.dir()
project/
  README.md
>>> src = Folder('src')
>>> src.append('script.py')
>>> tree.append(src)
>>> tree.dir()
project/
  README.md
  src/
    script.py
```

Built-in types cover most use cases

When you are about to create a new class that acts like a sequence or a mapping, think about its features and look over the existing built-in types. The `collections` module extends basic built-in types with many useful containers. You will end up using one of them most of the time.

Accessing methods from superclasses

`super` is a built-in class that can be used to access an attribute belonging to an object's superclass.

 The Python official documentation lists `super` as a built-in function. But it's a built-in class, even if it is used like a function:

```
>>> super
<class 'super'>
```

Its usage is a bit confusing when you are used to accessing a class attribute or method by calling the parent class directly and passing `self` as the first argument. This is really old pattern but still can be found in some codebases (especially in legacy projects). See the following code:

```
class Mama:  # this is the old way
    def says(self):
        print('do your homework')


class Sister(Mama):
    def says(self):
        Mama.says(self)
        print('and clean your bedroom')
```

When run in an interpreter session it gives following result:

```
>>> Sister().says()
do your homework
and clean your bedroom
```

Look particularly at the line `Mama.says(self)`, where we use the technique just described to call the `says()` method of the superclass (that is, the `Mama` class), and pass `self` as the argument. This means, the `says()` method belonging to `Mama` will be called. But the instance on which it will be called is provided as the `self` argument, which is an instance of `Sister` in this case.

Instead, the `super` usage would be:

```
class Sister(Mama):
    def says(self):
        super(Sister, self).says()
        print('and clean your bedroom')
```

Alternatively, you can also use the shorter form of the `super()` call:

```
class Sister(Mama):
    def says(self):
        super().says()
        print('and clean your bedroom')
```

The shorter form of `super` (without passing any arguments) is allowed inside the methods but `super` is not limited to methods. It can be used in any place of code where a call to the given instance superclass method implementation is required. Still, if `super` is not used inside the method, then its arguments are mandatory:

```
>>> anita = Sister()
>>> super(anita.__class__, anita).says()
do your homework
```

The last and most important thing that should be noted about `super` is that its second argument is optional. When only the first argument is provided, then `super` returns an unbounded type. This is especially useful when working with `classmethod`:

```
class Pizza:
    def __init__(self, toppings):
        self.toppings = toppings

    def __repr__(self):
        return "Pizza with " + " and ".join(self.toppings)

    @classmethod
    def recommend(cls):
        """Recommend some pizza with arbitrary toppings,"""
        return cls(['spam', 'ham', 'eggs'])


class VikingPizza(Pizza):
    @classmethod
    def recommend(cls):
        """Use same recommendation as super but add extra spam"""
        recommended = super(VikingPizza).recommend()
        recommended.toppings += ['spam'] * 5
        return recommended
```

Note that the zero-argument `super()` form is also allowed for methods decorated with the `classmethod` decorator. `super()` called without arguments in such a method is treated as having only the first argument defined.

The use cases presented earlier are very simple to follow and understand, but when you face a multiple inheritance schema, it becomes hard to use super. Before explaining these problems, understanding when super should be avoided and how the **Method Resolution Order (MRO)** works in Python is important.

Old-style classes and super in Python 2

super() in Python 2 works almost exactly the same. The only difference in call signature is that the shorter, zero-argument form is not available, so at least one of the expected arguments must be provided always.

Another important thing for programmers who want to write cross-version compatible code is that super in Python 2 works only for new-style classes. The earlier versions of Python did not have a common ancestor for all classes in the form of object. The old behavior was left in every Python 2.x branch release for backwards compatibility, so in those versions, if the class definition has no ancestor specified, it is interpreted as an old-style class and it cannot use super:

```
class OldStyle1:
    pass


class OldStyle2():
    pass
```

The new-style class in Python 2 must explicitly inherit from the object or other new-style class:

```
class NewStyleClass(object):
    pass

class NewStyleClassToo(NewStyleClass):
    pass
```

Python 3 no longer maintains the concept of old-style classes, so any class that does not inherit from any other class implicitly inherits from object. This means that explicitly stating that a class inherits from object may seem redundant. The general good practice is to not include redundant code, but removing such redundancy in this case is a good approach only for projects that no longer target any of the Python 2 versions. Code that aims for cross-version compatibility of Python must always include object as an ancestor of base classes even if this is redundant in Python 3. Not doing so will result in such classes being interpreted as old style, and this will eventually lead to issues that are very hard to diagnose.

Understanding Python's Method Resolution Order

Python's Method Resolution Order is based on **C3**, the MRO built for the Dylan programming language (http://opendylan.org). The reference document, written by Michele Simionato, is located at http://www.python.org/download/releases/2.3/mro. It describes how C3 builds the **linearization** of a class, also called **precedence**, which is an ordered list of the ancestors. This list is used to seek an attribute. The C3 algorithm is described in more detail later in this section.

The MRO change was made to resolve an issue introduced with the creation of a common base type (object). Before the change to the C3 linearization method, if a class had two ancestors (refer to *Figure 1*), the order in which methods were resolved was quite simple to compute and track for simple cases that do not use the multiple inheritance model. Here is an example of code that under Python 2 would not use C3 as a Method Resolution Order:

```python
class Base1:
    pass


class Base2:
    def method(self):
        print('Base2')


class MyClass(Base1, Base2):
    pass
```

The following transcript from interactive session shows this method resolution at work:

```python
>>> MyClass().method()
Base2
```

When `MyClass().method()` is called, the interpreter looks for the method in `MyClass`, then `Base1`, and then eventually finds it in `Base2`:

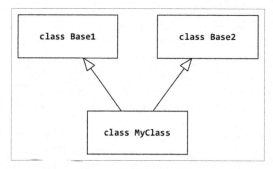

Figure 1 Classical hierarchy

When we introduce some `CommonBase` class on top of the two base classes (both `Base1` and `Base2` inherit from it, refer to *Figure 2*), things get more complicated. As a result, the simple resolution order that behaves according to the *left to right depth first* rule is getting back to the top through the `Base1` class before looking into the `Base2` class. This algorithm results in a counterintuitive output. In some cases, the method that is executed may not be the one that is the closest in the inheritance tree.

Such an algorithm is still available in Python 2 when old-style classes (not inheriting from `object`) are used. Here is an example of the old method resolution in Python 2 using old-style classes:

```
class CommonBase:
    def method(self):
        print('CommonBase')


class Base1(CommonBase):
    pass


class Base2(CommonBase):
    def method(self):
        print('Base2')


class MyClass(Base1, Base2):
    pass
```

The following transcript from interactive session shows that `Base2.method()` will not be called despite `Base2` is closer in the class hierarchy than `CommonBase`:

```
>>> MyClass().method()
CommonBase
```

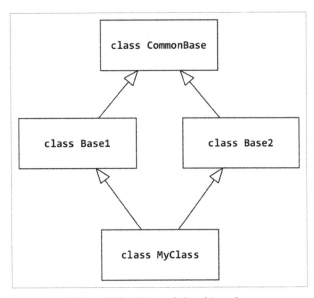

Figure 2 The Diamond class hierarchy

Such an inheritance scenario is extremely uncommon, so this is more a problem of theory than practice. The standard library does not structure the inheritance hierarchies in this way, and many developers think it is a bad practice. But with the introduction of `object` at the top of the types hierarchy, the multiple inheritance problem pops up on the C side of the language, resulting in conflicts when doing subtyping. Note also that every class in Python 3 has now the same common ancestor. Since making it work properly with the existing MRO involved too much work, a new MRO was a simpler and quicker solution.

So, the same example run under Python 3 gives a different result:

```
class CommonBase:
    def method(self):
        print('CommonBase')


class Base1(CommonBase):
    pass
```

```
class Base2(CommonBase):
    def method(self):
        print('Base2')


class MyClass(Base1, Base2):
    pass
```

And here is usage showing that C3 serialization will pick method of the closest ancestor:

```
>>> MyClass().method()
Base2
```

> Note that the above behavior cannot be replicated in Python 2 without the CommonBase class explicitly inheriting from object. The reasons why it may be useful to specify object as a class ancestor in Python 3 even if this is redundant were mentioned in the previous section, *Old-style classes and super in Python 2.*

The Python MRO is based on a recursive call over the base classes. To summarize the Michele Simionato paper referenced at the beginning of this section, the C3 symbolic notation applied to our example is:

```
L[MyClass(Base1, Base2)] =
        MyClass + merge(L[Base1], L[Base2], Base1, Base2)
```

Here, L[MyClass] is the linearization of the MyClass class, and merge is a specific algorithm that merges several linearization results.

So, a synthetic description would be, as Simionato says:

> *"The linearization of C is the sum of C plus the merge of the linearizations of the parents and the list of the parents"*

The merge algorithm is responsible for removing the duplicates and preserving the correct ordering. It is described in the paper like this (adapted to our example):

> *"Take the head of the first list, that is, L[Base1][0]; if this head is not in the tail of any of the other lists, then add it to the linearization of MyClass and remove it from the lists in the merge, otherwise look at the head of the next list and take it, if it is a good head.*
>
> *Then, repeat the operation until all the classes are removed or it is impossible to find good heads. In this case, it is impossible to construct the merge, Python 2.3 will refuse to create the class MyClass and will raise an exception."*

The `head` is the first element of a list and the `tail` contains the rest of the elements. For example, in `(Base1, Base2, ..., BaseN)`, `Base1` is the `head`, and `(Base2, ..., BaseN)` the `tail`.

In other words, C3 does a recursive depth lookup on each parent to get a sequence of lists. Then it computes a left-to-right rule to merge all lists with a hierarchy disambiguation, when a class is involved in several lists.

So the result is:

```
def L(klass):
    return [k.__name__ for k in klass.__mro__]


>>> L(MyClass)
['MyClass', 'Base1', 'Base2', 'CommonBase', 'object']
```

The `__mro__` attribute of a class (which is read-only) stores the result of the linearization computation, which is done when the class definition is loaded.

You can also call `MyClass.mro()` to compute and get the result. This is another reason why classes in Python 2 should be taken with extra case. While old-style classes in Python 2 have a defined order in which methods are resolved, they do not provide the `__mro__` attribute and the `mro()` method. So, despite the order of resolution, it is wrong to say that they have MRO. In most cases, whenever someone refers to MRO in Python, it means that they refer to the C3 algorithm described in this section.

super pitfalls

Back to `super`. Its usage, when using the multiple inheritance hierarchy, can be quite dangerous, mainly because of the initialization of classes. In Python, the base classes are not implicitly called in `__init__()`, and so it is up to the developer to call them. We will see a few examples.

Mixing super and explicit class calls

In the following example taken from James Knight's website (`http://fuhm.net/super-harmful`), a `C` class that calls its base classes using the `__init__()` method will make the `B` class be called twice:

```
class A:
    def __init__(self):
```

```
        print("A", end=" ")
        super().__init__()


class B:
    def __init__(self):
        print("B", end=" ")
        super().__init__()


class C(A, B):
    def __init__(self):
        print("C", end=" ")
        A.__init__(self)
        B.__init__(self)
```

Here is the output:

```
>>> print("MRO:", [x.__name__ for x in C.__mro__])
MRO: ['C', 'A', 'B', 'object']
>>> C()
C A B B <__main__.C object at 0x0000000001217C50>
```

This happens due to the A.__init__(self) call, which is made with the C instance, thus making the super(A, self).__init__() call the B.__init__() method. In other words, super should be used in the whole class hierarchy. The problem is that sometimes a part of this hierarchy is located in third-party code. Many related pitfalls on the hierarchy calls introduced by multiple inheritances can be found on James's page.

Unfortunately, you cannot be sure that external packages use super() in their code. Whenever you need to subclass some third-party class, it is always a good approach to take a look inside of its code and code of other classes in the MRO. This may be tedious, but as a bonus you get some information about the quality of code provided by such a package and more understanding of its implementation. You may learn something new that way.

Heterogeneous arguments

Another issue with `super` usage is the argument passing in initialization. How can a class call its base class `__init__()` code if it doesn't have the same signature? This leads to the following problem:

```python
class CommonBase:
    def __init__(self):
        print('CommonBase')
        super().__init__()


class Base1(CommonBase):
    def __init__(self):
        print('Base1')
        super().__init__()


class Base2(CommonBase):
    def __init__(self, arg):
        print('base2')
        super().__init__()


class MyClass(Base1 , Base2):
    def __init__(self, arg):
        print('my base')
        super().__init__(arg)
```

An attempt to create a `MyClass` instance will raise `TypeError` due to the mismatch of the parent classes' `__init__()` signatures:

```
>>> MyClass(10)
my base
Traceback (most recent call last):
  File "<stdin>", line 1, in <module>
  File "<stdin>", line 4, in __init__
TypeError: __init__() takes 1 positional argument but 2 were given
```

One solution would be to use arguments and keyword arguments packed with
`*args` and `**kwargs` magic so that all constructors pass along all the parameters
even if they do not use them:

```
class CommonBase:
    def __init__(self, *args, **kwargs):
        print('CommonBase')
        super().__init__()

class Base1(CommonBase):
    def __init__(self, *args, **kwargs):
        print('Base1')
        super().__init__(*args, **kwargs)

class Base2(CommonBase):
    def __init__(self, *args, **kwargs):
        print('base2')
        super().__init__(*args, **kwargs)

class MyClass(Base1 , Base2):
    def __init__(self, arg):
        print('my base')
        super().__init__(arg)
```

With this approach the parent class signatures will always match:

```
>>> _ = MyClass(10)
my base
Base1
base2
CommonBase
```

This is an awful fix though, because it makes all constructors accept any kind of
parameter. It leads to weak code, since anything can be passed and gone through.
Another solution is to use the explicit __init__() calls of specific classes in `MyClass`,
but this would lead to the first pitfall.

Best practices

To avoid all the mentioned problems, and until Python evolves in this field, we need
to take into consideration the following points:

- **Multiple inheritance should be avoided**: It can be replaced with some
  design patterns presented in *Chapter 14, Useful Design Patterns*.

- **super usage has to be consistent**: In a class hierarchy, `super` should be used everywhere or nowhere. Mixing `super` and classic calls is a confusing practice. People tend to avoid `super`, for their code to be more explicit.

- **Explicitly inherit from object in Python 3 if you target Python 2 too**: Classes without any ancestor specified are recognized as old-style classes in Python 2. Mixing old-style classes with new-style classes should be avoided in Python 2.

- **Class hierarchy has to be looked over when a parent class is called**: To avoid any problems, every time a parent class is called, a quick glance at the involved MRO (with `__mro__`) has to be done.

Advanced attribute access patterns

When many C++ and Java programmers first learn Python, they are surprised by Python's lack of a `private` keyword. The nearest concept is *name mangling*. Every time an attribute is prefixed by `__`, it is renamed by the interpreter on the fly:

```
class MyClass:
    __secret_value = 1
```

Accessing the `__secret_value` attribute by its initial name will raise an `AttributeError` exception:

```
>>> instance_of = MyClass()
>>> instance_of.__secret_value
Traceback (most recent call last):
  File "<stdin>", line 1, in <module>
AttributeError: 'MyClass' object has no attribute '__secret_value'
>>> dir(MyClass)
['_MyClass__secret_value', '__class__', '__delattr__', '__dict__', '__dir__', '__doc__', '__eq__', '__format__', '__ge__', '__getattribute__', '__gt__', '__hash__', '__init__', '__le__', '__lt__', '__module__', '__ne__', '__new__', '__reduce__', '__reduce_ex__', '__repr__', '__setattr__', '__sizeof__', '__str__', '__subclasshook__', '__weakref__']
>>> instance_of._MyClass__secret_value
1
```

This feature is provided to avoid name collision under inheritance, as the attribute is renamed with the class name as a prefix. It is not a real lock, since the attribute can be accessed through its composed name. This feature could be used to protect the access of some attributes, but in practice, __ should never be used. When an attribute is not public, the convention to use is a _ prefix. This does not call any mangling algorithm, but just documents the attribute as a private element of the class and is the prevailing style.

Other mechanisms are available in Python to build the public part of the class together with the private code. The descriptors and properties that are the key features to OOP design should be used to design a clean API.

Descriptors

A descriptor lets you customize what should be done when you refer to an attribute on an object.

Descriptors are the base of a complex attribute access in Python. They are used internally to implement properties, methods, class methods, static methods, and the `super` type. They are classes that define how attributes of another class can be accessed. In other words, a class can delegate the management of an attribute to another one.

The descriptor classes are based on three special methods that form the **descriptor protocol**:

- `__set__(self, obj, type=None)`: This is called whenever the attribute is set. In the following examples, we will refer to this as a **setter**.
- `__get__(self, obj, value)`: This is called whenever the attribute is read (referred to as a **getter**).
- `__delete__(self, obj)`: This is called when `del` is invoked on the attribute.

A descriptor that implements `__get__()` and `__set__()` is called a **data descriptor**. If it just implements `__get__()`, then it is called a **non-data descriptor**.

Methods of this protocol are in fact called by the object's special `__getattribute__` () method (do not confuse it with `__getattr__` (), which has a different purpose) on every attribute lookup. Whenever such a lookup is performed, either by using dotted notation in the form of `instance.attribute` or by using the `getattr(instance, 'attribute')` function call, the `__getattribute__` () method is implicitly invoked and it looks for an attribute in the following order:

1. It verifies if the attribute is a data descriptor on the class object of the instance.

2. If not, it looks to see if the attribute can be found in the `__dict__` of the instance object.

3. Finally, it looks to see if the attribute is a non-data descriptor on the class object of the instance.

In other words, data descriptors take precedence over `__dict__` lookup and `__dict__` lookup takes precedence over non-data descriptors.

To make it more clear, here is an example from the official Python documentation that shows how descriptors work on real code:

```python
class RevealAccess(object):
    """A data descriptor that sets and returns values
       normally and prints a message logging their access.
    """

    def __init__(self, initval=None, name='var'):
        self.val = initval
        self.name = name

    def __get__(self, obj, objtype):
        print('Retrieving', self.name)
        return self.val

    def __set__(self, obj, val):
        print('Updating', self.name)
        self.val = val


class MyClass(object):
    x = RevealAccess(10, 'var "x"')
    y = 5
```

And here is an example of using it in the interactive session:

```
>>> m = MyClass()
>>> m.x
Retrieving var "x"
10
>>> m.x = 20
Updating var "x"
>>> m.x
Retrieving var "x"
20
>>> m.y
5
```

The preceding example clearly shows that if a class has the data descriptor for the given attribute, then the descriptor's __get__() method is called to return the value every time the instance attribute is retrieved, and __set__() is called whenever a value is assigned to such an attribute. Although the case for the descriptor's __del__ method is not shown in the preceding example, it should be obvious now: it is called whenever an instance attribute is deleted with the del instance.attribute statement or the delattr(instance, 'attribute') call.

The difference between data and non-data descriptors is important due to the fact stated at the beginning. Python already uses the descriptor protocol to bind class functions to instances as a methods. They also power the mechanism behind the classmethod and staticmethod decorators. This is because, in fact, the function objects are non-data descriptors too:

```
>>> def function(): pass
>>> hasattr(function, '__get__')
True
>>> hasattr(function, '__set__')
False
```

And this is also true for functions created with lambda expressions:

```
>>> hasattr(lambda: None, '__get__')
True
>>> hasattr(lambda: None, '__set__')
False
```

So, without __dict__ taking precedence over non-data descriptors, we would not be able to dynamically override specific methods on already constructed instances at runtime. Fortunately, thanks to how descriptors work in Python. It is available, so developers may use a popular technique called monkey-patching to change the way how instances work without the need of subclassing.

Real-life example – lazily evaluated attributes

One example usage of descriptors may be to delay initialization of the class attribute to the moment when it is accessed from the instance. This may be useful if initialization of such attributes depends on the global application context. The other case is when such initialization is simply expensive but it is not known whether it will be used anyway when the class is imported. Such a descriptor could be implemented as follows:

```python
class InitOnAccess:
    def __init__(self, klass, *args, **kwargs):
        self.klass = klass
        self.args = args
        self.kwargs = kwargs
        self._initialized = None

    def __get__(self, instance, owner):
        if self._initialized is None:
            print('initialized!')
            self._initialized = self.klass(*self.args,
            **self.kwargs)
        else:
            print('cached!')
        return self._initialized
```

And here is example usage:

```python
>>> class MyClass:
...     lazily_initialized = InitOnAccess(list, "argument")
...
>>> m = MyClass()
>>> m.lazily_initialized
initialized!
['a', 'r', 'g', 'u', 'm', 'e', 'n', 't']
>>> m.lazily_initialized
cached!
['a', 'r', 'g', 'u', 'm', 'e', 'n', 't']
```

The official OpenGL Python library available on PyPI under the `PyOpenGL` name uses a similar technique to implement `lazy_property` that is both a decorator and a data descriptor:

```python
class lazy_property(object):
    def __init__(self, function):
        self.fget = function

    def __get__(self, obj, cls):
        value = self.fget(obj)
        setattr(obj, self.fget.__name__, value)
        return value
```

Such an implementation is similar to using the `property` decorator (described later), but the function that is wrapped with it is executed only once and then the class attribute is replaced with a value returned by such a property. Such a technique is often useful when the developer needs to fulfill the following two requirements at the same time:

- An object instance needs to be stored as a class attribute shared between its instances to save resources

- This object cannot be initialized on import time because its creation process depends on some global application state/context

In the case of applications written using OpenGL, this is very often true. For example, the creation of shaders in OpenGL is expensive because it requires compilation of code written in **GLSL (OpenGL Shading Language)**. It is reasonable to create them only once and include their definition in close proximity to classes that require them. On the other hand, shader compilation cannot be performed without having initialized the OpenGL context, so it is hard to define and compile them reliably in global module namespace at import time.

The following example shows the possible usage of the modified version of PyOpenGL's `lazy_property` decorator (here `lazy_class_attribute`) in some imaginary OpenGL-based application. The highlighted change to the original `lazy_property` decorator was required in order to allow sharing the attribute between different class instances:

```python
import OpenGL.GL as gl
from OpenGL.GL import shaders


class lazy_class_attribute(object):
    def __init__(self, function):
        self.fget = function
```

```python
    def __get__(self, obj, cls):
        value = self.fget(obj or cls)
        # note: storing in class object not its instance
        #       no matter if its a class-level or
        #       instance-level access
        setattr(cls, self.fget.__name__, value)
        return value


class ObjectUsingShaderProgram(object):
    # trivial pass-through vertex shader implementation
    VERTEX_CODE = """
        #version 330 core
        layout(location = 0) in vec4 vertexPosition;
        void main(){
            gl_Position =  vertexPosition;
        }
    """
    # trivial fragment shader that results in everything
    # drawn with white color
    FRAGMENT_CODE = """
        #version 330 core
        out lowp vec4 out_color;
        void main(){
            out_color = vec4(1, 1, 1, 1);
        }
    """

    @lazy_class_attribute
    def shader_program(self):
        print("compiling!")
        return shaders.compileProgram(
            shaders.compileShader(
                self.VERTEX_CODE, gl.GL_VERTEX_SHADER
            ),
            shaders.compileShader(
                self.FRAGMENT_CODE, gl.GL_FRAGMENT_SHADER
            )
        )
```

Like every advanced Python syntax feature, this one should also be used with caution and documented well in code. For unexperienced developers, the altered class behavior might be very confusing and unexpected because descriptors affect the very basic part of class behavior such as attribute access. Because of that, it is very important to make sure that all team members are familiar with descriptors and understand this concept well if it plays an important role in the project's codebase.

Properties

The properties provide a built-in descriptor type that knows how to link an attribute to a set of methods. A `property` takes four optional arguments: `fget`, `fset`, `fdel`, and `doc`. The last one can be provided to define a `docstring` that is linked to the attribute as if it were a method. Here is an example of a `Rectangle` class that can be controlled either by direct access to attributes that store two corner points or by using the `width`, and `height` properties:

```python
class Rectangle:
    def __init__(self, x1, y1, x2, y2):
        self.x1, self.y1 = x1, y1
        self.x2, self.y2 = x2, y2

    def _width_get(self):
        return self.x2 - self.x1

    def _width_set(self, value):
        self.x2 = self.x1 + value

    def _height_get(self):
        return self.y2 - self.y1

    def _height_set(self, value):
        self.y2 = self.y1 + value

    width = property(
        _width_get, _width_set,
        doc="rectangle width measured from left"
    )
    height = property(
        _height_get, _height_set,
        doc="rectangle height measured from top"
    )

    def __repr__(self):
```

```
        return "{}({}, {}, {}, {})".format(
            self.__class__.__name__,
            self.x1, self.y1, self.x2, self.y2
        )
```

The example usage of such defined properties in an interactive session is as follows:

```
>>> rectangle = Rectangle(10, 10, 25, 34)
>>> rectangle.width, rectangle.height
(15, 24)
>>> rectangle.width = 100
>>> rectangle
Rectangle(10, 10, 110, 34)
>>> rectangle.height = 100
>>> rectangle
Rectangle(10, 10, 110, 110)
help(Rectangle)
Help on class Rectangle in module chapter3:

class Rectangle(builtins.object)
 |  Methods defined here:
 |
 |  __init__(self, x1, y1, x2, y2)
 |      Initialize self.  See help(type(self)) for accurate signature.
 |
 |  __repr__(self)
 |      Return repr(self).
 |
 |  ----------------------------------------------------------
 |  Data descriptors defined here:
 |  (...)
 |
 |  height
 |      rectangle height measured from top
 |
 |  width
 |      rectangle width measured from left
```

The properties make it easier to write descriptors, but must be handled carefully when using inheritance over classes. The created attribute is made on the fly using the methods of the current class and will not use methods that are overridden in the derived classes.

For instance, the following example will fail to override the implementation of the `fget` method of the parent's class (`Rectangle`) `width` property:

```
>>> class MetricRectangle(Rectangle):
...     def _width_get(self):
...         return "{} meters".format(self.x2 - self.x1)
...
>>> Rectangle(0, 0, 100, 100).width
100
```

In order to solve this, the whole property simply needs to be overwritten in the derived class:

```
>>> class MetricRectangle(Rectangle):
...     def _width_get(self):
...         return "{} meters".format(self.x2 - self.x1)
...     width = property(_width_get, Rectangle.width.fset)
...
>>> MetricRectangle(0, 0, 100, 100).width
'100 meters'
```

Unfortunately, the preceding code has some maintainability issues. It can be a source of issue if the developer decides to change the parent class, but forgets about updating the property call. This is why overriding only parts of the property behavior is not advised. Instead of relying on the parent class's implementation, it is recommended to rewrite all the property methods in the derived classes, if there is need to change how they work. In most cases, this is the only option anyway, because usually the change to property `setter` behavior implies a change to the behavior of the `getter` as well.

Due to the preceding reason, the best syntax for creating properties is using `property` as a decorator. This will reduce the number of method signatures inside of the class and make code more readable and maintainable:

```
class Rectangle:
    def __init__(self, x1, y1, x2, y2):
        self.x1, self.y1 = x1, y1
        self.x2, self.y2 = x2, y2
```

```
    @property
    def width(self):
        """rectangle height measured from top"""
        return self.x2 - self.x1

    @width.setter
    def width(self, value):
        self.x2 = self.x1 + value

    @property
    def height(self):
        """rectangle height measured from top"""
        return self.y2 - self.y1

    @height.setter
    def height(self, value):
        self.y2 = self.y1 + value
```

Slots

An interesting feature that is almost never used by developers is slots. They allow you to set a static attribute list for a given class with the __slots__ attribute, and skip the creation of the __dict__ dictionary in each instance of the class. They were intended to save memory space for classes with very few attributes, since __dict__ is not created at every instance.

Besides this, they can help to design classes whose signature needs to be frozen. For instance, if you need to restrict the dynamic features of the language over a class, defining slots can help:

```
>>> class Frozen:
...     __slots__ = ['ice', 'cream']
...
>>> '__dict__' in dir(Frozen)
False
>>> 'ice' in dir(Frozen)
True
>>> frozen = Frozen()
>>> frozen.ice = True
>>> frozen.cream = None
>>> frozen.icy = True
Traceback (most recent call last):
  File "<input>", line 1, in <module>
AttributeError: 'Frozen' object has no attribute 'icy'
```

This feature should be used carefully. When a set of available attributes is limited using __slots__, it is much harder to add something to the object dynamically. Some techniques, such as monkey-patching, will not work with instances of classes that have slots defined. Fortunately, the new attributes can be added to the derived class if it does not have its own slots defined:

```
>>> class Unfrozen(Frozen):
...     pass
...
>>> unfrozen = Unfrozen()
>>> unfrozen.icy = False
>>> unfrozen.icy
False
```

Metaprogramming

There may be a good definition of metaprogramming from some academy paper that could be cited here, but this is rather a book about good software craftsmanship than about computer science theory. This is why we will use a simple one:

> *"Metaprogramming is a technique of writing computer programs that can treat themselves as data, so you can introspect, generate, and/or modify itself while running."*

Using this definition, we can distinguish two major approaches to metaprogramming in Python.

The first approach concentrates on the language's ability to introspect its basic elements such as functions, classes, or types and to create or modify them on the fly. Python gives a lot of tools to developers in this area. The easiest ones are decorators that allow to add additional functionality to the existing functions, methods, or classes. Next are special methods of classes that allow you to interfere with class instance process creation. The most powerful are metaclasses that allow programmers to even completely redesign the Python's implementation of the object-oriented programming paradigm. Here also, we have a good selection of different tools that allow programmers to work directly with code either in its raw plain text format or in the more programmatically accessible **Abstract Syntax Tree (AST)** form. This second approach is of course more complicated and difficult to work with but allows for really extraordinary things, such as extending Python's language syntax or even creating your own **Domain Specific Language (DSL)**.

Decorators – a method of metaprogramming

The decorator syntax is explained in *Chapter 2, Syntax Best Practices – below the Class Level*, as a simple pattern:

```
def decorated_function():
    pass
decorated_function = some_decorator(decorated_function)
```

This clearly shows what the decorator does. It takes a function object and modifies it at run time. As a result, a new function (or anything else) is created based on the previous function object with the same name. This may be even a complex operation that performs some introspection to give different results depending on how the original function is implemented. All this means is that decorators can be considered as a metaprogramming tool.

This are good news. Decorators are relatively easy to catch and in most cases make code shorter, easier to read, and also cheaper to maintain. Other metaprogramming tools available in Python are more difficult to grasp and master. Also, they might not make the code simple at all.

Class decorators

One of the less known syntax features of Python is the class decorator. The syntax and the way that they work is exactly the same as with function decorators mentioned in *Chapter 2, Syntax Best Practices – below the Class Level*. The only difference is that they are expected to return a class instead of the function object. Here is an example class decorator that modifies the __repr__() method to return the printable object representation that is shortened to some arbitrary number of characters:

```
def short_repr(cls):
    cls.__repr__ = lambda self: super(cls, self).__repr__()[:8]
    return cls


@short_repr
class ClassWithRelativelyLongName:
    pass
```

The following is what you will see in the output:

```
>>> ClassWithRelativelyLongName()
<ClassWi
```

Of course, the preceding code snippet is not an example of a good code by any means because it is too cryptic. Still, it shows how multiple language features explained in this chapter can be used together:

- Not only instances but also class objects can be modified at runtime
- Functions are descriptors too, so they can be added to the class at runtime because the actual binding instance is performed on the attribute lookup as part of the descriptor protocol
- The super() call can be used outside of a class definition scope as long as proper arguments are provided
- Finally, class decorators can be used on class definitions

The other aspects of the writing function decorators apply to the class decorators as well. Most importantly, they can use closures and be parametrized. Taking advantage of these facts, the previous example can be rewritten into a more readable and maintainable form:

```python
def parametrized_short_repr(max_width=8):
    """Parametrized decorator that shortens representation"""
    def parametrized(cls):
        """Inner wrapper function that is actual decorator"""
        class ShortlyRepresented(cls):
            """Subclass that provides decorated behavior"""
            def __repr__(self):
                return super().__repr__()[:max_width]

        return ShortlyRepresented

    return parametrized
```

The major drawback of using closures this way in class decorators is that the resulting objects are no longer instances of the class that was decorated but instances of the subclass created dynamically in the decorator function. Among others, this will affect the class's __name__ and __doc__ attributes:

```python
@parametrized_short_repr(10)
class ClassWithLittleBitLongerLongName:
    pass
```

Such usage of class decorators will result in following changes to the class metadata:

```python
>>> ClassWithLittleBitLongerLongName().__class__
<class 'ShortlyRepresented'>
>>> ClassWithLittleBitLongerLongName().__doc__
'Subclass that provides decorated behavior'
```

Unfortunately, this cannot be fixed as simply as explained in the *Introspection Preserving Decorators* section of *Chapter 2, Syntax Best Practices – below the Class Level*, using the additional `wraps` decorator. This makes use of the class decorators in this form limited in some circumstances. If no additional work is performed to preserve the old class's metadata, then this can break results of many automated documentation generation tools.

Still, despite this single caveat, class decorators are a simple and lightweight alternative to the popular mixin class pattern.

A mixin in Python is a class that is not meant to be instantiated, but is instead used to provide some reusable API or functionality to other existing classes. Mixin classes are almost always added using multiple inheritance in the form of:

```
class SomeConcreteClass(MixinClass, SomeBaseClass):
    pass
```

Mixins are useful design patterns that are used in many libraries. To name one, Django is one of the frameworks that uses them extensively. While useful and popular, the mixins can cause some trouble if not designed well, because, in most cases, they require the developer to rely on multiple inheritance. As was said earlier, Python handles multiple inheritance relatively well, thanks to the MRO. Anyway, it may be better to avoid subclassing multiple classes if it only does not require too much additional work and makes code simpler. This is why class decorators may be a good replacement of mixins.

Using the __new__() method to override instance creation process

The special method `__new__()` is a static method responsible for creating class instances. It is special-cased, so there is no need to declare it as a static using the `staticmethod` decorator. This `__new__(cls, [,...])` method is called prior to the `__init__()` initialization method. Typically, the implementation of overridden `__new__()` invokes its superclass version using `super().__new__()` with suitable arguments and modifies the instance before returning it:

```
class InstanceCountingClass:
    instances_created = 0
    def __new__(cls, *args, **kwargs):
        print('__new__() called with:', cls, args, kwargs)
        instance = super().__new__(cls)
        instance.number = cls.instances_created
        cls.instances_created += 1
```

```
        return instance

    def __init__(self, attribute):
        print('__init__() called with:', self, attribute)
        self.attribute = attribute
```

Here is the log of example interactive session that shows how our
`InstanceCountingClass` implementation works:

```
>>> instance1 = InstanceCountingClass('abc')
__new__() called with: <class '__main__.InstanceCountingClass'> ('abc',)
{}
__init__() called with: <__main__.InstanceCountingClass object at
0x101259e10> abc
>>> instance2 = InstanceCountingClass('xyz')
__new__() called with: <class '__main__.InstanceCountingClass'> ('xyz',)
{}
__init__() called with: <__main__.InstanceCountingClass object at
0x101259dd8> xyz
>>> instance1.number, instance1.instances_created
(0, 2)
>>> instance2.number, instance2.instances_created
(1, 2)
```

The __new__() method should usually return an instance of featured class but it is
also possible that it returns other class instances. If it does happen (different class
instance is returned) then the call to the __init__() method is skipped. This fact
is useful when there is a need to modify creation behavior of non-mutable class
instances such as some of Python's built-in types:

```
class NonZero(int):
    def __new__(cls, value):
        return super().__new__(cls, value) if value != 0 else None

    def __init__(self, skipped_value):
        # implementation of __init__ could be skipped in this case
        # but it is left to present how it may be not called
        print("__init__() called")
        super().__init__()
```

Let's see this in the interactive session:

```
>>> type(NonZero(-12))
__init__() called
<class '__main__.NonZero'>
>>> type(NonZero(0))
<class 'NoneType'>
>>> NonZero(-3.123)
__init__() called
-3
```

So, when to use `__new__()`? The answer is simple: only when `__init__()` is not enough. One such case was already mentioned. This is subclassing of non-mutable built-in Python types such as `int`, `str`, `float`, `frozenset`, and so on. It's because there is no way to modify such a nonmutable object instance in the `__init__()` method once it is created.

Some programmers can argue that `__new__()` may be useful for performing important object initialization that may be missed if the user forgets to use `super()`. The `__init__()` call is the overridden initialization method. While it sounds reasonable, this has a major drawback. If such an approach is used, then it becomes harder for the programmer to explicitly skip previous initialization steps if this is the already desired behavior. It also breaks an unspoken rule of all initializations performed in `__init__()`.

Because `__new__()` is not constrained to return the same class instance, it can be easily abused. Irresponsible usage of this method might do a lot of harm to the code, so it should always be used carefully and backed with extensive documentation. Generally, it is better to search for other solutions that may be available for the given problem, instead of affecting object creation in a way that will break basic programmers' expectations. Even overridden initialization of non-mutable types mentioned earlier can be replaced with more predictable and well-established design patterns, such as the Factory Method, which is described in *Chapter 14, Useful Design Patterns*.

There is at least one aspect of Python programming where extensive usage of the `__new__()` method is well justified. These are metaclasses that are described in the next section.

Metaclasses

Metaclass is a Python feature that is considered by many as one of the most difficult thing in this language and thus avoided by a great number of developers. In reality, it is not as complicated as it sounds once you understand few basic concepts. As a reward, knowing this feature grants the ability to do some things that were not possible using other approaches.

Metaclass is a type (class) that defines other types (classes). The most important thing to know in order to understand how they work is that classes that define object instances are objects too. So, if they are objects, then they have an associated class. The basic type of every class definition is simply the built-in `type` class. Here is a simple diagram that should make it clear:

Figure 3 How classes are typed

In Python, it is possible to substitute the metaclass for a class object with our own type. Usually, the new metaclass is still the subclass of the `type` class (refer to *Figure 4*) because not doing so would make the resulting classes highly incompatible with other classes in terms of inheritance.

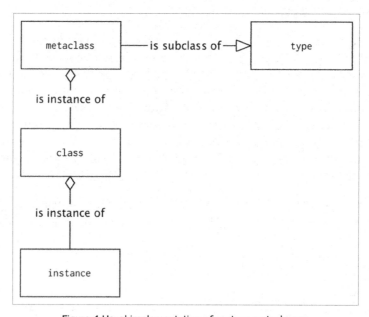

Figure 4 Usual implementation of custom metaclasses

The general syntax

The call to the built-in `type()` class can be used as a dynamic equivalent of the class statement. It creates a new class object given its name, its base classes, and a mapping containing its attributes:

```
def method(self):
    return 1

klass = type('MyClass', (object,), {'method': method})
```

The following is the output:

```
>>> instance = klass()
>>> instance.method()
1
```

This is equivalent to the explicit definition of the class:

```
class MyClass:
    def method(self):
        return 1
```

Here is what you will get:

```
>>> instance = MyClass()
>>> instance.method()
1
```

Every class created with the class statement implicitly uses `type` as its metaclass. This default behavior can be changed by providing the `metaclass` keyword argument to the class statement:

```
class ClassWithAMetaclass(metaclass=type):
    pass
```

The value provided as a `metaclass` argument is usually another class object, but it can be any other callable that accepts the same arguments as the `type` class and is expected to return another class object. The call signature is `type(name, bases, namespace)`, which is explained as follows:

- name: This is the name of class that will be stored in the __name__ attribute
- bases: This is the list of parent classes that will become the __bases__ attribute and will be used to construct the MRO of a newly created class

- `namespace`: This is a namespace (mapping) with definitions for the class body that will become the `__dict__` attribute

One way of thinking about metaclasses is the `__new__()` method, but at a higher level of class definition.

Despite the fact that functions that explicitly call `type()` can be used in place of metaclasses, the usual approach is to use a different class that inherits from `type` for this purpose. The common template for a metaclass is as follows:

```python
class Metaclass(type):
    def __new__(mcs, name, bases, namespace):
        return super().__new__(mcs, name, bases, namespace)

    @classmethod
    def __prepare__(mcs, name, bases, **kwargs):
        return super().__prepare__(name, bases, **kwargs)

    def __init__(cls, name, bases, namespace, **kwargs):
        super().__init__(name, bases, namespace)

    def __call__(cls, *args, **kwargs):
        return super().__call__(*args, **kwargs)
```

The `name`, `bases`, and `namespace` arguments have the same meaning as in the `type()` call explained earlier, but each of these four methods can have different purposes:

- `__new__(mcs, name, bases, namespace)`: This is responsible for the actual creation of the class object in the same way as it does for ordinary classes. The first positional argument is a metaclass object. In the preceding example, it would simply be a `Metaclass`. Note that `mcs` is the popular naming convention for this argument.

- `__prepare__(mcs, name, bases, **kwargs)`: This creates an empty namespace object. By default, it returns an empty `dict`, but it can be overridden to return any other mapping type. Note that it does not accept `namespace` as an argument because before calling it the namespace does not exist.

- `__init__(cls, name, bases, namespace, **kwargs)`: This is not seen popularly in metaclass implementations but has the same meaning as in ordinary classes. It can perform additional class object initialization once it was created with `__new__()`. The first positional argument is now named `cls` by convention to mark that this is already a created class object (metaclass instance) and not a metaclass object. When `__init__()` gets called, the class was already constructed and so this method can do less things than the `__new__()` method. Implementing such a method is very similar to using class decorators, but the main difference is that `__init__()` will be called for every subclass, while class decorators are not called for subclasses.

- `__call__(cls, *args, **kwargs)`: This is called when an instance of a metaclass is called. The instance of a metaclass is a class object (refer to *Figure 3*); it is invoked when you create new instances of a class. This can be used to override the default way how class instances are created and initialized.

Each of the preceding methods can accept additional extra keyword arguments here represented by `**kwargs`. These arguments can be passed to the metaclass object using extra keyword arguments in the class definition in the form of the following code:

```
class Klass(metaclass=Metaclass, extra="value"):
    pass
```

Such amount of information can be overwhelming at the beginning without proper examples, so let's trace the creation of metaclasses, classes, and instances with some `print()` calls:

```
class RevealingMeta(type):
    def __new__(mcs, name, bases, namespace, **kwargs):
        print(mcs, "__new__ called")
        return super().__new__(mcs, name, bases, namespace)

    @classmethod
    def __prepare__(mcs, name, bases, **kwargs):
        print(mcs, "__prepare__ called")
        return super().__prepare__(name, bases, **kwargs)

    def __init__(cls, name, bases, namespace, **kwargs):
        print(cls, "__init__ called")
        super().__init__(name, bases, namespace)

    def __call__(cls, *args, **kwargs):
        print(cls, "__call__ called")
        return super().__call__(*args, **kwargs)
```

Using `RevealingMeta` as a metaclass to create a new class definition will give the following output in the Python interactive session:

```
>>> class RevealingClass(metaclass=RevealingMeta):
...     def __new__(cls):
...         print(cls, "__new__ called")
...         return super().__new__(cls)
...     def __init__(self):
...         print(self, "__init__ called")
...         super().__init__()
...
<class 'RevealingMeta'> __prepare__ called
<class 'RevealingMeta'> __new__ called
<class 'RevealingClass'> __init__ called
>>> instance = RevealingClass()
<class 'RevealingClass'> __call__ called
<class 'RevealingClass'> __new__ called
<RevealingClass object at 0x1032b9fd0> __init__ called
```

New Python 3 syntax for metaclasses

Metaclasses are not a new feature and are available in Python since version 2.2. Anyway, the syntax of this changed significantly and this change is neither backwards nor forwards compatible. While the new syntax is:

```
class ClassWithAMetaclass(metaclass=type):
    pass
```

In Python 2, this must be written as follows:

```
class ClassWithAMetaclass(object):
    __metaclass__ = type
```

Class statements in Python 2 do not accept keyword arguments, so Python 3 syntax for defining `metaclasses` will raise the `SyntaxError` exception on import. It is still possible to write a code using metaclasses that will run on both Python versions, but it requires some extra work. Fortunately, compatibility-related packages such as `six` provide simple and reusable solutions to this problem:

```
from six import with_metaclass

class Meta(type):
    pass
```

```
class Base(object):
    pass


class MyClass(with_metaclass(Meta, Base)):
    pass
```

The other important difference is the lack of the __prepare__() hook in Python 2 metaclasses. Implementing such a function will not raise any exceptions under Python 2 but is pointless because it will not be called in order to provide a clean namespace object. This is why packages that need to maintain Python 2 compatibility need to rely on more complex tricks if they want to achieve things that are a lot easier to implement using __prepare__(). For instance, the Django REST Framework (http://www.django-rest-framework.org) uses the following approach to preserve the order in which attributes are added to a class:

```
class SerializerMetaclass(type):
    @classmethod
    def _get_declared_fields(cls, bases, attrs):
        fields = [(field_name, attrs.pop(field_name))
                    for field_name, obj in list(attrs.items())
                    if isinstance(obj, Field)]
        fields.sort(key=lambda x: x[1]._creation_counter)

        # If this class is subclassing another Serializer, add
        # that Serializer's fields.
        # Note that we loop over the bases in *reverse*.
        # This is necessary in order to maintain the
        # correct order of fields.
        for base in reversed(bases):
            if hasattr(base, '_declared_fields'):
                fields = list(base._declared_fields.items()) +
                    fields

        return OrderedDict(fields)

    def __new__(cls, name, bases, attrs):
        attrs['_declared_fields'] = cls._get_declared_fields(
            bases, attrs
        )
        return super(SerializerMetaclass, cls).__new__(
            cls, name, bases, attrs
        )
```

This is the workaround if the default namespace type, which is `dict`, does not guarantee to preserve the order of the key-value tuples. The `_creation_counter` attribute is expected to be in every instance of the `Field` class. This `Field.creation_counter` attribute is created in the same way as `InstanceCountingClass.instance_number` that was presented in the section about the `__new__()` method. This is a rather complex solution that breaks a single responsibility principle by sharing its implementation across two different classes only to ensure a trackable order of attributes. In Python 3, this could be simpler because `__prepare__()` can return other mapping types such as `OrderedDict`:

```python
from collections import OrderedDict


class OrderedMeta(type):
    @classmethod
    def __prepare__(cls, name, bases, **kwargs):
        return OrderedDict()

    def __new__(mcs, name, bases, namespace):
        namespace['order_of_attributes'] = list(namespace.keys())
        return super().__new__(mcs, name, bases, namespace)


class ClassWithOrder(metaclass=OrderedMeta):
    first = 8
    second = 2
```

Here is what you will see:

```python
>>> ClassWithOrderedAttributes.order_of_attributes
['__module__', '__qualname__', 'first', 'second']
>>> ClassWithOrderedAttributes.__dict__.keys()
dict_keys(['__dict__', 'first', '__weakref__', 'second',
'order_of_attributes', '__module__', '__doc__'])
```

 For more examples, there's a great introduction to metaclass programming in Python 2 by David Mertz, which is available at `http://www.onlamp.com/pub/a/python/2003/04/17/metaclasses.html`.

Metaclass usage

Metaclasses once mastered are a powerful feature but always complicate the code. They might also make the code less robust that is intended to work on any kind of class. For instance, you might encounter bad interactions when slots are used in the class, or when some base class already implements a metaclass, which conflicts with what yours does. They just do not compose well.

For simple things like changing the read/write attributes or adding new ones, metaclasses can be avoided in favor of simpler solutions such as properties, descriptors, or class decorators.

It is also true that often metaclasses can be replaced with other simpler approaches, but there are situations where things cannot be easily done without them. For instance, it is hard to imagine Django's ORM implementation built without extensive use of metaclasses. It could be possible, but it is rather unlikely that the resulting solution would be similarly easy to use. And frameworks are the place where metaclasses are really well-suited. They usually have a lot of complex solutions that are not easy to understand and follow, but eventually allow other programmers to write more condensed and readable code that operates on a higher level of abstraction.

Metaclass pitfalls

Like some other advanced Python features, metaclasses are very elastic and can be easily abused. While the call signature of the class is rather strict, Python does not enforce the type of the return parameter. It can be anything as long as it accepts incoming arguments on calls and has the required attributes whenever it is needed.

One such object that can be *anything-anywhere* is the instance of the Mock class provided in the unittest.mock module. Mock is not a metaclass and also does not inherit from the type class. It also does not return the class object on instantiating. Still, it can be included as a metaclass keyword argument in the class definition and this will not raise any issues, despite, it is pointless to do so:

```
>>> from unittest.mock import Mock
>>> class Nonsense(metaclass=Mock):  # pointless, but illustrative
...     pass
...
>>> Nonsense
<Mock spec='str' id='4327214664'>
```

The preceding example, of course, completely does not make sense and will fail on any attempt to instantiate such a `Nonsense` pseudo-class. It is still important to know that such things are possible because issues with `metaclass` types that do not result in the creation of the `type` subclass are sometimes very hard to spot and understand. As a proof, here is a traceback of the exception raised when we try to create a new instance of the `Nonsense` class presented earlier:

```
>>> Nonsense()
Traceback (most recent call last):
  File "<stdin>", line 1, in <module>
  File "/Library/Frameworks/Python.framework/Versions/3.5/lib/
python3.5/unittest/mock.py", line 917, in __call__
    return _mock_self._mock_call(*args, **kwargs)
  File "/Library/Frameworks/Python.framework/Versions/3.5/lib/python3.5/
unit
test/mock.py", line 976, in _mock_call
    result = next(effect)
StopIteration
```

Some tips on code generation

As already mentioned, dynamic code generation is the most difficult approach to code generation. There are some tools in Python that allow you to generate and execute code or even do some modifications to the already compiled code objects. A complete book could be written about this and even that will not exhaust the topic completely.

Various projects, such as **Hy** (mentioned later), show that even whole languages can be re-implemented in Python using code generation techniques. This proves that the possibilities are practically limitless. Knowing how vast this topic is and how badly it is riddled with various pitfalls, I won't even try to give detailed suggestions on how to create code this way or to provide useful code samples.

Anyway, knowing what is possible may be useful for you if you plan to study this field deeper by yourself. So, treat this section only as a short summary of possible starting points for further learning. Most of it is flavored with many warnings in case you would like to eagerly jump into calling `exec()` and `eval()` in your own project.

exec, eval, and compile

Python provides three built-in functions to manually execute, evaluate, and compile arbitrary Python code:

- `exec(object, globals, locals)`: This allows you to dynamically execute the Python code. `object` should be a string or a code object (see the `compile()` function). The `globals` and `locals` arguments provide global and local namespaces for the executed code and are optional. If they are not provided, then the code is executed in the current scope. If provided, `globals` must be dictionary, while `locals` might be any mapping object; it always returns `None`.

- `eval(expression, globals, locals)`: This is used to evaluate the given expression returning its value. It is similar to `exec()`, but it accepts that `expression` should be a single Python expression and not a sequence of statements. It returns the value of the evaluated expression.

- `compile(source, filename, mode)`: This compiles the source into the code object or AST object. The code to be compiled is provided as a string in the source argument. The filename should be the file from which the code was read. If it has no file associated because its source was created dynamically, then `<string>` is the value that is commonly used. Mode should be either exec (sequence of statements), `eval` (single expression), or `single` (a single interactive statement such as in Python interactive session).

The `exec()` and `eval()` functions are the easiest to start with when trying to dynamically generate code because they can operate on strings. If you already know how to program in Python, then you may know how to correctly generate a working source code programmatically. I hope you do.

The most useful in the context of metaprogramming is obviously `exec()` because it allows us to execute any sequence of Python statements. And the word *any* should be alarming for you. Even `eval()`, which only allows evaluation of expressions in the hands of a skillful programmer (when fed with the user input), can lead to serious security holes. Note that crashing the Python interpreter is the least scary scenario you should be afraid of. Introducing vulnerability to remote execution exploits due to irresponsible use of `exec()` and `eval()` can cost you your image as a professional developer, or even your job.

Even if used with a trusted input, there is a long list of little details about `exec()` and `eval()` that is too long to be included here, but might affect how your application works in the ways would not expect. Armin Ronacher has a good article that lists the most important of them called *Be careful with exec and eval in Python* (refer to http://lucumr.pocoo.org/2011/2/1/exec-in-python/).

Despite all these frightening warnings, there are natural situations where the usage of exec() and eval() is really justified. The popular statement about when you have to use them is: *you will know*. In other words, in case of even the tiniest doubt, you should not use them and try to find a different solution.

eval() and untrusted input

The signature of the eval() function might make you think that if you provide empty globals and locals namespaces and wrap it with proper try ... except statements, then it will be reasonably safe. There could be nothing more wrong. Ned Batcheler has written a very good article in which he shows how to cause an interpreter segmentation fault in the eval() call even with erased access to all Python built-ins (http://nedbatchelder.com/blog/201206/eval_really_is_dangerous.html). This is a single proof that both exec() and eval() should never be used with untrusted input.

Abstract Syntax Tree

The Python syntax is converted to **Abstract Syntax Tree (AST)** before it is compiled to byte code. This is a tree representation of the abstract syntactic structure of the source code. The processing of Python grammar is available thanks to the built-in ast module. Raw AST of Python code can be created using the compile() function with the ast.PyCF_ONLY_AST flag, or using the ast.parse() helper. Direct translation in reverse is not that simple and there is no function provided in the built-ins for that. Some projects, such as PyPy, do such things though.

The ast module provides some helper functions that allow working with the AST:

```
>>> tree = ast.parse('def hello_world(): print("hello world!")')
>>> tree
<_ast.Module object at 0x00000000038E9588>
>>> ast.dump(tree)
"Module(
    body=[
        FunctionDef(
            name='hello_world',
            args=arguments(
                args=[],
                vararg=None,
                kwonlyargs=[],
                kw_defaults=[],
```

```
            kwarg=None,
            defaults=[]
        ),
        body=[
            Expr(
                value=Call(
                    func=Name(id='print', ctx=Load()),
                    args=[Str(s='hello world!')],
                    keywords=[]
                )
            )
        ],
        decorator_list=[],
        returns=None
    )
  ]
)"
```

The output of `ast.dump()` in the preceding example was reformatted to increase the readability and better show the tree-like structure of the AST. It is important to know that the AST can be modified before being passed to the `compile()` call that gives many new possibilities. For instance, new syntax nodes can be used for additional instrumentation such as test coverage measurement. It is also possible to modify the existing code tree in order to add new semantics to the existing syntax. Such a technique is used by the MacroPy project (`https://github.com/lihaoyi/macropy`) to add syntactic macros to Python using the already existing syntax (refer to *Figure 5*):

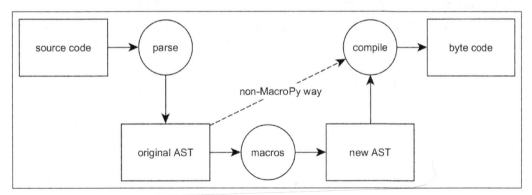

Figure 5: How MacroPy adds syntactic macros to Python modules on import

AST can also be created in a purely artificial manner and there is no need to parse any source at all. This gives Python programmers the ability to create Python bytecode for custom domain-specific languages or even completely implement other existing programming languages on top of Python VM.

Import hooks

Taking advantage of the MacroPy's ability to modify original AST would not be as easy as using the `import macropy.activate` statement if it would not somehow override the Python import behavior. Fortunately, Python provides a way to intercept imports using two kinds of import hooks:

- **Meta hooks**: These are called before any other `import` processing has occurred. Using meta hooks, you can override the way how `sys.path` is processed or even frozen and built-in modules. In order to add new meta hook, a new **meta path finder** object must be added to the `sys.meta_path` list.

- **Import path hooks**: These are called as part of `sys.path` processing. They are used if the path item associated with the given hook is encountered. The import path hooks are added by extending the `sys.path_hooks` list with a new **path finder** object.

The details on implementing both path finders and meta path finders are extensively implemented in the official Python documentation (`https://docs.python.org/3/reference/import.html`). The official documentation should be your primary resource if you want to interact with imports on that level. It's so because import machinery in Python is rather complex and any attempt to summarize it in a few paragraphs would inevitably fail. Treat this section rather as a note that such things are possible and as a reference to more detailed information.

Projects using code generation patterns

It is really hard to find a really usable implementation of the library that relies on code generation patterns that is not only an experiment or simple proof of concepts. The reasons for that situation are fairly obvious:

- Deserved fear of the `exec()` and `eval()` functions because if used irresponsibly they can cause real disasters

- Successful code generation is simply very difficult because it requires a deep understanding of the featured language and exceptional programming skills in general

Despite these difficulties, there are some projects that successfully take this approach either to improve performance or achieve things that would be impossible by other means.

Falcon's compiled router

Falcon (http://falconframework.org/) is a minimalist Python WSGI web framework for building fast and lightweight APIs. It strongly encourages REST architectural style that is currently very popular around the Web. It is a good alternative to other rather heavy frameworks such as Django or Pyramid. It is also a strong competitor to other micro-frameworks that aim for simplicity such as Flask, Bottle, and web2py.

One of its features is its very simple routing mechanism. It is not as complex as the routing provided by Django urlconf and does not provide as many features but in most cases is just enough for any API that follows the REST architectural design. What is most interesting about falcon's routing is that the actual router is implemented using the code generated from the list of routes provided to the object that defines the API configuration. This is the effort to make routing fast.

Consider this very short API example taken from falcon's web documentation:

```python
# sample.py
import falcon
import json


class QuoteResource:
    def on_get(self, req, resp):
        """Handles GET requests"""
        quote = {
            'quote': 'I\'ve always been more interested in '
                     'the future than in the past.',
            'author': 'Grace Hopper'
        }

        resp.body = json.dumps(quote)

api = falcon.API()
api.add_route('/quote', QuoteResource())
```

The highlighted call to the `api.add_route()` method in brief words translates to updating the whole dynamically generated router code tree, compiling using `compile()` and generating the new route-finding function using `eval()`. Looking at the `__code__` attribute of the `api._router._find()` function shows that it was generated from the string and that it changes with every call to `api.add_route()`:

```
>>> api._router._find.__code__
<code object find at 0x00000000033C29C0, file "<string>", line 1>
>>> api.add_route('/none', None)
>>> api._router._find.__code__
<code object find at 0x00000000033C2810, file "<string>", line 1>
```

Hy

Hy (`http://docs.hylang.org/`) is the dialect of Lisp written entirely in Python. Many similar projects implementing other code in Python usually try only to tokenize the plain form of code provided either as a file-like object or string and interpret it as a series of explicit Python calls. Unlike others, Hy can be considered a language that runs fully in the Python run-time environment just as Python does. Code written in Hy can use the existing built-in modules and external packages and vice versa. Code written with Hy can be imported back to Python.

In order to embed Lisp in Python, Hy translates Lisp code directly to Python Abstract Syntax Tree. Import interoperability is achieved using import hook that is registered once the Hy module is imported in Python. Every module with the `.hy` extension is treated as the Hy module and can be imported like the ordinary Python module. Thanks to this fact, the following "hello world" program is written in this Lisp dialect:

```
;; hyllo.hy
(defn hello [] (print "hello world!"))
```

It can be imported and executed by the following Python code:

```
>>> import hy
>>> import hyllo
>>> hyllo.hello()
hello world!
```

If we dig deeper and try to disassemble `hyllo.hello` using the built-in `dis` module, we will notice that the byte code of the Hy function does not differ significantly from its pure Python counterpart:

```
>>> import dis
>>> dis.dis(hyllo.hello)
  2           0 LOAD_GLOBAL        0 (print)
              3 LOAD_CONST         1 ('hello world!')
              6 CALL_FUNCTION      1 (1 positional, 0 keyword pair)
              9 RETURN_VALUE
>>> def hello(): print("hello world!")
>>> dis.dis(hello)
  1           0 LOAD_GLOBAL        0 (print)
              3 LOAD_CONST         1 ('hello world!')
              6 CALL_FUNCTION      1 (1 positional, 0 keyword pair)
              9 POP_TOP
             10 LOAD_CONST         0 (None)
             13 RETURN_VALUE
```

Summary

This chapter presented the best syntax practices related with classes. It started with basic information on how to subclass built-in types and call the method from superclasses. After that, more advanced concepts of object oriented programing in Python were presented. These were useful syntax features that focus on instance attribute access: descriptors and properties. It was shown how they can be used to create cleaner and more maintainable code. Slots too were featured, with an important note that they should always be used with caution.

The rest of the chapter explored the vast topic of metaprogramming in Python. The syntax features that favor the various metaprogramming patterns such as decorators and metaclasses were described in detail with some examples taken from real-life code.

The other important aspect of metaprogramming in the form of dynamic code generation was described only briefly as it is too vast to fit in the limited space of this book. However, it should be a good starting point that gives a quick summary of the possible options in that field.

4
Choosing Good Names

Most of the standard library was built keeping usability in mind. For instance, working with built-in types is done naturally and was designed to be easy to use. Python, in this case, can be compared to the pseudocode you might think about when working on a program. Most of the code can be read out loud. For instance, this snippet should be understandable by anyone:

```
my_list = []

if 'd' not in my_list:
    my_list.append('d')
```

This is one of the reasons why writing Python is so easy when compared to other languages. When you are writing a program, the flow of your thoughts is quickly translated into lines of code.

This chapter focuses on the best practices for writing code that is easy to understand and use, through:

- The usage of naming conventions, described in **PEP 8**
- The set of naming best practices
- The short summary of popular tools that allow you to check for compliance with styling guides

PEP 8 and naming best practices

PEP 8 (http://www.python.org/dev/peps/pep-0008) provides a style guide for writing Python code. Besides some basic rules such as space indentation, maximum line length, and other details concerning the code layout, PEP 8 also provides a section on naming conventions that most of the codebases follow.

This section provides a quick summary of this PEP, and adds to it a naming best-practice guide for each kind of element. You should still consider reading of PEP 8 document as mandatory.

Why and when to follow PEP 8?

If you are creating a new software package that is intended to be open-sourced, then the answer is simple: always. PEP 8 is de facto the standard code style for most of the open source software in Python. If you want to accept any collaboration from other programmers, then you should definitely stick to PEP 8, even if you have different views on the best code style guidelines. Doing so has the benefit of making it a lot easier for other developers to jump straight into your project. Code will be easier to read for newcomers because it will be consistent in style with most of the other Python open source packages.

Also, starting with full PEP 8 compliance saves you time and trouble in the future. If you want to release your code to the public, you will eventually face suggestions from fellow programmers to switch to PEP 8. Arguments as to whether it is really necessary to do so for a particular project tend to be never-ending flame wars that are impossible to win. This is the sad truth, but you may eventually be forced to be consistent with this style guide in order to not lose contributors.

Also, restyling of the whole project's codebase, if it is in a mature state of development, might require a tremendous amount of work. In some cases, such restyling might require changing almost every line of code. While most of the changes can be automated (indentation, newlines, and trailing whitespaces), such massive code overhaul usually introduces a lot of conflicts in every version control workflow that is based on branching. It is also very hard to review so many changes at once. These are the reasons why many open source projects have a rule that style fixing changes should always be included in separate pull/merge requests or patches that do not affect any feature or bug.

Beyond PEP 8 – team-specific style guidelines

Despite providing a comprehensive set of style guidelines, PEP 8 still leaves some freedom for the developers. Especially in terms of nested data literals and multiline function calls that require long lists of arguments. Some teams may decide that they require additional styling rules and the best option is to formalize them in some kind of document that is available for every team member.

Also, in some situations, it may be impossible, or economically infeasible, to be strictly consistent with PEP 8 in some old projects that had no style guide defined. Such projects will still benefit from formalization of the actual coding conventions even if they do not reflect the official set of PEP 8 rules. Remember, what is more important than consistency with PEP 8 is consistency within the project. If rules are formalized and available as a reference for every programmer, then it is way easier to keep consistency within a project and organization.

Naming styles

The different naming styles used in Python are:

- CamelCase
- mixedCase
- UPPERCASE, and UPPER_CASE_WITH_UNDERSCORES
- lowercase and lower_case_with_underscores
- _leading and trailing_ underscores, and sometimes __doubled__ underscores

Lowercase and uppercase elements are often a single word, and sometimes a few words concatenated. With underscores, they are usually abbreviated phrases. Using a single word is better. The leading and trailing underscores are used to mark the privacy and special elements.

These styles are applied to:

- Variables
- Functions and methods
- Properties
- Classes
- Modules
- Packages

Variables

There are two kinds of variables in Python:

- Constants
- Public and private variables

Constants

For constant global variables, an uppercase with an underscore is used. It informs the developer that the given variable represents a constant value.

 There are no real constants in Python like those in C++, where `const` can be used. You can change the value of any variable. That's why Python uses a naming convention to mark a variable as a constant.

For example, the `doctest` module provides a list of option flags and directives (`http://docs.python.org/lib/doctest-options.html`) that are small sentences, clearly defining what each option is intended for:

```
from doctest import IGNORE_EXCEPTION_DETAIL
from doctest import REPORT_ONLY_FIRST_FAILURE
```

These variable names seem rather long, but it is important to clearly describe them. Their usage is mostly located in initialization code rather than in the body of the code itself, so this verbosity is not annoying.

 Abbreviated names obfuscate the code most of the time. Don't be afraid of using complete words when an abbreviation seems unclear.

Some constants' names are also driven by the underlying technology. For instance, the `os` module uses some constants that are defined on C side, such as the `EX_XXX` series, that defines Unix exit code numbers. The same name code can be found, for example, in the system's `sysexits.h` C headers file:

```
import os
import sys


sys.exit(os.EX_SOFTWARE)
```

Another good practice when using constants is to gather them at the top of a module that uses them and combine them under new variables when they are intended for such operations:

```
import doctest
TEST_OPTIONS = (doctest.ELLIPSIS |
                doctest.NORMALIZE_WHITESPACE |
                doctest.REPORT_ONLY_FIRST_FAILURE)
```

Naming and usage

Constants are used to define a set of values the program relies on, such as the default configuration filename.

A good practice is to gather all the constants in a single file in the package. That is how Django works, for instance. A module named settings.py provides all the constants:

```
# config.py
SQL_USER = 'tarek'
SQL_PASSWORD = 'secret'
SQL_URI = 'postgres://%s:%s@localhost/db' % (
    SQL_USER, SQL_PASSWORD
)
MAX_THREADS = 4
```

Another approach is to use a configuration file that can be parsed with the ConfigParser module, or an advanced tool such as ZConfig, which is the parser used in Zope to describe its configuration files. But some people argue that it is rather an overkill to use another file format in a language such as Python, where a file can be edited and changed as easily as a text file.

For options that act like flags, a common practice is to combine them with Boolean operations, as the doctest and re modules do. The pattern taken from doctest is quite simple:

```
OPTIONS = {}


def register_option(name):
    return OPTIONS.setdefault(name, 1 << len(OPTIONS))


def has_option(options, name):
    return bool(options & name)

# now defining options
BLUE = register_option('BLUE')
RED = register_option('RED')
WHITE = register_option('WHITE')
```

You will get:

```
>>> # let's try them
>>> SET = BLUE | RED
>>> has_option(SET, BLUE)
```

```
True
>>> has_option(SET, WHITE)
False
```

When such a new set of constants is created, avoid using a common prefix for them, unless the module has several sets. The module name itself is a common prefix. Another solution would be to use the Enum class from the built-in enum module and simply rely on the set collection instead of the binary operators. Unfortunately, the Enum class has limited applications in code that targets old Python releases because the enum module was provided in Python 3.4 version.

 Using binary bit-wise operations to combine options is common in Python. The inclusive OR (|) operator will let you combine several options in a single integer, and the AND (&) operator will let you check that the option is present in the integer (refer to the has_option function).

Public and private variables

For global variables that are mutable and freely available through imports, a lowercase letter with an underscore should be used when they need to be protected. But these kinds of variables are not used frequently, since the module usually provides getters and setters to work with them when they need to be protected. A leading underscore, in that case, can mark the variable as a private element of the package:

```
_observers = []

def add_observer(observer):
    _observers.append(observer)


def get_observers():
    """Makes sure _observers cannot be modified."""
    return tuple(_observers)
```

Variables that are located in functions and methods follow the same rules, and are never marked as private, since they are local to the context.

For class or instance variables, using the private marker (the leading underscore) has to be done only if making the variable a part of the public signature does not bring any useful information, or is redundant.

In other words, if the variable is used internally in the method to provide a public feature, and is dedicated to this role, it is better to make it private.

For instance, the attributes that are powering a property are good private citizens:

```
class Citizen(object):
    def __init__(self):
        self._message = 'Rosebud...'

    def _get_message(self):
        return self._message

    kane = property(_get_message)
```

Another example would be a variable that keeps an internal state. This value is not useful for the rest of the code, but participates in the behavior of the class:

```
class UnforgivingElephant(object):
    def __init__(self, name):
        self.name = name
        self._people_to_stomp_on = []

    def get_slapped_by(self, name):
        self._people_to_stomp_on.append(name)
        print('Ouch!')

    def revenge(self):
        print('10 years later...')
        for person in self._people_to_stomp_on:
            print('%s stomps on %s' % (self.name, person))
```

Here is what you will see in interactive session:

```
>>> joe = UnforgivingElephant('Joe')
>>> joe.get_slapped_by('Tarek')
Ouch!
>>> joe.get_slapped_by('Bill')
Ouch!
>>> joe.revenge()
10 years later...
Joe stomps on Tarek
Joe stomps on Bill
```

Functions and methods

Functions and methods should be in lowercase with underscores. This rule was not always true in the old standard library modules. Python 3 did a lot of reorganizations to the standard library, so most of its functions and methods have a consistent case. Still, for some modules like threading, you can access the old function names that used *mixedCase* (for example, currentThread). This was left to allow easier backwards compatibility, but if you don't need to run your code in older versions of Python, then you should avoid using these old names.

This way of writing methods was common before the lowercase norm became the standard, and some frameworks, such as Zope and Twisted, are also using *mixedCase* for methods. The community of developers working with them is still quite large. So the choice between *mixedCase* and lowercase with an underscore is definitely driven by the library you are using.

As a Zope developer, it is not easy to stay consistent because building an application that mixes pure Python modules and modules that import Zope code is difficult. In Zope, some classes mix both conventions because the code base is still evolving and Zope developers try to adopt the common conventions accepted by so many.

A decent practice in this kind of library environment is to use *mixedCase* only for elements that are exposed in the framework, and to keep the rest of the code in PEP 8 style.

It is also worth noting that developers of the Twisted project took a completely different approach to this problem. The Twisted project, same as Zope, predates the PEP 8 document. It was started when there were no official guidelines for code style, so it had its own. Stylistic rules about the indentation, docstrings, line lengths, and so on could be easily adopted. On the other hand, updating all the code to match naming conventions from PEP 8 would result in completely broken backwards compatibility. And doing that for such a large project as Twisted is infeasible. So Twisted adopted as much of PEP 8 as possible and left things like *mixedCase* for variables, functions, and methods as part of its own coding standard. And this is completely compatible with the PEP 8 suggestion because it specifically says that consistency within a project is more important than consistency with PEP 8 style guide.

The private controversy

For private methods and functions, a leading underscore is conventionally added. This rule was quite controversial because of the name-mangling feature in Python. When a method has two leading underscores, it is renamed on the fly by the interpreter to prevent a name collision with a method from any subclass.

So some people tend to use a double leading underscore for their private attributes to avoid name collision in the subclasses:

```
class Base(object):
    def __secret(self):
        print("don't tell")

    def public(self):
        self.__secret()
```

```
class Derived(Base):
    def __secret(self):
        print("never ever")
```

You will see:

```
>>> Base.__secret
Traceback (most recent call last):
  File "<input>", line 1, in <module>
AttributeError: type object 'Base' has no attribute '__secret'
>>> dir(Base)
['_Base__secret', ..., 'public']
>>> Derived().public()
don't tell
```

The original motivation for name mangling in Python was not to provide a private gimmick, like in C++, but to make sure that some base classes implicitly avoid collisions in subclasses, especially in multiple inheritance contexts. But using it for every attribute obfuscates the code in private, which is not Pythonic at all.

Therefore, some people opined that the explicit name mangling should always be used:

```
class Base:
    def _Base_secret(self):  # don't do this !!!
        print("you told it ?")
```

This duplicates the class name all over the code and so __ should be preferred.

But the best practice, as the **BDFL** (Guido, the **Benevolent Dictator For Life**, see http://en.wikipedia.org/wiki/BDFL) said, is to avoid using name mangling by looking at the __mro__ (method resolution order) value of a class before writing a method in a subclass. Changing the base class private methods has to be done carefully.

For more information on this topic, an interesting thread occurred in the Python-Dev mailing list many years ago, where people argued on the utility of name mangling and its fate in the language. It can be found at http://mail.python.org/pipermail/python-dev/2005-December/058555.html.

Special methods

Special methods (https://docs.python.org/3/reference/datamodel.html#special-method-names) start and end with a double underscore, and no normal method should use this convention. Some developers used to call them *dunder* methods as a portmanteau of double-underscore. They are used for operator overloading, container definitions, and so on. For the sake of readability, they should be gathered at the beginning of class definitions:

```python
class WeirdInt(int):
    def __add__(self, other):
        return int.__add__(self, other) + 1

    def __repr__(self):
        return '<weirdo %d>' % self

    # public API
    def do_this(self):
        print('this')

    def do_that(self):
        print('that')
```

For a normal method, you should never use these kinds of names. So don't invent a name for a method such as this:

```python
class BadHabits:
    def __my_method__(self):
        print('ok')
```

Arguments

Arguments are in lowercase, with underscores if needed. They follow the same naming rules as variables.

Properties

The names of properties are in lowercase, or in lowercase with underscores. Most of the time, they represent an object's state, which can be a noun or an adjective, or a small phrase when needed:

```python
class Connection:
    _connected = []

    def connect(self, user):
        self._connected.append(user)

    @property
    def connected_people(self):
        return ', '.join(self._connected)
```

When run on interactive session:

```
>>> connection = Connection()
>>> connection.connect('Tarek')
>>> connection.connect('Shannon')
>>> print(connection.connected_people)
Tarek, Shannon
```

Classes

The names of classes are always in CamelCase, and may have a leading underscore when they are private to a module.

The class and instance variables are often noun phrases, and form a usage logic with the method names that are verb phrases:

```
class Database:
    def open(self):
        pass


class User:
    pass
```

Here is an example usage in interactive session:

```
>>> user = User()
>>> db = Database()
>>> db.open()
```

Modules and packages

Besides the special module __init__, the module names are in lowercase with no underscores.

The following are some examples from the standard library:

- os
- sys
- shutil

When the module is private to the package, a leading underscore is added. Compiled C or C++ modules are usually named with an underscore and imported in pure Python modules.

Package names follow the same rules, since they act like more structured modules.

The naming guide

A common set of naming rules can be applied on variables, methods, functions, and properties. The names of classes and modules also play an important role in namespace construction, and in turn in code readability. This mini-guide provides common patterns and antipatterns for picking their names.

Using the has or is prefix for Boolean elements

When an element holds a Boolean value, the `is` and `has` prefixes provide a natural way to make it more readable in its namespace:

```
class DB:
    is_connected = False
    has_cache = False
```

Using plurals for variables that are collections

When an element is holding a collection, it is a good idea to use a plural form. Some mappings can also benefit from this when they are exposed like sequences:

```
class DB:
    connected_users = ['Tarek']
    tables = {
        'Customer': ['id', 'first_name', 'last_name']
    }
```

Using explicit names for dictionaries

When a variable holds a mapping, you should use an explicit name when possible. For example, if a `dict` holds a person's address, it can be named `persons_addresses`:

```
persons_addresses = {'Bill': '6565 Monty Road',
                     'Pamela': '45 Python street'}
persons_addresses['Pamela']
'45 Python street'
```

Avoiding generic names

Using terms such as `list`, `dict`, `sequence`, or `elements`, even for local variables, is evil if your code is not building a new abstract datatype. It makes the code hard to read, understand, and use. Using a built-in name has to be avoided as well, to avoid shadowing it in the current namespace. Generic verbs should also be avoided, unless they have a meaning in the namespace.

Instead, domain-specific terms should be used:

```
def compute(data):  # too generic
    for element in data:
        yield element ** 2


def squares(numbers):  # better
    for number in numbers:
        yield number ** 2
```

There is also a list of prefixes and suffixes that despite being very common in programming should be, in fact, avoided in function and class names:

- Manager
- Object
- Do, handle, or perform

The reason for this is that they are vague, ambiguous, and do not add any value to the actual name. Jeff Atwood, the co-founder of Discourse and Stack Overflow, has a very good article on this topic, which can be found on his blog at http://blog.codinghorror.com/i-shall-call-it-somethingmanager/.

There is also a list of package names that should be avoided. Everything that does not give any clue about its content can do a lot of harm to the project in the long term. Names such as misc, tools, utils, common, or core have a very strong tendency to become endless bags of various unrelated code pieces of very poor quality that seem to grow in size exponentially. In most cases, the existence of such a module is a sign of laziness or lack of enough design efforts. Enthusiasts of such module names can simply forestall the future and rename them to trash or dumpster because this is exactly how their teammates will eventually treat such modules.

In most cases, it is almost always better to have more small modules, even with very little content, but with names that well reflect what is inside. To be honest, there is nothing inherently wrong with names such as utils and common and it is possible to use them responsibly. But the reality shows that in many cases they instead become a stub for dangerous structural antipatterns that proliferate very fast. And if you don't act fast enough, you may not ever be able get rid of them. So the best approach is simply to avoid such risky organizational patterns and nip them in the bud if introduced by other people working on a project.

Avoiding existing names

It is bad practice to use names that already exist in the context because it makes reading and, more specifically, debugging very confusing:

```
>>> def bad_citizen():
...     os = 1
...     import pdb; pdb.set_trace()
...     return os
...
>>> bad_citizen()
> <stdin>(4)bad_citizen()
(Pdb) os
1
(Pdb) import os
(Pdb) c
<module 'os' from '/Library/Frameworks/Python.framework/Versions/2.5/lib/python2.5/os.pyc'>
```

In this example, the os name was shadowed by the code. Both built-ins and module names from the standard library should be avoided.

Try to create original names, even if they are local to the context. For keywords, a trailing underscore is a way to avoid a collision:

```
def xapian_query(terms, or_=True):
    """if or_ is true, terms are combined with the OR clause"""
    ...
```

Note that class is often replaced by klass or cls:

```
def factory(klass, *args, **kwargs):
    return klass(*args, **kwargs)
```

Best practices for arguments

The signatures of functions and methods are the guardians of code integrity. They drive its usage and build its API. Besides the naming rules that we have seen previously, special care has to be taken for arguments. This can be done through three simple rules:

- Build arguments by iterative design
- Trust the arguments and your tests
- Use *args and **kwargs magic arguments carefully

Building arguments by iterative design

Having a fixed and well-defined list of arguments for each function makes the code more robust. But this can't be done in the first version, so arguments have to be built by iterative design. They should reflect the precise use cases the element was created for, and evolve accordingly.

For instance, when some arguments are appended, they should have default values wherever possible, to avoid any regression:

```
class Service:   # version 1
    def _query(self, query, type):
        print('done')

    def execute(self, query):
        self._query(query, 'EXECUTE')

>>> Service().execute('my query')
done


import logging

class Service(object):   # version 2
    def _query(self, query, type, logger):
        logger('done')

    def execute(self, query, logger=logging.info):
        self._query(query, 'EXECUTE', logger)

>>> Service().execute('my query')      # old-style call
>>> Service().execute('my query', logging.warning)
WARNING:root:done
```

When the argument of a public element has to be changed, a deprecation process is to be used, which is presented later in this section.

Trust the arguments and your tests

Given the dynamic typing nature of Python, some developers use assertions at the top of their functions and methods to make sure the arguments have proper content:

```
def division(dividend, divisor):
    assert isinstance(dividend, (int, float))
    assert isinstance(divisor, (int, float))
    return dividend / divisor
```

```
>>> division(2, 4)
0.5
>>> division(2, None)
Traceback (most recent call last):
  File "<input>", line 1, in <module>
  File "<input>", line 3, in division
AssertionError
```

This is often done by developers who are used to static typing and feel that something is missing in Python.

This way of checking arguments is a part of the **Design by Contract (DbC**, see `http://en.wikipedia.org/wiki/Design_By_Contract`) programming style, where preconditions are checked before the code is actually run.

The two main problems with this approach are:

- DbC's code explains how it should be used, making it less readable
- This can make it slower, since the assertions are made on each call

The latter can be avoided with the `"-O"` option of the interpreter. In that case, all assertions are removed from the code before the byte code is created, so that the checking is lost.

In any case, assertions have to be done carefully, and should not be used to bend Python to a statically typed language. The only use case for this is to protect the code from being called nonsensically.

A healthy Test-Driven Development style provides a robust base code in most cases. Here, the functional and unit tests validate all the use cases the code is created for.

When code in a library is used by external elements, making assertions can be useful, as the incoming data might break things up or even create damage. This happens for code that deals with databases or the filesystem.

Another approach to this is **fuzz testing** (`http://en.wikipedia.org/wiki/Fuzz_testing`), where random pieces of data are sent to the program to detect its weaknesses. When a new defect is found, the code can be fixed to take care of that, together with a new test.

Let's take care that a code base, which follows the TDD approach, evolves in the right direction, and gets increasingly robust, since it is tuned every time a new failure occurs. When it is done in the right way, the list of assertions in the tests becomes similar in some way to the list of pre-conditions.

Using *args and **kwargs magic arguments carefully

The *args and **kwargs arguments can break the robustness of a function or method. They make the signature fuzzy, and the code often starts to build a small argument parser where it should not:

```
def fuzzy_thing(**kwargs):

    if 'do_this' in kwargs:
        print('ok i did')

    if 'do_that' in kwargs:
        print('that is done')

    print('errr... ok')

>>> fuzzy_thing(do_this=1)
ok i did
errr... ok
>>> fuzzy_thing(do_that=1)
that is done
errr... ok
>>> fuzzy_thing(hahaha=1)
errr... ok
```

If the argument list gets long and complex, it is tempting to add magic arguments. But this is more a sign of a weak function or method that should be broken into pieces or refactored.

When *args is used to deal with a sequence of elements that are treated the same way in the function, asking for a unique container argument, such as an iterator, is better:

```
def sum(*args):  # okay
    total = 0
    for arg in args:
        total += arg
    return total


def sum(sequence):  # better!
    total = 0
    for arg in sequence:
        total += arg
    return total
```

For `**kwargs`, the same rule applies. It is better to fix the named arguments to make the method's signature meaningful:

```python
def make_sentence(**kwargs):
    noun = kwargs.get('noun', 'Bill')
    verb = kwargs.get('verb', 'is')
    adj = kwargs.get('adjective', 'happy')
    return '%s %s %s' % (noun, verb, adj)



def make_sentence(noun='Bill', verb='is', adjective='happy'):
    return '%s %s %s' % (noun, verb, adjective)
```

Another interesting approach is to create a container class that groups several related arguments to provide an execution context. This structure differs from `*args` or `**kwargs` because it can provide internals that work over the values and can evolve independently. The code that uses it as an argument will not have to deal with its internals.

For instance, a web request passed on to a function is often represented by an instance of a class. This class is in charge of holding the data passed by the web server:

```python
def log_request(request):  # version 1
    print(request.get('HTTP_REFERER', 'No referer'))

def log_request(request):  # version 2
    print(request.get('HTTP_REFERER', 'No referer'))
    print(request.get('HTTP_HOST', 'No host'))
```

Magic arguments cannot be avoided sometimes, especially in meta-programming. For instance, they are indispensable in the creation of decorators that work on functions with any kind of signature. More globally, anywhere where working with unknown data that just traverses the function, the magic arguments are great:

```python
import logging

def log(**context):
    logging.info('Context is:\n%s\n' % str(context))
```

Class names

The name of a class has to be concise, precise, so that it is sufficient to understand from it what the class does. A common practice is to use a suffix that informs about its type or nature, for example:

- **SQL**Engine
- **Mime**Types
- **String**Widget
- **Test**Case

For base or abstract classes, a **Base** or **Abstract** prefix can be used as follows:

- **Base**Cookie
- **Abstract**Formatter

The most important thing is to be consistent with the class attributes. For example, try to avoid redundancy between the class and its attributes' names:

```
>>> SMTP.smtp_send()   # redundant information in the namespace
>>> SMTP.send()        # more readable and mnemonic
```

Module and package names

The module and package names inform about the purpose of their content. The names are short, in lowercase, and without underscores:

- sqlite
- postgres
- sha1

They are often suffixed with `lib` if they are implementing a protocol:

```
import smtplib
import urllib
import telnetlib
```

They also need to be consistent within the namespace, so their usage is easier:

```
from widgets.stringwidgets import TextWidget   # bad
from widgets.strings import TextWidget         # better
```

Again, always avoid using the same name as that of one of the modules from the standard library.

When a module is getting complex, and contains a lot of classes, it is good practice to create a package and split the module's elements in other modules.

The __init__ module can also be used to put back some APIs at the top level as it will not impact its usage, but will help with re-organizing the code into smaller parts. For example, consider the __init__ module in a `foo` package with the following content:

```
from .module1 import feature1, feature2
from .module2 import feature3
```

This will allow users to import features directly, as shown in the following code:

```
from foo import feature1, feature2, feature3
```

But beware that this can increase your chances to get circular dependencies, and that the code added in the __init__ module will be instantiated. So use it with care.

Useful tools

Part of the previous conventions and practices can be controlled and worked out with the following tools:

- **Pylint**: This is a very flexible source code analyzer
- **pep8** and **flake8**: These are a small code style checker, and a wrapper that adds to it some more useful features, like static analysis and complexity measurement

Pylint

Besides some quality assurance metrics, Pylint allows you to check whether a given source code is following a naming convention. Its default settings correspond to PEP 8, and a Pylint script provides a shell report output.

To install Pylint, you can use `pip`:

```
$ pip install pylint
```

After this step, the command is available and can be run against a module, or several modules, using wildcards. Let's try it on Buildout's `bootstrap.py` script:

```
$ wget -O bootstrap.py https://bootstrap.pypa.io/bootstrap-buildout.py -q
$ pylint bootstrap.py
No config file found, using default configuration
```

```
************* Module bootstrap
C: 76, 0: Unnecessary parens after 'print' keyword (superfluous-parens)
C: 31, 0: Invalid constant name "tmpeggs" (invalid-name)
C: 33, 0: Invalid constant name "usage" (invalid-name)
C: 45, 0: Invalid constant name "parser" (invalid-name)
C: 74, 0: Invalid constant name "options" (invalid-name)
C: 74, 9: Invalid constant name "args" (invalid-name)
C: 84, 4: Import "from urllib.request import urlopen" should be placed at
the top of the module (wrong-import-position)

...


Global evaluation
-----------------
Your code has been rated at 6.12/10
```

Real Pylint's output is a bit longer and has been truncated here.

Notice that Pylint can give you bad rates or complaints. For instance, an import statement that is not used by the code of the module itself is perfectly fine in some cases (having it available in the namespace).

Making calls to libraries that are using mixedCase for methods can also lower your rating. In any case, the global evaluation is not as important. Pylint is just a tool that points the possible improvements.

The first thing to do to fine-tune Pylint is to create a `.pylinrc` configuration file in your projects directory, with the `-generate-rcfile` option:

```
$ pylint --generate-rcfile > .pylintrc
```

This configuration file is self-documenting (every possible option is described with comment) and should already contain every available configuration option.

Besides checking for compliance with some arbitrary coding standards, Pylint can also give additional information about the overall code quality, like:

- Code duplication metrics
- Unused variables and imports
- Missing function, method, or class docstrings
- Too long function signatures

The list of available checks that are enabled by default is very long. It is important to know that some of the rules are arbitrary and will not easily apply to every codebase. Remember that consistency is always more valuable than compliance with some arbitrary standards. Fortunately, Pylint is very tunable, so if your team uses some naming and coding conventions that are different than assumed by default, you can easily configure it to check for consistency with these conventions.

pep8 and flake8

`pep8` is a tool that has only one purpose: it provides only a stylecheck against code conventions from PEP 8. This is the main difference from Pylint, which has many additional features. This is the best option for programmers that are interested in automated code style checking only for PEP 8 standard, without any additional tool configuration, like in Pylint's case.

`pep8` can be installed with `pip`:

```
$ pip install pep8
```

When run on the Buildout's `bootstrap.py` script, it will give a short list of code style violations:

```
$ wget -O bootstrap.py https://bootstrap.pypa.io/bootstrap-buildout.py -q
$ pep8 bootstrap.py
bootstrap.py:118:1: E402 module level import not at top of file
bootstrap.py:119:1: E402 module level import not at top of file
bootstrap.py:190:1: E402 module level import not at top of file
bootstrap.py:200:1: E402 module level import not at top of file
```

The main difference from Pylint's output is its length. `pep8` concentrates only on style, so it does not provide any other warning, like unused variables, too long function names, or missing docstrings. It also does not give any rating. And it really makes sense because there is no such thing as partial consistency. Any, even the slightest, violation of style guidelines makes the code immediately inconsistent.

Output of `pep8` is simpler than Pylint's and easier to parse, so it may be a better choice if you want to integrate it with some continuous integration solutions, like Jenkins. If you are missing some static analysis features, there is the `flake8` package that is a wrapper on `pep8` and few other tools that is easily extendable and provides a more extensive suite of features:

- McCabe complexity measurement
- Static analysis via `pyflakes`
- Disabling whole files or single lines using comments

Summary

This chapter explained the most accepted coding conventions by pointing to the official Python style guide (the PEP 8 document). The official style guide was complemented by some naming suggestions that will make your future code more explicit, and also a few useful tools that are indispensable in keeping the code style consistent.

All of this prepares us for the first practical topic of the book—writing and distributing packages. In the next chapter we will learn how to publish our very own package on a public PyPI repository, and also how to leverage the power of the packaging ecosystem in your private organization.

5
Writing a Package

This chapter focuses on a repeatable process to write and release Python packages. Its intentions are:

- To shorten the time needed to set up everything before starting the real work
- To provide a standardized way to write packages
- To ease the use of a test-driven development approach
- To facilitate the releasing process

It is organized into the following four parts:

- A **common pattern** for all packages that describes the similarities between all Python packages, and how `distutils` and `setuptools` play a central role
- What **namespace packages** are and why they can be useful
- How to register and upload packages in the **Python Package Index (PyPI)** with emphasis on security and common pitfalls
- The **stand-alone executables** as an alternative way to package and distribute Python applications

Creating a package

Python packaging can be a bit overwhelming at first. The main reason for that is the confusion about proper tools for creating Python packages. Anyway, once you create your first package, you will see that this is not as hard as it looks. Also, knowing proper, state-of-the art packaging tools helps a lot.

You should know how to create packages even if you are not interested in distributing your code as open source. Knowing how to make your own will give you more insight into the packaging ecosystem and will help you to work with third-party code available on PyPI that you are probably using.

Also, having your closed source project or its components available as source distribution packages can help you to deploy your code in different environments. Advantages of leveraging the Python packaging ecosystem in code deployment will be described in more detail in the next chapter. Here we will focus on proper tools and techniques to create such distributions.

The confusing state of Python packaging tools

The state of Python packaging was very confusing for a long time and it took many years to bring organization to this topic. Everything started with the distutils package introduced in 1998 that was later enhanced by setuptools in 2003. These two projects started a long and knotted story of forks, alternative projects, and complete rewrites that tried to once and for all fix Python's packaging ecosystem. Unfortunately, most of these attempts never succeeded. The effect was quite the opposite. Each new project that aimed to supersede setuptools or distutils only added up to the already huge confusion around packaging tools. Some of such forks were merged back to their ancestors (like distribute that was a fork of setuptools) but some were left abandoned (like distutils2).

Fortunately, this state is gradually changing. An organization called **Python Packaging Authority** (**PyPA**) was formed to bring back the order and organization to the packaging ecosystem. **Python Packaging User Guide** (https://packaging.python.org), maintained by PyPA, is the authoritative source of information about the latest packaging tools and best practices. Treat it as the best source of information about packaging and a complementary reading to this chapter. The guide also contains a detailed history of changes and new projects related to packaging, so it will be useful if you already know a bit but want to make sure you still use the proper tools.

Stay away from other popular Internet resources, such as **The Hitchhiker's Guide to Packaging**. It is old, not maintained, and mostly obsolete. It may be interesting only for historical reasons and the Python Packaging User Guide is in fact a fork of this old resource.

The current landscape of Python packaging thanks to PyPA

PyPA, besides providing an authoritative guide for packaging, also maintains packaging projects and the standardization process for new official aspects of packaging. All of PyPA's projects can be found under a single organization on GitHub: https://github.com/pypa.

Some of them were already mentioned in the book. The most notable are:

- `pip`
- `virtualenv`
- `twine`
- `warehouse`

Note that most of them were started outside of this organization and only moved under PyPA patronage as mature and widespread solutions.

Thanks to PyPA engagement, the progressive abandoning of the eggs format in favor of wheels for built distributions is already happening. The future may bring us even more fresh breath. PyPA is actively working on `warehouse`, which aims to completely replace current PyPI implementations. This will be a huge step in packaging history because `pypi` is so old and neglected a project that only a few of us can imagine gradually improving it without a total rewrite.

Tool recommendations

Python Packaging User Guide gives a few suggestions on recommended tools for working with packages. They can be generally divided into two groups: tools for installing packages and tools for package creation and distribution.

Utilities from the first group recommended by PyPA were already mentioned in *Chapter 1, Current Status of Python*, but let's repeat them here for the sake of consistency:

- Use `pip` for installing packages from PyPI
- Use `virtualenv` or `venv` for application-level isolation of the Python environment

The Python Packaging User Guide recommendations of tools for package creation and distribution are as follows:

- Use `setuptools` to define projects and create **source distributions**
- Use **wheels** in favor of **eggs** to create **built distributions**
- Use `twine` to upload package distributions to PyPI

Project configuration

It should be obvious that the easiest way to organize the code of big applications is to split it into several packages. This makes the code simpler, and easier to understand, maintain, and change. It also maximizes the reusability of each package. They act like components.

setup.py

The root directory of a package that has to be distributed contains a `setup.py` script. It defines all metadata as described in the `distutils` module, combined as arguments in a call to the standard `setup()` function. Despite `distutils` is a standard library module, it is recommended that you use the `setuptools` package instead, which provides several enhancements to the standard `distutils`.

Therefore, the minimum content for this file is:

```
from setuptools import setup

setup(
    name='mypackage',
)
```

`name` gives the full name of the package. From there, the script provides several commands that can be listed with the `--help-commands` option:

```
$ python3 setup.py --help-commands
Standard commands:
  build          build everything needed to install
  clean          clean up temporary files from 'build' command
  install        install everything from build directory
  sdist          create a source distribution (tarball, zip file)
  register       register the distribution with the PyP
  bdist          create a built (binary) distribution
  check          perform some checks on the package
  upload         upload binary package to PyPI

Extra commands:
  develop        install package in 'development mode'
  alias          define a shortcut to invoke one or more commands
  test           run unit tests after in-place build
  bdist_wheel    create a wheel distribution
```

```
usage: setup.py [global_opts] cmd1 [cmd1_opts] [cmd2 [cmd2_opts] ...]
   or: setup.py --help [cmd1 cmd2 ...]
   or: setup.py --help-commands
   or: setup.py cmd --help
```

The actual list of commands is longer and can vary depending on the available `setuptools` extensions. It was truncated to show only those that are most important and relevant to this chapter. **Standard commands** are the built-in commands provided by `distutils`, whereas **extra commands** are the ones created by third-party packages such as `setuptools` or any other package that defines and registers a new command. One such extra command registered by another package is `bdist_wheel` provided by the `wheel` package.

setup.cfg

The `setup.cfg` file contains default options for commands of the `setup.py` script. This is very useful if the process for building and distributing the package is more complex and requires many optional arguments to be passed to the `setup.py` commands. This allows you to store such default parameters in code on a per-project basis. This will make your distribution flow independent from the project and also provide transparency about how your package was built and distributed to the users and other team members.

The syntax for the `setup.cfg` file is the same as provided by the built-in `configparser` module so it is similar to the popular Microsoft Windows INI files. Here is an example of the setup configuration file that provides some `global`, `sdist`, and `bdist_wheel` command defaults:

```
[global]
quiet=1

[sdist]
formats=zip,tar

[bdist_wheel]
universal=1
```

This example configuration will ensure that source distributions will always be created with two formats (ZIP and TAR) and built wheel distributions will be created as universal wheels (Python version independent). Also, most of output will be suppressed on every command by the global `quiet` switch. Note that this is only for demonstration purposes and it may not be a reasonable choice to suppress the output for every command by default.

MANIFEST.in

When building a distribution with `sdist` command, `distutils` browses the package directory looking for files to include in the archive. `distutils` will include:

- All Python source files implied by the `py_modules`, `packages`, and `scripts` options

- All C source files listed in the `ext_modules` option

Files that match the glob pattern `test/test*.py` are: `README`, `README.txt`, `setup.py`, and `setup.cfg`.

Besides, if your package is under subversion or CVS, `sdist` will browse folders such as `.svn` to look for files to include. Integration with other version control systems is also possible through extensions. `sdist` builds a `MANIFEST` file that lists all files and includes them into the archive.

Let's say you are not using these version control systems, and need to include more files. Now you can define a template called `MANIFEST.in` in the same directory as that of `setup.py` for the `MANIFEST` file, where you indicate to `sdist` which files to include.

This template defines one inclusion or exclusion rule per line, for example:

```
include HISTORY.txt
include README.txt
include CHANGES.txt
include CONTRIBUTORS.txt
include LICENSE
recursive-include *.txt *.py
```

The full list of the `MANIFEST.in` commands can be found in official `distutils` documentation.

Most important metadata

Besides the name and the version of the package being distributed, the most important arguments `setup` can receive are:

- `description`: This includes a few sentences to describe the package

- `long_description`: This includes a full description that can be in reStructuredText

- `keywords`: This is a list of keywords that define the package

- `author`: This is the author's name or organization

- `author_email`: This is the contact e-mail address
- `url`: This is the URL of the project
- `license`: This is the license (GPL, LGPL, and so on)
- `packages`: This is a list of all names in the package; `setuptools` provides a small function called `find_packages` that calculates this
- `namespace_packages`: This is a list of namespaced packages

Trove classifiers

PyPI and `distutils` provide a solution for categorizing applications with the set of classifiers called **trove classifiers**. All the classifiers form a tree-like structure. Each classifier is a form of string where every namespace is separated by the `::` substring. Their list is provided to the package definition as a `classifiers` argument to the `setup()` function. Here is an example list of classifiers for some project available on PyPI (here `solrq`):

```
from setuptools import setup

setup(
    name="solrq",
    # (...)

    classifiers=[
        'Development Status :: 4 - Beta',
        'Intended Audience :: Developers',
        'License :: OSI Approved :: BSD License',
        'Operating System :: OS Independent',
        'Programming Language :: Python',
        'Programming Language :: Python :: 2',
        'Programming Language :: Python :: 2.6',
        'Programming Language :: Python :: 2.7',
        'Programming Language :: Python :: 3',
        'Programming Language :: Python :: 3.2',
        'Programming Language :: Python :: 3.3',
        'Programming Language :: Python :: 3.4',
        'Programming Language :: Python :: Implementation :: PyPy',
        'Topic :: Internet :: WWW/HTTP :: Indexing/Search',
    ],
)
```

They are completely optional in the package definition but provide a useful extension to the basic metadata available in the `setup()` interface. Among others, trove classifiers may provide information about supported Python versions or systems, the development stage of the project, or the license under which the code is released. Many PyPI users search and browse the available packages by categories so a proper classification helps packages to reach their target.

Trove classifiers serve an important role in the whole packaging ecosystem and should never be ignored. There is no organization that verifies packages classification, so it is your responsibility to provide proper classifiers for your packages and not introduce chaos to the whole package index.

At the time of writing this book, there are 608 classifiers available on PyPI that are grouped into nine major categories:

- Development status
- Environment
- Framework
- Intended audience
- License
- Natural language
- Operating system
- Programming language
- Topic

New classifiers are added from time to time, so it is possible that these numbers will be different at the time you read it. The full list of currently available trove classifiers is available with the `setup.py register --list-classifiers` command.

Common patterns

Creating a package for distribution can be a tedious task for inexperienced developers. Most of the metadata that `setuptools` or `distuitls` accept in their `setup()` function call can be provided manually, ignoring the fact that this may be available in other parts of the project:

```
from setuptools import setup

setup(
    name="myproject",
    version="0.0.1",
```

```
        description="mypackage project short description",
        long_description="""
            Longer description of mypackage project
            possibly with some documentation and/or
            usage examples
        """,
        install_requires=[
            'dependency1',
            'dependency2',
            'etc',
        ]
    )
```

While this will definitely work, it is hard to maintain in the long term and leaves a place for future mistakes and inconsistencies. Both setuptools and distutils cannot automatically pick various metadata information from the project sources, so you need to provide them by yourself. There are some common patterns among the Python community for solving the most popular problems like dependency management, version/readme inclusion, and so on. It is worth knowing at least a few of them because they are so popular that they could be considered as packaging idioms.

Automated inclusion of version string from package

The **PEP 440 (Version Identification and Dependency Specification)** document specifies a standard for version and dependency specification. It is a long document that covers accepted version specification schemes and how version matching and comparison in Python packaging tools should work. If you are using or plan to use a complex project version numbering scheme, then reading this document is obligatory. If you are using a simple scheme that consists of one, two, three, or more numbers separated by dots, then you can let go the reading of PEP 440. If you don't know how to choose the proper versioning scheme, I greatly recommend following semantic versioning that was already mentioned in *Chapter 1*, *Current Status of Python*.

The other problem is where to include that version specifier for a package or module. There is PEP 396 (Module Version Numbers), which deals exactly with this problem. Note that it is only informational and has *deferred* status, so it is not a part of the standards track. Anyway, it describes what seems to be a *de facto* standard now. According to PEP 396, if a package or module has a version specified, it should be included as a __version__ attribute of a package root (__init__.py) or module file. Another de facto standard is to also include the VERSION attribute that contains the tuple of version parts. This helps users to write compatibility code because such version tuples can be easily compared if the versioning scheme is simple enough.

So many packages available on PyPI follow both standards. Their __init__.py files contain version attributes that look like the following:

```
# version as tuple for simple comparisons
VERSION = (0, 1, 1)
# string created from tuple to avoid inconsistency
__version__ = ".".join([str(x) for x in VERSION])
```

The other suggestion of deferred PEP 396 is that the version provided in the distutils' setup() function should be derived from __version__, or vice versa. Python Packaging User Guide features multiple patterns for a single-sourcing project version and each of them has its own advantages and limitations. My personal favorite is rather long and is not included in the PyPA's guide but has the advantage of limiting the complexity to setup.py script only. This boiler plate assumes that the version specifier is provided by the VERSION attribute of package's __init__ module and extracts this data for inclusion in the setup() call. Here is the excerpt from some imaginary package's setup.py script that presents this approach:

```python
from setuptools import setup
import os


def get_version(version_tuple):
    # additional handling of a,b,rc tags, this can
    # be simpler depending on your versioning scheme
    if not isinstance(version_tuple[-1], int):
        return '.'.join(
            map(str, version_tuple[:-1])
        ) + version_tuple[-1]

    return '.'.join(map(str, version_tuple))

# path to the packages __init__ module in project
# source tree
init = os.path.join(
    os.path.dirname(__file__), 'src', 'some_package',
    '__init__.py'
)

version_line = list(
    filter(lambda l: l.startswith('VERSION'), open(init))
)[0]
```

```
# VERSION is a tuple so we need to eval its line of code.
# We could simply import it from the package but we
# cannot be sure that this package is importable before
# finishing its installation
VERSION = get_version(eval(version_line.split('=')[-1]))

setup(
    name='some-package',
    version=VERSION,
    # ...
)
```

README file

Python Packaging Index can display a project's readme or the value of long_
description on the package page in PyPI portal. You can write this description
using reStructuredText (http://docutils.sourceforge.net/rst.html) markup,
so it will be formatted to HTML on upload. Unfortunately, only reStructuredText is
currently available as a documentation markup on PyPI. This is unlikely to change in
the near future. More likely, additional markup languages will be supported when
we see the warehouse project replacing completely current PyPI implementations.
Unfortunately, the final release of warehouse is still unknown.

Still, many developers want to use different markup languages for various reasons.
The most popular choice is Markdown, which is the default markup language on
GitHub—the place where most open source Python development currently happens.
So, usually, GitHub and Markdown enthusiasts either ignore this problem or
provide two independent documentation texts. Descriptions provided to PyPI are
either short versions of what is available on the project's GitHub page or it is plain
unformatted Markdown that does not present well on PyPI.

If you want to use something different than reStructuredText markup language for
your project's README, you can still provide it as a project description on the PyPI
page in a readable form. The trick lies in using the pypandoc package to translate
your other markup language into reStructuredText while uploading the package to
Python Package Index. It is important to do it with a fallback to plain content of your
readme file, so the installation won't fail if the user has no pypandoc installed:

```
try:
    from pypandoc import convert

    def read_md(f):
        return convert(f, 'rst')
```

```
except ImportError:
    convert = None
    print(
        "warning: pypandoc module not found, could not convert
        Markdown to RST"
    )

    def read_md(f):
        return open(f, 'r').read()  # noqa

README = os.path.join(os.path.dirname(__file__), 'README.md')

setup(
    name='some-package',
    long_description=read_md(README),
    # ...
)
```

Managing dependencies

Many projects require some external packages to be installed and/or used. When
the list of dependencies is very long there comes a question as to how to manage it.
The answer in most cases is very simple. Do not over-engineer the problem. Keep it
simple and provide the list of dependencies explicitly in your setup.py script:

```
from setuptools import setup
setup(
    name='some-package',
    install_requires=['falcon', 'requests', 'delorean']
    # ...
)
```

Some Python developers like to use requirements.txt files for tracking lists of
dependencies for their packages. In some situations, you might find a reason for
doing that but in most cases this is a relic of times where the code of that project was
not properly packaged. Anyway, even such notable projects as Celery still stick to
this convention. So if you are not willing to change your habits or you are somehow
forced to use requirement files, then at least do it properly. Here is one of the popular
idioms for reading the list of dependencies from the requirements.txt file:

```
from setuptools import setup
import os

def strip_comments(l):
    return l.split('#', 1)[0].strip()
```

```
def reqs(*f):
    return list(filter(None, [strip_comments(l) for l in open(
        os.path.join(os.getcwd(), *f)).readlines()]))


setup(
    name='some-package',
    install_requires=reqs('requirements.txt')
    # ...
)
```

The custom setup command

distutils allows you to create new commands. A new command can be registered with an entry point, which was introduced by setuptools as a simple way to define packages as plug-ins.

An entry point is a named link to a class or a function that is made available through some APIs in setuptools. Any application can scan for all registered packages and use the linked code as a plug-in.

To link the new command, the entry_points metadata can be used in the setup call:

```
setup(
    name="my.command",
    entry_points="""
        [distutils.commands]
        my_command = my.command.module.Class
    """
)
```

All named links are gathered in named sections. When distutils is loaded, it scans for links that were registered under distutils.commands.

This mechanism is used by numerous Python applications that provide extensibility.

Working with packages during development

Working with setuptools is mostly about building and distributing packages. However, you still need to know how to use them to install packages directly from project sources. And the reason for that is simple. It is good to test if your packaging code works properly before submitting a package to PyPI. And the simplest way to test it is by installing it. If you will send a broken package to the repository, then in order to re-upload it, you need to increase the version number.

Testing if your code is packaged properly before the final distribution saves you from unnecessary version number inflation and obviously from wasted time. Also, installation directly from your own sources using `setuptools` may be essential when working on multiple related packages at the same time.

setup.py install

The `install` command installs the package into Python environment. It will try to build the package if no previous build was made and then inject the result into the Python tree. When a source distribution is provided, it can be uncompressed in a temporary folder and then installed with this command. The `install` command will also install dependencies that are defined in the `install_requires` metadata. This is done by looking at the packages in the Python Package Index.

An alternative to the bare `setup.py` script when installing a package is to use `pip`. Since it is a tool that is recommended by PyPA, you should use it even when installing a package in your local environment for development purposes. In order to install a package from local sources, run the following command:

```
pip install <project-path>
```

Uninstalling packages

Amazingly, `setuptools` and `distutils` lack the `uninstall` command. Fortunately, it is possible to uninstall any Python package using `pip`:

```
pip uninstall <package-name>
```

Uninstalling can be a dangerous operation when attempted on system-wide packages. This is another reason why it is so important to use virtual environments for any development.

setup.py develop or pip -e

Packages installed with `setup.py install` are copied to the site-packages directory of your current environment. This means whenever you make a change to the sources of that package, you are required to re-install it. This is often a problem during intensive development because it is very easy to forget about the need to perform installation again. This is why `setuptools` provides an extra `develop` command that allows us to install packages in **development mode**. This command creates a special link to project sources in the deployment directory (site-packages) instead of copying the whole package there. Package sources can be edited without need of re-installation and it is available in `sys.path` as it were installed normally.

`pip` also allows installing packages in such a mode. This installation option is called *editable mode* and can be enabled with the `-e` parameter in the `install` command:

```
pip install -e <project-path>
```

Namespace packages

The Zen of Python, which you can read by writing `import this` in the interpreter session, says the following about namespaces:

> *Namespaces are one honking great idea – let's do more of those!*

And this can be understood in at least two ways. The first is a namespace in the context of the language. We all use namespaces without even knowing:

- The global namespace of a module
- The local namespace of the function or method invocation
- The built-in name's namespace

The other kind of namespaces can be provided at packaging levels. These are **namespaced packages**. This is often an overlooked feature that can be very useful in structuring the package ecosystem in your organization or in a very large project.

Why is it useful?

Namespace packages can be understood as a way of grouping related packages or modules higher than a meta-package level, where each of these packages can be installed independently.

Namespace packages are especially useful if you have your application components developed, packaged, and versioned independently but you still want to access them from the same namespace. This helps to make clear to which organization or project every package belongs. For instance, for some imaginary Acme company, the common namespace could be `acme`. The result could lead to the creation of the general `acme` namespace package that will serve as a container for other packages from this organization. For example, if someone from Acme wants to contribute to this namespace with, for example, an SQL-related library, he can create a new `acme.sql` package that registers itself in `acme`.

It is important to know the difference between normal and namespace packages and what problems they solve. Normally (without namespace packages), you would create a package acme with an sql subpackage/submodule with the following file structure:

```
$ tree acme/
acme/
├── acme
│   ├── __init__.py
│   └── sql
│       └── __init__.py
└── setup.py

2 directories, 3 files
```

Whenever you want to add a new subpackage, let's say templating, you are forced to include it in the source tree of acme:

```
$ tree acme/
acme/
├── acme
│   ├── __init__.py
│   ├── sql
│   │   └── __init__.py
│   └── templating
│       └── __init__.py
└── setup.py

3 directories, 4 files
```

Such an approach makes independent development of acme.sql and acme.templating almost impossible. The setup.py script will also have to specify all dependencies for every subpackage, so it is impossible (or at least very hard) to have an installation of just some of the acme components optionally. Also, it is an unresolvable issue if some of the subpackages have conflicting requirements.

With namespace packages, you can store the source tree for each of these
subpackages independently:

```
$ tree acme.sql/
acme.sql/
├── acme
│    └── sql
│         └── __init__.py
└── setup.py


2 directories, 2 files
```

```
$ tree acme.templating/
acme.templating/
├── acme
│    └── templating
│         └── __init__.py
└── setup.py


2 directories, 2 files
```

You can also register them independently in PyPI or any package index you use.
Users can choose which of the subpackages they want to install from the acme
namespace but they never install the general acme package (it does not exist):

```
$ pip install acme.sql acme.templating
```

Note that independent source trees are not enough to create namespace packages
in Python. You need a bit of additional work if you don't want your packages to
overwrite each other. Also, proper handling may be different depending on the
Python language version you target. Details of that are described in the next
two sections.

PEP 420 – implicit namespace packages

If you use and target only Python 3, then there is good news for you. **PEP 420 (Implicit Namespace Packages)** introduced a new way to define namespace packages. It is a part of the standards track and became an official part of the language since the 3.3 version. In short, every directory that contains Python packages or modules (including namespace packages too) is considered a namespace package if it does not contain the __init__.py file. So, the following are examples of file structures presented in the previous section:

```
$ tree acme.sql/
acme.sql/
├── acme
│   └── sql
│       └── __init__.py
└── setup.py

2 directories, 2 files
```

```
$ tree acme.templating/
acme.templating/
├── acme
│   └── templating
│       └── __init__.py
└── setup.py

2 directories, 2 files
```

They are enough to define that acme is a namespace package in Python 3.3 and later. Minimal setup.py scripts using setup tools will look like the following:

```
from setuptools import setup


setup(
    name='acme.templating',
    packages=['acme.templating'],
)
```

Unfortunately, `setuptools.find_packages()` does not support PEP 420 at the time of writing this book. Anyway, this may change in the future. Also, a requirement to explicitly define a list of packages seems to be a very small price for easy integration of namespace packages.

Namespace packages in previous Python versions

There is no way to make the namespaces packages in PEP 420 layout to work in Python versions older than 3.3. Still, this concept is very old and commonly used in such mature projects like Zope, so it is definitely possible to use them but without implicit definition. In older versions of Python, there are several ways to define that the package should be treated as a namespace.

The simplest one is to create a file structure for each component that resembles an ordinary package layout without namespace packages and leave everything to `setuptools`. So, the example layout for `acme.sql` and `acme.templating` could be the following:

```
$ tree acme.sql/
acme.sql/
├── acme
│   ├── __init__.py
│   └── sql
│       └── __init__.py
└── setup.py

2 directories, 3 files

$ tree acme.templating/
acme.templating/
├── acme
│   ├── __init__.py
│   └── templating
│       └── __init__.py
└── setup.py

2 directories, 3 files
```

Note that for both `acme.sql` and `acme.templating`, there is an additional source file `acme/__init__.py`. This must be left empty. The `acme` namespace package will be created if we provide this name as a value of the `namespace_packages` keyword argument of the `setuptools.setup()` function:

```
from setuptools import setup

setup(
    name='acme.templating',
    packages=['acme.templating'],
    namespace_packages=['acme'],
)
```

Easiest does not mean best. `setuptools`, in order to register a new namespace, will call for the `pkg_resources.declare_namespace()` function in your `__init__.py` file. It will happen even if the `__init__.py` file is empty. Anyway, as the official documentation says, it is your own responsibility to declare namespaces in the `__init__.py` file, and this implicit behavior of `setuptools` may be dropped in the future. In order to be safe and "future-proof", you need to add the following line to the file `acme/__init__.py`:

```
__import__('pkg_resources').declare_namespace(__name__)
```

Uploading a package

Packages will be useless without an organized way to store, upload, and download them. Python Packaging Index is the main source of open source packages in the Python community. Anyone can freely upload new packages and the only requirement is to register on the PyPI site — https://pypi.python.org/pypi.

You are not limited, of course, to only this index and all packaging tools support the usage of alternative package repositories. This is especially useful for distributing closed source code among internal organizations or for deployment purposes. Details of such packaging usage with instructions on how to create your own package index will be explained in the next chapter. Here we focus only on open-source uploads to PyPI with only a little mention on how to specify alternative repositories.

PyPI – Python Package Index

Python Package Index is, as already mentioned, the official source of open source package distributions. Downloading from it does not require any account or permission. The only thing you need is a package manager that can download new distributions from PyPI. Your preferred choice should be `pip`.

Uploading to PyPI – or other package index

Anyone can register and upload packages to PyPI provided that he or she has an account registered. Packages are bound to the user, so, by default, only the user that registered the name of the package is its admin and can upload new distributions. This could be a problem for bigger projects, so there is an option to design other users as package maintainers so that they are able to upload new distributions.

The easiest way to upload a package is to use the `upload` command of the `setup.py` script:

```
$ python setup.py <dist-commands> upload
```

Here, `<dist-commands>` is a list of commands that creates distribution to upload. Only distributions created during the same `setup.py` execution will be uploaded to the repository. So, if you would upload source distribution, built distribution, and wheel package at once, then you need to issue the following command:

```
$ python setup.py sdist bdist bdist_wheel upload
```

When uploading using `setup.py`, you cannot reuse already built distributions and are forced to rebuild them on every upload. This might make some sense but can be inconvenient for large or complex projects in which creation of the distribution may actually take a considerable amount of time. Another problem of `setup.py` `upload` is that it can use plaintext HTTP or unverified HTTPS connection on some Python versions. This is why `twine` is recommended as a secure replacement for `setup.py upload`.

Twine is the utility for interacting with PyPI that currently serves only one purpose—securely uploading packages to the repository. It supports any packaging format and always ensures that the connection is secure. It also allows you to upload files that were already created, so you are able to test distributions before the release. An example usage of `twine` still requires invoking `setup.py` for building distributions:

```
$ python setup.py sdist bdist_wheel
$ twine upload dist/*
```

If you have not yet registered this package, then the upload will fail because you need to register it first. This can also be done using `twine`:

```
$ twine register dist/*
```

.pypirc

`.pypirc` is a configuration file that stores information about Python packages repositories. It should be located in your home directory. The format for this file is as follows:

```
[distutils]
index-servers =
    pypi
    other

[pypi]
repository: <repository-url>
username: <username>
password: <password>

[other]
repository: https://example.com/pypi
username: <username>
password: <password>
```

The `distutils` section should have the `index-servers` variable that lists all sections describing all the available repositories and credentials to them. There are only three variables that can be modified for each repository section:

- `repository`: This is the URL of the package repository (it defaults to `https://www.python.org/pypi`)
- `username`: This is the username for authorization in the given repository
- `password`: This is the user password for authorization in plaintext

Note that storing your repository password in plaintext may not be the wisest security choice. You can always leave it blank and you will be prompted for it whenever it is necessary.

The `.pypirc` file should be respected by every packaging tool built for Python. While this may not be true for every packaging-related utility out there, it is supported by the most important ones such as `pip`, `twine`, `distutils`, and `setuptools`.

Source packages versus built packages

There are generally two types of distributions for Python packages:

- Source distributions
- Built (binary) distributions

Source distributions are the simplest and most platform independent. For pure Python packages, it is a no-brainer. Such a distribution contains only Python sources and these should be already highly portable.

A more complex situation is when your package introduces some extensions written, for example, in C. Source distributions will still work provided that the package user has a proper development toolchain in his/her environment. This consists mostly of the compiler and proper C header files. For such cases, the built distribution format may be better suited because it may provide already built extensions for specific platforms.

sdist

The `sdist` command is the simplest command available. It creates a release tree where everything needed to run the package is copied. This tree is then archived in one or many archive files (often, it just creates one tarball). The archive is basically a copy of the source tree.

This command is the easiest way to distribute a package from the target system independently. It creates a `dist` folder with the archives in it that can be distributed. To be able to use it, an extra argument has to be passed to `setup` to provide a version number. If you don't give it a `version` value, it will use `version = 0.0.0`:

```
from setuptools import setup

setup(name='acme.sql', version='0.1.1')
```

This number is useful to upgrade an installation. Every time a package is released, the number is raised so that the target system knows it has changed.

Let's run the `sdist` command with this extra argument:

```
$ python setup.py sdist
running sdist
...
creating dist
tar -cf dist/acme.sql-0.1.1.tar acme.sql-0.1.1
```

```
gzip -f9 dist/acme.sql-0.1.1.tar
removing 'acme.sql-0.1.1' (and everything under it)
$ ls dist/
acme.sql-0.1.1.tar.gz
```

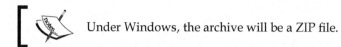 Under Windows, the archive will be a ZIP file.

The version is used to mark the name of the archive, which can be distributed and installed on any system that has Python. In the `sdist` distribution, if the package contains C libraries or extensions, the target system is responsible for compiling them. This is very common for Linux-based systems or Mac OS because they commonly provide a compiler, but it is less usual to have it under Windows. That's why a package should always be distributed with a prebuilt distribution as well, when it is intended to run under several platforms.

bdist and wheels

To be able to distribute a prebuilt distribution, `distutils` provides the `build` command, which compiles the package in four steps:

- `build_py`: This builds pure Python modules by byte-compiling them and copying them into the build folder.
- `build_clib`: This builds C libraries, when the package contains any, using C compiler and creating a static library in the build folder.
- `build_ext`: This builds C extensions and puts the result in the build folder like `build_clib`.
- `build_scripts`: This builds the modules that are marked as scripts. It also changes the interpreter path when the first line was set (`!#`) and fixes the file mode so that it is executable.

Each of these steps is a command that can be called independently. The result of the compilation process is a build folder that contains everything needed for the package to be installed. There's no cross-compiler option yet in the `distutils` package. This means that the result of the command is always specific to the system it was built on.

When some C extensions have to be created, the build process uses the system compiler and the Python header file (`Python.h`). This **include** file is available from the time Python was built from the sources. For a packaged distribution, an extra package for your system distribution is probably required. At least in popular Linux distributions, it is often named `python-dev`. It contains all the necessary header files for building Python extensions.

The C compiler used is the system compiler. For a Linux-based system or Mac OS X, this would be **gcc** or **clang** respectively. For Windows, Microsoft Visual C++ can be used (there's a free command-line version available) and the open-source project MinGW can be used as well. This can be configured in distutils.

The build command is used by the bdist command to build a binary distribution. It calls build and all the dependent commands, and then creates an archive in the same way as sdist does.

Let's create a binary distribution for acme.sql under Mac OS X:

```
$ python setup.py bdist
running bdist
running bdist_dumb
running build
...
running install_scripts
tar -cf dist/acme.sql-0.1.1.macosx-10.3-fat.tar .
gzip -f9 acme.sql-0.1.1.macosx-10.3-fat.tar
removing 'build/bdist.macosx-10.3-fat/dumb' (and everything under it)
$ ls dist/
acme.sql-0.1.1.macosx-10.3-fat.tar.gz    acme.sql-0.1.1.tar.gz
```

Notice that the newly created archive's name contains the name of the system and the distribution it was built under (*Mac OS X 10.3*).

The same command called under Windows will create a specific distribution archive:

```
C:\acme.sql> python.exe setup.py bdist
...
C:\acme.sql> dir dist
25/02/2008  08:18    <DIR>          .
25/02/2008  08:18    <DIR>          ..
25/02/2008  08:24           16 055 acme.sql-0.1.win32.zip
             1 File(s)         16 055 bytes
             2 Dir(s)  22 239 752 192 bytes free
```

If a package contains C code, apart from a source distribution, it's important to release as many different binary distributions as possible. At the very least, a Windows binary distribution is important for those who don't have a C compiler installed.

A binary release contains a tree that can be copied directly into the Python tree. It mainly contains a folder that is copied into Python's `site-packages` folder. It may also contain cached bytecode files (`*.pyc` files on Python 2 and `__pycache__/*.pyc` on Python 3).

The other kind of built distributions are "wheels" provided by the `wheel` package. When installed (for example, using `pip`), `wheel` adds a new `bdist_wheel` command to the `distutils`. It allows creating platform-specific distributions (currently only for Windows and Mac OS X) that provides alternatives to normal `bdist` distributions. It was designed to replace another distribution introduced earlier by `setuptools` – eggs. Eggs are now obsolete so won't be featured here. The list of advantages of using wheels is quite long. Here are the ones that are mentioned in the Python Wheels page (`http://pythonwheels.com/`):

- Faster installation for pure python and native C extension packages
- Avoids arbitrary code execution for installation. (Avoids `setup.py`)
- Installation of a C extension does not require a compiler on Windows or OS X
- Allows better caching for testing and continuous integration
- Creates `.pyc` files as part of the installation to ensure they match the Python interpreter used
- More consistent installs across platforms and machines

According to PyPA recommendation, wheels should be your default distribution format. Unfortunately, platform-specific wheels for Linux are not available yet so if you have to distribute packages with C extensions, then you need to create `sdist` distribution for Linux users.

Standalone executables

Creating standalone executables is a commonly overlooked topic in materials that cover packaging of Python code. This is mainly because Python lacks proper tools in its standard library that could allow programmers to create simple executables that could be run by users without the need to install the Python interpreter.

Compiled languages have a big advantage over Python in that they allow creation of an executable application for the given system architecture that could be run by users in a way that does not require them to have any knowledge of the underlying technology. Python code, when distributed as a package, requires the Python interpreter in order to be run. This creates a big inconvenience for users who do not have enough technical proficiency.

Developer-friendly operating systems such as Mac OS X or most Linux distributions come with Python pre-installed. So, for their users, the Python-based application still could be distributed as a source package that relies on specific **interpreter directive** in the main script file, which is popularly called **shebang**. For most Python applications, this takes the following form:

```
#!/usr/bin/env python
```

Such directive, when used as a first line of script, will mark it to be interpreted by default by the Python version for the given environment. This can, of course, take a more detailed form, which requires a specific Python version such as `python3.4`, `python3`, or `python2`. Note that this will work in most popular POSIX systems, but isn't portable at all by definition. This solution relies on the existence of specific Python versions and also availability of `env` executable exactly at `/usr/bin/env`. Both of these assumptions may fail on some operating systems. Also, shebangs will not work on Windows at all. Additionally, bootstrapping of the Python environment on Windows can be a challenge even for experienced developers, so you cannot expect that nontechnical users will be able to do that by themselves.

The other thing to consider is the simple user experience in the desktop environment. Users usually expect that applications can be run from the desktop by simply clicking on them. Not every desktop environment will support that with Python applications distributed as a source.

Therefore, it would be best if we are able to create a binary distribution that would work as any other compiled executable. Fortunately, it is possible to create an executable that has both the Python interpreter and our project embedded. This allows users to open our application without caring about Python or any other dependency.

When are standalone executables useful?

Standalone executables are useful in situations where simplicity of user experience is more important than the user's ability to interfere with applications' code. Note that the fact that you are distributing application as executable only makes code reading or modification harder—not impossible. It is not a way to secure applications code and should only be used as a way to make interacting with an application simpler.

Standalone executables should be a preferred way of distributing applications for nontechnical end users and also seems to be the only reasonable way of distributing a Python application for Windows.

Standalone executables are usually a good choice for:

- Applications that depend on specific Python versions that may not be easily available on the target operating systems
- Applications that rely on modified precompiled CPython sources
- Applications with graphical interfaces
- Projects that have many binary extensions written in different languages
- Games

Popular tools

Python does not have any built-in support for building standalone executables. Fortunately, there are some community projects solving that problem with varied success. The four most notable are:

- PyInstaller
- cx_Freeze
- py2exe
- py2app

Each one of them is slightly different in use and also each one of them has slightly different limitations. Before choosing your tool, you need to decide which platform you want to target, because every packaging tool can support only a specific set of operating systems.

The best case scenario is if you make such a decision at the very beginning of the project's life. None of these tools, of course, require deep interaction in your code, but if you start building standalone packages early, you can automate the whole process and save future integration time and costs. If you leave this for later, you may find yourself in a situation where the project is built in such a sophisticated way that none of the available tools will work. Providing a standalone executable for such a project will be problematic and will take a lot of your time.

PyInstaller

PyInstaller (`http://www.pyinstaller.org/`) is by far the most advanced program to freeze Python packages into standalone executables. It provides the most extensive multiplatform compatibility among every available solution at the moment, so it is the most recommended one. Platforms that PyInstaller supports are:

- Windows (32-bit and 64-bit)
- Linux (32-bit and 64-bit)
- Mac OS X (32-bit and 64-bit)
- FreeBSD, Solaris, and AIX

Supported versions of Python are Python 2.7 and Python 3.3, 3.4, and 3.5. It is available on PyPI, so it can be installed in your working environment using `pip`. If you have problems installing it this way, you can always download the installer from the project's page.

Unfortunately, cross-platform building (cross-compilation) is not supported so if you want to build your standalone executable for a specific platform, then you need to perform building on that platform. This is not a big trouble today with the advent of many virtualization tools. If you don't have a specific system installed on your computer, you can always use Vagrant that will provide you with the desired operating system as a virtual machine.

Usage for simple applications is easy. Let's assume our application is contained in the script named `myscript.py`. This is a simple "Hello world!" application. We want to create a standalone executable for Windows users and we had our sources located under `D://dev/app` in the filesystem. Our application can be bundled with the following short command:

```
$ pyinstaller myscript.py

2121 INFO: PyInstaller: 3.1
2121 INFO: Python: 2.7.10
2121 INFO: Platform: Windows-7-6.1.7601-SP1
2121 INFO: wrote D:\dev\app\myscript.spec
2137 INFO: UPX is not available.
2138 INFO: Extending PYTHONPATH with paths
['D:\\dev\\app', 'D:\\dev\\app']
2138 INFO: checking Analysis
```

```
2138 INFO: Building Analysis because out00-Analysis.toc is non
existent
2138 INFO: Initializing module dependency graph...
2154 INFO: Initializing module graph hooks...
2325 INFO: running Analysis out00-Analysis.toc
(...)
25884 INFO: Updating resource type 24 name 2 language 1033
```

PyInstaller's standard output is quite long even for simple applications, so it was truncated in the preceding example for the sake of brevity. If run on Windows, the resulting structure of directories and files will be as follows:

```
$ tree /0066
|    myscript.py
|    myscript.spec
|
├────build
|    └────myscript
|             myscript.exe
|             myscript.exe.manifest
|             out00-Analysis.toc
|             out00-COLLECT.toc
|             out00-EXE.toc
|             out00-PKG.pkg
|             out00-PKG.toc
|             out00-PYZ.pyz
|             out00-PYZ.toc
|             warnmyscript.txt
|
└────dist
     └────myscript
              bz2.pyd
              Microsoft.VC90.CRT.manifest
              msvcm90.dll
              msvcp90.dll
              msvcr90.dll
              myscript.exe
```

```
myscript.exe.manifest
python27.dll
select.pyd
unicodedata.pyd
_hashlib.pyd
```

The `dist/myscript` directory contains the built application that can now be distributed to the users. Note that the whole directory must be distributed. It contains all additional files that are required to run our application (DLLs, compiled extension libraries, and so on). A more compact distribution can be obtained with the `--onefile` switch of the `pyinstaller` command:

```
$ pyinstaller --onefile myscript.py
(...)
$ tree /f
├─────build
│      └─────myscript
│              myscript.exe.manifest
│              out00-Analysis.toc
│              out00-EXE.toc
│              out00-PKG.pkg
│              out00-PKG.toc
│              out00-PYZ.pyz
│              out00-PYZ.toc
│              warnmyscript.txt
│
└─────dist
        myscript.exe
```

When built with the `--onefile` option, the only file you need to distribute to other users is the single executable found in the `dist` directory (here, `myscript.exe`). For small applications, this is probably the preferred option.

One of the side effects of running the `pyinstaller` command is the creation of the `*.spec` file. This is an autogenerated Python module containing specification on how to create executables from your sources. For example, we already used this in the following code:

```python
# -*- mode: python -*-

block_cipher = None


a = Analysis(['myscript.py'],
             pathex=['D:\\dev\\app'],
             binaries-None,
             datas=None,
             hiddenimports=[],
             hookspath=[],
             runtime_hooks=[],
             excludes=[],
             win_no_prefer_redirects=False,
             win_private_assemblies=False,
             cipher=block_cipher)
pyz = PYZ(a.pure, a.zipped_data,
             cipher=block_cipher)
exe = EXE(pyz,
          a.scripts,
          a.binaries,
          a.zipfiles,
          a.datas,
          name='myscript',
          debug=False,
          strip=False,
          upx=True,
          console=True )
```

This `.spec` file contains all `pyinstaller` arguments specified earlier. This is very useful if you have performed a lot of customizations to your build because this can be used instead of building scripts that would have to store your configuration. Once created, you can use it as an argument to the `pyinstaller` command instead of your Python script:

```
$ pyinstaller.exe myscript.spec
```

Note that this is a real Python module, so you can extend it and perform more complex customizations to the building procedure using a language that you already know. Customizing the .spec file is especially useful when you are targeting many different platforms. Also, not all of the pyinstaller options are available through the command-line arguments and can be used only when modifying .spec file.

PyInstaller is an extensive tool, which by its usage is very simple for the great majority of programs. Anyway, the thorough reading of its documentation is recommended if you are interested in using it as a tool to distribute your applications.

cx_Freeze

cx_Freeze (http://cx-freeze.sourceforge.net/) is another tool for creating standalone executables. It is a simpler solution than PyInstaller, but also supports the three major platforms:

- Windows
- Linux
- Mac OS X

Same as PyInstaller, it does not allow us to perform cross-platform builds, so you need to create your executables on the same operating system you are distributing to. The major disadvantage of cx_Freeze is that it does not allow us to create real single-file executables. Applications built with it need to be distributed with related DLL files and libraries. Assuming that we have the same application as featured in the *PyInstaller* section, the example usage is very simple as well:

```
$ cxfreeze myscript.py

copying C:\Python27\lib\site-packages\cx_Freeze\bases\Console.exe ->
D:\dev\app\dist\myscript.exe

copying C:\Windows\system32\python27.dll ->
D:\dev\app\dist\python27.dll

writing zip file D:\dev\app\dist\myscript.exe

(...)
copying C:\Python27\DLLs\bz2.pyd -> D:\dev\app\dist\bz2.pyd

copying C:\Python27\DLLs\unicodedata.pyd ->
D:\dev\app\dist\unicodedata.pyd
```

Resulting structure of files is as follows:

```
$ tree /f
|    myscript.py
|
└───dist
        bz2.pyd
        myscript.exe
        python27.dll
        unicodedata.pyd
```

Instead of providing the own format for build specification (like PyInstaller does), cx_Freeze extends the distutils package. This means you can configure how your standalone executable is built with the familiar setup.py script. This makes cx_Freeze very convenient if you already distribute your package using setuptools or distutils because additional integration requires only small changes to your setup.py script. Here is an example of such a setup.py script using cx_Freeze. setup() for creating standalone executables on Windows:

```python
import sys
from cx_Freeze import setup, Executable

# Dependencies are automatically detected, but it might need fine
tuning.
build_exe_options = {"packages": ["os"], "excludes": ["tkinter"]}

setup(
    name="myscript",
    version="0.0.1",
    description="My Hello World application!",
    options={
        "build_exe": build_exe_options
    },
    executables=[Executable("myscript.py")]
)
```

With such a file, the new executable can be created using the new build_exe command added to the setup.py script:

```
$ python setup.py build_exe
```

The usage of cx_Freeze seems a bit easier than PyInstaller's and `distutils` integration is a very useful feature. Unfortunately this project may cause some troubles for inexperienced developers:

- Installation using `pip` may be problematic under Windows
- The official documentation is very brief and lacking in some places

py2exe and py2app

py2exe (`http://www.py2exe.org/`) and py2app (`https://pythonhosted.org/py2app/`) are two other programs that integrate with Python packaging either via `distutils` or `setuptools` in order to create standalone executables. Here they are mentioned together because they are very similar in both usage and their limitations. The major drawback of py2exe and py2app is that they target only a single platform:

- py2exe allows building Windows executables
- py2app allows building Mac OS X apps

Because the usage is very similar and requires only modification of the `setup.py` script, these packages seem to complement each other. The documentation of py2app projects the following example of the `setup.py` script that allows to build standalone executables with the right tool (either py2exe or py2app), depending on the platform used:

```python
import sys
from setuptools import setup

mainscript = 'MyApplication.py'

if sys.platform == 'darwin':
    extra_options = dict(
        setup_requires=['py2app'],
        app=[mainscript],
        # Cross-platform applications generally expect sys.argv to
        # be used for opening files.
        options=dict(py2app=dict(argv_emulation=True)),
    )
elif sys.platform == 'win32':
    extra_options = dict(
        setup_requires=['py2exe'],
        app=[mainscript],
    )
```

```
else:
    extra_options = dict(
        # Normally unix-like platforms will use "setup.py install"
        # and install the main script as such
        scripts=[mainscript],
    )

setup(
    name="MyApplication",
    **extra_options
)
```

With such a script, you can build your Windows executable using the `python setup.py py2exe` command and Mac OS X app using `python setup.py py2app`. Cross compilation is of course not possible.

Despite some limitations and less elasticity than PyInstaller or cx_Freeze, it is good to know that there are always py2exe and py2app projects. In some cases, PyInstaller or cx_Freeze might fail to build executable for the project properly. In such situations, it is always worth checking whether other solutions can handle our code.

Security of Python code in executable packages

It is important to know that standalone executables does not make application code secure by any means. It is not an easy task to decompile the embedded code from such executable files, but it is doable for sure. What is even more important is that the results of such de-compilation (if done with proper tools) might look strikingly similar to original sources.

This fact makes standalone Python executables not a viable solution for closed source projects where leaking of the application code could harm the organization. So, if your whole business can be copied simply by copying the source code of your application, then you should think of other ways to distribute the application. Maybe providing software as a service will be a better choice for you.

Making decompilation harder

As already said, there is no reliable way to secure applications from de-compilation with the tools available at the moment. Still, there are some ways to make this process harder. But harder does not mean less probable. For some of us, the most tempting challenges are the hardest ones. And we all know that the eventual prize in this challenge is very high: the code that you tried to secure.

Usually the process of de-compilation consists of a few steps:

1. Extracting the project's binary representation of bytecode from standalone executables.
2. Mapping of a binary representation to bytecode of a specific Python version.
3. Translation of bytecode to AST.
4. Recreation of sources directly from AST.

Providing the exact solutions for deterring developers from such reverse-engineering of standalone executables would be pointless for obvious reasons. So here are only some ideas for hampering of the de-compilation process or devaluating its results:

- Removing any code metadata available at runtime (docstrings), so the eventual results will be a bit less readable

- Modifying the bytecode values used by the CPython interpreter so that conversion from binary to bytecode and later to AST requires more effort

- Using a version of CPython sources modified in such a complex way that even if decompiled sources of the application are available they are useless without decompiling the modified CPython binary

- Using obfuscation scripts on sources before bundling them into executables, which will make sources less valuable after the de-compilation

Such solutions make the development process a lot harder. Some of the above ideas require a very deep understanding of Python runtime but each one of them is riddled with many pitfalls and disadvantages. Mostly, they only defer what is inevitable. Once your trick is broken, it renders all your additional efforts a waste of time and resources.

The only reliable way to not allow your closed code leak outside of your application is to not ship it directly to users in any form. And this is only true if other aspects of your organization's security stay airtight.

Summary

This chapter described details of Python's packaging ecosystem. Now, after reading it, you should know which tools suit your packaging needs and also which types of distributions your project requires. You should also know the popular techniques for common problems and how to provide useful metadata to your project.

We also discussed the topic of standalone executables that are very useful, especially in distributing desktop applications.

Next chapter will extensively rely on what we have learned here to show how to efficiently deal with code deployments in a reliable and automated way.

6
Deploying Code

Even the perfect code (if it exists) is useless if it is not being run. So in order to serve a purpose, our code needs to be installed on the target machine (computer) and executed. The process of making a specific version of your application or service available to the end users is called deployment.

In case of desktop applications, this seems to be simple — your job ends on providing a downloadable package with optional installer, if necessary. It is the user's responsibility to download and install it in his/her environment. Your responsibility is to make this process as easy and convenient as possible. Proper packaging is still not a simple task, but some tools were already explained in the previous chapter.

Surprisingly, things get more complicated when your code is not a product per se. If your application only provides a service that is being sold to the users, then it is your responsibility to run it on your own infrastructure. This scenario is typical for a web application or any "X as a Service" product. In such a situation, the code is deployed to set off remote machines that usually are hardly physically accessible to the developers. This is especially true if you are already a user of cloud computing services such as **Amazon Web Services** (**AWS**) or Heroku.

In this chapter, we will concentrate on the aspect of code deployment to remote hosts because of the very high popularity of Python in the field of building various web-related services and products. Despite the high portability of this language, it has no specific quality that would make its code easily deployable. What matters the most is how your application is built and what processes you use to deploy it to the target environments. So this chapter will focus on the following topics:

- What are the main challenges in deploying the code to remote environments
- How to build applications in Python that are easily deployable
- How to reload web services without downtime

- How to leverage Python packaging ecosystem in code deployment
- How to properly monitor and instrument code that runs remotely

The Twelve-Factor App

The main requirement for painless deployment is building your application in a way that ensures that this process will be simple and as streamlined as possible. This is mostly about removing obstacles and encouraging well-established practices. Following such common practices is especially important in organizations where only specific people are responsible for development (developers team or Dev for short) and different people are responsible for deploying and maintaining the execution environments (operations team or Ops for short).

All tasks related to server maintenance, monitoring, deployment, configuration, and so on are often put to one single bag called operations. Even in organizations that have no separate teams for operational tasks, it is common that only some of the developers are authorized to do deployment tasks and maintain the remote servers. The common name for such a position is DevOps. Also, it isn't such an unusual situation that every member of the development team is responsible for operations, so everyone in such a team can be called DevOps. Anyway, no matter how your organization is structured and what the responsibilities of each developer are, everyone should know how operations work and how code is deployed to the remote servers because, in the end, the execution environment and its configuration is a hidden part of the product you are building.

The following common practices and conventions are important mainly for the following reasons:

- At every company people quit and new ones are hired. By using best approaches, you are making it easier for fresh team members to jump into the project. You can never be sure that new employees are already familiar with common practices for system configuration and running applications in a reliable way, but you at least make their fast adaptation more probable.
- In organizations where only some people are responsible for deployments, it simply reduces the friction between the operations and development teams.

A good source of such practices that encourage building easily deployable apps is a manifesto called **Twelve-Factor App**. It is a general language-agnostic methodology for building software-as-a-service apps. One of its purposes is making applications easier to deploy, but it also highlights other topics, such as maintainability and making applications easier to scale.

As its name says, the Twelve-Factor App consists of 12 rules:

- **Codebase**: One codebase tracked in revision control, many deploys
- **Dependencies**: Explicitly declare and isolate dependencies
- **Config**: Store config in the environment
- **Backing services**: Treat backing services as attached resources
- **Build, release, run**: Strictly separate build and run stages
- **Processes**: Execute the app as one or more stateless processes
- **Port binding**: Export services via port binding
- **Concurrency**: Scale out via the process model
- **Disposability**: Maximize robustness with fast startup and graceful shutdown
- **Dev/prod parity**: Keep development, staging, and production as similar as possible
- **Logs**: Treat logs as event streams
- **Admin processes**: Run admin/management tasks as one-off processes

Extending each of these rules here is a bit pointless because the official page of Twelve-Factor App methodology (`http://12factor.net/`) contains extensive rationale for every app factor with examples of tools for different frameworks and environments.

This chapter tries to stay consistent with the above manifesto, so we will discuss some of them in detail when necessary. The techniques and examples that are presented may sometimes slightly diverge from these 12 factors, but remember that these rules are not carved in stone. They are great as long as they serve the purpose. In the end, what matters is the working application (product) and not being compatible with some arbitrary methodology.

Deployment automation using Fabric

For very small projects, it may be possible to do deploy your code "by hand", that is, by manually typing the sequence of commands through the remote shell that are necessary to install a new version of code and execute it on a remote shell. Anyway, even for an average-sized project, this is error prone, tedious, and should be considered a waste of most the precious resource you have, your own time.

The solution for that is automation. The simple rule of thumb could be if you needed to perform the same task manually at least twice, you should automate it so you won't need to do it for the third time. There are various tools that allow you to automate different things:

- Remote execution tools such as Fabric are used for on-demand automated execution of code on multiple remote hosts.

- Configuration management tools such as Chef, Puppet, CFEngine, Salt, and Ansible are designed for automatized configuration of remote hosts (execution environments). They can be used to set up backing services (databases, caches, and so on), system permissions, users, and so on. Most of them can be used also as a tool for remote execution like Fabric, but depending on their architecture, this may be more or less easy.

Configuration management solutions is a complex topic that deserves a separate book. The truth is that the simplest remote execution frameworks have the lowest entry barrier and are the most popular choice, at least for small projects. In fact, every configuration management tool that provides a way to declaratively specify configuration of your machines has a remote execution layer implemented somewhere deep inside.

Also, depending on some of the tools, thanks to their design, it may not be best suited for actual automated code deployment. One such example is Puppet, which really discourages the explicit running of any shell commands. This is why many people choose to use both types of solution to complement each other: configuration management for setting up system-level environment and on-demand remote execution for application deployment.

Fabric (`http://www.fabfile.org/`) is so far the most popular solution used by Python developers to automate remote execution. It is a Python library and command-line tool for streamlining the use of SSH for application deployment or systems administration tasks. We will focus on it because it is relatively easy to start with. Be aware that, depending on your needs, it may not be the best solution to your problems. Anyway, it is a great example of a utility that can add some automation to your operations, if you don't have any yet.

Fabric and Python 3

This book encourages you to develop only in Python 3 (if it is possible) with notes about older syntax features and compatibility caveats only to make the eventual version switch a bit more painless. Unfortunately, Fabric, at the time of writing this book, still has not been officially ported to Python 3. Enthusiasts of this tool are being told for at least a few years that there is ongoing Fabric 2 development that will bring a compatibility update. This is said to be a total rewrite with a lot of new features but there is no official open repository for Fabric 2 and almost no one has seen its code. Core Fabric developers do not accept any pull requests for Python 3 compatibility in the current development branch of this project and close every feature request for it. Such an approach to the development of popular open source projects is at best disturbing. The history of this issue does not give us a high chance of seeing the official release of Fabric 2 soon. Such secret development of a new Fabric release raises many questions.

Regardless of anyone's opinions, this fact does not diminish the usefulness of Fabric in its current state. So there are two options if you already decided to stick with Python 3: use a fully compatible and independent fork (`https://github.com/mathiasertl/fabric/`) or write your application in Python 3 and maintain Fabric scripts in Python 2. The best approach would be to do it in a separate code repository.

You could of course automate all the work using only Bash scripts, but this is very tedious and error-prone. Python has more convenient ways of string processing and encourages code modularization. Fabric is in fact only a tool for gluing execution of commands via SSH, so some knowledge about how the command-line interface and its utilities work in your environment is still required.

To start working with Fabric, you need to install the `fabric` package (using `pip`) and create a script named `fabfile.py` that is usually located in the root of your project. Note that `fabfile` can be considered a part of your project configuration. So if you want to strictly follow the Twelve-Factor App methodology, you should not maintain its code in the source tree of the deployed application. Complex projects are in fact very often built from various components maintained as separate codebases, so it is another reason why it is a good approach to have one separate repository for all of the project component configurations and Fabric scripts. This makes deployment of different services more consistent and encourages good code reuse.

An example `fabfile` that defines a simple deployment procedure will look like this:

```python
# -*- coding: utf-8 -*-
import os

from fabric.api import *  # noqa
from fabric.contrib.files import exists


# Let's assume we have private package repository created
# using 'devpi' project
PYPI_URL = 'http://devpi.webxample.example.com'

# This is arbitrary location for storing installed releases.
# Each release is a separate virtual environment directory
# which is named after project version. There is also a
# symbolic link 'current' that points to recently deployed
# version. This symlink is an actual path that will be used
# for configuring the process supervision tool e.g.:
# .
# ├── 0.0.1
# ├── 0.0.2
# ├── 0.0.3
# ├── 0.1.0
# └── current -> 0.1.0/

REMOTE_PROJECT_LOCATION = "/var/projects/webxample"

env.project_location = REMOTE_PROJECT_LOCATION

# roledefs map out environment types (staging/production)
env.roledefs = {
    'staging': [
        'staging.webxample.example.com',
    ],
    'production': [
        'prod1.webxample.example.com',
        'prod2.webxample.example.com',
    ],
}


def prepare_release():
```

```
    """ Prepare a new release by creating source distribution and
    uploading to out private package repository
    """
    local('python setup.py build sdist upload -r {}'.format(
        PYPI_URL
    ))


def get_version():
    """ Get current project version from setuptools """
    return local(
        'python setup.py --version', capture=True
    ).stdout.strip()


def switch_versions(version):
    """ Switch versions by replacing symlinks atomically """
    new_version_path = os.path.join(REMOTE_PROJECT_LOCATION,
    version)
    temporary = os.path.join(REMOTE_PROJECT_LOCATION, 'next')
    desired = os.path.join(REMOTE_PROJECT_LOCATION, 'current')

    # force symlink (-f) since probably there is a one already
    run(
        "ln -fsT {target} {symlink}"
        "".format(target=new_version_path, symlink=temporary)
    )
    # mv -T ensures atomicity of this operation
    run("mv -Tf {source} {destination}"
        "".format(source=temporary, destination=desired))


@task
def uptime():
    """
    Run uptime command on remote host - for testing connection.
    """
    run("uptime")


@task
def deploy():
    """ Deploy application with packaging in mind """
    version = get_version()
```

```
    pip_path = os.path.join(
        REMOTE_PROJECT_LOCATION, version, 'bin', 'pip'
    )

    prepare_release()

    if not exists(REMOTE_PROJECT_LOCATION):
        # it may not exist for initial deployment on fresh host
        run("mkdir -p {}".format(REMOTE_PROJECT_LOCATION))

    with cd(REMOTE_PROJECT_LOCATION):
        # create new virtual environment using venv
        run('python3 -m venv {}'.format(version))

        run("{} install webxample=={} --index-url {}".format(
            pip_path, version, PYPI_URL
        ))


    switch_versions(version)
    # let's assume that Circus is our process supervision tool
    # of choice.
    run('circusctl restart webxample')
```

Every function decorated with `@task` is treated as an available subcommand to the `fab` utility provided with the `fabric` package. You can list all the available subcommands using the `-l` or `--list` switch:

```
$ fab --list
Available commands:


    deploy  Deploy application with packaging in mind
    uptime  Run uptime command on remote host - for testing connection.
```

Now you can deploy the application to the given environment type with just a single shell command:

```
$ fab -R production deploy
```

Note that the preceding `fabfile` serves only illustrative purposes. In your own code, you might want to provide extensive failure handling and also try to reload the application without the need to restart the web worker process. Also, some of the techniques presented here may be obvious right now but will be explained later in this chapter. These are:

- Deploying an application using the private package repository
- Using Circus for process supervision on the remote host

Your own package index or index mirror

There are three main reasons why you might want to run your own index of Python packages:

- The official Python Package Index does not have any availability guarantees. It is run by Python Software Foundation thanks to numerous donations. Because of that, it very often means that this site can be down. You don't want to stop your deployment or packaging process in the middle due to PyPI outage.

- It is useful to have reusable components written in Python properly packaged even for the closed source that will never be published publicly. It simplifies the code base because packages that are used across the company for different projects do not need to be vendored. You can simply install them from the repository. This simplifies maintenance for such shared code and might reduce development costs for the whole company if it has many teams working on different projects.

- It is very good practice to have your entire project packaged using `setuptools`. Then, deployment of the new application version is often as simple as running `pip install --update my-application`.

Code vendoring

Code vendoring is a practice of including sources of the external package in the source code (repository) of other projects. It is usually done when the project's code depends on a specific version of some external package that may also be required by other packages (and in a completely different version). For instance, the popular `requests` package vendors some version of `urllib3` in its source tree because it is very tightly coupled to it and is also very unlikely to work with any other version of `urllib3`. An example of a module that is particularly often vendored by others is `six`. It can be found in sources of numerous popular projects such as Django (`django.utils.six`), Boto (`boto.vedored.six`), or Matplotlib (`matplotlib.externals.six`).

Although vendoring is practiced even by some large and successful open source projects, it should be avoided if possible. This has justifiable usage only in certain circumstances and should not be treated as a substitute for package dependency management.

PyPI mirroring

The problem of PyPI outages can be somehow mitigated by allowing the installation tools to download packages from one of its mirrors. In fact, the official Python Package Index is already served through **CDN (Content Delivery Network)**, so it is intrinsically mirrored. This does not change the fact that it seems to have some bad days from time to time when any attempt to download a package fails. Using unofficial mirrors is not a solution here because it might raise some security concerns.

The best solution is to have your own PyPI mirror that will have all the packages you need. The only party that will use it is you, so it will be much easier to ensure proper availability. The other advantage is that whenever this service gets down, you don't need to rely on someone else to bring it up. The mirroring tool maintained and recommended by PyPA is **bandersnatch** (`https://pypi.python.org/pypi/bandersnatch`). It allows you to mirror the whole content of Python Package Index and it can be provided as the `index-url` option for the repository section in the `.pypirc` file (as explained in the previous chapter). This mirror does not accept uploads and does not have the web part of PyPI. Anyway, beware! A full mirror might require hundreds of gigabytes of storage and its size will continue to grow over time.

But why stop on a simple mirror while we have a much better alternative? There is a very small chance that you will require a mirror of the whole package index. Even with a project that has hundreds of dependencies, it will be only a minor fraction of all the available packages. Also, not being able to upload your own private package is a huge limitation of such a simple mirror. It seems that the added value of using bandersnatch is very low for such a high price. And this is true in most situations. If the package mirror is to be maintained only for single of few projects, a much better approach is to use **devpi** (`http://doc.devpi.net/`). It is a PyPI-compatible package index implementation that provides both:

- A private index to upload nonpublic packages
- Index mirroring

The main advantage of devpi over bandersnatch is how it handles mirroring. It can of course do a full generic mirror of other indexes, like bandersnatch does, but it is not its default behavior. Instead of doing rather expensive backup of the whole repository, it maintains mirrors for packages that were already requested by clients. So whenever a package is requested by the installation tool (`pip`, `setuptools`, and `easyinstall`), if it does not exist in the local mirror, the devpi server will attempt to download it from the mirrored index (usually PyPI) and serve. Once the package is downloaded, the devpi will periodically check for its updates to maintain a fresh state of its mirror.

The mirroring approach leaves a slight risk of failure when you request a new package that has not yet been mirrored and the upstream package index has an outage. Anyway, this risk is reduced thanks to the fact that in most deploys you will depend only on packages that were already mirrored in the index. The mirror state for packages that were already requested has eventual consistency with PyPI and new versions will be downloaded automatically. This seems to be a very reasonable tradeoff.

Deployment using a package

Modern web applications have a lot of dependencies and often require a lot of steps to properly install on the remote host. For instance, the typical bootstrapping process for a new version of the application on a remote host consists of the following steps:

- Create new virtual environment for isolation
- Move the project code to the execution environment
- Install the latest project requirements (usually from the `requirements.txt` file)
- Synchronize or migrate the database schema

- Collect static files from project sources and external packages to the desired location

- Compile localization files for applications available in different languages

For more complex sites, there might be lot of additional tasks mostly related to frontend code:

- Generate CSS files using preprocessors such as SASS or LESS

- Perform minification, obfuscation, and/or concatenation of static files (JavaScript and CSS files)

- Compile code written in JavaScript superset languages (CoffeeScript, TypeScript, and so on) to native JS

- Preprocess response template files (minification, style inlining, and so on)

All of these steps can be easily automated using tools such as Bash, Fabric, or Ansible but it is not a good idea to do everything on remote hosts where the application is being installed. Here are the reasons:

- Some of the popular tools for processing static assets can be either CPU- or memory-intensive. Running them in production environments can destabilize your application execution.

- These tools very often will require additional system dependencies that may not be required for normal operation of your projects. These are mostly additional runtime environments such as JVM, Node, or Ruby. This adds complexity to configuration management and increases the overall maintenance costs.

- If you are deploying your application to multiple servers (tenths, hundredths, thousands), you are simply repeating a lot of work that could be done once. If you have your own infrastructure, then you may not experience a huge increase in costs, especially if you perform deployments in periods of low traffic. But if you run cloud computing services in the pricing model that charges you extra for spikes in load or generally for execution time, then this additional cost may be substantial on a proper scale.

- Most of these steps just take a lot of time. You are installing your code on a remote server, so the last thing you want is to have your connection interrupted by some network issue. By keeping the deployment process quick, you are lowering the chance of deploy interruption.

For obvious reasons, the results of the mentioned deployment steps can't be included in your application code repository. Simply, there are things that must be done with every release and you can't change that. It is obviously a place for proper automation but the clue is to do it in the right place and at the right time.

Most of the things such as static collection and code/asset preprocessing can be done locally or in a dedicated environment, so the actual code that is deployed to the remote server requires only a minimal amount of on-site processing. The most notable deployment steps either in the process of building a distribution or installing a package are:

- Installation of Python dependencies and transferring static assets (CSS files and JavaScript) to the desired location can be handled as a part of the `install` command of the `setup.py` script

- Preprocessing code (processing JavaScript supersets, minification/ obfuscation/concatenation of assets, and running SASS or LESS) and things such as localized text compilation (for example, `compilemessages` in Django) can be a part of the `sdist/bdist` command of the `setup.py` script

Inclusion of preprocessed code other than Python can be easily handled with the proper `MANIFEST.in` file. Dependencies are of course best provided as an `install_requires` argument of the `setup()` function call from the `setuptools` package.

Packaging the whole application of course will require some additional work from you like providing your own custom `setuptools` commands or overriding the existing ones, but gives you a lot of advantages and makes project deployment a lot faster and reliable.

Let's use a Django-based project (in Django 1.9 version) as an example. I have chosen this framework because it seems to be the most popular Python project of this type, so there is a high chance that you already know it a bit. A typical structure of files in such a project might look like the following:

```
$ tree . -I __pycache__ --dirsfirst
.
├── webxample
│   ├── conf
│   │   ├── __init__.py
│   │   ├── settings.py
│   │   ├── urls.py
│   │   └── wsgi.py
│   ├── locale
│   │   ├── de
│   │   │   └── LC_MESSAGES
│   │   │       └── django.po
│   │   ├── en
```

```
|   |   |       └── LC_MESSAGES
|   |   |               └── django.po
|   |   └── pl
|   |       └── LC_MESSAGES
|   |               └── django.po
|   ├── myapp
|   |   ├── migrations
|   |   |   └── __init__.py
|   |   ├── static
|   |   |   ├── js
|   |   |   |   └── myapp.js
|   |   |   └── sass
|   |   |           └── myapp.scss
|   |   ├── templates
|   |   |   ├── index.html
|   |   |   └── some_view.html
|   |   ├── __init__.py
|   |   ├── admin.py
|   |   ├── apps.py
|   |   ├── models.py
|   |   ├── tests.py
|   |   └── views.py
|   ├── __init__.py
|   └── manage.py
├── MANIFEST.in
├── README.md
└── setup.py
```

15 directories, 23 files

Note that this slightly differs from the usual Django project template. By default, the package that contains the WSGI application, the settings module, and the URL configuration has the same name as the project. Because we decided to take the packaging approach, this would be named `webxample`. This can cause some confusion, so it is better to rename it `conf`.

Without digging into the possible implementation details, let's just make a few simple assumptions:

- Our example application has some external dependencies. Here, it will be two popular Django packages: `djangorestframework` and `django-allauth`, plus one non-Django package: `gunicorn`.

- `djangorestframework` and `django-allauth` are provided as INSTALLED_ APPS in the `webexample.webexample.settings` module.

- The application is localized in three languages (German, English, and Polish) but we don't want to store the compiled `gettext` messages in the repository.

- We are tired of vanilla CSS syntax, so we decided to use the more powerful SCSS language that we translate to CSS using SASS.

Knowing the structure of the project, we can write our `setup.py` script in a way that make `setuptools` handle:

- Compilation of SCSS files under `webxample/myapp/static/scss`

- Compilation of `gettext` messages under `webexample/locale` from `.po` to `.mo` format

- Installation of requirements

- A new script that provides an entry point to the package, so we will have the custom command instead of the `manage.py` script

We have a bit of luck here. Python binding for `libsass`, a C/C++ port of SASS engine, provides a handful integration with `setuptools` and `distutils`. With only little configuration, it provides a custom `setup.py` command for running the SASS compilation:

```
from setuptools import setup

setup(
    name='webxample',
    setup_requires=['libsass >= 0.6.0'],
    sass_manifests={
        'webxample.myapp': ('static/sass', 'static/css')
    },
)
```

So instead of running the `sass` command manually or executing a subprocess in the `setup.py` script we can type `python setup.py build_scss` and have our SCSS files compiled to CSS. This is still not enough. It makes our life a bit easier but we want the whole distribution to be fully automated so there is only one step for creating new releases. To achieve this goal, we are forced to override a bit some of the existing `setuptools` distribution commands.

The example `setup.py` file that handles some of the project preparation steps through packaging might look like this:

```
import os

from setuptools import setup
from setuptools import find_packages
from distutils.cmd import Command
from distutils.command.build import build as _build

try:
    from django.core.management.commands.compilemessages \
        import Command as CompileCommand
except ImportError:
    # note: during installation django may not be available
    CompileCommand = None


# this environment is requires
os.environ.setdefault(
    "DJANGO_SETTINGS_MODULE", "webxample.conf.settings"
)


class build_messages(Command):
    """ Custom command for building gettext messages in Django
    """
    description = """compile gettext messages"""
    user_options = []

    def initialize_options(self):
        pass

    def finalize_options(self):

        pass
```

```python
    def run(self):
        if CompileCommand:
            CompileCommand().handle(
                verbosity=2, locales=[], exclude=[]
            )
        else:
            raise RuntimeError("could not build translations")


class build(_build):
    """ Overriden build command that adds additional build steps
    """
    sub_commands = [
        ('build_messages', None),
        ('build_sass', None),
    ] + _build.sub_commands


setup(
    name='webxample',
    setup_requires=[
        'libsass >= 0.6.0',
        'django >= 1.9.2',
    ],
    install_requires=[
        'django >= 1.9.2',
        'gunicorn == 19.4.5',
        'djangorestframework == 3.3.2',
        'django-allauth == 0.24.1',
    ],
    packages=find_packages('.'),
    sass_manifests={
        'webxample.myapp': ('static/sass', 'static/css')
    },
    cmdclass={
        'build_messages': build_messages,
        'build': build,
    },
    entry_points={
        'console_scripts': {
            'webxample = webxample.manage:main',
        }
    }
)
```

With such an implementation, we can build all assets and create source distribution of a package for the webxample project using this single terminal command:

```
$ python setup.py build sdist
```

If you already have your own package index (created with devpi) you can add the install subcommand or use twine so this package will be available for installation with pip in your organization. If we look into a structure of source distribution created with our setup.py script, we can see that it contains the compiled gettext messages and CSS style sheets generated from SCSS files:

```
$ tar -xvzf dist/webxample-0.0.0.tar.gz 2> /dev/null
$ tree webxample-0.0.0/ -I    pycache__ --dirsfirst
webxample-0.0.0/
├── webxample
│   ├── conf
│   │   ├── __init__.py
│   │   ├── settings.py
│   │   ├── urls.py
│   │   └── wsgi.py
│   ├── locale
│   │   ├── de
│   │   │   └── LC_MESSAGES
│   │   │       ├── django.mo
│   │   │       └── django.po
│   │   ├── en
│   │   │   └── LC_MESSAGES
│   │   │       ├── django.mo
│   │   │       └── django.po
│   │   └── pl
│   │       └── LC_MESSAGES
│   │           ├── django.mo
│   │           └── django.po
│   ├── myapp
│   │   ├── migrations
│   │   │   └── __init__.py
│   │   ├── static
│   │   │   ├── css
```

```
|    |    |    |    └── myapp.scss.css
|    |    |    └── js
|    |    |        └── myapp.js
|    |    ├── templates
|    |    |    ├── index.html
|    |    |    └── some_view.html
|    |    ├── __init__.py
|    |    ├── admin.py
|    |    ├── apps.py
|    |    ├── models.py
|    |    ├── tests.py
|    |    └── views.py
|    ├── __init__.py
|    └── manage.py
├── webxample.egg-info
|    ├── PKG-INFO
|    ├── SOURCES.txt
|    ├── dependency_links.txt
|    ├── requires.txt
|    └── top_level.txt
├── MANIFEST.in
├── PKG-INFO
├── README.md
├── setup.cfg
└── setup.py
```

```
16 directories, 33 files
```

The additional benefit of using this approach is that we were able to provide our own entry point for the project in place of Django's default manage.py script. Now we can run any Django management command using this entry point, for instance:

```
$ webxample migrate
$ webxample collectstatic
$ webxample runserver
```

This required a little change in the `manage.py` script for compatibility with the `entry_points` argument in `setup()`, so the main part of its code is wrapped with the `main()` function call:

```python
#!/usr/bin/env python3
import os
import sys


def main():
    os.environ.setdefault(
        "DJANGO_SETTINGS_MODULE", "webxample.conf.settings"
    )

    from django.core.management import execute_from_command_line

    execute_from_command_line(sys.argv)


if __name__ == "__main__":
    main()
```

Unfortunately, a lot of frameworks (including Django) are not designed with the idea of packaging your projects that way in mind. It means that depending on the advancement of your application, converting it to a package may require a lot of changes. In Django, this often means rewriting many of the implicit imports and updating a lot of configuration variables in your settings file.

The other problem is the consistency of releases created using Python packaging. If different team members are authorized to create application distribution, it is crucial that this process takes place in the same replicable environment, especially when you do a lot of asset preprocessing; it is possible that the package created in two different environments will not look the same even if created from the same code base. This may be due to different version of tools used during the build process. The best practice is to move the distribution responsibility to a continuous integration/delivery system such as Jenkins or Buildbot. The additional advantage is that you can assert that the package passes all required tests before going to distribution. You can even make the automated deployment as a part of such continuous delivery system.

Despite this, distributing your code as Python packages using `setuptools` is not simple and effortless; it will greatly simplify your deployments, so it is definitely worth trying. Note that this is also in line with the detailed recommendation of the sixth rule in the Twelve-Factor App: execute the app as one or more stateless processes (`http://12factor.net/processes`).

Common conventions and practices

There is a set of common conventions and practices for deployment that not every developer may know but that are obvious for anyone who has done some operations in their life. As explained in the chapter introduction, it is crucial to know at least a few of them even if you are not responsible for code deployment and operations because it will allow you to make better design decisions during the development.

The filesystem hierarchy

The most obvious conventions that may come into your mind are probably about filesystem hierarchy and user naming. If you are looking for such suggestions here, then you will be disappointed. There is of course a **Filesystem Hierarchy Standard** that defines the directory structure and directory contents in Unix and Unix-like operating systems, but it is really hard to find an actual OS distribution that is fully compliant with FHS. If system designers and programmers cannot obey such standards, it is very hard to expect the same from its administrators. In my experience, I've seen application code deployed almost everywhere where it is possible, including nonstandard custom directories in the root filesystem level. Almost always, the people behind such decisions had really strong arguments for doing so. The only suggestions in this matter that I can give to you are as follows:

- Choose wisely and avoid surprises
- Be consistent across all the available infrastructure of your project
- Try to be consistent across your organization (the company you work in)

What really helps is to document conventions for your project. Just remember to make sure that this documentation is accessible for every interested team member and that everyone knows such a document exists.

Isolation

Reasons for isolation as well as recommended tools were already discussed in *Chapter 1, Current Status of Python*. For the purpose of deployments, there is only one important thing to add. You should always isolate project dependencies for each release of your application. In practice it means that whenever you deploy a new version of the application, you should create a new isolated environment for this release (using `virtualenv` or `venv`). Old environments should be left for some time on your hosts, so in case of issues you can easily perform a rollback to one of the older versions of your application.

Creating fresh environments for each release helps in managing their clean state and compliance with a list of provided dependencies. By fresh environment we mean creating a new directory tree in the filesystem instead of updating already existing files. Unfortunately, it may make it a bit harder to perform things such as a graceful reload of services, which is much easier to achieve if the environment is updated in-place.

Using process supervision tools

Applications on remote servers usually are never expected to quit. If it is the web application, its HTTP server process will indefinitely wait for new connections and requests and will exit only if some unrecoverable error occurs.

It is of course not possible to run it manually in the shell and have a never-ending SSH connection. Using `nohup`, `screen`, or `tmux` to semi-daemonize the process is not an option. Doing so is like designing your service to fail.

What you need is to have some process supervision tool that can start and manage your application process. Before choosing the right one you need to make sure it:

- Restarts the service if it quits
- Reliably tracks its state
- Captures its `stdout`/`stderr` streams for logging purposes
- Runs a process with specific user/group permissions
- Configures system environment variables

Most of the Unix and Linux distributions have some built-in tools/subsystems for process supervision, such as `initd` scripts, `upstart`, and `runit`. Unfortunately, in most cases they are not well suited for running user-level application code and are really hard to maintain. Especially writing reliable `init.d` scripts is a real challenge because it requires a lot of Bash scripting that is hard to do right. Some Linux distributions such as Gentoo have a redesigned approach to `init.d` scripts, so writing them is a lot easier. Anyway, locking yourself to a specific OS distribution just for the purpose of a single process supervision tool is not a good idea.

Two popular tools in the Python community for managing application processes are Supervisor (`http://supervisord.org`) and Circus (`https://circus.readthedocs.org/en/latest/`). They are both very similar in configuration and usage. Circus is a bit younger than Supervisor because it was created to address some weaknesses of the latter. They both can be configured in simple INI-like configuration format. They are not limited to running Python processes and can be configured to manage any application. It is hard to say which one is better because they both provide very similar functionality.

Anyway, Supervisor does not run on Python 3, so it does not get our blessing. While it is not a problem to run Python 3 processes under Supervisor's control, I will take it as an excuse and feature only the example of the Circus configuration.

Let's assume that we want to run the webxample application (presented previously in this chapter) using `gunicorn` webserver under Circus control. In production, we would probably run Circus under applicable system-level process supervision tools (`initd`, `upstart`, and `runit`), especially if it was installed from the system packages repository. For the sake of simplicity, we will run this locally inside of the virtual environment. The minimal configuration file (here named `circus.ini`) that allows us to run our application in Circus looks like this:

```
[watcher:webxample]
cmd = /path/to/venv/dir/bin/gunicorn webxample.conf.wsgi:application
numprocesses = 1
```

Now, the `circus` process can be run with this configuration file as the execution argument:

```
$ circusd circus.ini
2016-02-15 08:34:34 circus[1776] [INFO] Starting master on pid 1776
2016-02-15 08:34:34 circus[1776] [INFO] Arbiter now waiting for commands
2016-02-15 08:34:34 circus[1776] [INFO] webxample started
[2016-02-15 08:34:34 +0100] [1778] [INFO] Starting gunicorn 19.4.5
[2016-02-15 08:34:34 +0100] [1778] [INFO] Listening at:
http://127.0.0.1:8000 (1778)
[2016-02-15 08:34:34 +0100] [1778] [INFO] Using worker: sync
[2016-02-15 08:34:34 +0100] [1781] [INFO] Booting worker with pid: 1781
```

Now you can use the `circusctl` command to run an interactive session and control all managed processes using simple commands. Here is an example of such a session:

```
$ circusctl
circusctl 0.13.0
webxample: active
(circusctl) stop webxample
ok
(circusctl) status
webxample: stopped
(circusctl) start webxample
ok
(circusctl) status
webxample: active
```

Of course, both of the mentioned tools have a lot more features available. All of them are explained in their documentation, so before making your choice, you should read them carefully.

Application code should be run in user space

Your application code should be always run in user space. This means it must not be executed under super-user privileges. If you designed your application following Twelve-Factor App, it is possible to run your application under a user that has almost no privileges. The conventional name for a user that owns no files and is in no privileged groups is `nobody`, anyway the actual recommendation is to create a separate user for each application daemon. The reason for that is system security. It is to limit the damage that a malicious user can do if it gains control over your application process. In Linux, processes of the same user can interact with each other, so it is important to have different applications separated at the user level.

Using reverse HTTP proxies

Multiple Python WSGI-compliant web servers can easily serve HTTP traffic all by themselves without the need for any other web server on top of them. It is still very common to hide them behind a reverse proxy such as Nginx for various reasons:

- TLS/SSL termination is usually better handled by top-level web servers such as Nginx and Apache. The Python application can then speak only simple HTTP protocol (instead of HTTPS), so complexity and configuration of secure communication channels is left for the reverse proxy.

- Unprivileged users cannot bind low ports (in the range of 0-1000), but HTTP protocol should be served to the users on port 80, and HTTPS should be served on port 443. To do this, you must run the process with super-user privileges. Usually, it is safer to have your application serving on high port or on Unix Domain Socket and use that as an upstream for a reverse proxy that is run under the more privileged user.

- Usually, Nginx can serve static assets (images, JS, CSS, and other media) more efficiently than Python code. If you configure it as a reverse proxy, then it is only few more lines of configuration to serve static files through it.

- When single host needs to serve multiple applications from different domains, Apache or Nginx are indispensable for creating virtual hosts for different domains served on the same port.

- Reverse proxies can improve performance by adding an additional caching layer or can be configured as simple load-balancers.

Some of the web servers actually are recommended to be run behind a proxy, such as Nginx. For example, `gunicorn` is a very robust WSGI-based server that can give exceptional performance results if its clients are fast as well. On the other hand, it does not handle slow clients well, so it is easily susceptible to denial-of-service attacks based on slow client connection. Using a proxy server that is able to buffer slow clients is the best way to solve this problem.

Reloading processes gracefully

The ninth rule of the Twelve-Factor App methodology deals with process disposability and says that you should maximize robustness with fast startup times and graceful shutdowns. While a fast startup time is quite self-explanatory, graceful shutdowns require some additional discussion.

In the scope of web applications, if you terminate the server process in a nongraceful way, it will quit immediately without time to finish processing requests and reply with the proper responses to connected clients. In the best case scenario, if you use some kind of reverse proxy, then the proxy might reply to the connected clients with some generic error response (for example, 502 Bad Gateway), even though it is not the right way to notify users that you have restarted your application and have deployed a new release.

According to the Twelve-Factor App, the web serving process should be able to quit gracefully upon receiving Unix SIGTERM signal (for example, `kill -TERM <process-id>`). This means the server should stop accepting new connections, finish processing all the pending requests, and then quit with some exit code when there is nothing more to do.

Obviously, when all of the serving processes quit or start their shutdown procedure, you are not able to process new requests any longer. This means your service will still experience an outage, so there is an additional step you need to perform—start new workers that will be able to accept new connections while the old ones are gracefully quitting. Various Python WSGI-compliant web server implementations allow reloading the service gracefully without any downtime. The most popular are Gunicorn and uWSGI:

- Gunicorn's master process, upon receiving the SIGHUP signal (`kill -HUP <process-pid>`), will start new workers (with new code and configuration) and attempt a graceful shutdown on the old ones.

- uWSGI has at least three independent schemes for doing graceful reloads. Each of them is too complex to explain briefly, but its official documentation provides full information on all the possible options.

Graceful reloads are today a standard in deploying web applications. Gunicorn seems to have an approach that is the easiest to use but also leaves you with the least flexibility. Graceful reloads in uWSGI on the other hand allow much better control on reloads but require more effort to automate and setup. Also, how you handle graceful reloads in your automated deploys is also affected on what supervision tools you use and how they are configured. For instance, in Gunicorn, graceful reloads are as simple as:

```
kill -HUP <gunicorn-master-process-pid>
```

But if you want to properly isolate project distributions by separating virtual environments for each release and configure process supervision using symbolic links (as presented in the fabfile example earlier), you will shortly notice that this does not work as expected. For more complex deployments, there is still no solution available that will just work for you out-of-the-box. You will always need to do a bit of hacking and sometimes this will require a substantial level of knowledge about low-level system implementation details.

Code instrumentation and monitoring

Our work does not end with writing an application and deploying it to the target execution environment. It is possible to write an application that after deployment will not require any further maintenance, although it is very unlikely. In reality, we need to ensure that it is properly observed for errors and performance.

To be sure that our product works as expected, we need to properly handle application logs and monitor the necessary application metrics. This often includes:

- Monitoring web application access logs for various HTTP status codes
- A collection of process logs that may contain information about runtime errors and various warnings
- Monitoring system resources (CPU load, memory, and network traffic) on remote hosts where the application is run
- Monitoring application-level performance and metrics that are business performance indicators (customer acquisition, revenue, and so on)

Luckily there are a lot of free tools available for instrumenting your code and monitoring its performance. Most of them are very easy to integrate.

Logging errors – sentry/raven

No matter how precisely your application is tested, the truth is painful. Your code will eventually fail at some point. This can be anything—unexpected exception, resource exhaustion, some backing service crashing, network outage, or simply an issue in the external library. Some of the possible issues, such as resource exhaustion, can be predicted and prevented with proper monitoring, but there will be always something that passes your defences no matter how much you try.

What you can do is be well prepared for such scenarios and make sure that no error passes unnoticed. In most cases, any unexpected failure scenario results in an exception raised by the application and logged through the logging system. This can be `stdout`, `sderr`, file, or whatever output you have configured for logging. Depending on your implementation, this may or may not result in the application quitting with some system exit code.

You could, of course, depend only on such logs stored in files for finding and monitoring your application errors. Unfortunately, observing errors in textual logs is quite painful and does not scale well beyond anything more complex than running code in development. You will eventually be forced to use some services designed for log collection and analysis. Proper log processing is very important for other reasons that will be explained a bit later but does not work well for tracking and debugging production errors. The reason is simple. The most common form of error logs is just Python stack trace. If you stop only on that, you will soon realize that it is not enough to find the root cause of your issues—especially when errors occur in unknown patterns or in certain load conditions.

What you really need is as much context information about error occurrence as possible. It is also very useful to have a full history of errors that have occurred in the production environment that you can browse and search in some convenient way. One of the most common tools that gives such capabilities is Sentry (`https://getsentry.com`). It is a battle-tested service for tracking exceptions and collecting crash reports. It is available as open source, is written in Python, and originated as a tool for backend web developers. Now it has outgrown its initial ambitions and has support for many more languages, including PHP, Ruby, and JavaScript, but still stays the most popular tool of choice for most Python web developers.

Exception stack tracebacks in web applications

It is common that web applications do not exit on unhandled exceptions because HTTP servers are obliged to return an error response with a status code from the 5XX group if any server error occurs. Most Python web frameworks do such things by default. In such cases, the exception is in fact handled but on a lower framework-level. Anyway, this, in most cases, will still result in the exception stack trace being printed (usually on standard output).

Sentry is available in a paid software-as-a-service model, but it is open source, so it can be hosted for free on your own infrastructure. The library that provides integration with Sentry is `raven` (available on PyPI). If you haven't worked with it yet, want to test it but have no access to your own Sentry server, then you can easily signup for a free trial on Sentry's on-premise service site. Once you have access to a Sentry server and have created a new project, you will obtain a string called DSN, or Data Source Name. This DSN string is the minimal configuration setting needed to integrate your application with sentry. It contains protocol, credentials, server location, and your organization/project identifier in the following form:

```
'{PROTOCOL}://{PUBLIC_KEY}:{SECRET_KEY}@{HOST}/{PATH}{PROJECT_ID}'
```

Once you have DSN, the integration is pretty straightforward:

```
from raven import Client

client = Client('https://<key>:<secret>@app.getsentry.com/<project>')

try:
    1 / 0
except ZeroDivisionError:
    client.captureException()
```

Raven has numerous integrations with the most popular Python frameworks, such as Django, Flask, Celery, and Pyramid, to make integration easier. These integrations will automatically provide additional context that is specific to the given framework. If your web framework of choice does not have dedicated support, the `raven` package provides generic WSGI middleware that makes it compatible with any WSGI-based web servers:

```
from raven import Client
from raven.middleware import Sentry
```

```
# note: application is some WSGI application object defined earlier
application = Sentry(
    application,
    Client('https://<key>:<secret>@app.getsentry.com/<project>')
)
```

The other notable integration is the ability to track messages logged through Python's built-in `logging` module. Enabling such support requires only a few additional lines of code:

```
from raven.handlers.logging import SentryHandler
from raven.conf import setup_logging

client = Client('https://<key>:<secret>@app.getsentry.com/<project>')
handler = SentryHandler(client)
setup_logging(handler)
```

Capturing `logging` messages may have some not obvious caveats, so make sure to read the official documentation on that topic if you are interested in such a feature. This should save you from unpleasant surprises.

The last note is about running your own Sentry as a way to save some money. "There ain't no such thing as a free lunch." You will eventually pay additional infrastructure costs and Sentry will be just another service to maintain. *Maintenance = additional work = costs*! As your application grows, the number of exceptions grow, so you will be forced to scale Sentry as you scale your product. Fortunately, this is a very robust project, but will not give you any value if overwhelmed with too much load. Also, keeping Sentry prepared for a catastrophic failure scenario where thousands of crash reports per second can be sent is a real challenge. So you must decide which option is really cheaper for you, and whether you have enough resources and wit to do all of this by yourself. There is of course no such dilemma if security policies in your organization deny sending any data to third parties. If so, just host it on your own infrastructure. There are costs of course, but ones that are definitely worth paying.

Monitoring system and application metrics

When it comes to monitoring performance, the amount of tools to choose from may be overwhelming. If you have high expectations, then it is possible that you will need to use a few of them at the same time.

Munin (http://munin-monitoring.org) is one of the popular choices used by many organizations regardless of the technology stack they use. It is a great tool for analyzing resource trends and provides a lot of useful information even with default installation without additional configuration. Its installation consists of two main components:

- The Munin master that collects metrics from other nodes and serves metrics graphs

- The Munin node that is installed on a monitored host, which gathers local metrics and sends it to the Munin master

Master, node, and most of the plugins are written in Perl. There are also node implementations in other languages: munin-node-c is written in C (https://github.com/munin-monitoring/munin-c) and munin-node-python is written in Python (https://github.com/agroszer/munin-node-python). Munin comes with a huge number of plugins available in its contrib repository. This means it provides out-of-the-box support for most of the popular databases and system services. There are even plugins for monitoring popular Python web servers such as uWSGI, and Gunicorn.

The main drawback of Munin is the fact it serves graphs as static images and actual plotting configuration is included in specific plugin configurations. This does not help in creating flexible monitoring dashboards and comparing metric values from different sources at the same graph. But this is the price we need to pay for simple installation and versatility. Writing your own plugins is quite simple. There is the munin-python package (http://python-munin.readthedocs.org/en/latest/) that helps writing Munin plugins in Python.

Unfortunately, the architecture of Munin that assumes that there is always a separate monitoring daemon process on every host that is responsible for collection of metrics may not be the best solution for monitoring custom application performance metrics. It is indeed very easy to write your own Munin plugins, but under the assumption that the monitoring process can already report its performance statistics in some way. If you want to collect some custom application-level metrics, it might be necessary to aggregate and store them in some temporary storage until reporting to a custom Munin plugin. It makes creation of custom metrics more complicated, so you might want to consider other solutions for this purpose.

The other popular solution that makes it especially easy to collect custom metrics is StatsD (`https://github.com/etsy/statsd`). It's a network daemon written in Node.js that listens to various statistics such as counters, timers, and gauges. It is very easy to integrate, thanks to the simple protocol based on UDP. It is also easy to use the Python package named `statsd` for sending metrics to the StatsD daemon:

```
>>> import statsd
>>> c = statsd.StatsClient('localhost', 8125)
>>> c.incr('foo')  # Increment the 'foo' counter.
>>> c.timing('stats.timed', 320)  # Record a 320ms 'stats.timed'.
```

Because UDP is connectionless, it has a very low performance overhead on the application code so it is very suitable for tracking and measuring custom events inside the application code.

Unfortunately, StatsD is the only metrics collection daemon, so it does not provide any reporting features. You need other processes that are able to process data from StatsD in order to see the actual metrics graphs. The most popular choice is Graphite (`http://graphite.readthedocs.org`). It does mainly two things:

- Stores numeric time-series data
- Renders graphs of this data on demand

Graphite provides you with the ability to save graph presets that are highly customizable. You can also group many graphs into thematic dashboards. Graphs are, similarly to Munin, rendered as static images, but there is also the JSON API that allows other frontends to read graph data and render it by other means. One of the great dashboard plugins integrated with Graphite is Grafana (`http://grafana.org`). It is really worth trying because it has way better usability than plain Graphite dashboards. Graphs provided in Grafana are fully interactive and easier to manage.

Graphite is unfortunately a bit of a complex project. It is not a monolithic service and consists of three separate components:

- **Carbon**: This is a daemon written using Twisted that listens for time-series data
- **whisper**: This is a simple database library for storing time-series data
- **graphite webapp**: This is a Django web application that renders graphs on-demand as static images (using Cairo library) or as JSON data

When used with the StatsD project, the `statsd` daemon sends its data to `carbon` daemon. This makes the full solution a rather complex stack of various applications, where each of them is written using a completely different technology. Also, there are no preconfigured graphs, plugins, and dashboards available, so you will need to configure everything by yourself. This is a lot of work at the beginning and it is very easy to miss something important. This is the reason why it might be a good idea to use Munin as a monitoring backup even if you decide to have Graphite as your core monitoring service.

Dealing with application logs

While solutions such as Sentry are usually way more powerful than ordinary textual output stored in files, logs will never die. Writing some information to a standard output or file is one of the simplest things that an application can do and this should never be underestimated. There is a risk that messages sent to Sentry by raven will not get delivered. The network can fail. Sentry's storage can get exhausted or may not be able to handle incoming load. Your application might crash before any message is sent (with segmentation fault, for example). These are only a few of the possible scenarios. What is less likely is your application won't be able to log messages that are going to be written to the filesystem. It is still possible, but let's be honest. If you face such a condition where logging fails, probably you have a lot more burning issues than some missing log messages.

Remember that logs are not only about errors. Many developers used to think about logs only as a source of data that is useful when debugging issues and/or which can be used to perform some kind of forensics. Definitely, less of them try to use it as a source for generating application metrics or to do some statistical analysis. But logs may be a lot more useful than that. They can be even the core of the product implementation. A great example of building a product with logs is the Amazon article presenting an example architecture for a real-time bidding service, where everything is centered around access log collection and processing. See `https://aws.amazon.com/blogs/aws/real-time-ad-impression-bids-using-dynamodb/`.

Basic low-level log practices

The Twelve-Factor App says that logs should be treated as event streams. So a log file is not a log per se, but only an output format. The fact that they are streams means they represent time ordered events. In raw, they are typically in a text format with one line per event, although in some cases they may span multiple lines. This is typical for any backtraces related to run-time errors.

According to the Twelve-Factor App methodology, the application should never be aware of the format in which logs are stored. This means that writing to the file, or log rotation and retention should never be maintained by the application code. These are the responsibilities of the environment in which applications are run. This may be confusing because a lot of frameworks provide functions and classes for managing log files as well as rotation, compression, and retention utilities. It is tempting to use them because everything can be contained in your application codebase, but actually it is an anti-pattern that should be really avoided.

The best conventions for dealing with logs can be closed in a few rules:

- The application should always write logs unbuffered to the standard output (`stdout`)
- The execution environment should be responsible for the collection and routing of logs to the final destination

The main part of the mentioned execution environment is usually some kind of process supervision tool. The popular Python solutions, such as Supervisor or Circus, are the first ones responsible for dealing with log collection and routing. If logs are to be stored in the local filesystem, then only they should write to actual log files.

Both Supervisor and Circus are also capable of handling log rotation and retention for managed processes but you should really consider whether this is a path that you want to go. Successful operations are mostly about simplicity and consistency. Logs of your own application are probably not the only ones that you want to process and archive. If you use Apache or Nginx as a reverse proxy, you might want to collect their access logs. You might also want to store and process logs for caches and databases. If you are running some popular Linux distribution, then the chances are very high that each of these services have their own log files processed (rotated, compressed, and so on) by the popular utility named `logrotate`. My strong recommendation is to forget about Supervisor's and Circus' log rotation capabilities for the sake of consistency with other system services. `logrotate` is way more configurable and also supports compression.

logrotate and Supervisor/Circus

There is an important thing to know when using `logrotate` with Supervisor or Circus. The rotation of logs will always happen while the process Supervisor still has an open descriptor to rotated logs. If you don't take proper countermeasures, then new events will be still written to file descriptor that was already deleted by `logrotate`. As a result, nothing more will be stored in a filesystem. Solutions to this problem are quite simple. Configure `logrotate` for log files of processes managed by Supervisor or Circus with the `copytruncate` option. Instead of moving the log file after rotation, it will copy it and truncate the original file to zero size in-place. This approach does not invalidate any of existing file descriptors and processes that are already running can write to log files uninterrupted. The Supervisor can also accept the `SIGUSR2` signal that will make it reopen all the file descriptors. It may be included as the `postrotate` script in the `logrotate` configuration. This second approach is more economical in the terms of I/O operations but is also less reliable and harder to maintain.

Tools for log processing

If you have no experience of working with large amounts of logs, you will eventually gain it when working with a product that has some substantial load. You will shortly notice that a simple approach based on storing them in files and backing in some persistent storage for later retrieval is not enough. Without proper tools, this will become crude and expensive. Simple utilities such as `logrotate` help you only to ensure that the hard disk is not overflown by the ever-increasing amount of new events, but splitting and compressing log files only helps in the data archival process but does not make data retrieval or analysis simpler.

When working with distributed systems that span multiple nodes, it is nice to have a single central point from which all logs can be retrieved and analyzed. This requires a log processing flow that goes way beyond simple compression and backing up. Fortunately this is a well-known problem so there are many tools available that aim to solve it.

One of the popular choices among many developers is **Logstash**. This is the log collection daemon that can observe active log files, parse log entries and send them to the backing service in a structured form. The choice of backing stays almost always the same—**Elasticsearch**. Elasticsearch is the search engine built on top of Lucene. Among text search capabilities, it has a unique data aggregation framework that fits extremely well into the purpose of log analysis.

The other addition to this pair of tools is **Kibana**. It is a very versatile monitoring, analysis, and visualization platform for Elasticsearch. The way how these three tools complement each other is the reason why they are almost always used together as a single stack for log processing.

The integration of existing services with Logstash is very simple because it can listen on existing log files changes for the new events with only minimal changes in your logging configuration. It parses logs in textual form and has preconfigured support for some of the popular log formats, such as Apache/Nginx access logs. The only problem with Logstash is that it does not handle log rotation well, and this is a bit surprising. Forcing a process to reopen its file descriptors by sending one of the defined Unix signals (usually SIGHUP or SIGUSR1) is a pretty well-established pattern. It seems that every application that deals with logs (exclusively) should know that and be able to process various log file rotation scenarios. Sadly, Logstash is not one of them, so if you want to manage log retention with the logrotate utility, remember to rely heavily on its copytruncate option. The Logstash process can't handle situations when the original log file was moved or deleted, so without the copytruncate option it wouldn't be able to receive new events after log rotation. Logstash can of course handle different inputs of log streams such as UDP packets, TCP connections, or HTTP requests.

The other solution that seems to fill some of Logstash gaps is Fluentd. It is an alternative log collection daemon that can be used interchangeably with Logstash in the mentioned log monitoring stack. It also has an option to listen and parse log events directly in log files, so minimal integration requires only a little effort. In contrast to Logstash, it handles reloads very well and does not even need to be signaled if log files were rotated. Anyway, the biggest advantage comes from using one of its alternative log collection options that will require some substantial changes to logging configuration in your application.

Fluentd really treats logs as event streams (as recommended by the Twelve-Factor App). The file-based integration is still possible but it is only kind of backward compatibility for legacy applications that treat logs mainly as files. Every log entry is an event and it should be structured. Fluentd can parse textual logs and has multiple plugin options to handle:

- Common formats (Apache, Nginx, and syslog)
- Arbitrary formats specified using regular expressions or handled with custom parsing plugins
- Generic formats for structured messages such as JSON

The best event format for Fluentd is JSON because it adds the least amount of overhead. Messages in JSON can be also passed almost without any change to the backing service like Elasticsearch or the database.

The other very useful feature of Fluentd is the ability to pass event streams using transports other than a log file written to the disk. Most notable built-in input plugins are:

- `in_udp`: With this plugin every log event is sent as UDP packets
- `in_tcp`: With this plugin events are sent through TCP connection
- `in_unix`: With this plugin events are sent through Unix Domain Socket (names socket)
- `in_http`: With this plugin events are sent as HTTP POST requests
- `in_exec`: With this plugin Fluentd process executes an external command periodically to pull events in the JSON or MessagePack format
- `in_tail`: With this plugin Fluentd process listens for an event in a textual file

Alternative transports for log events may be especially useful in situations where you need to deal with poor I/O performance of machine storage. It is very often on cloud computing services that the default disk storage has a very low number of **IOPS (Input Output Operations Per Second)** and you need to pay a lot of money for better disk performance. If your application outputs large amount of log messages, you can easily saturate your I/O capabilities even if the data size is not very high. With alternate transports, you can use your hardware more efficiently because you leave the responsibility of data buffering only to a single process—log collector. When configured to buffer messages in memory instead of disk, you can even completely get rid of disk writes for logs, although this may greatly reduce the consistency guarantees of collected logs.

Using different transports seems to be slightly against the 11th rule of the Twelve-Factor App methodology. Treat logs as event streams when explained in detail suggests that the application should always log only through a single standard output stream (`stdout`). It is still possible to use alternate transports without breaking this rule. Writing to `stdout` does not necessarily mean that this stream must be written to file. You can leave your application logging that way and wrap it with an external process that will capture this stream and pass it directly to Logstash or Fluentd without engaging the filesystem. This is an advanced pattern that may not be suitable for every project. It has an obvious disadvantage of higher complexity, so you need to consider by yourself whether it is really worth doing.

Summary

Code deployment is not a simple topic and you should already know that after reading this chapter. Extensive discussion of this problem could easily take a few books. Even though we limited our scope exclusively to web application, we have barely scratched the surface. This chapter takes as a basis the Twelve-Factor App methodology. We discussed in detail only a few of them: log treatment, managing dependencies, and separating build/run stages.

After reading this chapter, you should know how to properly automate your deployment process, taking into consideration best practices, and be able to add proper instrumentation and monitoring for code that is run on your remote hosts.

7
Python Extensions in Other Languages

When writing Python-based applications, you are not limited to the Python language alone. There are tools such as Hy, mentioned briefly in *Chapter 3, Syntax Best Practices – above the Class Level*. It allows you to write modules, packages, or even whole applications with some other language (dialect of Lisp) that will run in Python virtual machine. Although it gives you the ability to express program logic with completely different syntax, it is still quite the same language because it compiles to the same bytecode. It means that it has the same limitations as ordinary Python code:

- Threading usability is greatly reduced due to the existence of GIL
- It is not compiled
- It does not provide static typing and possible optimizations that come with it

The solution that helps in overcoming such core limitations are extensions that are entirely written in a different language and expose their interface through Python extension APIs.

This chapter will discuss the main reasons for writing your own extensions in other languages and introduce you to the popular tools that help to create them. You will learn:

- How to write simple extensions in C using the Python/C API
- How to do the same using Cython
- What are the main challenges and problems introduced by extensions
- How to interface with compiled dynamic libraries without creating dedicated extensions and using only Python code

Different language means – C or C++

When we talk about extensions in different languages, we think almost exclusively about C and C++. Even tools such as Cython or Pyrex that provide Python language supersets only for the purpose of extensions are in fact source-to-source compilers that generate the C code from extended Python-like syntax.

It's true that you can use dynamic/shared libraries written in any language in Python if only such compilation is possible and so it goes a way beyond C and C++. But shared libraries are intrinsically generic. They can be used in any language that supports their loading. So, even if you write such a library in a completely different language (let's say Delphi or Prolog), it is hard to name such library a Python extension if it does not use the Python/C API.

Unfortunately, writing your own extensions only in C or C++ using the bare Python/C API is quite demanding. Not only because it requires a good understanding of one of the two languages that are relatively hard to master, but also because it requires exceptional amount of boilerplate. There is a lot of repetitive code that must be written only to provide an interface that will glue your implemented logic with Python and its datatypes. Anyway, it is good to know how pure C extensions are built because:

- You will understand better how Python works in general
- One day you may need to debug or maintain a native C/C++ extension
- It helps with understanding how higher-level tools for building extensions work

How do extensions in C or C++ work

Python interpreter is able to load extensions from dynamic/shared libraries if they provide an applicable interface using Python/C API. This API must be incorporated in source code of extension using the `Python.h` C header file that is distributed with Python sources. In many distributions of Linux, this header file is contained in a separate package (for example, `python-dev` in Debian/Ubuntu) but under Windows, it is distributed by default and can be found in the `includes/` directory of your Python installation.

Python/C API traditionally changes with every release of Python. In most cases, these are only additions of new features to the API, so it is typically source-compatible. Anyway, in most cases, they are not binary compatible due to changes in the **Application Binary Interface (ABI)**. This means that extensions must be built separately for every version of Python. Note also that different operating systems have noncompatible ABIs, so this makes it practically impossible to create a binary distribution for every possible environment. This is the reason why most Python extensions are distributed in source form.

Since Python 3.2, a subset of Python/C API has been defined to have stable ABIs. It is possible then to build extensions using this limited API (with a stable ABI), so extensions can be built only once and will work with any version of Python higher than or equal to 3.2 without the need for recompilation. Anyway, this limits the amount of API features and does not solve the problems of older Python versions or the distribution of the extension in binary form to environments using different operating systems. So this is a trade-off, and price of the stable ABI seems to be a bit high for very low gain.

One thing you need to know is that Python/C API is a feature that is limited to CPython implementations. Some efforts were made to bring extension support to alternative implementations such as PyPI, Jython, or IronPython, but it seems that there is no viable solution for them at the moment. The only alternative Python implementation that should deal easily with extensions is Stackless Python because it is in fact only a modified version of CPython.

C extensions for Python need to be compiled into shared/dynamic libraries before they will be available to use because obviously there is no native way to import C/C++ code into Python directly from sources. Fortunately, `distutils` and `setuptools` provide helpers to define compiled extensions as modules so compilation and distribution can be handled using the `setup.py` script as if they were ordinary Python packages. This is an example of the `setup.py` script from the official documentation that handles the packaging of simple packages with built extensions:

```python
from distutils.core import setup, Extension


module1 = Extension(
    'demo',
    sources=['demo.c']
)


setup(
    name='PackageName',
    version='1.0',
    description='This is a demo package',
    ext_modules=[module1]
)
```

Once prepared that way, there is one additional step required in your distribution flow:

```
python setup.py build
```

This will compile all your extensions provided as the `ext_modules` argument according to all additional compiler settings provided with the `Extension()` call. The compiler that will be used is the one that is default for your environment. This compilation step is not required if the package is going to be distributed with source distribution. In that case, you need to be sure that the target environment has all compilation prerequisites, such as a compiler, header files, and additional libraries that are going to be linked to the binary (if your extension needs any). More details of packaging the Python extensions will be explained later in the *Challenges* section.

Why you might want to use extensions

It's not easy to say when it is a reasonable decision to write extensions in C/C++. The general rule of thumb could be, *never, unless you have no other choice*. But this is a very subjective statement that leaves a lot of room for interpretation of what is not doable in Python. In fact, it is hard to find a thing that cannot be done using pure Python code, but there are some problems where extensions may be especially useful:

- Bypassing **GIL (Global Interpreter Lock)** in the Python threading model
- Improving performance in critical code sections
- Integrating third-party dynamic libraries
- Integrating source code written in different languages
- Creating custom datatypes

For example, the core language constraints such as GIL can easily be overcome with a different approach to concurrency, such as green threads or multiprocessing instead of a threading model.

Improving performance in critical code sections

Let's be honest. Python is not chosen by developers because of performance. It does not execute quickly, but allows you to develop quickly. Still, no matter how performant we are as programmers, thanks to this language, we may sometimes find a problem that may not be solved efficiently using pure Python.

In most cases, solving performance problems is really only about choosing proper algorithms and data structures and not about limiting the constant factor of language overhead. And it is not actually a good solution to rely on extensions in order to shave off some CPU cycles if the code is already written poorly or does not use proper algorithms. It is often possible that performance can be improved to an acceptable level without the need to increase the complexity of your project by looping in another language to the stack. And if it is possible, it should be done that way in the first place. Anyway, it is also very likely that even with *state of the art* algorithmic approach and the best suited data structures that are available to our disposal, we will not be able to fit some arbitrary technological constraints using Python alone.

The example field that puts some well-defined limits on the application's performance is the **Real Time Bidding** (**RTB**) business. In short, the whole RTB is about buying and selling advertisement inventory (places for ads) in a way similar to real auctions or stock exchanges. The trading usually takes place through some ad exchange service that sends information about available inventory to **demand-side platforms** (**DSP**) interested in buying them. And this is the place where things get exciting. Most ad exchanges use the OpenRTB protocol (which is based on HTTP) for communication with potential bidders where DSP is the site responsible for serving responses to its HTTP requests. And ad exchanges always put very limited time constraints (usually between 50 and 100 ms) on the whole process—from the first TPC packet received to the last byte written by the server. To spice things up, it is not uncommon for DSP platforms to process tens of thousands of requests per second. Being able to push the time of request processing even by a few milliseconds is the *to be or not to be* in this business. This means that porting even trivial code to C may be reasonable in that situation but only if it's a part of some performance bottleneck and cannot be improved any further algorithmically. As someone once said:

> *"You can't beat a loop written in C."*

Integrating existing code written in different languages

A lot of useful libraries have been written during the short history of computer science. It would be a great loss to forget about all that heritage every time a new programming language pops out, but it is also impossible to reliably port any piece of software that was ever written to any available language.

The C and C++ languages seem to be the most important languages that provide a lot of libraries and implementation that you would like to integrate in your application code without the need to port them completely to Python. Fortunately, CPython is already written in C, so the most natural way to integrate such code is precisely through custom extensions.

Integrating third-party dynamic libraries

Integration of code written using different technologies does not end with C/C++. A lot of libraries, especially third-party software with closed sources, are distributed as compiled binaries. In C, it is really easy to load such shared/dynamic libraries and call their functions. This means that you can use any C library as long as you wrap it with extensions using Python/C API.

This, of course, is not the only solution and there are tools such as `ctypes` or CFFI that allow you to interact with dynamic libraries using pure Python without the need of writing extensions in C. Very often, the Python/C API may still be a better choice because it provides a better separation between the integration layer (written in C) and the rest of the application.

Creating custom datatypes

Python provides a very versatile selection of built-in datatypes. Some of them really use state of the art internal implementations (at least in CPython) that are specifically tailored for usage in the Python language. The number of basic types and collections available out-of-the-box may look impressive for newcomers, but it is clear that it does not cover all of our possible needs.

You can, of course, create many custom data structures in Python either by basing them completely on some built-in types or by building them from scratch as completely new classes. Unfortunately, for some applications that may heavily rely on such custom data structures, the performance might not be enough. The whole power of complex collections such as `dict` or `set` comes from their underlying C implementation. Why not do the same and implement some of your custom data structures in C too?

Writing extensions

As already said, writing extensions is not a simple task but in exchange for your hard work, it can give you a lot of advantages. The easiest and recommended approach to your own extensions is to use tools such as Cython or Pyrex or simply integrate the existing dynamic libraries with `ctypes` or `cffi`. These projects will increase your productivity and also make code easier to develop, read, and maintain.

Anyway, if you are new to this topic, it is good to know that you can start your adventure with extensions by writing one using nothing more than bare C code and Python/C API. This will improve your understanding of how extensions work and will also help you to appreciate the advantages of alternative solutions. For the sake of simplicity, we will take a simple algorithmic problem as an example and try to implement it using three different approaches:

- Writing a pure C extension
- Using Cython
- Using Pyrex

Our problem will be finding the *nth* number of the Fibonacci sequence. It is very unlikely that you would like to create compiled extensions solely for this problem, but it is very simple so it will serve as a very good example of wiring any C function to Python/C APIs. Our only goals are clarity and simplicity, so we won't try to provide the most efficient solution. Once we know this, our reference implementation of the Fibonacci function implemented in Python looks as follows:

```
"""Python module that provides fibonacci sequence function"""


def fibonacci(n):
    """Return nth Fibonacci sequence number computed recursively.
    """
    if n < 2:
        return 1
    else:
        return fibonacci(n - 1) + fibonacci(n - 2)
```

Note that this is one of the most simple implementations of the `fibonnaci()` function and a lot of improvements could be applied to it. We refuse to improve our implementation (using a memoization pattern, for instance) though because this is not the purpose of our example. In the same manner, we won't optimize our code later when discussing implementations in C or Cython even though the compiled code gives many more possibilities to do so.

Pure C extensions

Before we fully dive into the code examples of Python extensions written in C, here is a huge warning. If you want to extend Python with C, you need to already know both of these languages well. This is especially true for C. Lack of proficiency with it can lead to real disasters because it can be easily mishandled.

If you have decided that you need to write C extension for Python, I assume that you already know the C language to a level that will allow you to fully understand the examples that are presented. Nothing other than Python/C API details will be explained here. This book is about Python and not any other language. If you don't know C at all, you should definitely not try to write your own Python extensions in C until you gain enough experience and skills. Leave it to others and stick with Cython or Pyrex because they are a lot safer from the beginner's perspective. This is mostly because Python/C API, despite having been crafted with great care, is definitely not a good introduction to C.

As proposed earlier, we will try to port the `fibonacci()` function to C and expose it to Python code as an extension. The bare implementation without the wiring to Python/C API that is analogous to the previous Python example could be roughly as follows:

```
long long fibonacci(unsigned int n) {
    if (n < 2) {
        return 1;
    } else {
        return fibonacci(n - 2) + fibonacci(n - 1);
    }
}
```

And here is the example of a complete, fully functional extension that exposes this single function in a compiled module:

```
#include <Python.h>


long long fibonacci(unsigned int n) {
    if (n < 2) {
        return 1;
    } else {
        return fibonacci(n-2) + fibonacci(n-1);
    }
}

static PyObject* fibonacci_py(PyObject* self, PyObject* args) {
    PyObject *result = NULL;
    long n;

    if (PyArg_ParseTuple(args, "l", &n)) {
        result = Py_BuildValue("L", fibonacci((unsigned int)n));
    }
```

```
        return result;
    }


    static char fibonacci_docs[] =
        "fibonacci(n): Return nth Fibonacci sequence number "
        "computed recursively\n";


    static PyMethodDef fibonacci_module_methods[] = {
        {"fibonacci", (PyCFunction)fibonacci_py,
         METH_VARARGS, fibonacci_docs},
        {NULL, NULL, 0, NULL}
    };


    static struct PyModuleDef fibonacci_module_definition = {
        PyModuleDef_HEAD_INIT,
        "fibonacci",
        "Extension module that provides fibonacci sequence function",
        -1,
        fibonacci_module_methods
    };


    PyMODINIT_FUNC PyInit_fibonacci(void) {
        Py_Initialize();

        return PyModule_Create(&fibonacci_module_definition);
    }
```

The preceding example might be a bit overwhelming at first glance because we had to add four times more code just to make the `fibonacci()` C function accessible from Python. We will discuss every bit of that code later, so don't worry. But before we do that, let's see how it can be packaged and executed in Python. The minimal `setuptools` configuration for our module needs to use the `setuptools.Extension` class in order to instruct the interpreter how our extension is compiled:

```
from setuptools import setup, Extension


setup(
    name='fibonacci',
    ext_modules=[
        Extension('fibonacci', ['fibonacci.c']),
    ]
)
```

The build process for the extension can be initialized with Python's `setup.py` build command, but will also be automatically performed on package installation. The following transcript presents the result of installation in development mode and a simple interactive session where our compiled `fibonacci()` function is inspected and executed:

```
$ ls -1a
fibonacci.c
setup.py


$ pip install -e .
Obtaining file:///Users/swistakm/dev/book/chapter7
Installing collected packages: fibonacci
  Running setup.py develop for fibonacci
Successfully installed Fibonacci


$ ls -1ap
build/
fibonacci.c
fibonacci.cpython-35m-darwin.so
fibonacci.egg-info/
setup.py


$ python
Python 3.5.1 (v3.5.1:37a07cee5969, Dec  5 2015, 21:12:44)
[GCC 4.2.1 (Apple Inc. build 5666) (dot 3)] on darwin
Type "help", "copyright", "credits" or "license" for more information.
>>> import fibonacci
>>> help(fibonacci.fibonacci)


Help on built-in function fibonacci in fibonacci:

fibonacci.fibonacci = fibonacci(...)
    fibonacci(n): Return nth Fibonacci sequence number computed
recursively
```

```
>>> [fibonacci.fibonacci(n) for n in range(10)]
[1, 1, 2, 3, 5, 8, 13, 21, 34, 55]
>>>
```

A closer look at Python/C API

Since we know how to properly package, compile, and install custom C extensions and we are sure that it works as expected, now it is the right time to discuss our code in detail.

The extensions module starts with a single C preprocessor directive that includes the Python.h header file:

```
#include <Python.h>
```

This pulls the whole Python/C API and is everything you need to include to be able to write your extensions. In more realistic cases, your code will require a lot more preprocessor directives to take benefit from C standard library functions or to integrate other source files. Our example was simple, so no more directives were required.

Next we have the core of our module:

```
long long fibonacci(unsigned int n) {
    if (n < 2) {
        return 1;
    } else {
        return fibonacci(n - 2) + fibonacci(n - 1);
    }
}
```

The preceding fibonacci() function is the only part of our code that does something useful. It is pure C implementation that Python by default can't understand. The rest of our example will create the interface layer that will expose it through Python/C API.

The first step of exposing this code to Python is the creation of the C function that is compatible with the CPython interpreter. In Python, everything is an object. This means that C functions called in Python also need to return real Python objects. Python/C APIs provide a PyObject type and every callable must return the pointer to it. The signature of our function is:

```
static PyObject* fibonacci_py(PyObject* self, PyObject* args)s
```

Note that the preceding signature does not specify the exact list of arguments but only PyObject* args that will hold the pointer to the structure that contains the tuple of the provided values. The actual validation of the argument list must be performed inside of the function body and this is exactly what fibonacci_py() does. It parses the args argument list assuming it is the single unsigned int type and uses that value as an argument to the fibonacci() function to retrieve the Fibonacci sequence element:

```
static PyObject* fibonacci_py(PyObject* self, PyObject* args) {
    PyObject *result = NULL;
    long n;

    if (PyArg_ParseTuple(args, "l", &n)) {
        result = Py_BuildValue("L", fibonacci((unsigned int)n));
    }

    return result;
}
```

The preceding example function has some serious bugs, which the eyes of an experienced developer should spot very easily. Try to find it as an exercise in working with C extensions. For now, we leave it as it is for the sake of brevity. We will try to fix it later when discussing details of dealing with errors in the *Exception handling* section.

The "l" string in the PyArg_ParseTuple(args, "l", &n) call means that we expect args to contain only a single long value. In case of failure, it will return NULL and store information about the exception in the per-thread interpreter state. The details of exception handling will be described a bit later in the *Exception handling* section.

The actual signature of the parsing function is int PyArg_ParseTuple(PyObject *args, const char *format, ...) and what goes after the format string is a variable length list of arguments that represents parsed value output (as pointers). This is analogous to how the scanf() function from the C standard library works. If our assumption fails and the user provides an incompatible arguments list, then PyArg_ParseTuple() will raise the proper exception. This is a very convenient way to encode function signatures once you get used to it but has a huge downside when compared to plain Python code. Such Python call signatures implicitly defined by the PyArg_ParseTuple() calls cannot be easily inspected inside of the Python interpreter. You need to remember this fact when using code provided as extensions.

As already said, Python expects objects to be returned from callables. This means that we cannot return a raw `long long` value obtained from the `fibonacci()` function as a result of `fibonacci_py()`. Such an attempt would not even compile and there is no automatic casting of basic C types to Python objects. The `Py_BuildValue(*format, ...)` function must be used instead. It is the counterpart of `PyArg_ParseTuple()` and accepts a similar set of format strings. The main difference is that the list of arguments is not a function output but an input, so actual values must be provided instead of pointers.

After `fibonacci_py()` is defined, most of the heavy work is done. The last step is to perform module initialization and add metadata to our function that will make usage a bit simpler for users. This is the boilerplate part of our extension code that for some simple examples, such as this one, can take more place than actual functions that we want to expose. In most cases, it simply consists of some static structures and one initialization function that will be executed by the interpreter on module import.

At first, we create a static string that will be a content of Python docstring for the `fibonacci_py()` function:

```
static char fibonacci_docs[] =
    "fibonacci(n): Return nth Fibonacci sequence number "
    "computed recursively\n";
```

Note that this could be *inlined* somewhere later in `fibonacci_module_methods`, but it is a good practice to have docstrings separated and stored in close proximity to the actual function definition that they refer to.

The next part of our definition is the array of the `PyMethodDef` structures that define methods (functions) that will be available in our module. This structure contains exactly four fields:

- `char* ml_name`: This is the name of the method.
- `PyCFunction ml_meth`: This is the pointer to the C implementation of the function.
- `int ml_flags`: This includes the flags indicating either the calling convention or binding convention. The latter is applicable only for definition of class methods.
- `char* ml_doc`: This is the pointer to the content of method/function docstring.

Such an array must always end with a sentinel value of {NULL, NULL, 0, NULL} that indicates its end. In our simple case, we created the static PyMethodDef fibonacci_module_methods[] array that contains only two elements (including the sentinel value):

```
static PyMethodDef fibonacci_module_methods[] = {
    {"fibonacci", (PyCFunction)fibonacci_py,
     METH_VARARGS, fibonacci_docs},
    {NULL, NULL, 0, NULL}
};
```

And this is how the first entry maps to the PyMethodDef structure:

- ml_name = "fibonacci": Here, the fibonacci_py() C function will be exposed as a Python function under the fibonacci name

- ml_meth = (PyCFunction)fibonacci_py: Here, the casting to PyCFunction is simply required by Python/C API and is dictated by the call convention defined later in ml_flags

- ml_flags = METH_VARARGS: Here, the METH_VARARGS flag indicates that the calling convention of our function accepts a variable list of arguments and no keyword arguments

- ml_doc = fibonacci_docs: Here, the Python function will be documented with the content of the fibonacci_docs string

When an array of function definitions is complete, we can create another structure that contains the definition of the whole module. It is described using the PyModuleDef type and contains multiple fields. Some of them are useful only for more complex scenarios, where fine-grained control over the module initialization process is required. Here we are interested only in the first five of them:

- PyModuleDef_Base m_base: This should always be initialized with PyModuleDef_HEAD_INIT.

- char* m_name: This is the name of the newly created module. In our case it is fibonacci.

- char* m_doc: This is the pointer to the docstring content for the module. We usually have only a single module defined in one C source file, so it is OK to inline our documentation string in the whole structure.

- `Py_ssize_t m_size`: This is the size of the memory allocated to keep the module state. This is only used when support for multiple subinterpreters or multiphase initialization is required. In most cases, you don't need that and it is gets the value `-1`.

- `PyMethodDef* m_methods`: This is a pointer to the array containing module-level functions described by the `PyMethodDef` values. It could be NULL if the module does not expose any functions. In our case, it is `fibonacci_module_methods`.

The other fields are explained in detail in the official Python documentation (refer to `https://docs.python.org/3/c-api/module.html`) but are not needed in our example extension. They should be set to NULL if not required and they will be initialized with that value implicitly when not specified. This is why our module description contained in the `fibonacci_module_definition` variable can take this simple five-element form:

```
static struct PyModuleDef fibonacci_module_definition = {
    PyModuleDef_HEAD_INIT,
    "fibonacci",
    "Extension module that provides fibonacci sequence function",
    -1,
    fibonacci_module_methods
};
```

The last piece of code that crowns our work is the module initialization function. This must follow a very specific naming convention, so the Python interpreter can easily pick it when the dynamic/shared library is loaded. It should be named `PyInit_name`, where *name* is your module name. So it is exactly the same string that was used as the `m_base` field in the `PyModuleDef` definition and as the first argument of the `setuptools.Extension()` call. If you don't require a complex initialization process for the module, it takes a very simple form, exactly like in our example:

```
PyMODINIT_FUNC PyInit_fibonacci(void) {
    return PyModule_Create(&fibonacci_module_definition);
}
```

The `PyMODINIT_FUNC` macro is a preprocessor macro that will declare the return type of this initialization function as `PyObject *` and add any special linkage declarations if required by the platform.

Calling and binding conventions

As explained in the *A closer look at Python/C API* section, the `ml_flags` bitfield of the `PyMethodDef` structure contains flags for calling and binding conventions. **Calling convention flags** are:

- `METH_VARARGS`: This is a typical convention for the Python function or method that only accepts arguments as its parameters. The type provided as the `ml_meth` field for such a function should be `PyCFunction`. The function will be provided with two arguments of the `PyObject*` type. The first is either the `self` object (for methods) or the `module` object (for module functions). A typical signature for the C function with that calling convention is `PyObject* function(PyObject* self, PyObject* args)`.

- `METH_KEYWORDS`: This is the convention for the Python function that accepts keyword arguments when called. Its associated C type is `PyCFunctionWithKeywords`. The C function must accept three arguments of the `PyObject*` type: self, args, and a dictionary of keyword arguments. If combined with `METH_VARARGS`, the first two arguments have the same meaning as for the previous calling convention, otherwise args will be NULL. The typical C function signature is: `PyObject* function(PyObject* self, PyObject* args, PyObject* keywds)`.

- `METH_NOARGS`: This is the convention for Python functions that do not accept any other argument. The C function should be of the `PyCFunction` type, so the signature is the same as that of the `METH_VARARGS` convention (two `self` and `args` arguments). The only difference is that args will always be NULL, so there is no need to call `PyArg_ParseTuple()`. This cannot be combined with any other calling convention flag.

- `METH_O`: This is the shorthand for functions and methods accepting single object arguments. The type of C function is again `PyCFunction`, so it accepts two `PyObject*` arguments: `self` and `args`. Its difference from `METH_VARARGS` is that there is no need to call `PyArg_ParseTuple()` because `PyObject*` provided as args will already represent the single argument provided in the Python call to that function. This also cannot be combined with any other calling convention flag.

A function that accepts keywords is described either with METH_KEYWORDS or a bitwise combination of calling convention flags in the form of METH_VARARGS | METH_KEYWORDS. If so, it should parse its arguments with PyArg_ParseTupleAndKeywords() instead of PyArg_ParseTuple() or PyArg_UnpackTuple(). Here is an example module with a single function that returns None and accepts two named keyword arguments that are printed on standard output:

```
#include <Python.h>

static PyObject* print_args(PyObject *self, PyObject *args,
PyObject *keywds)
{
    char *first;
    char *second;

    static char *kwlist[] = {"first", "second", NULL};

    if (!PyArg_ParseTupleAndKeywords(args, keywds, "ss", kwlist,
                                     &first, &second))
        return NULL;

    printf("%s %s\n", first, second);

    Py_INCREF(Py_None);
    return Py_None;
}


static PyMethodDef module_methods[] = {
    {"print_args", (PyCFunction)print_args,
     METH_VARARGS | METH_KEYWORDS,
     "print provided arguments"},
    {NULL, NULL, 0, NULL}
};


static struct PyModuleDef module_definition = {
    PyModuleDef_HEAD_INIT,
    "kwargs",
    "Keyword argument processing example",
    -1,
    module_methods
};


PyMODINIT_FUNC PyInit_kwargs(void) {
    return PyModule_Create(&module_definition);
}
```

Argument parsing in Python/C API is very elastic and is extensively described in the official documentation at `https://docs.python.org/3.5/c-api/arg.html`. The format argument in `PyArg_ParseTuple()` and `PyArg_ParseTupleAndKeywords()` allows fine grained control over argument number and types. Every advanced calling convention known in Python can be coded in C with this API including:

- Functions with default values for arguments
- Functions with arguments specified as keyword-only
- Functions with a variable number of arguments

The **binding convention flags** are `METH_CLASS`, `METH_STATIC`, and `METH_COEXIST`, are reserved for methods, and cannot be used to describe module functions. The first two are quite self-explanatory. They are the C counterparts of `classmethod` and `staticmethod` decorators and change the meaning of the `self` argument passed to the C function.

`METH_COEXIST` allows loading a method in place of the existing definition. It is useful very rarely. This is mostly when you would like to provide an implementation of the C method that would be generated automatically from the other features of the type that was defined. Python documentation gives an example of the `__contains__()` wrapper method that would be generated if the type has the `sq_contains` slot defined. Unfortunately, defining your own classes and types using Python/C API is beyond the scope of this introductory chapter. We will cover creating your own types in extensions later when discussing Cython because doing that in pure C requires way too much boilerplate code and leaves a lot of room for making mistakes.

Exception handling

C, unlike Python, or even C++ does not have syntax for raising and catching exceptions. All error handling is usually handled with function return values and optional global state for storing details that can explain the cause of the last failure.

Exception handling in Python/C API is built around that simple principle. There is a global per thread indicator of the last error that occurred and functioned in the C API. It is set to describe the cause of a problem. There is also a standardized way to inform the caller of a function if this state was changed during the call:

- If the function is supposed to return a pointer, it returns `NULL`
- If the function is supposed to return an `int` type, it returns `-1`

The only exceptions from the preceding rules in Python/C API are the `PyArg_*()` functions that return `1` to indicate success and `0` to indicate failure.

To see how this works in practice, let's recall our `fibonacci_py()` function from the example in the previous sections:

```
static PyObject* fibonacci_py(PyObject* self, PyObject* args) {
    PyObject *result = NULL;
    long n;

    if (PyArg_ParseTuple(args, "l", &n)) {
        result = Py_BuildValue("L", fibonacci((unsigned int) n));
    }

    return result;
}
```

Lines that somehow take part in our error handling are highlighted. It starts at the very beginning with the initialization of the `result` variable that is supposed to store the return value of our function. It is initialized with NULL that, as we already know, is an indicator of error. And this is how you will usually code your extensions, assuming that error is the default state of your code.

Later we have the `PyArg_ParseTuple()` call that will set error info in case of an exception and return 0. This is part of the `if` statement and in that case we don't do anything more and return NULL. Whoever calls our function will be notified about the error.

`Py_BuildValue()` can also raise an exception. It is supposed to return `PyObject*` (pointer), so in case of failure it gives NULL. We can simply store it as our result variable and pass further as a return value.

But our job does not end with caring for exceptions raised by Python/C API calls. It is very probable that you will need to inform the extension user that some other kind of error or failure occurred. Python/C API has multiple functions that help you to raise an exception, but the most common one is `PyErr_SetString()`. It sets an error indicator with the given exception type with an additional string provided as the error cause explanation. The full signature of this function is:

```
void PyErr_SetString(PyObject* type, const char* message)
```

I have already said that implementation of our `fibonacci_py()` function has serious bug. Now is the right time to fix it. Fortunately, we have proper tools to do that. The problem lies in insecure casting of the `long` type to `unsigned int` in the following lines:

```
    if (PyArg_ParseTuple(args, "l", &n)) {
        result = Py_BuildValue("L", fibonacci((unsigned int) n));
    }
```

Thanks to the `PyArg_ParseTuple()` call, the first and only argument will be interpreted as a `long` type (the `"l"` specifier) and stored in the local n variable. Then it is cast to `unsigned int` so the issue will occur if the user calls the `fibonacci()` function from Python with a negative value. For instance, `-1`, as a signed 32-bit integer, will be interpreted as `4294967295` when cast to an unsigned 32-bit integer. Such a value will cause deep recursion and will result in stack overflow and a segmentation fault. Note that the same may happen if the user gives an arbitrarily large positive argument. We cannot fix this without a complete redesign of the C `fibonacci()` function, but we can at least try to ensure that argument that is passed meets some preconditions. Here we check if the value of the n argument is greater than or equal to zero and we raise a `ValueError` exception if that's not true:

```
static PyObject* fibonacci_py(PyObject* self, PyObject* args) {
    PyObject *result = NULL;
    long n;
    long long fib;

    if (PyArg_ParseTuple(args, "l", &n)) {
        if (n<0) {
            PyErr_SetString(PyExc_ValueError,
                            "n must not be less than 0");
        } else {
            result = Py_BuildValue("L", fibonacci((unsigned
            int)n));
        }
    }

    return result;
}
```

The last note is that the global error state does not clear by itself. Some of the errors can be handled gracefully in your C functions (same as using the `try ... except` clause in Python) and you need to be able to clear the error indicator if it is no longer valid. The function for that is `PyErr_Clear()`.

Releasing GIL

I have already mentioned that extensions can be a way to bypass Python GIL. There is a famous limitation of the CPython implementation stating that only one thread at a time can execute Python code. While multiprocessing is the suggested approach to circumvent this problem, it may not be a good solution for some highly parallelizable algorithms due to the resource overhead of running additional processes.

Because extensions are mostly used in cases where a bigger part of the work is performed in pure C without any calls to Python/C API, it is possible (even advisable) to release GIL in some application sections. Thanks to this, you can still benefit from having multiple CPU cores and multithreaded application design. The only thing you need to do is to wrap blocks of code that are known to not use any of Python/C API calls or Python structures with specific macros provided by Python/C API. These two preprocessor macros are provided to simplify the whole procedure of releasing and reacquiring the Global Interpreter Lock:

- `Py_BEGIN_ALLOW_THREADS`: This declares the hidden local variable where the current thread state is saved and it releases GIL

- `Py_END_ALLOW_THREADS`: This reacquires GIL and restores the thread state from the local variable declared with the previous macro

When we look carefully at our `fibonacci` extension example, we can clearly see that the `fibonacci()` function does not execute any Python code and does not touch any of the Python structures. This means that the `fibonacci_py()` function that simply wraps the `fibonacci(n)` execution could be updated to release GIL around that call:

```
static PyObject* fibonacci_py(PyObject* self, PyObject* args) {
    PyObject *result = NULL;
    long n;
    long long fib;

    if (PyArg_ParseTuple(args, "l", &n)) {
        if (n<0) {
            PyErr_SetString(PyExc_ValueError,
                            "n must not be less than 0");
        } else {
            Py_BEGIN_ALLOW_THREADS;
            fib = fibonacci(n);
            Py_END_ALLOW_THREADS;

            result = Py_BuildValue("L", fib);
        }
    }

    return result;
}
```

Reference counting

Finally, we come to the important topic of memory management in Python. Python has its own garbage collector, but it is designed only to solve the issue of cyclic references in the **reference counting** algorithm. Reference counting is the primary method of managing the deallocation of objects that are no longer needed.

Python/C API documentation introduces an *ownership of references* to explain how it deals with deallocation of objects. Objects in Python are never owned and they are always shared. The actual creation of objects is managed by Python's memory manager. It is the component of CPython interpreter that is responsible for allocating and deallocating memory for objects that are stored in a private heap. What can be owned instead is a reference to the object.

Every object in Python that is represented by a reference (`PyObject *` pointer) has an associated reference count. When it goes to zero, it means that no one holds any valid reference to the object and the deallocator associated with its type can be called. Python/C API provides two macros for increasing and decreasing reference counts: `Py_INCREF()`, and `Py_DECREF()`. But before we discuss their details, we need to understand a few more terms related to reference ownership:

- **Passing of ownership**: Whenever we say that the function *passes the ownership* over a reference, it means that it has already increased the reference count and it is the responsibility of the caller to decrease the count when the reference to the object is no longer needed. Most of the functions that return the newly created objects, such as `Py_BuildValue`, do that. If that object is going to be returned from our function to another caller, then the ownership is passed again. We do not decrease the reference count in that case because it is no longer our responsibility. This is why the `fibonacci_py()` function does not call `Py_DECREF()` on the `result` variable.

- **Borrowed references**: The *borrowing* of references happens when the function receives a reference to some Python object as an argument. The reference count for such a reference should never be decreased in that function unless it was explicitly increased in its scope. In our `fibonacci_py()` function the `self` and `args` arguments are such borrowed references and thus we do not call `PyDECREF()` on them. Some of the Python/C API functions may also return borrowed references. The notable examples are `PyTuple_GetItem()` and `PyList_GetItem()`. It is often said that such references are *unprotected*. There is no need to dispose of its ownership unless it will be returned as a function's return value. In most cases, extra care should be taken if we use such borrowed references as arguments of other Python/C API calls. It may be necessary in some circumstances to additionally protect such references with additional `Py_INCREF()` before using as argument to other function and then calling `Py_DECREF()` when it is no longer needed.

- **Stolen references**: It is also possible for the Python/C API function to *steal* the reference instead of *borrowing* it when provided as a call argument. This is the case of exactly two functions: `PyTuple_SetItem()` and `PyList_SetItem()`. They fully take over the responsibility of the reference passed to them. They do not increase the reference count by themselves but will call `Py_DECREF()` when the reference is no longer needed.

Keeping an eye on the reference counts is one of the hardest things when writing complex extensions. Some of the not-so-obvious issues may not be noticed until the code is run in a multithreaded setup.

The other common problem is caused by the very nature of Python's object model and the fact that some functions return borrowed references. When the reference count goes to zero, the deallocation function is executed. For user-defined classes, it is possible to define a __del__() method that will be called at that moment. This can be any Python code and it is possible that it will affect other objects and their reference counts. The official Python documentation gives the following example of code that may be affected by this problem:

```
void bug(PyObject *list) {
    PyObject *item = PyList_GetItem(list, 0);

    PyList_SetItem(list, 1, PyLong_FromLong(0L));
    PyObject_Print(item, stdout, 0); /* BUG! */
}
```

It looks completely harmless, but the problem is in fact that we cannot know what elements the list object contains. When `PyList_SetItem()` sets a new value on the `list[1]` index, the ownership of the object that was previously stored at that index is disposed. If it was the only existing reference, the reference count will become 0 and the object will become deallocated. It is possible that it was some user-defined class with a custom implementation of the __del__() method. A serious issue will occur if in the result of such a __del__() execution `item[0]` will be removed from the list. Note that `PyList_GetItem()` returns a *borrowed* reference! It does not call `Py_INCREF()` before returning a reference. So in that code, it is possible that `PyObject_Print()` will be called with a reference to an object that no longer exists. This will cause a segmentation fault and crash the Python interpreter.

The proper approach is to protect borrowed references for the whole time we need them because there is a possibility that any call in-between may cause deallocation of any other object—even if they are seemingly unrelated:

```
void no_bug(PyObject *list) {
    PyObject *item = PyList_GetItem(list, 0);
```

```
    Py_INCREF(item);
    PyList_SetItem(list, 1, PyLong_FromLong(0L));
    PyObject_Print(item, stdout, 0);
    Py_DECREF(item);
}
```

Cython

Cython is both an optimizing static compiler and the name of a programming language that is a superset of Python. As a compiler, it can perform *source to source* compilation of native Python code and its Cython dialect to Python C extensions using Python/C API. It allows you to combine the power of Python and C without the need to manually deal with Python/C API.

Cython as a source to source compiler

For extensions created using Cython, the major advantage you will get is using the superset language that it provides. Anyway, it is possible to create extensions from plain Python code using *source to source* compilation. This is the simplest approach to Cython because it requires almost no changes to the code and can give some significant performance improvements at a very low development cost.

Cython provides a simple `cythonize` utility function that allows you to easily integrate the compilation process with `distutils` or `setuptools`. Let's assume that we would like to compile a pure Python implementation of our `fibonacci()` function to a C extension. If it is located in the `fibonacci` module, the minimal `setup.py` script could be as follows:

```
from setuptools import setup
from Cython.Build import cythonize

setup(
    name='fibonacci',
    ext_modules=cythonize(['fibonacci.py'])
)
```

Cython used as a source compilation tool for the Python language has another benefit. Source to source compilation to extensions can be a fully optional part of source distribution installation process. If the environment where the package needs to be installed does not have Cython or any other building prerequisites, it can be installed as a normal *pure Python* package. The user should not notice any functional difference in the behavior of code distributed that way.

A common approach for distributing extensions built with Cython is to include both Python/Cython sources and C code that would be generated from these source files. This way the package can be installed in three different ways depending on the existence of building prerequisites:

- If the installation environment has Cython available, the extension C code is generated from the Python/Cython sources that are provided

- If Cython is not available but there are available building prerequisites (C compiler, Python/C API headers), the extension is built from distributed pre-generated C files

- If neither of the preceding prerequisites is available but the extension is created from pure Python sources, the modules are installed like ordinary Python code, and the compilation step is skipped

Note that Cython documentation says that including generated C files as well as Cython sources is the recommended way of distributing Cython extensions. The same documentation says that Cython compilation should be disabled by default because the user may not have the required version of Cython in his environment and this may result in unexpected compilation issues. Anyway, with the advent of environment isolation, this seems to be a less worrying problem today. Also, Cython is a valid Python package that is available on PyPI, so it can easily be defined as your project requirement in a specific version. Including such a prerequisite is, of course, a decision with serious implications and should be considered very carefully. The safer solution is to leverage the power of the `extras_require` feature in the `setuptools` package and allow the user to decide whether he wants to use Cython with a specific environment variable:

```
import os

from distutils.core import setup
from distutils.extension import Extension

try:
    # cython source to source compilation available
    # only when Cython is available
    import Cython
    # and specific environment variable says
    # explicitly that Cython should be used
    # to generate C sources
    USE_CYTHON = bool(os.environ.get("USE_CYTHON"))

except ImportError:
    USE_CYTHON = False
```

```
ext = '.pyx' if USE_CYTHON else '.c'

extensions = [Extension("fibonacci", ["fibonacci"+ext])]

if USE_CYTHON:
    from Cython.Build import cythonize
    extensions = cythonize(extensions)

setup(
    name='fibonacci',
    ext_modules=extensions,
    extras_require={
        # Cython will be set in that specific version
        # as a requirement if package will be intalled
        # with '[with-cython]' extra feature
        'cython': ['cython==0.23.4']
    }
)
```

The `pip` installation tool supports the installation of packages with the *extras* option by adding the `[extra-name]` suffix to the package name. For the preceding example, the optional Cython requirement and compilation during the installation from local sources can be enabled using the following command:

```
$ USE_CYTHON=1 pip install .[with-cython]
```

Cython as a language

Cython is not only a compiler but also a superset of the Python language. Superset means that any valid Python code is allowed and it can be further updated with additional features, such as support for calling C functions or declaring C types on variables and class attributes. So any code written in Python is also written in Cython. This explains why ordinary Python modules can be so easily compiled to C using the Cython compiler.

But we won't stop on that simple fact. Instead of saying that our reference `fibonacci()` function is also code for valid extensions in this superset of Python, we will try to improve it a bit. This won't be any real optimization to our function design but some minor updates that will allow it to benefit from being written in Cython.

Cython sources use a different file extension. It is .pyx instead of .py. Let's assume that we still want to implement our Fibbonacci sequence. The content of fibonacci.pyx might look like this:

```
"""Cython module that provides fibonacci sequence function."""


def fibonacci(unsigned int n):
    """Return nth Fibonacci sequence number computed
    recursively."""
    if n < 2:
        return n
    else:
        return fibonacci(n - 1) + fibonacci(n - 2)
```

As you can see, the only thing that has really changed is the signature of the fibonacci() function. Thanks to optional static typing in Cython, we can declare the n argument as unsigned int, and this should slightly improve the way our function works. Additionally, it does a lot more than we did previously when writing extensions by hand. If the argument of the Cython function is declared with a static type, then the extension will automatically handle conversion and overflow errors by raising proper exceptions:

```
>>> from fibonacci import fibonacci
>>> fibonacci(5)
5
>>> fibonacci(-1)
Traceback (most recent call last):
  File "<stdin>", line 1, in <module>
  File "fibonacci.pyx", line 21, in fibonacci.fibonacci (fibonacci.c:704)
OverflowError: can't convert negative value to unsigned int
>>> fibonacci(10 ** 10)
Traceback (most recent call last):
  File "<stdin>", line 1, in <module>
  File "fibonacci.pyx", line 21, in fibonacci.fibonacci (fibonacci.c:704)
OverflowError: value too large to convert to unsigned int
```

We already know that Cython compiles only *source to source* and the generated code uses the same Python/C API that we would use when writing C code for extensions by hand. Note that `fibonacci()` is a recursive function, so it calls itself very often. This will mean that although we declared a static type for input argument, during the recursive call it will treat itself like any other Python function. So `n-1` and `n-2` will be packed back into the Python object and then passed to the hidden wrapper layer of the internal `fibonacci()` implementation that will again bring it back to the `unsigned int` type. This will happen again and again until we reach the final depth of recursion. This is not necessarily a problem but involves a lot more argument processing than really required.

We can cut off the overhead of Python function calls and argument processing by delegating more of the work to a pure C function that does not know anything about Python structures. We did this previously when creating C extensions with pure C and we can do that in Cython too. We can use the `cdef` keyword to declare C-style functions that accept and return only C types:

```
cdef long long fibonacci_cc(unsigned int n):
    if n < 2:
        return n
    else:
        return fibonacci_cc(n - 1) + fibonacci_cc(n - 2)


def fibonacci(unsigned int n):
    """ Return nth Fibonacci sequence number computed recursively
    """
    return fibonacci_cc(n)
```

We can go even further. With a plain C example, we finally showed how to release GIL during the call of our pure C function, so the extension was a bit nicer for multithreaded applications. In previous examples, we have used `Py_BEGIN_ALLOW_THREADS` and `Py_END_ALLOW_THREADS` preprocessor macros from Python/C API headers to mark section of code as free from Python calls. The Cython syntax is a lot shorter and easier to remember. GIL can be released around the section of code using a simple `with nogil` statement:

```
def fibonacci(unsigned int n):
    """ Return nth Fibonacci sequence number computed recursively
    """
    with nogil:
        result = fibonacci_cc(n)

    return fibonacci_cc(n)
```

You can also mark the whole C style function as safe to call without GIL:

```
cdef long long fibonacci_cc(unsigned int n) nogil:
    if n < 2:
        return n
    else:
        return fibonacci_cc(n - 1) + fibonacci_cc(n - 2)
```

It is important to know that such functions cannot have Python objects as arguments or return types. Whenever a function marked as `nogil` needs to perform any Python/C API call, it must acquire GIL using the `with gil` statement.

Challenges

To be honest, I started my adventure with Python only because I was tired of all the difficulty of writing software in C and C++. In fact, it is very common that programmers start to learn Python when they realize that other languages do not deliver what the users need. Programming in Python, when compared to C, C++, or Java, is a breeze. Everything seems to be simple and well designed. You might think that there are no places where you can trip and there are no other programming languages required anymore.

And of course nothing could be more wrong. Yes, Python is an amazing language with a lot of cool features and it is used in many fields. But it does not mean that it is perfect and does not have any downsides. It is easy to understand and write, but this easiness comes with a price. It is not as slow as many think, but will never be as fast as C. It is highly portable, but its interpreter is not available on as many architectures as compilers for other languages are. We could go with that list forever.

One of the solutions to that problem is to write extensions, so we can bring of some of the advantages of *good old* C back to Python. And in most cases, it works well. The question is: are we really using Python because we want to extend it with C? The answer is *no*. This is only an inconvenient necessity in situations where we don't have any better option.

Additional complexity

It is not a secret that developing applications in many different languages is not an easy task. Python and C are completely different technologies and it is very hard to find anything that they have in common. It is also true that there is no application that is free of bugs. If extensions become common in your codebase, debugging can become painful. Not only because debugging of C code requires completely different workflow and tools, but also because you will need to switch context between two different languages very often.

We are all humans and all have limited cognitive capabilities. There are, of course, people who can handle multiple layers of abstraction and technology stacks at the same time efficiently but they seem to be very rare specimens. No matter how skilled you are, there is always an additional price to pay for maintaining such hybrid solutions. This will either involve extra effort and time required to switch between C and Python, or additional stress that will make you eventually less efficient.

According to the TIOBE index, C is still one of the most popular programming languages. Despite this fact, it is very common for Python programmers to know very little or almost nothing about it. Personally, I think that C should be *lingua franca* in the programming world, but my opinion is very unlikely to change anything in this matter. Python also is so seductive and easy to learn that a lot of programmers forget about all their previous experiences and completely switch to the new technology. And programming is not like riding a bike. This particular skill erodes faster if not used and polished sufficiently. Even programmers with strong C background are risking to gradually lose their previous knowledge if they decide to dive into Python for too long. All of the above leads to one simple conclusion—it is harder to find people who will be able to understand and extend your code. For open source packages, this means fewer voluntary contributors. In closed source, this means that not all of your teammates will be able to develop and maintain extensions without breaking things.

Debugging

When it comes to failures, extensions may break, very badly. Static typing gives you a lot of advantages over Python and allows you to catch a lot of issues during the compilation step that would be hard to notice in Python without a rigorous testing routine and full test coverage. On the other hand, all memory management must be performed manually. And faulty memory management is the main reason of most programming errors in C. In the best case scenario, such mistakes will only result in some memory leaks that will gradually eat all of your environment resources. The best case does not mean easy to handle. Memory leaks are really tricky to find without using proper external tools such as Valgrind. Anyway, in most cases, the memory management issues in your extension's code will result in a segmentation fault that is unrecoverable in Python and will cause the interpreter to crash without raising any exception. This means that you will eventually need to arm up with additional tools that most Python programmers don't need to use. This adds complexity to your development environment and workflow.

Interfacing with dynamic libraries without extensions

Thanks to `ctypes` (a module in the standard library) or `cffi` (an external package), you can integrate just about every compiled dynamic/shared library in Python no matter in what language it was written. And you can do that in pure Python without any compilation steps, so this is an interesting alternative to writing extensions in C.

This does not mean you don't need to know anything about C. Both solutions require from you a reasonable understanding of C and how dynamic libraries work in general. On the other hand, they remove the burden of dealing with Python reference counting and greatly reduce the risk of making painful mistakes. Also interfacing with C code through `ctypes` or `cffi` is more portable than writing and compiling the C extension module.

ctypes

`ctypes` is the most popular module to call functions from dynamic or shared libraries without the need of writing custom C extensions. The reason for that is obvious. It is part of the standard library, so it is always available and does not require any external dependencies. It is a **foreign function interface** (FFI) library and provides an API for creating C-compatible datatypes.

Loading libraries

There are four types of dynamic library loaders available in `ctypes` and two conventions to use them. The classes that represent dynamic and shared libraries are `ctypes.CDLL`, `ctypes.PyDLL`, `ctypes.OleDLL`, and `ctypes.WinDLL`. The last two are only available on Windows, so we won't discuss them here. The differences between `CDLL` and `PyDLL` are as follows:

- `ctypes.CDLL`: This class represents loaded shared libraries. The functions in these libraries use the standard calling convention, and are assumed to return `int`. GIL is released during the call.

- `ctypes.PyDLL`: This class works like `CDLL`, but GIL is not released during the call. After execution, the Python error flag is checked and an exception is raised if it is set. It is only useful when directly calling functions from Python/C API.

To load a library, you can either instantiate one of the preceding classes with proper arguments or call the `LoadLibrary()` function from the submodule associated with a specific class:

- `ctypes.cdll.LoadLibrary()` for `ctypes.CDLL`
- `ctypes.pydll.LoadLibrary()` for `ctypes.PyDLL`
- `ctypes.windll.LoadLibrary()` for `ctypes.WinDLL`
- `ctypes.oledll.LoadLibrary()` for `ctypes.OleDLL`

The main challenge when loading shared libraries is how to find them in a portable way. Different systems use different suffixes for shared libraries (`.dll` on Windows, `.dylib` on OS X, `.so` on Linux) and search for them in different places. The main offender in this area is Windows, that does not have a predefined naming scheme for libraries. Because of that, we won't discuss the details of loading libraries with `ctypes` on this system and concentrate mainly on Linux and Mac OS X that deal with this problem in a consistent and similar way. If you are anyway interested in Windows platform, refer to the official `ctypes` documentation that has plenty of information about supporting that system (refer to `https://docs.python.org/3.5/library/ctypes.html`).

Both library loading conventions (the `LoadLibrary()` function and specific library-type classes) require you to use the full library name. This means all the predefined library prefixes and suffixes need to be included. For example, to load the C standard library on Linux, you need to write the following:

```
>>> import ctypes
>>> ctypes.cdll.LoadLibrary('libc.so.6')
<CDLL 'libc.so.6', handle 7f0603e5f000 at 7f0603d4cbd0>
```

Here, for Mac OS X, this would be:

```
>>> import ctypes
>>> ctypes.cdll.LoadLibrary('libc.dylib')
```

Fortunately, the `ctypes.util` submodule provides a `find_library()` function that allows to load a library using its name without any prefixes or suffixes and will work on any system that has a predefined scheme for naming shared libraries:

```
>>> import ctypes
>>> from ctypes.util import find_library
>>> ctypes.cdll.LoadLibrary(find_library('c'))
<CDLL '/usr/lib/libc.dylib', handle 7fff69b97c98 at 0x101b73ac8>
>>> ctypes.cdll.LoadLibrary(find_library('bz2'))
```

```
<CDLL '/usr/lib/libbz2.dylib', handle 10042d170 at 0x101b6ee80>
>>> ctypes.cdll.LoadLibrary(find_library('AGL'))
<CDLL '/System/Library/Frameworks/AGL.framework/AGL', handle 101811610 at
0x101b73a58>
```

Calling C functions using ctypes

When the library is successfully loaded, the common pattern is to store it as a module-level variable with the same name as library. The functions can be accessed as object attributes, so calling them is like calling a Python function from any other imported module:

```
>>> import ctypes
>>> from ctypes.util import import find_library
>>>
>>> libc = ctypes.cdll.LoadLibrary(find_library('c'))
>>>
>>> libc.printf(b"Hello world!\n")
Hello world!
13
```

Unfortunately, all the built-in Python types except integers, strings, and bytes are incompatible with C datatypes and thus must be wrapped in the corresponding classes provided by the `ctypes` module. Here is the full list of compatible datatypes that comes from the `ctypes` documentation:

ctypes type	C type	Python type
c_bool	_Bool	bool (1)
c_char	char	1-character bytes object
c_wchar	wchar_t	1-character string
c_byte	char	int
c_ubyte	unsigned char	int
c_short	short	int
c_ushort	unsigned short	int
c_int	int	int
c_uint	unsigned int	int
c_long	long	int
c_ulong	unsigned long	int
c_longlong	__int64 or long long	int

ctypes type	C type	Python type
c_ulonglong	unsigned __int64 or unsigned long long	int
c_size_t	size_t	int
c_ssize_t	ssize_t or Py_ssize_t	int
c_float	float	float
c_double	double	float
c_longdouble	long double	float
c_char_p	char * (NUL terminated)	bytes object or None
c_wchar_p	wchar_t * (NUL terminated)	string or None
c_void_p	void *	int or None

As you can see, the preceding table does not contain dedicated types that would reflect any of the Python collections as C arrays. The recommended way to create types for C arrays is to simply use the multiplication operator with the desired basic ctypes type:

```
>>> import ctypes
>>> IntArray5 = ctypes.c_int * 5
>>> c_int_array = IntArray5(1, 2, 3, 4, 5)
>>> FloatArray2 = ctypes.c_float * 2
>>> c_float_array = FloatArray2(0, 3.14)
>>> c_float_array[1]
3.140000104904175
```

Passing Python functions as C callbacks

It is a very popular design pattern to delegate part of the work of function implementation to custom callbacks provided by the user. The most known function from the C standard library that accepts such callbacks is a qsort() function that provides a generic implementation of the **Quicksort** algorithm. It is rather unlikely that you would like to use this algorithm instead of the default Python **Timsort** that is more suited for sorting Python collections. Anyway, qsort() seems to be a canonical example of an efficient sorting algorithm and a C API that uses the callback mechanism that is found in many programming books. This is why we will try to use it as an example of passing the Python function as a C callback.

The ordinary Python function type will not be compatible with the callback function type required by the `qsort()` specification. Here is the signature of `qsort()` from the BSD `man` page that also contains the type of accepted callback type (the `compar` argument):

```
void qsort(void *base, size_t nel, size_t width,
           int (*compar)(const void *, const void *));
```

So in order to execute `qsort()` from `libc`, you need to pass:

- `base`: This is the array that needs to be sorted as a `void*` pointer.
- `nel`: This is the number of elements as `size_t`.
- `width`: This is the size of the single element in the array as `size_t`.
- `compar`: This is the pointer to the function that is supposed to return `int` and accepts two `void*` pointers. It points to the function that compares the size of two elements being sorted.

We already know from the *Calling C functions using ctypes* section how to construct the C array from other `ctypes` types using the multiplication operator. `nel` should be `size_t`, and it maps to Python `int`, so it does not require any additional wrapping and can be passed as `len(iterable)`. The `width` value can be obtained using the `ctypes.sizeof()` function once we know the type of our `base` array. The last thing we need to know is how to create the pointer to the Python function compatible with the `compar` argument.

The `ctypes` module contains a `CFUNTYPE()` factory function that allows us to wrap Python functions and represents them as C callable function pointers. The first argument is the C return type that the wrapped function should return. It is followed by the variable list of C types that the function accepts as its arguments. The function type compatible with the `compar` argument of `qsort()` will be:

```
CMPFUNC = ctypes.CFUNCTYPE(
    # return type
    ctypes.c_int,
    # first argument type
    ctypes.POINTER(ctypes.c_int),
    # second argument type
    ctypes.POINTER(ctypes.c_int),
)
```

> CFUNTYPE() uses the cdecl calling convention, so it is compatible only with the CDLL and PyDLL shared libraries. The dynamic libraries on Windows that are loaded with WinDLL or OleDLL use the stdcall calling convention. This means that the other factory must be used to wrap Python functions as C callable function pointers. In ctypes, it is WINFUNCTYPE().

To wrap everything up, let's assume that we want to sort a randomly shuffled list of integer numbers with a qsort() function from the standard C library. Here is the example script that shows how to do that using everything that we have learned about ctypes so far:

```python
from random import shuffle

import ctypes
from ctypes.util import find_library

libc = ctypes.cdll.LoadLibrary(find_library('c'))

CMPFUNC = ctypes.CFUNCTYPE(
    # return type
    ctypes.c_int,
    # first argument type
    ctypes.POINTER(ctypes.c_int),
    # second argument type
    ctypes.POINTER(ctypes.c_int),
)

def ctypes_int_compare(a, b):
    # arguments are pointers so we access using [0] index
    print(" %s cmp %s" % (a[0], b[0]))

    # according to qsort specification this should return:
    # * less than zero if a < b
    # * zero if a == b
    # * more than zero if a > b
    return a[0] - b[0]

def main():
    numbers = list(range(5))
    shuffle(numbers)
    print("shuffled: ", numbers)
```

```
# create new type representing array with length
# same as the length of numbers list
NumbersArray = ctypes.c_int * len(numbers)
# create new C array using a new type
c_array = NumbersArray(*numbers)

libc.qsort(
    # pointer to the sorted array
    c_array,
    # length of the array
    len(c_array),
    # size of single array element
    ctypes.sizeof(ctypes.c_int),
    # callback (pointer to the C comparison function)
    CMPFUNC(ctypes_int_compare)
)
print("sorted:    ", list(c_array))


if __name__ == "__main__":
    main()
```

The comparison function provided as a callback has an additional `print` statement, so we can see how it is executed during the sorting process:

```
$ python ctypes_qsort.py
shuffled:  [4, 3, 0, 1, 2]
 4 cmp 3
 4 cmp 0
 3 cmp 0
 4 cmp 1
 3 cmp 1
 0 cmp 1
 4 cmp 2
 3 cmp 2
 1 cmp 2
sorted:    [0, 1, 2, 3, 4]
```

CFFI

CFFI is a Foreign Function Interface for Python that is an interesting alternative to `ctypes`. It is not a part of the standard library but is easily available as a `cffi` package on PyPI. It is different from `ctypes` because it puts more emphasis on reusing plain C declarations instead of providing extensive Python APIs in a single module. It is way more complex and also has a feature that also allows you to automatically compile some parts of your integration layer into extensions using C compiler. So it can be used as a hybrid solution that fills the gap between C extensions and `ctypes`.

Because it is a very large project, it is impossible to shortly introduce it in a few paragraphs. On the other hand, it would be a shame to not say something more about it. We have already discussed one example of integrating the `qsort()` function from the standard library using `ctypes`. So, the best way to show the main differences between these two solutions will be to re-implement the same example with `cffi`. I hope that one block of code is worth more than a few paragraphs of text:

```python
from random import shuffle

from cffi import FFI

ffi = FFI()

ffi.cdef("""
void qsort(void *base, size_t nel, size_t width,
        int (*compar)(const void *, const void *));
""")
C = ffi.dlopen(None)


@ffi.callback("int(void*, void*)")
def cffi_int_compare(a, b):
    # Callback signature requires exact matching of types.
    # This involves less more magic than in ctypes
    # but also makes you more specific and requires
    # explicit casting
    int_a = ffi.cast('int*', a)[0]
    int_b = ffi.cast('int*', b)[0]
    print(" %s cmp %s" % (int_a, int_b))

    # according to qsort specification this should return:
    # * less than zero if a < b
    # * zero if a == b
    # * more than zero if a > b
    return int_a - int_b


def main():
    numbers = list(range(5))
```

```
    shuffle(numbers)
    print("shuffled: ", numbers)

    c_array = ffi.new("int[]", numbers)

    C.qsort(
        # pointer to the sorted array
        c_array,
        # length of the array
        len(c_array),
        # size of single array element
        ffi.sizeof('int'),
        # callback (pointer to the C comparison function)
        cffi_int_compare,
    )
    print("sorted:   ", list(c_array))

if __name__ == "__main__":
    main()
```

Summary

This chapter explained one of the most advanced topics in the book. We discussed the reasons and tools for building Python extensions. We started from writing pure C extensions that depend only on Python/C API and then re-implemented them with Cython to show how easy it can be if you only choose the proper tool.

There are still some reasons for doing things *the hard way* and using nothing more than the pure C compiler and the Python.h headers. Anyway, the best recommendation is to use tools such as Cython or Pyrex (not featured here) because it will make your codebase more readable and maintainable. It will also save you from most of the issues caused by incautious reference counting and memory management.

Our discussion of extensions ended with the presentation of ctypes and CFFI as an alternative way to solve the problems of integrating shared libraries. Because they do not require writing custom extensions to call functions from compiled binaries, they should be your tools of choice for doing that—especially if you don't need to use custom C code.

In next chapter, we will take a short rest from low-level programming techniques and delve into topics that are no less important—code management and version control systems.

8
Managing Code

Working on a software project that involves more than one person is tough. Everything slows down and gets harder. This happens for several reasons. This chapter will expose these reasons and will try to provide some ways to fight against them.

This chapter is divided into two parts, which explain:

- How to work with a version control system
- How to set up continuous development processes

First of all, a code base evolves so much that it is important to track all the changes that are made, even more so when many developers work on it. That is the role of a **version control system**.

Next, several brains that are not directly wired together can still work on the same project. They have different roles and work on different aspects. Therefore, a lack of global visibility generates a lot of confusion about what is going on and what is being done by others. This is unavoidable, and some tools have to be used to provide continuous visibility and mitigate the problem. This is done by setting up a series of tools for continuous development processes such as **continuous integration** or **continuous delivery**.

Now we will discuss these two aspects in detail.

Version control systems

Version control systems (**VCS**) provide a way to share, synchronize, and back up any kind of file. They are categorized into two families:

- Centralized systems
- Distributed systems

Centralized systems

A centralized version control system is based on a single server that holds the files and lets people check in and check out the changes that are made to those files. The principle is quite simple—everyone can get a copy of the files on his/her system and work on them. From there, every user can *commit* his/her changes to the server. They will be applied and the *revision* number will be raised. The other users will then be able to get those changes by synchronizing their *repository* copy through an *update*.

The repository evolves through all the commits, and the system archives all revisions into a database to undo any change or provide information on what has been done:

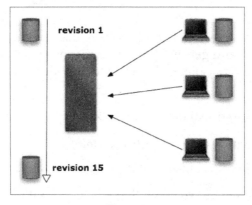

Figure 1

Every user in this centralized configuration is responsible for synchronizing his/her local repository with the main one in order to get the other user's changes. This means that some conflicts can occur when a locally modified file has been changed and checked in by someone else. A conflict resolution mechanism is carried out, in this case on the user system, as shown in the following figure:

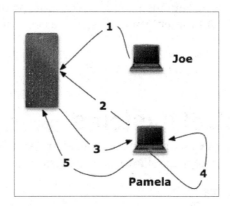

Figure 2

This will help you understand better:

1. Joe checks in a change.
2. Pamela attempts to check in a change on the same file.
3. The server complains that her copy of the file is out of date.
4. Pamela updates her local copy. The version control software may or may not be able to merge the two versions seamlessly (that is, without a conflict).
5. Pamela commits a new version that contains the latest changes made by Joe and her own.

This process is perfectly fine on small-sized projects that involve a few developers and a small number of files. But it becomes problematic for bigger projects. For instance, a complex change involves a lot of files, which is time consuming, and keeping everything local before the whole work is done is unfeasible. The problems of such approach are:

- It is dangerous because the user may keep his/her computer changes that are not necessarily backed up
- It is hard to share with others until it is checked in and sharing it before it is done would leave the repository in an unstable state, and so the other users would not want to share

Centralized VCS has resolved this problem by providing *branches* and *merges*. It is possible to fork from the main stream of revisions to work on a separated line and then to get back to the main stream.

In *Figure 3*, Joe starts a new branch from revision 2 to work on a new feature. The revisions are incremented in the main stream and in his branch every time a change is checked in. At revision 7, Joe has finished his work and commits his changes into the trunk (the main branch). This requires, most of the time, some conflict resolution.

But in spite of their advantages, centralized VCS has several pitfalls:

- Branching and merging is quite hard to deal with. It can become a nightmare.
- Since the system is centralized, it is impossible to commit changes offline. This can lead to a huge, single commit to the server when the user gets back online. Lastly, it doesn't work very well for projects such as Linux, where many companies permanently maintain their own branch of the software and there is no central repository that everyone has an account on.

For the latter, some tools are making it possible to work offline, such as SVK, but a more fundamental problem is how the centralized VCS works.

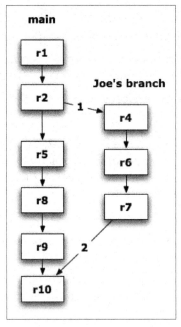

Figure 3

Despite these pitfalls, centralized VCS is still quite popular among many companies mainly due to inertia of corporate environments. The main examples of centralized VCSes used by many organizations are **Subversion (SVN)** and **Concurrent Version System (CVS)**. The obvious issues with centralized architecture for version control systems is the reason why most of the open source communities have already switched to the more reliable architecture of **Distributed VCS (DVCS)**.

Distributed systems

Distributed VCS is the answer to the centralized VCS deficiencies. It does not rely on a main server that people work with, but on peer-to-peer principles. Everyone can hold and manage his/her own independent repository for a project and synchronize it with other repositories:

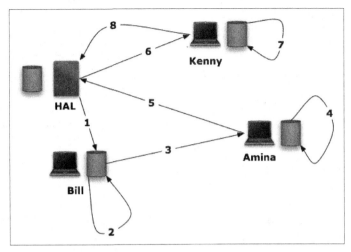

Figure 4

In *Figure 4*, we can see an example of such a system in use:

1. Bill *pulls* the files from HAL's repository.
2. Bill makes some changes on the files.
3. Amina *pulls* the files from Bill's repository.
4. Amina changes the files too.
5. Amina *pushes* the changes to HAL.
6. Kenny *pulls* the files from HAL.
7. Kenny makes changes.
8. Kenny regularly *pushes* his changes to HAL.

The key concept is that people *push* and *pull* the files to or from other repositories, and this behavior changes according to the way people work and the way the project is managed. Since there is no main repository anymore, the maintainer of the project needs to define a strategy for people to *push* and *pull* the changes.

Furthermore, people have to be a bit smarter when they work with several repositories. In most distributed version control systems, revision numbers are local to each repository, and there are no global revision numbers anyone can refer to. Therefore, *tags* have to be used to make things clearer. They are textual labels that can be attached to a revision. Lastly, users are responsible for backing up their own repositories, which is not the case in a centralized infrastructure where the administrator usually sets back up strategies.

Distributed strategies

A central server is, of course, still desirable with a DVCS if you're working in a company setting with everyone working toward the same goal. But the purpose of that server is completely different than in centralized VCS. It is simply a hub that allows all developers to share their changes in a single place rather than pull and push between each other's repositories. Such a single central repository (often called *upstream*) serves also as a backup for all the changes tracked in the individual repositories of all team members.

Different approaches can be applied to sharing code with the central repository in DVCS. The simplest one is to set up a server that acts like a regular centralized server, where every member of the project can push his/her changes into a common stream. But this approach is a bit simplistic. It does not take full advantage of the distributed system, since people will use push and pull commands in the same way as they would with a centralized system.

Another approach consists of providing several repositories on a server with different levels of access:

- An **unstable repository** is where everyone can push changes.

- A **stable repository** is read-only for all members except the release managers. They are allowed to pull changes from the unstable repository and decide what should be merged.

- Various **release repositories** correspond to the releases and are read-only, as we will see later in the chapter.

This allows people to contribute, and managers to review, the changes before they make it to the stable repository. Anyway, depending on the tools used, this may be too much of an overhead. In many distributed version control systems, this can also be handled with a proper branching strategy.

The other strategies can be made up, since DVCS provides infinite combinations. For instance, the Linux Kernel, which is using Git (http://git-scm.com/), is based on a star model, where Linus Torvalds is maintaining the official repository and pulls the changes from a set of developers he trusts. In this model, people who wish to push changes to the kernel will, hopefully, try to push them to the trusted developers so that they reach Linus through them.

Centralized or distributed?

Just forget about the centralized version control systems.

Let's be honest. Centralized version control systems are relict of the past. In a time when most of us have the opportunity to work remotely full-time, it is unreasonable to be constrained by all the deficiencies of centralized VCS. For instance, with CVS or SVN you can't track the changes when offline. And that's silly. What should you do when the Internet connection at your workplace is temporarily broken or the central repository goes down? Should you forget about all your workflow and just allow changes to pile up until the situation changes and then just commit it as a one huge blob of unstructured updates? No!

Also, most of the centralized version control systems do not handle branching schemes efficiently. And branching is a very useful technique that allows you to limit the number of merge conflicts in the projects where many people work on multiple features. Branching in SVN is so ridiculous that most of the developers try to avoid it at all costs. Instead, most of the centralized VCS provides some file-locking primitives that should be considered the anti-pattern for any version control system. The sad truth about every version control tool is that if it contains a dangerous option, someone in your team will start using it on a daily basis eventually. And locking is one such feature that in return of fewer merge conflicts will drastically reduce the productivity of your whole team. By choosing a version control system that does not allow for such bad workflows, you are making a situation, which makes it more likely that your developers will use it effectively.

Use Git if you can

Git is currently the most popular distributed version control system. It was created by Linus Torvalds for maintaining versions of the Linux kernel when its core developers needed to resign from proprietary BitKeeper that was used previously.

If you have not used any of the version control systems then you should start with Git from the beginning. If you already use some other tools for version control, learn Git anyway. You should definitely do that even if your organization is unwilling to switch to Git in the near future, otherwise you risk becoming a living fossil.

I'm not saying that Git is the ultimate and best DVCS version control system. It surely has some disadvantages. Most of all, it is not an easy-to-use tool and is very challenging for newcomers. Git's steep learning curve is already a source of many jokes online. There may be some version control systems that may perform better for a lot of projects and the full list of open source Git contenders would be quite long. Anyway, Git is currently the most popular DVCS, so the *network effect* really works in its favor.

Briefly speaking, the network effect causes that the overall benefit of using popular tools is greater than using others, even if slightly better, precisely due to its high popularity (this is how VHS killed Betamax). It is very probable that people in your organization, as well as new hires, are somewhat proficient with Git, so the cost of integrating exactly this DVCS will be lower than trying something less popular.

Anyway, it is still always good to know something more and familiarizing yourself with other DVCS won't hurt you. The most popular open source rivals of Git are Mercurial, Bazaar, and Fossil. The first one is especially neat because it is written in Python and was the official version control system for CPython sources. There are some signs that it may change in the near future, so CPython developers may already use Git by the time you read this book. But it really does not matter. Both systems are great. If there would be no Git, or it were less popular, I would definitely recommend Mercurial. There is evident beauty in its design. It's definitely not as powerful as Git, but a lot easier to master for beginners.

Git flow and GitHub flow

The very popular and standardized methodology for working with Git is simply called **Git flow**. Here is the brief description of the main rules of that flow:

- There is a main working branch, usually called `develop`, where all the developments for the latest version of the application occurs.

- New project features are implemented in separate branches called *feature branches* that always start from the `develop` branch. When work on a feature is finished and the code is properly tested, this branch is merged back to `develop`.

- When the code in `develop` is stabilized (without known bugs) and there is a need for new application release, a new *release branch* is created. This release branch usually requires additional tests (extensive QA tests, integration tests, and so on) so new bugs will be definitely found. If additional changes (such as bug fixes) are included in a release branch, they need to eventually be merged back to the `develop` branch.

- When code on a *release branch* is ready to be deployed/released, it is merged to the `master` branch and the latest commit on the `master` is labeled with an appropriate version tag. No other branches but `release` branches can be merged to the `master`. The only exceptions are hot fixes that need to be immediately deployed or released.

- Hot fixes that require urgent release are always implemented on separate branches that start from the `master`. When the fix is done, it is merged to both the `develop` and `master` branches. Merging of the hot fix branch is done like it were an ordinary release branch, so it must be properly tagged and the application version identifier should be modified accordingly.

The visual example of *Git flow* in action is presented in *Figure 5*. For those that have never worked in such a way, and have also never used distributed version control systems, this may be a bit overwhelming. Anyway, it is really worth trying in your organization if you don't have any formalized workflow. It has multiple benefits and also solves real problems. It is especially useful for teams of multiple programmers that are working on many separate features and when continuous support for multiple releases needs to be provided.

This methodology is also handy if you want to implement continuous delivery using continuous deployment processes because it is always clear in your organization and which version of code represents a deliverable release of your application or service. It is also a great tool for open source projects because it provides great transparency to both the users and the active contributors.

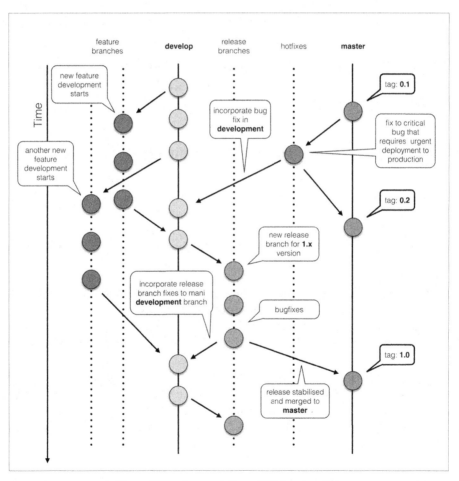

Figure 5 Visual presentation of Git flow in action

So, if you think that this short summary of *Git flow* makes a bit of sense and it did not scare you yet, then you should dig deeper into online resources on that topic. It is really hard to say who the original author of the preceding workflow is, but most online sources point to Vincent Driessen. Thus, the best starting material to learn about *Git flow* is his online article titled *A successful Git branching model* (refer to `http://nvie.com/posts/a-successful-git-branching-model/`).

Like every other popular methodology, *Git flow* gained a lot of criticism over the Internet from programmers that do not like it. The most commented thing about Vincent Driessen's article is the rule (strictly technical) saying that every merge should create a new artificial commit representing that merge. Git has an option to do *fast forward* merges and Vincent discourages that option. This is, of course, an unsolvable problem because the best way to perform merges is a completely subjective matter to the organization Git is being used in. Anyway, the real issue of *Git flow* is that it is noticeably complicated. The full set of rules is really long, so it is easy to make some mistakes. It is very probable that you would like to choose something simpler.

One such flow is used at GitHub and described by Scott Chacon on his blog (refer to `http://scottchacon.com/2011/08/31/github-flow.html`). It is referred to as **GitHub flow** and is very similar to *Git flow*:

- Anything in the master branch is deployable
- The new features are implemented on separate branches

The main difference from *Git flow* is simplicity. There is only one main development branch (`master`) and it is always stable (in contrast to the `develop` branch in *Git flow*). There are also no release branches and a big emphasis is placed on tagging the code. There is no such need at GitHub because, as they say, when something is merged into the master it is usually deployed to production immediately. Diagram presenting an example of GitHub flow in action is shown in *Figure 6*.

GitHub flow seems like a good and lightweight workflow for teams that want to have a continuous deployment process setup for their project. Such a workflow is, of course, not viable for any project that has a strong notion of release (with strict version numbers)—at least without any modifications. It is important to know that the main assumption of the *always deployable* `master` branch is that it cannot be ensured without proper automated testing and a building procedure. This is what continuous integration systems take care of and we will discuss that a bit later. The following is a diagram presenting an example of GitHub flow in action:

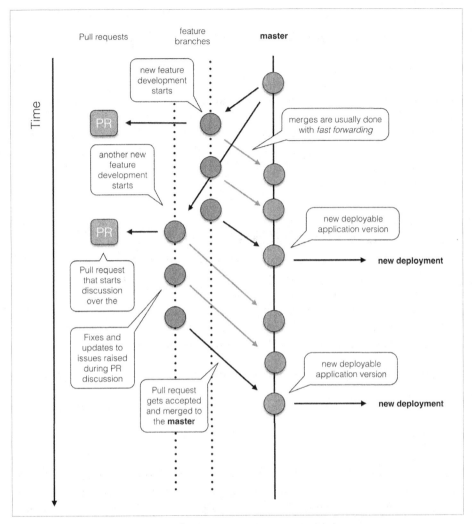

Figure 6 Visual presentation of GitHub flow in action

Note that both *Git flow* and *GitHub flow* are only branching strategies, so despite having *Git* in their names, they are not limited to that single DVCS solution. It's true that the official article describing *Git flow* mentions specific `git` command parameters that should be used when performing a merge, but the general idea can be easily applied to almost any other distributed version control system. In fact, due to the way it is suggested to handle merges, Mercurial seems like a better tool to use for this specific branching strategy! The same applies to *GitHub flow*. This is the only branching strategy sprinkled with a bit of specific development culture, so it can be used in any version control system that allows you to easily create and merge branches of code.

As a last comment, remember that no methodology is carved in stone and no one forces you to use it. They are created to solve some existing problems and keep you from making common mistakes. You can take all of their rules or modify some of them to your own needs. They are great tools for beginners that may easily get into common pitfalls. If you are not familiar with any version control system, you should then start with a lightweight methodology like *GitHub flow* without any custom modification. You should start thinking about more complex workflows only when you get enough experience with Git, or any other tool of your choice. Anyway, as you will gain more and more proficiency, you will eventually realize that there is no perfect workflow that suits every project. What works well in one organization does not need to work well in others.

Continuous development processes

There are some processes that can greatly streamline your development and reduce a time in getting the application ready to be released or deployed to the production environment. They often have `continuous` in their name, and we will discuss the most important and popular ones in this section. It is important to highlight that they are strictly technical processes, so they are almost unrelated to project management technologies, although they can highly dovetail with the latter.

The most important processes we will mention are:

- Continuous integration
- Continuous delivery
- Continuous deployment

The order of listing is important because each one of them is an extension of the previous one. Continuous deployment could be simply considered even a variation of continuous delivery. We will discuss them separately anyway, because what is only a minor difference for one organization may be critical in others.

The fact that these are technical processes means that their implementation strictly depends on the usage of proper tools. The general idea behind each of them is rather simple, so you could build your own continuous integration/delivery/deployment tools, but the best approach is to choose something that is already built. This way, you can focus more on building your product instead of the tool chain for continuous development.

Continuous integration

Continuous integration, often abbreviated as **CI**, is a process that takes benefit from automated testing and version control systems to provide a fully automatic integration environment. It can be used with centralized version control systems but in practice it spreads its wings only when a good DVCS tool is being used to manage the code.

Setting up a repository is the first step towards continuous integration, which is a set of software practices that have emerged from **eXtreme Programming** (**XP**). The principles are clearly described on Wikipedia (`http://en.wikipedia.org/wiki/ Continuous_integration#The_Practices`) and define a way to make sure the software is easy to build, test, and deliver.

The first and most important requirement to implement continuous integration is to have a fully automated workflow that can test the whole application in the given revision in order to decide if it is technically correct. Technically correct means that it is free of known bugs and that all the features work as expected.

The general idea behind CI is that tests should always be run before merging to the mainstream development branch. This could be handled only through formal arrangements in the development team, but practice shows that this is not a reliable approach. The problem is that, as programmers, we tend to be overconfident and are unable to look critically at our code. If continuous integration is built only on team arrangements, it will inevitably fail because some of the developers will eventually skip their testing phase and commit possibly faulty code to the mainstream development branch that should always remain stable. And, in reality, even simple changes can introduce critical issues.

The obvious solution is to utilize a dedicated build server that automatically runs all the required application tests whenever the codebase changes. There are many tools that streamline this process and they can be easily integrated with version control hosting services such as GitHub or Bitbucket and self-hosted services such as GitLab. The benefit of using such tools is that the developer may locally run only the selected subset of tests (that, according to him, are related to his current work) and leave a potentially time consuming whole suite of integration tests for the build server. This really speeds up the development but still reduces the risk that new features will break the existing stable code found in the mainstream code branch.

Another plus of using a dedicated build server is that tests can be run in the environment that is closer to the production. Developers should also use environments that match the production as closely as possible and there are great tools for that (Vagrant, for instance); it is, however, hard to enforce this in any organization. You can easily do that on one dedicated build server or even on a cluster of build servers. Many CI tools make that even less problematic by utilizing various virtualization tools that help to ensure that tests are run always in the same, and completely fresh, testing environment.

Having a build server is also a must if you create desktop or mobile applications that must be delivered to users in binary form. The obvious thing to do is to always perform such a building procedure in the same environment. Almost every CI system takes into account the fact that applications often need to be downloaded in binary form after testing/building is done. Such building results are commonly referred to as **build artifacts**.

Because CI tools originated in times where most of the applications were written in compiled languages, they mostly use the term "building" to describe their main activity. For languages such as C or C++, this is obvious because applications cannot be run and tested if it is not built (compiled). For Python, this makes a bit less sense because most of the programs are distributed in a source form and can be run without any additional building step. So, in the scope of our language, the *building* and *testing* terms are often used interchangeably when talking about continuous integration.

Testing every commit

The best approach to continuous integration is to perform the whole test suite on every change pushed to the central repository. Even if one programmer pushed a series of multiple commits in a single branch, it very often makes sense to test each change separately. If you decide to test only the latest changeset in a single repository push, then it will be harder to find sources of possible regression problems introduced somewhere in the middle.

Of course, many DVCS such as Git or Mercurial allow you to limit time spent on searching regression sources by providing commands to *bisect* the history of changes, but in practice it is much more convenient to do that automatically as part of your continuous integration process.

Of course there is the issue of projects that have very long running test suites that may require tens of minutes or even hours to complete. One server may be not enough to perform all the builds on every commit made in the given time frame. This will make waiting for results even longer. In fact, long running tests is a problem on its own that will be described later in the *Problem 2 – too long building time* section. For now, you should know that you should always strive to test every commit pushed to the repository. If you have no power to do that on a single server, then set up the whole building cluster. If you are using a paid service, then pay for a higher pricing plan with more parallel builds. Hardware is cheap. Your developers' time is not. Eventually, you will save more money by having faster parallel builds and a more expensive CI setup than you would save on skipping tests for selected changes.

Merge testing through CI

Reality is complicated. If the code on a feature branch passes all the tests, it does not mean that the build will not fail when it is merged to a stable mainstream branch. Both of the popular branching strategies mentioned in the *Git flow and GitHub flow* sections assume that code merged to the master branch is always tested and deployable. But how can you be sure that this assumption is met if you have not perform the merge yet? This is a lesser problem for *Git flow* (if implemented well and used precisely) due to its emphasis on release branches. But it is a real problem for the simple *GitHub flow* where merging to master is often related with conflicts and is very likely to introduce regressions in tests. Even for *Git flow*, this is a serious concern. This is a complex branching model, so for sure people will make mistakes when using it. So, you can never be sure that the code on master will pass the tests after merging if you won't take the special precautions.

One of the solutions to this problem is to delegate the duty of merging feature branches into a stable mainstream branch to your CI system. In many CI tools, you can easily set up an on-demand building job that will locally merge a specific feature branch to the stable branch and push it to the central repository only if it passed all the tests. If the build fails, then such a merge will be reverted, leaving the stable branch untouched. Of course, this approach gets more complex in fast paced projects where many feature branches are developed simultaneously because there is a high risk of conflicts that can't be resolved automatically by any CI system. There are, of course, solutions to that problem, like rebasing in Git.

Such an approach to merging anything into the stable branch in a version control system is practically a must if you are thinking about going further and implementing continuous delivery processes. It is also required if you have a strict rule in your workflow stating that everything in a stable branch is releasable.

Matrix testing

Matrix testing is a very useful tool if your code needs to be tested in different environments. Depending on your project needs, the direct support of such a feature in your CI solution may be less or more required.

The easiest way to explain the idea of matrix testing is to take the example of some open source Python package. Django, for instance, is the project that has a strictly specified set of supported Python language versions. The 1.9.3 version lists the Python 2.7, Python 3.4, and Python 3.5 versions as required in order to run Django code. This means that every time Django core developers make a change to the project, the full tests suite must be executed on these three Python versions in order to back this claim. If even a single test fails on one environment, the whole build must be marked as failed because the backwards compatibility constraint was possibly broken. For such a simple case, you do not need any support from CI. There is a great Tox tool (refer to `https://tox.readthedocs.org/`) that, among other features, allows you to easily run test suites in different Python versions in isolated virtual environments. This utility can also be easily used in local development.

But this was only the simplest example. It is not uncommon that the application must be tested in multiple environments where completely different parameters must be tested. To name a few:

- Different operating systems
- Different databases
- Different versions of backing services
- Different types of filesystems

The full set of combinations forms a multi-dimensional environment parameter matrix, and this is why such a setup is called matrix testing. When you need such a deep testing workflow, it is very possible that you require some integrated support for matrix testing in your CI solution. With a large number of possible combinations, you will also require a highly parallelizable building process because every run over the matrix will require a large amount of work from your building server. In some cases, you will be forced to do some tradeoff if your test matrix has too many dimensions.

Continuous delivery

Continuous delivery is a simple extension of the continuous integration idea. This approach to software engineering aims to ensure that the application can be released reliably at any time. The goal of continuous delivery is to release software in short circles. It generally reduces both costs and the risk of releasing software by allowing the incremental delivery of changes to the application in production.

The main prerequisites for building successful continuous delivery processes are:

- A reliable continuous integration process
- An automated process of deployment to the production environment (if the project has a notion of the production environment)
- A well-defined version control system workflow or branching strategy that allows you to easily define what version of software represents releasable code

In many projects, the automated tests are not enough to reliably tell if the given version of the software is really ready to be released. In such cases, the additional manual user acceptance tests are usually performed by skilled QA staff. Depending on your project management methodology, this may also require some approval from the client. This does not mean that you can't use *Git flow*, *GitHub flow*, or a similar branching strategy, if some of your acceptance tests must be performed manually by humans. This only changes the semantics of your stable and release branches from *ready to be deployed* to *ready for user acceptance tests and approval*.

Also, the previous paragraph does not change the fact that code deployment should always be automated. We already discussed some of the tools and benefits of automation in *Chapter 6*, *Deploying Code*. As stated there, it will always reduce the cost and risk of a new release. Also, most of the available CI tools allow you to set up special build targets that, instead of testing, will perform automated deployment for you. In most continuous delivery processes, this is usually triggered manually (on demand) by authorized staff members when they are sure there is required approval and all acceptance tests ended with success.

Continuous deployment

Continuous deployment is a process that takes continuous delivery to the next level. It is a perfect approach for projects where all acceptance tests are automated and there is no need for manual approval from the client. In short, once code is merged to the stable branch (usually `master`), it is automatically deployed to the production environment.

This approach seems to be very nice and robust but is not often used because it is very hard to find a project that does not need manual QA testing and someone's approval before a new version is released. Anyway, it is definitely doable and some companies claim to be working in that way.

In order to implement continuous deployment, you need the same basic prerequisites as the continuous delivery process. Also, a more careful approach to merging into a stable branch is very often required. What gets merged into the `master` in continuous integration usually goes instantly to the production. Because of that, it is reasonable to handoff the merging task to your CI system, as explained in the *Merge testing through CI* section.

Popular tools for continuous integration

There is a tremendous variety of choices for CI tools nowadays. They greatly vary on ease of use and available features, and almost each one of them has some unique features that others will lack. So, it is hard to give a good general recommendation because each project has completely different needs and also a different development workflow. There are, of course, some great free and open source projects, but paid hosted services are also worth researching. It's because although open source software such as Jenkins or Buildbot are freely available to install without any fee, it is false thinking that they are free to run. Both hardware and maintenance are added costs of having your own CI system. In some circumstances, it may be less expensive to pay for such a service instead of paying for additional infrastructure and spending time on resolving any issues in open source CI software. Still, you need to make sure that sending your code to any third-party service is in line with security policies at your company.

Here we will review some of the popular free open source tools, as well as paid hosted services. I really don't want to advertise any vendor, so we will discuss only those that are available without any fees for open source projects to justify this rather subjective selection. No best recommendation will be given, but we will point out both the good and bad sides of any solution. If you are still in doubt, the next section that describes common continuous integration pitfalls should help you in making good decisions.

Jenkins

Jenkins (`https://jenkins-ci.org`) seems to be the most popular tool for continuous integration. It is also one of the oldest open source projects in this field, in pair with Hudson (the development of these two projects split and Jenkins is a fork of Hudson).

Figure 7 Preview of Jenkins main interface

Jenkins is written in Java and was initially designed mainly for building projects written in the Java language. It means that for Java developers, it is a perfect CI system, but you will need to struggle a bit if you want to use it with other technology stack.

One big advantage of Jenkins is its very extensive list of features that Jenkins have implemented straight out of the box. The most important one, from the Python programmer's point of view, is the ability to understand test results. Instead of giving only plain binary information about build success, Jenkins is able to present the results of all tests that were executed during a run in the form of tables and graphs. This will, of course, not work automatically and you need to provide those results in a specific format (by default, Jenkins understands JUnit files) during your build. Fortunately, a lot of Python testing frameworks are able to export results in a machine-readable format.

The following is an example presentation of unit test results in Jenkins in its web UI:

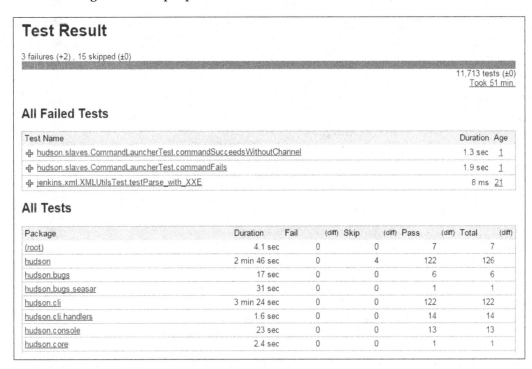

Test Result

3 failures (+2) , 15 skipped (±0)

11,713 tests (±0)
Took 51 min.

All Failed Tests

Test Name	Duration	Age
⊹ hudson.slaves.CommandLauncherTest.commandSucceedsWithoutChannel	1.3 sec	1
⊹ hudson.slaves.CommandLauncherTest.commandFails	1.9 sec	1
⊹ jenkins.xml.XMLUtilsTest.testParse_with_XXE	8 ms	21

All Tests

Package	Duration	Fail	(diff)	Skip	(diff)	Pass	(diff)	Total	(diff)
(root)	4.1 sec	0		0		7		7	
hudson	2 min 46 sec	0		4		122		126	
hudson.bugs	17 sec	0		0		6		6	
hudson.bugs.seasar	31 sec	0		0		1		1	
hudson.cli	3 min 24 sec	0		0		122		122	
hudson.cli.handlers	1.6 sec	0		0		14		14	
hudson.console	23 sec	0		0		13		13	
hudson.core	2.4 sec	0		0		1		1	

Figure 8 Presentation of unit test results in Jenkins

The following screenshot illustrates how Jenkins presents additional build information such as trends or downloadable artifacts:

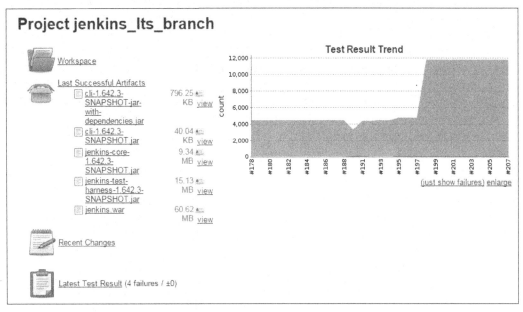

Figure 9 Test result trends graph on example Jenkins project

Surprisingly, most of Jenkins' power does not come from its built-in features but from a huge repository of free plugins. What is available from clean installation may be great for Java developers but programmers using different technologies will need to spend a lot of time to make it suited for their project. Even support for Git is provided by some plugin.

It is great that Jenkins is so easily extendable, but this has also some serious downsides. You will eventually depend on installed plugins to drive your continuous integration process and these are developed independently from Jenkins core. Most authors of popular plugins try to keep them up to date and compatible with the latest releases of Jenkins. Nevertheless, the extensions with smaller communities will be updated less frequently, and some day you may be either forced to resign from them or postpone the update of the core system. This may be a real problem when there is urgent need for an update (security fix, for instance), but some of the plugins that are critical for your CI process will not work with the new version.

The basic Jenkins installation that provides you with a master CI server is also capable of performing builds. This is different from other CI systems that put more emphasis on distribution and create a strict separation from master and slave build servers. This is both good and bad. On the one side, it allows you to set up a wholly working CI server in a few minutes. Jenkins, of course, supports deferring work to build slaves, so you can scale out in future whenever it is needed. On the other hand, it is very common that Jenkins is underperforming because it is deployed in single-server settings, and its users complain regarding performance without providing it enough resources. It is not hard to add new building nodes to the Jenkins cluster. It seems that this is rather a mental challenge than a technical problem for those that got used to the single-server setup.

Buildbot

Buildbot (`http://buildbot.net/`) is a software written in Python that automates the compile and test cycles for any kind of software project. It is configurable in a way that every change made on a source code repository generates some builds and launches some tests and then provides some feedback:

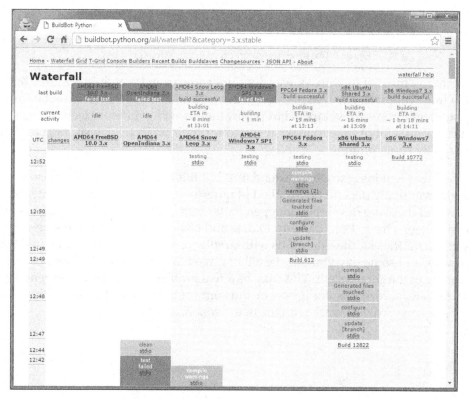

Figure 10 Buildbot's Waterfall view for CPython 3.x branch

This tool is used, for instance, by CPython core and can be seen at
`http://buildbot.python.org/all/waterfall?&category=3.x.stable`.

The default Buildbot's representation of build results is a Waterfall view, as shown in *Figure 10*. Each column corresponds to a **build** composed of **steps** and is associated with some **build slaves**. The whole system is driven by the build master:

- The build master centralizes and drives everything
- A build is a sequence of steps used to build an application and run tests over it
- A **step** is an atomic command, for example:
  - Check out the files of a project
  - Build the application
  - Run tests

A build slave is a machine that is in charge of running a build. It can be located anywhere as long as it can reach the build master. Thanks to this architecture, Buildbot scales very well. All of heavy lifting is done on build slaves and you can have as many of them as you want.

Very simple and clear design makes Buildbot very flexible. Each build step is just a single command. Buildbot is written in Python but it is completely language agnostic. So the build step can be absolutely anything. The process exit code is used to decide if the step ended as a success and all standard output of the step command is captured by default. Most of the testing tools and compilers follow good design practices, and they indicate failures with proper exit codes and return readable error/warning messages on `sdout` or `stderr` output streams. If it's not true, you can usually easily wrap them with a Bash script. In most cases, this is a simple task. Thanks to this, a lot of projects can be integrated with Buildbot with only minimal effort.

The next advantage of Buildbot is that it supports many version control systems out of the box without the need to install any additional plugins:

- CVS
- Subversion
- Perforce
- Bzr
- Darcs
- Git
- Mercurial
- Monotone

The main disadvantage of Buildbot is its lack of higher-level presentation tools for presenting build results. For instance, other projects, such as Jenkins, can take the notion of unit tests run during the build. If you feed them with test results data presented in the proper format (usually XML), they can present all the tests in a readable form like tables and graphs. Buildbot does not have such a built-in feature and this is the price it pays for its flexibility and simplicity. If you need some extra bells and whistles, you need to build them by yourself or search for some custom extension. On the other hand, thanks to such simplicity, it is easier to reason about Buildbot's behavior and maintain it. So, there is always a tradeoff.

Travis CI

Travis CI (`https://travis-ci.org/`) is a continuous integration system sold in Software as a Service form. It is a paid service for enterprises but can be used completely for free in open source projects hosted on GitHub.

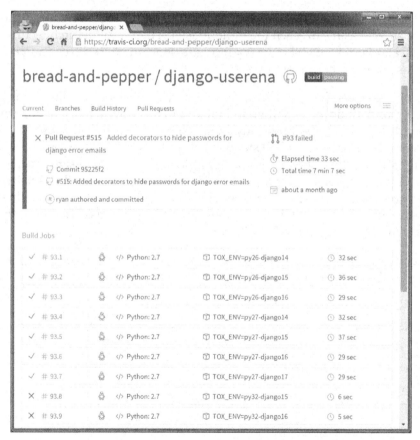

Figure 11 Travis CI page for django-userena project showing failed builds in its build matrix

Naturally, this is the free part of its pricing plan that made it very popular. Currently, it is one of the most popular CI solutions for projects hosted on GitHub. But the biggest advantage over older projects such as Buildbot or Jenkins, is how the build configuration is stored. All build definition is provided in a single `.travis.yml` file in the root of the project repository. Travis works only with GitHub, so if you have enabled such integration, your project will be tested on every commit if there is only a `.travis.yml` file.

Having the whole CI configuration for a project in its code repository is really a great approach. This makes the whole process a lot clearer for the developers and also allows for more flexibility. In systems where build configuration must be provided to build a server separately (using web interface or through server configuration), there is always some additional friction when something new needs to be added to the testing rig. In some organizations, where only selected staff are authorized to maintain the CI system, this really slows the process of adding new build steps down. Also, sometimes there is a need to test different branches of the code with completely different procedures. When build configuration is available in project sources, it is a lot easier to do so.

The other great feature of Travis is the emphasis it puts on running builds in clean environments. Every build is executed in a completely fresh virtual machine, so there is no risk of some persisted state that would affect build results. Travis uses a rather big virtual machine image, so you have a lot of open source software and programming environments available without the need of additional installs. In this isolated environment, you have full administrative rights so you can download and install anything you need to perform your build and the syntax of the `.travis.yml` file makes it very easy. Unfortunately, you do not have a lot of choice over the operating system available as the base of your testing environment. Travis does not allow to provide your own virtual machine images, so you must rely on the very limited options provided. Usually there is no choice at all and all the builds must be done in some version of Ubuntu or Mac OS X (still experimental at the time of writing the book). Sometimes there is an option to select some legacy version of the system or the preview of the new testing environment, but such a possibility is always temporary. There is always a way to bypass this. You can run another virtual machine inside of the one provided by Travis. This should be something that allows you to easily encode VM configuration in your project sources such as Vagrant or Docker. But this will add more time to your builds, so it is not the best approach you will take. Stacking virtual machines that way may not be the best and most efficient approach if you need to perform tests under different operating systems. If this is an important feature for you, then this is a sign that Travis is not a service for you.

The biggest downside of Travis is that it is completely locked to GitHub. If you would like to use it in your open source project, then this is not a big deal. For enterprises and closed source projects, this is mostly an unsolvable issue.

GitLab CI

GitLab CI is a part of a larger GitLab project. It is available as both a paid service (Enterprise Edition) and an open source project that you may host on your own infrastructure (Community Edition). The open source edition lacks some of the paid service features, but in most cases is everything that any company needs from the software that manages version control repositories and continuous integration.

GitLab CI is very similar in feature sets to the Travis. It is even configured with a very similar YAML syntax stored in the `.gitlab-ci.yml` file. The biggest difference is that the GitLab Enterprise Edition pricing model does not provide you with free accounts for open source projects. The Community Edition is open source by itself but you need to have some own infrastructure in order to run it.

When compared with Travis, the GitLab has an obvious advantage of having more control over the execution environment. Unfortunately, in the area of environment isolation, the default build runner in GitLab is a bit inferior. The process called Gitlab Runner executes all the build steps in the same environment it is run in, so it works more like Jenkins' or Buildbot's slave servers. Fortunately, it plays well with Docker, so you can easily add more isolation with container-based virtualization, but this will require some effort and additional setup. In Travis, you get full isolation out of the box.

Choosing the right tool and common pitfalls

As already said, there is no perfect CI tool that will suit every project and, most importantly, every organization and workflow it uses. I can give only a single suggestion for open source projects hosted on GitHub. For small code bases with platform independent code, **Travis CI** seems like the best choice. It is easy to start with and will give you almost instant gratification with a minimal amount of work.

For projects with closed sources, the situation is completely different. It is possible that you will need to evaluate a few CI systems in various setups until you are able decide which one is best for you. We discussed only four of the popular tools but it should be a rather representative group. To make your decision a bit easier, we will discuss some of the common problems related to continuous integration systems. In some of the available CI systems, it is more possible to make certain kinds of mistakes than in others. On the other hand, some of the problems may not be important to every application. I hope that by combining the knowledge of your needs with this short summary, it will be easier to make your first decision the right one.

Problem 1 – too complex build strategies

Some organizations like to formalize and structure things beyond the reasonable levels. In companies that create computer software, this is especially true in two areas: project management tools and build strategies on CI servers.

Excessive configuration of project management tools usually ends with issue processing workflows on JIRA (or any other management software) so complicated that they will never fit a single wall when expressed as graphs. If your manager has such configuration/control mania, you can either talk to him or switch him for another manager (read: quit your current job). Unfortunately, this does not reliably ensure any improvement in that matter.

But when it comes to CI, we can do more. Continuous integration tools are usually maintained and configured by us: developers. These are OUR tools that are supposed to improve OUR work. If someone has irresistible temptation to toggle every switch and turn every knob possible, then he should be kept away from configuration of CI systems, especially if his main job is to talk the whole day and make decisions.

There is really no need for making complex strategies to decide which commit or branch should be tested. No need to limit testing to specific tags. No need to queue commits in order to perform larger builds. No need to disable building via custom commit messages. Your continuous integration process should be simple to reason about. Test everything! Test always! That's all! If there are not enough hardware resources to test every commit, then add more hardware. Remember that the programmer's time is more expensive than silicon chips.

Problem 2 – too long building time

Long building times is a thing that kills performance of any developer. If you need to wait hours to know if your work was done properly, then there is no way you can be productive. Of course, having something else to do when your feature is being tested helps a lot. Anyway, as humans, we are really terrible at multitasking. Switching between different problems takes time and, in the end, reduces our programming performance to zero. It's simply hard to keep focus when working on multiple problems at once.

The solution is very simple: keep your builds fast at any price. At first, try to find bottlenecks and optimize them. If the performance of build servers is the problem, then try to scale out. If this does not help, then split each build into smaller parts and parallelize.

There are plenty of solutions to speed up slow build tests, but sometimes nothing can be done about that problem. For instance, if you have automated browser tests or need to perform long running calls to external services, then it is very hard to improve performance beyond some hard limit. For instance, when speed of automated acceptance test in your CI becomes a problem, then you can loosen the *test everything, test always* rule a bit. What matters the most for programmers are usually unit tests and static analysis. So, depending on your workflow, the slow browser tests may be sometimes deferred in time to the moment when release is being prepared.

The other solution to slow build runs is rethinking the overall architecture design of your application. If testing the application takes a lot of time, it is very often a sign that it should be split into a few independent components that can be developed and tested separately. Writing software as huge monoliths is one of the shortest paths to failure. Usually any software engineering process breaks on software that is not modularized properly.

Problem 3 – external job definitions

Some continuous integration systems, especially Jenkins, allow you to set up most of the build configurations and testing processes completely through web UI, without the need to touch the code repository. But you should really avoid putting anything more than simple entry points to the build steps/commands into externals systems. This is the kind of CI anti-pattern that can cause nothing more than troubles.

Your building and testing process is usually tightly tied to your codebase. If you store its whole definition in external system such as Jenkins or Buildbot, then it will be really hard to introduce changes to that process.

As an example of a problem introduced by global external build definition, let's assume that we have some open source project. The initial development was hectic and we did not care for any style guidelines. Our project was successful, so the development required another major release. After some time, we moved from 0.x version to 1.0 and decided to reformat all of your code to conform to PEP 8 guidelines. It is a good approach to have a static analysis check as part of CI builds, so we decided to add the execution of the pep8 tool to our build definition. If we had only a global external build configuration, then there would be a problem if some improvement needs to be done to the code in older versions. Let's say that there is a critical security issue that needs to be fixed in both branches of the application: 0.x and 1.y. We know that anything below version 1.0 wasn't compliant with the style guide and the newly introduced check against PEP 8 will mark the build as failed.

The solution to the problem is to keep the definition of your build process as close to the source as possible. With some CI systems (Travis CI and GitLab CI), you get that workflow by default. With other solutions (Jenkins and Buildbot) you need to take additional care in order to ensure that most of the build processes are included in your code instead of some external tool configuration. Fortunately, you have a lot of choices that allow that kind of automation:

- Bash scripts
- Makefiles
- Python code

Problem 4 – lack of isolation

We have discussed the importance of isolation when programming in Python many times already. We know that the best approach to isolate Python execution environment on the package level is to use virtual environments with `virtualenv` or `python -m venv`. Unfortunately, when testing code for the purpose of continuous integration processes, it is usually not enough. The testing environment should be as close as possible to the production environment and it is really hard to achieve that without additional system-level virtualization.

The main issues you may experience when not ensuring proper system-level isolation when building your application are:

- Some state persisted between builds either on the filesystem or in backing services (caches, databases, and so on)
- Multiple builds or tests interfacing with each other through the environment, filesystem or backing services
- Problems that would occur due to specific characteristics of the production operating system not caught on the build server

The preceding issues are particularly troublesome if you need to perform concurrent builds of the same application or even parallelize single builds.

Some Python frameworks (mostly Django) provide some additional level of isolation for databases that try to ensure the storage will be cleaned before running tests. There is also quite a useful extension for `py.test` called `pytest-dbfixtures` (refer to `https://github.com/ClearcodeHQ/pytest-dbfixtures`) that allows you to achieve that even more reliably. Anyway, such solutions add even more complexity to your builds instead of reducing it. Always clearing the virtual machine on every build (in the style of Travis CI) seems like a more elegant and simpler approach.

Summary

We have learned the following things in this chapter:

- What is the difference between centralized and distributed version control systems
- Why you should prefer distributed version control systems over centralized
- Why Git should be your first choice for DVCS
- What are the common workflows and branching strategies for Git
- What is continuous integration/delivery/deployment and what are the popular tools that allow you to implement these processes

The next chapter will explain how to clearly document your code.

9
Documenting Your Project

Documentation is the work that is often neglected by developers and sometimes by managers. This is often due to a lack of time towards the end of development cycles, and the fact that people think they are bad at writing. Some of them are bad indeed, but the majority of them are able to produce a fine documentation.

In any case, the result is a disorganized documentation made of documents that are written in a rush. Developers hate doing this kind of work most of the time. Things get even worse when the existing documents need to be updated. Many projects out there are just providing poor, out-of-date documentation because the manager does not know how to deal with it.

But setting up a documentation process at the beginning of the project and treating documents as if they were modules of code makes documenting easier. Writing can even be fun when a few rules are followed.

This chapter provides a few tips to start documenting your project through:

- The seven rules of technical writing that summarize the best practices
- A reStructuredText primer, which is a plain text markup syntax used in most of the Python projects
- A guide for building good project documentation

The seven rules of technical writing

Writing good documentation is easier in many aspects than writing code. Most developers think it is very hard, but by following a simple set of rules it becomes really easy.

We are not talking here about writing a book of poems but a comprehensive piece of text that can be used to understand a design, an API, or anything that makes up the codebase.

Every developer is able to produce such material, and this section provides seven rules that can be applied in all cases:

- **Write in two steps**: Focus on ideas and then on reviewing and shaping your text.
- **Target the readership**: Who is going to read it?
- **Use a simple style**: Keep it straight and simple. Use good grammar.
- **Limit the scope of the information**: Introduce one concept at a time.
- **Use realistic code examples**: "Foos" and "bars" should be avoided.
- **Use a light but sufficient approach**: You are not writing a book!
- **Use templates**: Help the readers to get habits.

These rules are mostly inspired and adapted from *Agile Documentation: A Pattern Guide to Producing Lightweight Documents for Software Projects, Wiley,* a book by Andreas Rüping that focuses on producing the best documentation in software projects.

Write in two steps

Peter Elbow, in *Writing With Power: Techniques for Mastering the Writing Process, Oxford University Press,* explains that it is almost impossible for any human being to produce a perfect text in one shot. The problem is that many developers write documentation and try to directly come up with some perfect text. The only way they succeed in this exercise is by stopping writing after every two sentences to read them back and doing some corrections. This means that they are focusing both on the content and the style of the text.

This is too hard for the brain and the result is often not as good as it could be. A lot of time and energy is spent in polishing the style and shape of the text before its meaning is completely thought through.

Another approach is to drop the style and organization of the text and focus on its content. All ideas are laid down on paper, no matter how they are written. The developer starts to write a continuous stream and does not pause when he or she makes grammatical mistakes, or for anything that is not about the content. For instance, it does not matter if the sentences are barely understandable as long as the ideas are written down. He or she just writes down what he wants to say with a rough organization.

By doing this, the developer focuses on what he or she wants to say and will probably get more content out of his or her mind than he or she initially thought they would.

Another side-effect when doing free writing is that other ideas that are not directly related to the topic will easily go through the mind. A good practice is to write them down on a second piece of paper or screen when they appear, so they are not lost, and then get back to the main writing.

The second step consists of reading back the whole text and polishing it so that it is comprehensible to everyone. Polishing a text means enhancing its style, correcting its faults, reorganizing it a bit, and removing any redundant information it has.

When the time dedicated to writing documentation is limited, a good practice is to split this time into two halves—one for writing the content and one to clean and organize the text.

 Focus on the content and then on style and cleanliness.

Target the readership

When writing content, there is a simple question the writer should consider: *Who is going to read it?*

This is not always obvious, as a technical text explains how a piece of software works and is often written for every person who might get and use the code. The reader can be a researcher who is looking for an appropriate technical solution to a problem or a developer who needs to implement a feature with it. A designer might also read it to know if the package fits his or her needs from an architectural point of view.

Good documentation should follow a simple rule—each text should have only one kind of reader.

This philosophy makes the writing easier. The writer precisely knows what kind of reader he or she is dealing with. He or she can provide concise and precise documentation that is not vaguely intended for all kinds of readers.

A good practice is to provide a small introductory text that explains in one sentence what the documentation is about and guides the reader to the appropriate part:

```
Atomisator is a product that fetches RSS feeds and saves them in a
database, with a filtering process.

If you are a developer, you might want to look at the API description
(api.txt)
```

```
If you are a manager, you can read the features list and the FAQ
(features.txt)

If you are a designer, you can read the architecture and
infrastructure notes (arch.txt)
```

By taking care of directing your readers in this way, you will probably produce better documentation.

[Know your readership before you start to write.]

Use a simple style

Seth Godin is one of the best-selling writers on marketing topics. You might want to read *Unleashing the Ideavirus, Hachette Books,* which is available for free on the Internet (http://www.sethgodin.com/ideavirus/downloads/IdeavirusReadandShare.pdf).

Some time ago, he made an analysis on his blog to try to understand why his books sold so well. He made a list of all the best sellers in the marketing area and compared the average number of words per sentences in each one of them.

He realized that his books had the lowest number of words per sentence (thirteen words). This simple fact, Seth explained, proved that readers prefer short and simple sentences, rather than long and stylish ones.

By keeping sentences short and simple, your writings will consume less brain power for their content to be extracted, processed, and then understood. Writing technical documentation aims to provide a software guide to readers. It is not a fiction story and should be closer to your microwave notice than to the latest Stephen King novel.

A few tips to keep in mind are:

- Use simple sentences. They should not be longer than two lines.
- Each paragraph should be composed of three or four sentences, at the most, that express one main idea. Let your text breathe.
- Don't repeat yourself too much. Avoid journalistic styles where ideas are repeated again and again to make sure they are understood.
- Don't use several tenses. The present tense is enough most of the time.
- Do not make jokes in the text if you are not a really fine writer. Being funny in a technical text is really hard, and few writers master it. If you really want to distill some humor, keep it in code examples and you will be fine.

You are not writing fiction, so keep the style as simple as possible.

Limit the scope of information

There's a simple sign of bad documentation in a software — you are looking for some information that you know is present somewhere but you cannot find it. After spending some time reading the table of contents, you are starting to grep the files trying several word combinations but cannot get what you are looking for.

This happens when writers are not organizing their texts in topics. They might provide tons of information, but it is just gathered in a monolithic or non-logical way. For instance, if a reader is looking for a big picture of your application, he or she should not have to read the API documentation — that is a low-level matter.

To avoid this effect, paragraphs should be gathered under a meaningful title for a given section, and the global document title should synthesize the content in a short phrase.

A table of contents could be made of all the section's titles.

A simple practice to compose your titles is to ask yourself, "What phrase would I type in Google to find this section?"

Use realistic code examples

Foo and *bar* are bad citizens. When a reader tries to understand how a piece of code works with a usage example, having an unrealistic example will make it harder to understand.

Why not use a real-world example? A common practice is to make sure that each code example can be cut and pasted in a real program.

To show an example of bad usage, let's assume we want to show how to use the `parse()` function:

```
>>> from atomisator.parser import parse
>>> # Let's use it:
>>> stuff = parse('some-feed.xml')
>>> next(stuff)
{'title': 'foo', 'content': 'blabla'}
```

A better example would be when the parser knows how to return a feed content with the parse function, available as a top-level function:

```
>>> from atomisator.parser import parse
>>> # Let's use it:
>>> my_feed = parse('http://tarekziade.wordpress.com/feed')
>>> next(my_feed)
{'title': 'eight tips to start with python', 'content': 'The first tip
is..., ...'}
```

This slight difference might sound overkill, but in fact it makes your documentation a lot more useful. A reader can copy those lines into a shell, understand that parse uses a URL as a parameter, and that it returns an iterator that contains blog entries.

Of course, giving a realistic example is not always possible or viable. This is especially true to very generic code. Even this book has few occurrences of vague foo and bar strings where the name context is unimportant. Anyway, you should always strive to reduce the amount of such unrealistic examples to minimum.

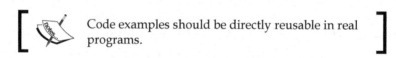

Code examples should be directly reusable in real programs.

Use a light but sufficient approach

In most agile methodologies, documentation is not the first citizen. Making software that works is the most important thing over detailed documentation. So a good practice, as Scott Ambler explains in his book *Agile Modeling: Effective Practices for eXtreme Programming and the Unified Process, John Wiley & Sons*, is to define the real documentation needs, rather than create an exhaustive set of documents.

For instance, let's see an example documentation of some simple project—ianitor—that is available on GitHub under https://github.com/ClearcodeHQ/ianitor. It is a tool that helps registering processes in the Consul service discovery cluster, so it is mostly aimed at system administrators. If you take a look at its documentation, you will realize that this is just a single document (the README.md file). It only explains how it works and how to use it. From the administrator's perspective, this is sufficient. They only need to know how to configure and run the tool and there is no other group of people expected to use ianitor. This document limits its scope by answering one question, "How do I use ianitor on my server?"

Use templates

Every page on Wikipedia is similar. There are boxes on the one side that are used to summarize dates or facts. At the beginning of the document is a table of contents with links that refer to anchors in the same text. There is always a reference section at the end.

Users get used to it. For instance, they know they can have a quick look at the table of contents, and if they do not find the info they are looking for, they will go directly to the reference section to see if they can find another website on the topic. This works for any page on Wikipedia. You learn the *Wikipedia way* to be more efficient.

So, using templates forces a common pattern for documents and therefore makes people more efficient in using them. They get used to the structure and know how to read it quickly.

Providing a template for each kind of document also provides a quick start for writers.

A reStructuredText primer

reStructuredText is also called reST (refer to `http://docutils.sourceforge.net/rst.html`). It is a plain text markup language widely used in the Python community to document packages. The great thing about reST is that the text is still readable since the markup syntax does not obfuscate the text like LaTeX would.

Here's a sample of such a document:

```
=====
Title
=====


Section 1
=========
This *word* has emphasis.


Section 2
=========


Subsection
::::::::::

Text.
```

reST comes in `docutils`, a package that provides a suite of scripts to transform a reST file to various formats, such as HTML, LaTeX, XML, or even S5, Eric Meyer's slide show system (refer to `http://meyerweb.com/eric/tools/s5`).

Writers can focus on the content and then decide how to render it, depending on the needs. For instance, Python itself is documented into reST, which is then rendered in HTML to build `http://docs.python.org`, and in various other formats.

The minimum elements one should know to start writing reST are:

- Section structure
- Lists
- Inline markup
- Literal block
- Links

This section is a really fast overview of the syntax. A quick reference is available for more information at: `http://docutils.sourceforge.net/docs/user/rst/quickref.html`, which is a good place to start working with reST.

To install reStructuredText, install `docutils`:

```
$ pip install docutils
```

For instance, the `rst2html` script provided by the `docutils` package will produce HTML output given a reST file:

```
$ more text.txt
Title
=====

content.

$ rst2html.py text.txt
<?xml version="1.0" encoding="utf-8" ?>
...
<html ...>
<head>
...
</head>
<body>
```

```
<div class="document" id="title">
<h1 class="title">Title</h1>
<p>content.</p>
</div>
</body>
</html>
```

Section structure

The document's title and its sections are underlined using nonalphanumeric characters. They can be overlined and underlined, and a common practice is to use this double markup for the title and keep a simple underline for sections.

The most used characters to underline a section title are in the following order of precedence: =, -, _, :, #, +, ^.

When a character is used for a section, it is associated with its level and it has to be used consistently throughout the document.

Consider the following code for example:

```
==============
Document title
==============


Introduction to the document content.


Section 1
=========

First document section with two subsections.

Note the ``=`` used as heading underline.


Subsection A
------------

First subsection (A) of Section 1.

Note the ``-`` used as heading underline.
```

```
Subsection B
------------
Second subsection (B) of Section 1.


Section 2
=========

Second section of document with one subsection.


Subsection C
------------

Subsection (C) of Section 2.
```

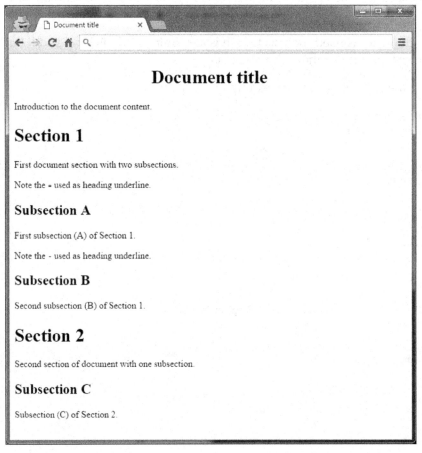

Figure 1 reStructuredText converted to HTML and rendered in the browser

Lists

reST provides readable syntax for bullet lists, enumerated lists, and definition lists with autoenumeration features:

```
Bullet list:

- one
- two
- three


Enumerated list:

1. one
2. two
#. auto-enumerated


Definition list:

one
    one is a number.

two
    two is also a number.
```

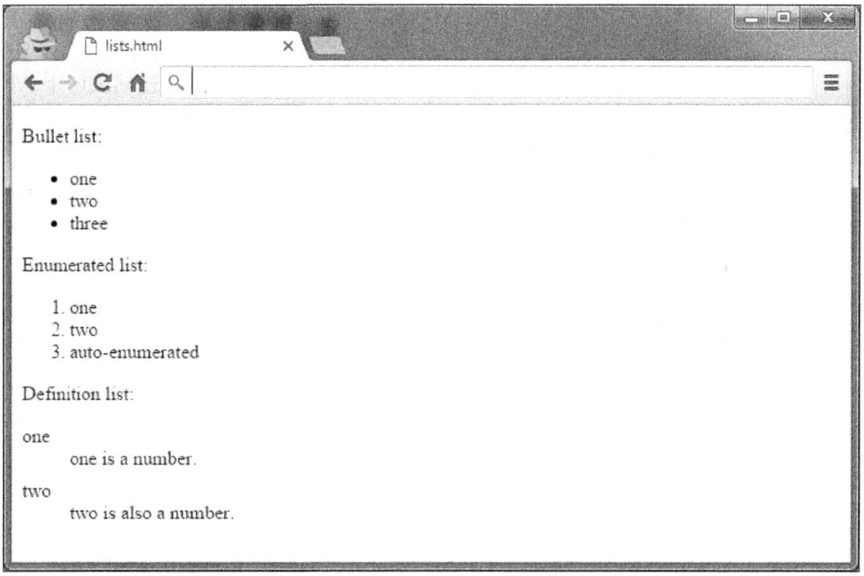

Figure 2 Different types of lists rendered as HTML

Inline markup

The text can be styled using an inline markup:

- `*emphasis*`: Italics
- `**strong emphasis**`: Boldface
- `` ``inline preformatted`` ``: Inline preformatted text (usually monospaced, terminal-like)
- `` `a text with a link`_ ``: This will be replaced by a hyperlink as long as it is provided in the document (see in the *Links* section)

Literal block

When you need to present some code examples, a literal block can be used. Two colons are used to mark the block, which is an indented paragraph:

```
This is a code example

::

    >>> 1 + 1
    2


Let's continue our text
```

 Don't forget to add a blank line after : : and after the block, otherwise it will not be rendered.

Notice that the colon characters can be put in a text line. In that case, they will be replaced by a single colon in various rendering formats:

```
This is a code example::

    >>> 1 + 1
    2


Let's continue our text
```

If you don't want to keep a single colon, you can insert a space between the leading text and : :. In that case, : : will be interpreted and totally removed.

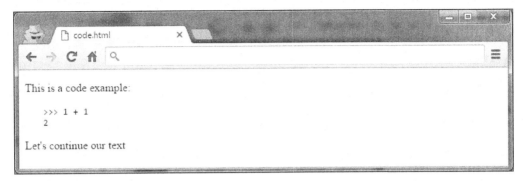

Figure 3 Code samples in reST rendered as HTML

Links

A text can be changed into an external link with a special line starting with two dots, as long as it is provided in the document:

```
Try `Plone CMS`_, it is great ! It is based on Zope_.

.. _`Plone CMS`: http://plone.org
.. _Zope: http://zope.org
```

A usual practice is to group the external links at the end of the document. When the text to be linked contains spaces, it has to be surrounded with ` (backtick) characters.

Internal links can also be used by adding a marker in the text:

```
This is a code example

.. _example:

::

    >>> 1 + 1
    2

Let's continue our text, or maybe go back to
the example_.
```

Sections are also targets that can be used:

```
===============
Document title
===============

Introduction to the document content.


Section 1
=========

First document section.


Section 2
=========

-> go back to `Section 1`_
```

Building the documentation

An easier way to guide your readers and your writers is to provide each one of them with helpers and guidelines, as we have learned in the previous section of this chapter.

From a writer's point of view, this is done by having a set of reusable templates together with a guide that describes how and when to use them in a project. It is called a **documentation portfolio**.

From a reader's point of view, it is important to be able to browse the documentation with no pain, and getting used to finding the information efficiently. It is done by building a **document landscape**.

Building the portfolio

There are many kinds of documents a software project can have, from low-level documents that refer directly to the code, to design papers that provide a high-level overview of the application.

For instance, Scott Ambler defines an extensive list of document types in his book, *Agile Modeling: Effective Practices for eXtreme Programming and the Unified Process*, *John Wiley & Sons*. He builds a portfolio from early specifications to operations documents. Even the project management documents are covered, so the whole documenting needs are built with a standardized set of templates.

Since a complete portfolio is tightly related to the methodologies used to build the software, this chapter will only focus on a common subset that you can complete with your specific needs. Building an efficient portfolio takes a long time as it captures your working habits.

A common set of documents in software projects can be classified into three categories:

- **Design**: This includes all the documents that provide architectural information and low-level design information, such as class diagrams or database diagrams

- **Usage**: This includes all the documents on how to use the software; this can be in the shape of a cookbook and tutorials or a module-level help

- **Operations**: This provides guidelines on how to deploy, upgrade, or operate the software

Design

The important point when creating such documents is to make sure the target readership is perfectly known and the content scope is limited. So, a generic template for design documents can provide a light structure with a little advice for the writer.

Such a structure might include:

- Title
- Author
- Tags (keywords)
- Description (abstract)
- Target (who should read this?)
- Content (with diagrams)
- References to other documents

The content should be three or four pages when printed, at the most, to be sure to limit the scope. If it gets bigger, it should be split into several documents or summarized.

The template also provides the author's name and a list of tags to manage its evolutions and ease its classification. This will be covered later in the chapter.

The example design document template in reST could be as follows:

```
==========================================
Design document title
==========================================

:Author: Document Author
:Tags: document tags separated with spaces

:abstract:

    Write here a small abstract about your design document.

.. contents ::


Audience
========

Explain here who is the target readership.


Content
=======

Write your document here. Do not hesitate to split it in several
sections.


References
==========

Put here references, and links to other documents.
```

Usage

The usage documentation describes how a particular part of the software is used. This documentation can describe low-level parts, such as how a function works, but also high-level parts, such as command-line arguments for calling the program. This is the most important part of documentation in framework applications, since the target readership is mainly the developers that are going to reuse the code.

The three main kinds of documents are:

- **Recipe**: This is a short document that explains how to do something. This kind of document targets one readership and focuses on one specific topic.
- **Tutorial**: This is a step-by-step document that explains how to use a feature of the software. This document can refer to recipes, and each instance is intended to one readership.
- **Module helper**: This is a low-level document that explains what a module contains. This document could be shown (for instance) when you call the `help` built-in over a module.

Recipe

A recipe answers a very specific problem and provides a solution to resolve it. For example, ActiveState provide a huge repository of Python recipes online where developers can describe how to do something in Python (refer to `http://code.activestate.com/recipes/langs/python/`). Such a set of recipes related to a single area/project is often called *cookbook*.

These recipes must be short and are structured like this:

- Title
- Submitter
- Last updated
- Version
- Category
- Description
- Source (the source code)
- Discussion (the text explaining the code)
- Comments (from the Web)

Often, they are one-screen long and do not go into great detail. This structure perfectly fits a software's needs and can be adapted in a generic structure, where the target readership is added and the category is replaced by tags:

- Title (short sentence)
- Author
- Tags (keywords)
- Who should read this?

- Prerequisites (other documents to read, for example)
- Problem (a short description)
- Solution (the main text, one or two screens)
- References (links to other documents)

The date and version are not useful here, since project documentation should be rather managed like a source code in the project. This means that the best way to handle the documentation is to manage it through the version control system. In most cases, this is exactly the same code repository as the one used for the project's code.

A simple reusable template for the recipes could be as follows:

```
===========
Recipe name
===========


:Author: Recipe Author
:Tags: document tags separated with spaces

:abstract:

    Write here a small abstract about your design document.

.. contents ::


Audience
========

Explain here who is the target readership.


Prerequisites
=============

Write the list of prerequisites for implementing this recipe. This
can be additional documents, software, specific libraries, environment
settings or just anything that is required beyond the obvious language
interpreter.


Problem
=======
```

```
Explain the problem that this recipe is trying to solve.


Solution
========

Give solution to problem explained earlier. This is the core of a
recipe.


References
==========

Put here references, and links to other documents.
```

Tutorial

A tutorial differs from a recipe in its purpose. It is not intended to resolve an isolated problem, but rather describes how to use a feature of the application step by step. This can be longer than a recipe and can concern many parts of the application. For example, Django provides a list of tutorials on its website. *Writing your first Django App, part 1* (refer to `https://docs.djangoproject.com/en/1.9/intro/tutorial01/`) explains in few screens how to build an application with Django.

A structure for such a document will be:

- Title (short sentence)
- Author
- Tags (words)
- Description (abstract)
- Who should read this?
- Prerequisites (other documents to read, for example)
- Tutorial (the main text)
- References (links to other documents)

Module helper

The last template that can be added in our collection is the module helper template. A module helper refers to a single module and provides a description of its contents, together with usage examples.

Some tools can automatically build such documents by extracting the docstrings and computing module help using `pydoc`, such as Epydoc (refer to `http://epydoc.sourceforge.net`). So it is possible to generate an extensive documentation based on API introspection. This kind of documentation is often provided in Python frameworks. For instance, Plone provides an `http://api.plone.org` server that keeps an up-to-date collection of module helpers.

The main problems with this approach are:

- There is no smart selection performed over the modules that are really interesting to the document
- The code can be obfuscated by the documentation

Furthermore, a module documentation provides examples that sometimes refer to several parts of the module and that are hard to split between the functions' and classes' docstrings. The module docstring could be used for that purpose by writing text at the top of the module. But this ends in having a hybrid file composed of a block of text rather than a block of code. This is rather obfuscating when the code represents less than 50% of the total length. If you are the author, this is perfectly fine. But when people try to read the code (not the documentation), they will have to skip the docstrings part.

Another approach is to separate the text in its own file. A manual selection can then be operated to decide which Python module will have its module helper file. The documents can then be separated from the code base and allowed to live their own life, as we will see in the next part. This is how Python is documented.

Many developers will disagree on the fact that doc and code separation is better than docstrings. This approach means that the documentation process is fully integrated in the development cycle; otherwise it will quickly become obsolete. The docstrings approach solves this problem by providing proximity between the code and its usage example but doesn't bring it to a higher level—a document that can be used as part of a plain documentation.

The template for a module helper is really simple, as it contains just a little metadata before the content is written. The target is not defined since it is the developers who wish to use the module:

- Title (module name)
- Author
- Tags (words)
- Content

The next chapter will cover test-driven development using doctests and module helpers.

Operations

Operation documents are used to describe how the software can be operated. Consider the following points for instance:

- Installation and deployment documents
- Administration documents
- Frequently Asked Questions (FAQ) documents
- Documents that explain how people can contribute, ask for help, or provide feedback

These documents are very specific but they can probably use the tutorial template defined in the earlier section.

Making your own portfolio

The templates that we discussed earlier are just a basis that you can use to document your software. With time, you will eventually develop your own templates and style for making documentation. But always keep in mind the light but sufficient approach for project documentation: each document added should have a clearly defined target readership and should fill a real need. Documents that don't add a real value should not be written.

Each project is unique and has different documentation needs. For example, small terminal tools with simple usage can definitely live with only a single README file as its document landscape. Having such a minimal single-document approach is completely fine if the target readers are precisely defined and consistently grouped (system administrators, for instance).

Also, do not apply the provided templates too rigorously. Some additional metadata provided as an example is really useful in either big projects or in strictly formalized teams. Tags, for instance, are intended to improve textual search in big documentations but will not provide any value in a documentation landscape consisting only of a few documents.

Also, including the document author is not always a good idea. Such an approach may be especially questionable in open source projects. In such projects, you will want the community to also contribute to documentation. In most cases, such documents are continuously updated whenever there is such a need by whoever makes the contribution. People tend to treat the document *author* also as the document *owner*. This may discourage people to update the documentation if every document has its author always specified. Usually, the version control software provides clearer and more transparent information about real document authors than explicitly provided metadata annotations. The situations where explicit authors are really recommended are various design documents, especially in projects where the design process is strictly formalized. The best example is the series of PEP documents with the Python language enhancement proposals.

Building the landscape

The document portfolio built in the previous section provides a structure at document level but does not provide a way to group and organize it to build the documentation the readers will have. This is what Andreas Rüping calls a document landscape, referring to the mental map the readers use when they browse documentation. He came up with the conclusion that the best way to organize documents is to build a logical tree.

In other words, the different kinds of documents composing the portfolio need to find a place to live within a tree of directories. This place must be obvious to the writers when they create the document and to the readers when they are looking for it.

A great help when browsing documentation is the index pages at each level that can drive writers and readers.

Building a document landscape is done in two steps:

- Building a tree for the producers (the writers)
- Building a tree for the consumers (the readers) on top of the producers' tree

This distinction between producers and consumers is important since they access the documents in different places and different formats.

Producer's layout

From a producer's point of view, each document is processed exactly like a Python module. It should be stored in the version control system and works like code. Writers do not care about the final appearance of their prose and where it is available, they just want to make sure that they are writing a document, so it is the single source of truth on the topic covered. reStructuredText files stored in a folder tree are available in the version control system together with the software code and are a convenient solution to building the documentation landscape for producers.

By convention, the docs folder is used as a root of documentation tree:

```
$ cd my-project
$ find docs
docs
docs/source
docs/source/design
docs/source/operations
docs/source/usage
docs/source/usage/cookbook
docs/source/usage/modules
docs/source/usage/tutorial
```

Notice that the tree is located in a source folder because the docs folder will be used as a root folder to set up a special tool in the next section.

From there, an index.txt file can be added at each level (besides the root), explaining what kind of documents the folder contains or summarizing what each subfolder contains. These index files can define a listing of the documents they contain. For instance, the operations folder can contain a list of operations documents available:

```
==========
Operations
==========


This section contains operations documents:

- How to install and run the project
- How to install and manage a database for the project
```

It is important to know that people tend to forget to update such lists of documents and tables of content. So it is better to have them updated automatically. In the next subsection, we will discuss one tool that, among many other features, can also handle this use case.

Consumer's layout

From a consumer's point of view, it is important to work out the index files and to present the whole documentation in a format that is easy to read and looks good. Web pages are the best pick and are easy to generate from reStructuredText files.

Sphinx (http://sphinx.pocoo.org) is a set of scripts and docutils extensions that can be used to generate an HTML structure from our text tree. This tool is used (for instance) to build the Python documentation, and many projects are now using it for their documentation. Among its built-in features, it produces a really nice browsing system, together with a light but sufficient client-side JavaScript search engine. It also uses pygments for rendering code examples, which produces really nice syntax highlights.

Sphinx can be easily configured to stick with the document landscape defined in the earlier section. It can be easily installed with pip as Sphinx package.

The easiest way to start working with Sphinx is to use the sphinx-quickstart script. This utility will generate a script together with Makefile, which can be used to generate the web documentation every time it is needed. It will interactively ask you some questions and then bootstrap the whole initial documentation source tree and configuration file. Once it is done, you can easily tweak it whenever you want. Let's assume we have already bootstrapped the whole Sphinx environment and we want to see its HTML representation. This can be easily done using the make html command:

```
project/docs$ make html
sphinx-build -b html -d _build/doctrees   . _build/html
Running Sphinx v1.3.6
making output directory...
loading pickled environment... not yet created
building [mo]: targets for 0 po files that are out of date
building [html]: targets for 1 source files that are out of date
updating environment: 1 added, 0 changed, 0 removed
reading sources... [100%] index
looking for now-outdated files... none found
pickling environment... done
checking consistency... done
preparing documents... done
writing output... [100%] index
generating indices... genindex
```

```
writing additional pages... search
copying static files... done
copying extra files... done
dumping search index in English (code: en) ... done
dumping object inventory... done
build succeeded.
Build finished. The HTML pages are in _build/html.
```

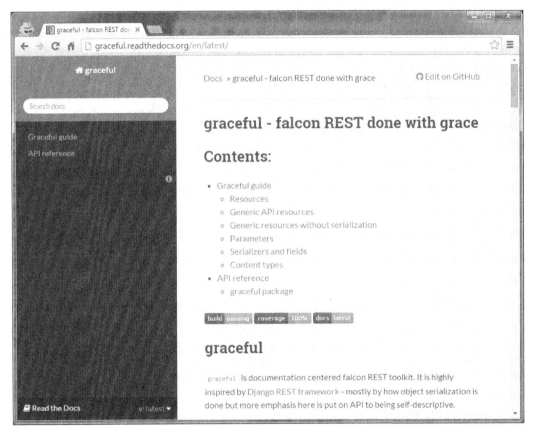

Figure 4 An example HTML version of documentation built with Sphinx –
http://graceful.readthedocs.org/en/latest/

Besides the HTML versions of the documents, the tool also builds automatic pages, such as a module list and an index. Sphinx provides a few `docutils` extensions to drive these features. The main ones are:

- A directive that builds a table of contents
- A marker that can be used to register a document as a module helper
- A marker to add an element in the index

Working on the index pages

Sphinx provides a `toctree` directive that can be used to inject a table of contents in a document with links to other documents. Each line must be a file with its relative path, starting from the current document. Glob-style names can also be provided to add several files that match the expression.

For example, the index file in the `cookbook` folder, which we have previously defined in the producer's landscape, can look like this:

```
========
Cookbook
========

Welcome to the Cookbook.

Available recipes:

.. toctree::
   :glob:
   *
```

With this syntax, the HTML page will display a list of all the reStructuredText documents available in the `cookbook` folder. This directive can be used in all the index files to build a browsable documentation.

Registering module helpers

For module helpers, a marker can be added so that it is automatically listed and available in the module's index page:

```
=======
session
=======

.. module:: db.session

The module session...
```

Notice that the db prefix here can be used to avoid module collision. Sphinx will use it as a module category and will group all modules that start with db. in this category.

Adding index markers

Another option can be used to fill the index page by linking the document to an entry:

```
=======
session
=======

.. module:: db.session

.. index::
   Database Access
   Session

The module session...
```

Two new entries, Database Access and Session, will be added in the index page.

Cross-references

Finally, Sphinx provides an inline markup to set cross-references. For instance, a link to a module can be done like this:

```
:mod:`db.session`
```

Here, :mod: is the module marker's prefix and `db.session` is the name of the module to be linked to (as registered previously); keep in mind that :mod: as well as the previous elements are the specific directives introduced in reSTructuredText by Sphinx.

Sphinx provides a lot more features that you can discover on its website. For instance, the *autodoc* feature is a great option to automatically extract your doctests to build the documentation. Refer to http://sphinx.pocoo.org.

Documentation building and continuous integration

Sphinx really improves the readability and experience of reading documentation from the consumer's point of view. As already said, it is especially helpful when some of its parts are tightly coupled to the code, so in the form of dosctrings or module helpers. While this approach really makes it easier to ensure that the source version of the documentation matches with the code it documents, it does not guarantee that documentation readership will have access to the latest and most up to date compiled version.

Having only minimal source representation is also not enough if the target readers of the documentation are not proficient enough with command-line tools and will not know how to build it into browsable and readable form. This is why it is important to build your documentation into a consumer-friendly form automatically whenever any change to the code repository is committed/pushed.

The best way to host the documentation built with Sphinx is to generate an HTML build and serve it as a static resource with your web server of choice. Sphinx provides proper `Makefile` to build HTML files with the `make html` command. Because `make` is a very common utility, it should be very easy to integrate this process with any continuous integration systems discussed in *Chapter 8, Managing Code*.

If you are documenting an open source project with Sphinx, then you will make your life a lot easier by using **Read the Docs** (`https://readthedocs.org/`). It is a free service for hosting documentation of open source Python projects with Sphinx. The configuration is completely hassle-free and it integrates very easily with two popular code hosting services: GitHub and Bitbucket. In practice, if you have your accounts properly connected and code repository properly set up, enabling documentation hosting on Read the Docs is a matter of just a few clicks.

Summary

This chapter explained in detail how to:

- Use a few rules for efficient writing
- Use reStructuredText, the Pythonista's LaTeX
- Build a document portfolio and landscape
- Use Sphinx to generate useful web documentations

The hardest thing to do when documenting a project is to keep it accurate and up to date. Making the documentation part of the code repository makes it a lot easier. From there, every time a developer changes a module, he or she should change the corresponding documentation as well.

This can be quite difficult in big projects, and adding a list of related documents in the header of the modules can help in that case.

A complementary approach to make sure the documentation is always accurate is to combine the documentation with tests through doctests. This is covered in the next chapter, which presents test-driven development principles and then document-driven development.

10
Test-Driven Development

Test-Driven Development (**TDD**) is a simple technique to produce high quality software. It is widely used in the Python community, but it is also very popular in other communities.

Testing is especially important in Python due to its dynamic nature. It lacks static typing so many, even minute, errors won't be noticed until the code is run and each of its line is executed. But the problem is not only how types in Python work. Remember that most bugs are not related to bad syntax usage, but rather to logical errors and subtle misunderstandings that can lead to major failures.

This chapter is split into two parts:

- *I don't test*, which advocates TDD and quickly describes how to do it with the standard library
- *I do test*, which is intended for developers who practice tests and wish to get more out of them

I don't test

If you have already been convinced to TDD, you should move to the next section. It will focus on advanced techniques and tools for making your life easier when working with tests. This part is mainly intended for those who are not using this approach and tries to advocate its usage.

Test-driven development principles

The test-driven development process, in its simplest form, consists of three steps:

1. Writing automated tests for a new functionality or improvement that has not been implemented yet.
2. Providing minimal code that just passes all the defined tests.
3. Refactoring code to meet the desired quality standards.

The most important fact to remember about this development cycle is that tests should be written before implementation. It is not an easy task for unexperienced developers, but it is the only approach which guarantees that the code you are going to write will be testable.

For example, a developer who is asked to write a function that checks whether the given number is a prime number, writes a few examples on how to use it and what the expected results are:

```
assert is_prime(5)
assert is_prime(7)
assert not is_prime(8)
```

The developer that implements the feature does not need to be the only one responsible for providing tests. The examples can be provided by another person as well. For instance, very often the official specifications of network protocols or cryptography algorithms provide test vectors that are intended to verify correctness of implementation. These are a perfect basis for test cases.

From there, the function can be implemented until the preceding examples work:

```
def is_prime(number):
    for element in range(2, number):
        if number % element == 0:
            return False
    return True
```

A bug or an unexpected result is a new example of usage the function should be able to deal with:

```
>>> assert not is_prime(1)
Traceback (most recent call last):
  File "<stdin>", line 1, in <module>
AssertionError
```

The code can be changed accordingly, until the new test passes:

```
def is_prime(number):
    if number in (0, 1):
        return False

    for element in range(2, number):
        if number % element == 0:
            return False

    return True
```

And more cases show that the implementation is still incomplete:

```
>>> assert not is_prime(-3)
Traceback (most recent call last):
  File "<stdin>", line 1, in <module>
AssertionError
```

The updated code is as follows:

```
def is_prime(number):
    if number < 0 or number in (0, 1):
        return False

    for element in range(2, number):
        if number % element == 0:
            return False

    return True
```

From there, all tests can be gathered in a test function, which is run every time the code evolves:

```
def test_is_prime():
    assert is_prime(5)
    assert is_prime(7)

    assert not is_prime(8)
    assert not is_prime(0)
    assert not is_prime(1)

    assert not is_prime(-1)
    assert not is_prime(-3)
    assert not is_prime(-6)
```

Every time we come up with a new requirement, the `test_is_prime()` function should be updated first to define the expected behavior of the `is_prime()` function. Then, the test is run to check if the implementation delivers the desired results. Only if the tests are known to be failing, there is a need to update code for the tested function.

Test-driven development provides a lot of benefits:

- It helps to prevent software regression
- It improves software quality
- It provides a kind of low-level documentation of code behavior
- It allows you to produce robust code faster in short development cycles

The best convention to deal in with test is to gather all of them in a single module or package (usually named `tests`) and have an easy way to run the whole suite using a single shell command. Fortunately, there is no need to build whole test tool chains all by yourself. Both Python standard library and Python Package Index come with plenty of test frameworks and utilities that allow you to build, discover, and run tests in a convenient way. We will discuss the most notable examples of such packages and modules later in this chapter.

Preventing software regression

We all face software regression issues in our developer lives. Software regression is a new bug introduced by a change. It manifests when features or functionalities that were known to be working in the previous versions of the software get broken and stop working at some point during project development.

The main reason for regressions is high complexity of software. At some point, it is impossible to guess what a single change in the codebase might lead to. Changing some code might break some other features and sometimes lead to vicious side effects, such as silently corrupting data. And high complexity is not only the problem of huge codebases. There is, of course, obvious correlation between the amount of code and its complexity, but even small projects (few hundredths/thousands lines of code) may have such convoluted architecture that it is hard to predict all consequences of relatively small changes.

To avoid regression, the whole set of features the software provides should be tested every time a change occurs. Without this, you are not able to reliably tell difference between bugs that have always existed in your software from the new ones introduced to parts that were working correctly just some time ago.

Opening up a codebase to several developers amplifies the problem, since each person will not be fully aware of all the development activities. While having a version control system prevents conflicts, it does not prevent all unwanted interactions.

TDD helps reduce software regression. The whole software can be automatically tested after each change. This will work as long as each feature has the proper set of tests. When TDD is properly done, the testbase grows together with the codebase.

Since a full test campaign can last for quite a long time, it is a good practice to delegate it to some continuous integration system which can do the work in the background. We discussed such solutions already in *Chapter 8, Managing Code*. Nevertheless, the local re-launching of the tests should be performed manually by the developer too, at least for the concerned modules. Relying only on continuous integration will have a negative effect on the developers' productivity. Programmers should be able to run selections of tests easily in their environments. This is the reason why you should carefully choose testing tools for the project.

Improving code quality

When a new module, class, or a function is written, a developer focuses on how to write it and how to produce the best piece of code he or she can. But while he or she is concentrating on algorithms, he or she might lose the user's point of view: How and when will his or her function be used? Are the arguments easy and logical to use? Is the name of the API right?

This is done by applying the tips described in the previous chapters, such as *Chapter 4, Choosing Good Names*. But the only way to do it efficiently is to write usage examples. This is the moment when the developer realizes if the code he or she wrote is logical and easy to use. Often, the first refactoring occurs right after the module, class, or function is finished.

Writing tests, which are use cases for the code, helps in having a user point of view. Developers will, therefore, often produce a better code when they use TDD. It is difficult to test gigantic functions and huge monolithic classes. Code that is written with testing in mind tends to be architected more cleanly and modularly.

Providing the best developer documentation

Tests are the best place for a developer to learn how software works. They are the use cases the code was primarily created for. Reading them provides a quick and deep insight into how the code works. Sometimes an example is worth a thousand words.

The fact that these tests are always up to date with the codebase makes them the best developer documentation that a piece of software can have. Tests don't go stale in the same way documentation does, otherwise they would fail.

Producing robust code faster

Writing without testing leads to long debugging sessions. A consequence of a bug in one module might manifest itself in a completely different part of the software. Since you don't know who to blame, you spend an inordinate amount of time debugging. It's better to fight small bugs one at a time when a test fails, because you'll have a better clue as to where the real problem is. And testing is often more fun than debugging because it is coding.

If you measure the time taken to fix the code together with the time taken to write it, it will usually be longer than the time a TDD approach would take. This is not obvious when you start a new piece of code. This is because the time taken to set up a test environment and write the first few tests is extremely long compared to the time taken just to write the first pieces of code.

But there are some test environments that are really hard to set up. For instance, when your code interacts with an LDAP or an SQL server, writing tests is not obvious at all. This is covered in the *Fakes and mocks* section in this chapter.

What kind of tests?

There are several kinds of tests that can be made on any software. The main ones are **acceptance tests** (or **functional tests**) and **unit tests**, and these are the ones that most people think of when discussing the topic of software testing. But there are a few other kinds of tests that you can use in your project. We will discuss some of them shortly in this section.

Acceptance tests

An acceptance test focuses on a feature and deals with the software like a black box. It just makes sure that the software really does what it is supposed to do, using the same media as that of the users and controlling the output. These tests are usually written out of the development cycle to validate that the application meets the requirements. They are usually run as a checklist over the software. Often, these tests are not done through TDD and are built by managers, QA staff, or even customers. In that case, they are often called **user acceptance tests**.

Still, they can and they should be done with TDD principles. Tests can be provided before the features are written. Developers get a pile of acceptance tests, usually made out of the functional specifications, and their job is to make sure the code will pass all of them.

The tools used to write those tests depend on the user interface the software provides. Some popular tools used by Python developers are:

Application type	Tool
Web application	Selenium (for Web UI with JavaScript)
Web application	`zope.testbrowser` (doesn't test JS)
WSGI application	`paste.test.fixture` (doesn't test JS)
Gnome Desktop application	dogtail
Win32 Desktop application	pywinauto

 For an extensive list of functional testing tools, Grig Gheorghiu maintains a wiki page at `https://wiki.python.org/moin/PythonTestingToolsTaxonomy`.

Unit tests

Unit tests are low-level tests that perfectly fit test-driven development. As the name suggests, they focus on testing software units. A software unit can be understood as the smallest testable piece of the application code. Depending on the application, the size may vary from whole modules to a single method or function, but usually unit tests are written for the smallest fragments of code possible. Unit tests usually isolate the tested unit (module, class, function, and so on) from the rest of the application and other units. When external dependencies are required, such as web APIs or databases, they are often replaced by fake objects or mocks.

Functional tests

Functional tests focus on whole features and functionalities instead of small code units. They are similar in their purpose to acceptance tests. The main difference is that functional tests do not necessarily need to use the same interface that a user does. For instance, when testing web applications, some of the user interactions (or its consequences) can be simulated by synthetic HTTP requests or direct database access, instead of simulating real page loading and mouse clicks.

This approach is often easier and faster than testing with tools used in *user acceptance tests*. The downside of limited functional tests is that they tend not to cover enough parts of the application where different abstraction layers and components meet. Tests that focus on such *meeting points* are often called integration tests.

Integration tests

Integration tests represent a higher level of testing than unit tests. They test bigger parts of code and focus on situations where many application layers or components meet and interact with each other. The form and scope of integration tests varies depending on the project's architecture and complexity. For example, in small and monolithic projects, this may be as simple as running more complex functional tests and allowing them to interact with real backing services (databases, caches, and so on) instead of mocking or faking them. For complex scenarios or products that are built from multiple services, the real integration tests may be very extensive and even require running the whole project in a big distributed environment that mirrors the production.

Integration tests are often very similar to functional tests and the border between them is very blurry. It is very common that integration tests are also logically testing separate functionalities and features.

Load and performance testing

Load tests and performance tests provide objective information about code efficiency rather than its correctness. The terms of load testing and performance testing are used by some interchangeably but the first one in fact refers to a limited aspect of performance. Load testing focuses on measuring how code behaves under some artificial demand (load). This is a very popular way of testing web applications where load is understood as web traffic from real users or programmatic clients. It is important to note that load tests tend to cover whole requests to the application so are very similar to integration and functional tests. This makes it important to be sure that tested application components are fully verified to be working correctly. Performance tests are generally all the tests that aim to measure code performance and can target even small units of code. So, load tests are only a specific subtype of performance tests.

They are special kind of tests because they do not provide binary results (failure/success) but only some performance quality measurement. This means that single results need to be interpreted and/or compared with results of different test runs. In some cases, the project requirements may set some hard time or resource constraints on the code but this does not change the fact that there is always some arbitrary interpretation involved in these kinds of testing approaches.

Load performance tests are a great tool during the development of any software that needs to fulfill some **Service Level Agreements** because it helps to reduce the risk of compromising the performance of critical code paths. Anyway, it should not be overused.

Code quality testing

Code quality does not have the arbitrary scale that would say for definite if it is bad or good. Unfortunately, the abstract concept of code quality cannot be measured and expressed in the form of numbers. But instead, we can measure various metrics of the software that are known to be highly correlated with the quality of code. To name a few:

- The number of code style violations
- The amount of documentation
- Complexity metrics, such as McCabe's cyclomatic complexity
- The number of static code analysis warnings

Many projects use code quality testing in their continuous integration workflows. The good and popular approach is to test at least basic metrics (static code analysis and code style violations) and not allow the merging of any code to the mainstream that makes these metrics lower.

Python standard test tools

Python provides two main modules in the standard library to write tests:

- `unittest` (https://docs.python.org/3/library/unittest.html): This is the standard and most common Python unit testing framework based on Java's JUnit and was originally written by Steve Purcell (formerly `PyUnit`)
- `doctest` (https://docs.python.org/3/library/doctest.html): This is a literate programing testing tool with interactive usage examples

unittest

`unittest` basically provides what JUnit does for Java. It offers a base class called `TestCase`, which has an extensive set of methods to verify the output of function calls and statements.

This module was created to write unit tests, but acceptance tests can also be written with it as long as the test uses the user interface. For instance, some testing frameworks provide helpers to drive tools such as Selenium on top of `unittest`.

Writing a simple unit test for a module using `unittest` is done by subclassing `TestCase` and writing methods with the `test` prefix. The final example from the *Test-driven development principles* section will look like this:

```
import unittest

from primes import is_prime


class MyTests(unittest.TestCase):
    def test_is_prime(self):
        self.assertTrue(is_prime(5))
        self.assertTrue(is_prime(7))

        self.assertFalse(is_prime(8))
        self.assertFalse(is_prime(0))
        self.assertFalse(is_prime(1))

        self.assertFalse(is_prime(-1))
        self.assertFalse(is_prime(-3))
        self.assertFalse(is_prime(-6))


if __name__ == "__main__":
    unittest.main()
```

The `unittest.main()` function is the utility that allows to make the whole module to be executable as a test suite:

```
$ python test_is_prime.py -v
test_is_prime (__main__.MyTests) ... ok


----------------------------------------------------------------------

Ran 1 test in 0.000s


OK
```

The `unittest.main()` function scans the context of the current module and looks for classes that subclass `TestCase`. It instantiates them, then runs all methods that start with the `test` prefix.

A good test suite follows the common and consistent naming conventions. For instance, if the `is_prime` function is included in the `primes.py` module, the test class could be called `PrimesTests` and put into the `test_primes.py` file:

```python
import unittest

from primes import is_prime


class PrimesTests(unittest.TestCase):
    def test_is_prime(self):
        self.assertTrue(is_prime(5))
        self.assertTrue(is_prime(7))

        self.assertFalse(is_prime(8))
        self.assertFalse(is_prime(0))
        self.assertFalse(is_prime(1))

        self.assertFalse(is_prime(-1))
        self.assertFalse(is_prime(-3))
        self.assertFalse(is_prime(-6))


if __name__ == '__main__':
    unittest.main()
```

From there, every time the `utils` module evolves, the `test_utils` module gets more tests.

In order to work, the `test_primes` module needs to have the `primes` module available in the context. This can be achieved either by having both modules in the same package by adding a tested module explicitly to the Python path. In practice, the `develop` command of `setuptools` is very helpful here.

Running tests over the whole application presupposes that you have a script that builds a **test campaign** out of all test modules. `unittest` provides a `TestSuite` class that can aggregate tests and run them as a test campaign, as long as they are all instances of `TestCase` or `TestSuite`.

In Python's past, there was convention that test module provides a `test_suite` function that returns a `TestSuite` instance either used in the `__main__` section, when the module is called by Command Prompt, or used by a test runner:

```python
import unittest

from primes import is_prime


class PrimesTests(unittest.TestCase):
    def test_is_prime(self):
        self.assertTrue(is_prime(5))

        self.assertTrue(is_prime(7))

        self.assertFalse(is_prime(8))
        self.assertFalse(is_prime(0))
        self.assertFalse(is_prime(1))

        self.assertFalse(is_prime(-1))
        self.assertFalse(is_prime(-3))
        self.assertFalse(is_prime(-6))


class OtherTests(unittest.TestCase):
    def test_true(self):
        self.assertTrue(True)


def test_suite():
    """builds the test suite."""
    suite = unittest.TestSuite()
    suite.addTests(unittest.makeSuite(PrimesTests))
    suite.addTests(unittest.makeSuite(OtherTests))

    return suite


if __name__ == '__main__':
    unittest.main(defaultTest='test_suite')
```

Running this module from the shell will print the test campaign output:

```
$ python test_primes.py -v
test_is_prime (__main__.PrimesTests) ... ok
test_true (__main__.OtherTests) ... ok


----------------------------------------------------------------------

Ran 2 tests in 0.001s


OK
```

The preceding approach was required in the older versions of Python when the unittest module did not have proper test discovery utilities. Usually, running of all tests was done by a global script that browses the code tree looking for tests and runs them. This is called **test discovery** and will be covered more extensively later in this chapter. For now, you should only know that unittest provides a simple command that can discover all tests from modules and packages with a test prefix:

```
$ python -m unittest -v
test_is_prime (test_primes.PrimesTests) ... ok
test_true (test_primes.OtherTests) ... ok


----------------------------------------------------------------------

Ran 2 tests in 0.001s


OK
```

If you use the preceding command, then there is no requirement to manually define the __main__ sections and invoke the unittest.main() function.

doctest

doctest is a module that extracts snippets in the form of interactive prompt sessions from docstrings or text files and replays them to check whether the example output is the same as the real one.

For instance, the text file with the following content could be run as a test:

```
Check addition of integers works as expected::

>>> 1 + 1
2
```

Let's assume this documentation file is stored in the filesystem under `test.rst` name. The `doctest` module provides some functions to extract and run the tests from such documentation:

```
>>> import doctest
>>> doctest.testfile('test.rst', verbose=True)
Trying:
    1 + 1
Expecting:
    2
ok
1 items passed all tests:
   1 tests in test.rst
1 tests in 1 items.
1 passed and 0 failed.
Test passed.
TestResults(failed=0, attempted=1)
```

Using `doctest` has many advantages:

- Packages can be documented and tested through examples
- Documentation examples are always up to date
- Using examples in doctests to write a package helps to maintain the user's point of view

However, doctests do not make unit tests obsolete; they should be used only to provide human-readable examples in documents. In other words, when the tests are concerning low-level matters or need complex test fixtures that would obfuscate the document, they should not be used.

Some Python frameworks such as Zope use doctests extensively, and they are at times criticized by people who are new to the code. Some doctests are really hard to read and understand, since the examples break one of the rules of technical writing—they cannot be taken and run in a simple prompt, and they need extensive knowledge. So, documents that are supposed to help newcomers are really hard to read because the code examples, which are doctests built through TDD, are based on complex test fixtures or even specific test APIs.

As explained in *Chapter 9, Documenting Your Project*, when you use doctests that are part of the documentation of your packages, be careful to follow the seven rules of technical writing.

At this stage, you should have a good overview of what TDD brings. If you are still not convinced, you should give it a try over a few modules. Write a package using TDD and measure the time spent on building, debugging, and then refactoring. You should find out quickly that it is truly superior.

I do test

If you are coming from the *I don't test* section and are now convinced to do test-driven development, then congratulations! You know the basics of test-driven development, but there are some more things you should learn before you will be able to efficiently use this methodology.

This section describes a few problems developers bump into when they write tests and some ways to solve them. It also provides a quick review of popular test runners and tools available in the Python community.

unittest pitfalls

The `unittest` module was introduced in Python 2.1 and has been massively used by developers since then. But some alternative test frameworks were created in the community by people who were frustrated with the weaknesses and limitations of `unittest`.

These are the common criticisms that are often made:

- The **framework is heavy to use** because:
    - You have to write all your tests in subclasses of `TestCase`
    - You have to prefix the method names with `test`
    - You are encouraged to use assertion methods provided in `TestCase` instead of plain `assert` statements and existing methods may not cover every use case

- The framework is hard to extend because it requires massive subclassing of its base classes or tricks such as decorators.

- Test fixtures are sometimes hard to organize because the `setUp` and `tearDown` facilities are tied to the `TestCase` level, though they run once per test. In other words, if a test fixture concerns many test modules, it is not simple to organize its creation and cleanup.
- It is not easy to run a test campaign over Python software. The default test runner (`python -m unittest`) indeed provides some test discovery but does not provide enough filtering capabilities. In practice, extra scripts have to be written to collect the tests, aggregate them, and then run them in a convenient way.

A lighter approach is needed to write tests without suffering from the rigidity of a framework that looks too much like its big Java brother, JUnit. Since Python does not require working with a 100% class-based environment, it is preferable to provide a more Pythonic test framework that is not based on subclassing.

A common approach would be:

- To provide a simple way to mark any function or any class as a test
- To extend the framework through a plug-in system
- To provide a complete test fixture environment for all test levels: the whole campaign, a group of tests at module level, and at test level
- To provide a test runner based on test discovery with an extensive set of options

unittest alternatives

Some third-party tools try to solve the problems just mentioned by providing extra features in the shape of `unittest` extensions.

Python wiki provides a very long list of various testing utilities and frameworks (refer to `https://wiki.python.org/moin/PythonTestingToolsTaxonomy`), but there are just two projects that are especially popular:

- `nose`: `http://nose.readthedocs.org`
- `py.test`: `http://pytest.org`

nose

`nose` is mainly a test runner with powerful discovery features. It has extensive options that allow running all kind of test campaigns in a Python application.

It is not a part of standard library but is available on PyPI and can be easily installed with pip:

```
pip install nose
```

Test runner

After installing nose, a new command called `nosetests` is available at the prompt. Running the tests presented in the first section of the chapter can be done directly with it:

```
nosetests -v
test_true (test_primes.OtherTests) ... ok
test_is_prime (test_primes.PrimesTests) ... ok
builds the test suite. ... ok


----------------------------------------------------------------------
Ran 3 tests in 0.009s


OK
```

nose takes care of discovering the tests by recursively browsing the current directory and building a test suite on its own. The preceding example at first glance does not look like any improvement over the simple `python -m unittest`. The difference will be noticeable if you run this command with the `--help` switch. You will notice that nose provides tens of parameters that allow you to control test discovery and execution.

Writing tests

nose goes a step further by running all classes and functions whose name matches the regular expression `((?:^|[b_.-])[Tt]est)` located in modules that match it too. Roughly, all callables that start with `test` and are located in a module that match the pattern will also be executed as a test.

For instance, this `test_ok.py` module will be recognized and run by `nose`:

```
$ more test_ok.py
def test_ok():
    print('my test')
$ nosetests -v
test_ok.test_ok ... ok
```

```
--------------------------------------------------------------
Ran 1 test in 0.071s
```

OK

Regular TestCase classes and doctests are executed as well.

Last, nose provides assertion functions that are similar to TestCase methods. But these are provided as functions that follow the PEP 8 naming conventions, rather than using the Java convention unittest uses (refer to http://nose.readthedocs.org/).

Writing test fixtures

nose supports three levels of fixtures:

- **Package level**: The setup and teardown functions can be added in the __init__.py module of a test's package containing all test modules
- **Module level**: A test module can have its own setup and teardown functions
- **Test level**: The callable can also have fixture functions using the with_setup decorator provided

For instance, to set a test fixture at the module and test level, use this code:

```
def setup():
    # setup code, launched for the whole module
    ...

def teardown():
    # teardown code, launched for the whole module
    ...

def set_ok():
    # setup code launched only for test_ok
    ...

@with_setup(set_ok)
def test_ok():
    print('my test')
```

Integration with setuptools and a plug-in system

Last, nose integrates smoothly with setuptools and so the test command can be used with it (python setup.py test). This integration is done by adding the test_suite metadata in the setup.py script:

```
setup(
    #...
    test_suite='nose.collector',
)
```

nose also uses setuptool's entry point machinery for developers to write nose plugins. This allows you to override or modify every aspect of the tool from test discovery to output formatting.

 A list of nose plugins is maintained at https://nose-plugins. jottit.com.

Wrap-up

nose is a complete testing tool that fixes many of the issues unittest has. It is still designed to use implicit prefix names for tests, which remains a constraint for some developers. While this prefix can be customized, it still requires one to follow a convention.

This convention over configuration statement is not bad and is a lot better than the boiler-plate code required in unittest. But using explicit decorators, for example, could be a nice way to get rid of the test prefix.

Also, the ability to extend nose with plugins makes it very flexible and allows a developer to customize the tool to meet his/her needs.

If your testing workflow requires overriding a lot of nose parameters, you can easily add a .noserc or a nose.cfg file in your home directory or project root. It will specify the default set of options for the nosetests command. For instance, a good practice is to automatically look for doctests during test run. An example of the nose configuration file that enables running doctests is as follows:

```
[nosetests]
with-doctest=1
doctest-extension=.txt
```

py.test

py.test is very similar to nose. In fact, the latter was inspired by py.test, so we will focus mainly on details that make these tools different from each other. The tool was born as part of a larger package called py but now these are developed separately.

Like every third-party package mentioned in this book, py.test is available on PyPI and can be installed with pip as pytest:

```
$ pip install pytest
```

From there, a new py.test command is available at the prompt that can be used exactly like nosetests. The tool uses similar pattern-matching and a test discovery algorithm to catch tests to be run. The pattern is stricter than that which nose uses and will only catch:

- Classes that start with Test, in a file that starts with test
- Functions that start with test, in a file that starts with test

 Be careful to use the right character case. If a function starts with a capital "T", it will be taken as a class, and thus ignored. And if a class starts with a lowercase "t", py.test will break because it will try to deal with it as a function.

The advantages of py.test are:

- The ability to easily disable some test classes
- A flexible and original mechanism for dealing with fixtures
- The ability to distribute tests among several computers

Writing test fixtures

py.test supports two mechanisms to deal with fixtures. The first one, modeled after xUnit framework, is similar to nose. Of course semantics differ a bit. py.test will look for three levels of fixtures in each test module as shown in following example:

```
def setup_module(module):
    """ Setup up any state specific to the execution
        of the given module.
    """


def teardown_module(module):
    """ Teardown any state that was previously setup
```

```
        with a setup_module method.
    """

def setup_class(cls):
    """ Setup up any state specific to the execution
        of the given class (which usually contains tests).
    """

def teardown_class(cls):
    """ Teardown any state that was previously setup
        with a call to setup_class.
    """

def setup_method(self, method):
    """ Setup up any state tied to the execution of the given
        method in a class. setup_method is invoked for every
        test method of a class.
    """

def teardown_method(self, method):
    """ Teardown any state that was previously setup
        with a setup_method call.
    """
```

Each function will get the current module, class, or method as an argument. The test fixture will, therefore, be able to work on the context without having to look for it, as with nose.

The alternative mechanism for writing fixtures with py.test is to build on the concept of dependency injection, allowing to maintain the test state in a more modular and scalable way. The non xUnit-style fixtures (setup/teardown procedures) always have unique names and need to be explicitly activated by declaring their use in test functions, methods, and modules in classes.

The simplest implementation of fixtures takes the form of a named function declared with the pytest.fixture() decorator. To mark a fixture as used in the test, it needs to be declared as a function or method argument. To make it more clear, consider the previous example of the test module for the is_prime function rewritten with the use of py.test fixtures:

```
import pytest

from primes import is_prime
```

```
@pytest.fixture()
def prime_numbers():
    return [3, 5, 7]


@pytest.fixture()
def non_prime_numbers():
    return [8, 0, 1]


@pytest.fixture()
def negative_numbers():
    return [-1, -3, -6]


def test_is_prime_true(prime_numbers):
    for number in prime_numbers:
        assert is_prime(number)


def test_is_prime_false(non_prime_numbers, negative_numbers):
    for number in non_prime_numbers:
        assert not is_prime(number)

    for number in non_prime_numbers:
        assert not is_prime(number)
```

Disabling test functions and classes

py.test provides a simple mechanism to disable some tests upon certain conditions. This is called skipping, and the pytest package provides the .skipif decorator for that purpose. If a single test function or a whole test class decorator needs to be skipped upon certain conditions, it needs to be defined with this decorator and with some value provided that verifies if the expected condition was met. Here is an example from the official documentation that skips running the whole test case class on Windows:

```
import pytest

@pytest.mark.skipif(
    sys.platform == 'win32',
    reason="does not run on windows"
)
```

```
class TestPosixCalls:

    def test_function(self):
        """will not be setup or run under 'win32' platform"""
```

You can, of course, predefine the skipping conditions in order to share them across your testing modules:

```
import pytest

skipwindows = pytest.mark.skipif(
    sys.platform == 'win32',
    reason="does not run on windows"
)


@skip_windows
class TestPosixCalls:

    def test_function(self):
        """will not be setup or run under 'win32' platform"""
```

If a test is marked in such a way, it will not be executed at all. However, in some cases, you want to run such a test and want to execute it, but you know, it is expected to fail under known conditions. For this purpose, a different decorator is provided. It is @mark.xfail and ensures that the test is always run, but it should fail at some point if the predefined condition occurs:

```
import pytest

@pytest.mark.xfail(
sys.platform == 'win32',
    reason="does not run on windows"
)
class TestPosixCalls:

    def test_function(self):
        """it must fail under windows"""
```

Using xfail is much stricter than skipif. Test is always executed and if it does not fail when it is expected to, then the whole py.test run will result in a failure.

Automated distributed tests

An interesting feature of `py.test` is its ability to distribute the tests across several computers. As long as the computers are reachable through SSH, `py.test` will be able to drive each computer by sending tests to be performed.

However, this feature relies on the network; if the connection is broken, the slave will not be able to continue working since it is fully driven by the master.

Buildbot, or other continuous integration tools, is preferable when a project has long test campaigns. But the `py.test` distributed model can be used for the ad hoc distribution of tests when you are working on an application that consumes a lot of resources to run the tests.

Wrap-up

`py.test` is very similar to `nose` since no boilerplate code is needed to aggregate the tests in it. It also has a good plugin system and there are a great number of extensions available on PyPI.

Lastly, `py.test` focuses on making the tests run fast and is truly superior compared to the other tools in this area. The other notable feature is the original approach to fixtures that really helps in managing a reusable library of fixtures. Some people may argue that there is too much magic involved but it really streamlines the development of a test suite. This single advantage of `py.test` makes it my tool of choice, so I really recommend it.

Testing coverage

Code coverage is a very useful metric that provides objective information on how well project code is tested. It is simply a measurement of how many and which lines of code are executed during all test executions. It is often expressed as a percentage and 100% coverage means that every line of code was executed during tests.

The most popular code coverage tool is called simply coverage and is freely available on PyPI. The usage is very simple and consists only of two steps. The first step is to run the coverage run command in your shell with the path to your script/program that runs all the tests as an argument:

```
$ coverage run --source . `which py.test` -v

===================== test session starts =====================
platformdarwin -- Python 3.5.1, pytest-2.8.7, py-1.4.31, pluggy-0.3.1 --
/Users/swistakm/.envs/book/bin/python3
cachedir: .cache
```

```
rootdir: /Users/swistakm/dev/book/chapter10/pytest, inifile:
plugins: capturelog-0.7, codecheckers-0.2, cov-2.2.1, timeout-1.0.0
collected 6 items


primes.py::pyflakes PASSED
primes.py::pep8 PASSED
test_primes.py::pyflakes PASSED
test_primes.py::pep8 PASSED
test_primes.py::test_is_prime_true PASSED
test_primes.py::test_is_prime_false PASSED


========= 6 passed, 1 pytest-warnings in 0.10 seconds ==========
```

The coverage run also accepts -m parameter that specifies a runnable module name instead of a program path that may be better for some testing frameworks:

```
$ coverage run -m unittest
$ coverage run -m nose
$ coverage run -m pytest
```

The next step is to generate a human-readable report of your code coverage from results cashed in the .coverage file. The coverage package supports a few output formats and the simplest one just prints an ASCII table in your terminal:

```
$ coverage report
Name              StmtsMiss  Cover
----------------------------------
primes.py              7    0    100%
test_primes.py        16    0    100%
----------------------------------
TOTAL                 23    0    100%
```

The other useful coverage report format is HTML that can be browsed in your web browser:

```
$ coverage html
```

The default output folder of this HTML report is `htmlcov/` in your working directory. The real advantage of the `coverage html` output is that you can browse annotated sources of your project with highlighted parts that have missing test coverage (as shown in *Figure 1*):

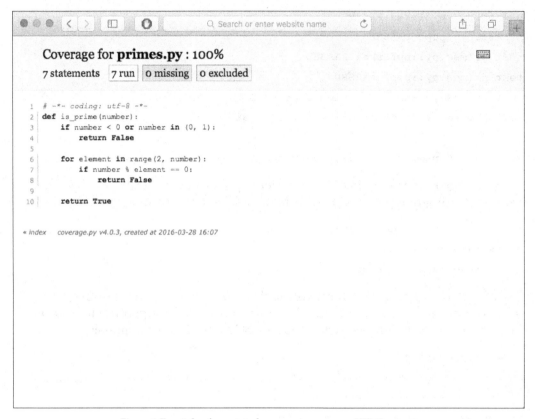

Figure 1 Example of annotated sources in coverage HTML report

You should remember that while you should always strive to ensure 100% test coverage, it is never a guarantee that code is tested perfectly and there is no place where code can break. It means only that every line of code was reached during execution, but not necessarily every possible condition was tested. In practice, it may be relatively easy to ensure full code coverage, but it is really hard to make sure that every branch of code was reached. This is especially true for the testing of functions that may have multiple combinations of `if` statements and specific language constructs like `list`/`dict`/`set` comprehensions. You should always care for good test coverage, but you should never treat its measurement as the final answer of how good your testing suite is.

Fakes and mocks

Writing unit tests presupposes that you isolate the unit of code that is being tested. Tests usually feed the function or method with some data and verify its return value and/or the side effects of its execution. This is mainly to make sure the tests:

- Are concerning an atomic part of the application, which can be a function, method, class, or interface
- Provide deterministic, reproducible results

Sometimes, the proper isolation of the program component is not obvious. For instance, if the code sends e-mails, it will probably call Python's `smtplib` module, which will work with the SMTP server through a network connection. If we want our tests to be reproducible and are just testing if e-mails have the desired content, then probably this should not happen. Ideally, unit tests should run on any computer with no external dependencies and side effects.

Thanks to Python's dynamic nature, it is possible to use **monkey patching** to modify the runtime code from the test fixture (that is, modify software dynamically at runtime without touching the source code) to **fake** the behavior of a third-party code or library.

Building a fake

A fake behavior in the tests can be created by discovering the minimal set of interactions needed for the tested code to work with the external parts. Then, the output is manually returned or uses a real pool of data that has been previously recorded.

This is done by starting an empty class or function and using it as a replacement. The test is then launched, and the fake is iteratively updated until it behaves correctly. This is possible thanks to nature of a Python type system. The object is considered compatible with the given type as long as it behaves as the expected type and does not need to be its ancestor via subclassing. This approach to typing in Python is called duck typing—if something behaves like a duck, it can be treated like a duck.

Let's take an example with a function called `send` in a module called `mailer` that sends e-mails:

```python
import smtplib
import email.message


def send(
    sender, to,
```

```
            subject='None',
            body='None',
            server='localhost'
    ):
        """sends a message."""
        message = email.message.Message()
        message['To'] = to
        message['From'] = sender
        message['Subject'] = subject
        message.set_payload(body)

        server = smtplib.SMTP(server)
        try:
            return server.sendmail(sender, to, message.as_string())
        finally:
            server.quit()
```

 py.test will be used to demonstrate fakes and mocks in this section.

The corresponding test can be:

```
from mailer import send


def test_send():
    res = send(
        'john.doe@example.com',
        'john.doe@example.com',
        'topic',
        'body'
    )
    assert res == {}
```

This test will pass and work as long as there is an SMTP server on the local host. If not, it will fail like this:

```
$ py.test --tb=short

========================= test session starts =========================
platform darwin -- Python 3.5.1, pytest-2.8.7, py-1.4.31, pluggy-0.3.1
rootdir: /Users/swistakm/dev/book/chapter10/mailer, inifile:
plugins: capturelog-0.7, codecheckers-0.2, cov-2.2.1, timeout-1.0.0
collected 5 items
```

```
mailer.py ..
test_mailer.py ..F


============================ FAILURES ============================
_____ test_send _____
test_mailer.py:10: in test_send
    'body'
mailer.py:19: in send
    server = smtplib.SMTP(server)
.../smtplib.py:251: in __init__
    (code, msg) = self.connect(host, port)
.../smtplib.py:335: in connect
    self.sock = self._get_socket(host, port, self.timeout)
.../smtplib.py:306: in _get_socket
    self.source_address)
.../socket.py:711: in create_connection
    raise err
.../socket.py:702: in create_connection
    sock.connect(sa)
E   ConnectionRefusedError: [Errno 61] Connection refused
======== 1 failed, 4 passed, 1 pytest-warnings in 0.17 seconds ========
```

A patch can be added to fake the SMTP class:

```
import smtplib
import pytest
from mailer import send


class FakeSMTP(object):
    pass


@pytest.yield_fixture()
def patch_smtplib():
    # setup step: monkey patch smtplib
    old_smtp = smtplib.SMTP
    smtplib.SMTP = FakeSMTP
```

```
        yield

        # teardown step: bring back smtplib to
        # its former state
        smtplib.SMTP = old_smtp


    def test_send(patch_smtplib):
        res = send(
            'john.doe@example.com',
            'john.doe@example.com',
            'topic',
            'body'
        )
        assert res == {}
```

In the preceding code, we have used a new `pytest.yield_fixture()` decorator. It allows us to use a generator syntax to provide both setup and teardown procedures in a single fixture function. Now our test suite can be run again with the patched version of `smtplib`:

```
$ py.test --tb=short -v

========================= test session starts =========================
platform darwin -- Python 3.5.1, pytest-2.8.7, py-1.4.31, pluggy-0.3.1 --
/Users/swistakm/.envs/book/bin/python3
cachedir: .cache
rootdir: /Users/swistakm/dev/book/chapter10/mailer, inifile:
plugins: capturelog-0.7, codecheckers-0.2, cov-2.2.1, timeout-1.0.0
collected 5 items


mailer.py::pyflakes PASSED
mailer.py::pep8 PASSED
test_mailer.py::pyflakes PASSED
test_mailer.py::pep8 PASSED
test_mailer.py::test_send FAILED


============================ FAILURES ============================
_____ test_send _____
test_mailer.py:29: in test_send
    'body'
```

```
mailer.py:19: in send
    server = smtplib.SMTP(server)
E   TypeError: object() takes no parameters
======= 1 failed, 4 passed, 1 pytest-warnings in 0.09 seconds =======
```

As we can see from the preceding transcript, our `FakeSMTP` class implementation is not complete. We need to update its interface to match the original SMTP class. According to the duck typing principle, we need only to provide interfaces that are required by the tested `send()` function:

```python
class FakeSMTP(object):
    def __init__(self, *args, **kw):
        # arguments are not important in our example
        pass

    def quit(self):
        pass

    def sendmail(self, *args, **kw):
        return {}
```

Of course, the fake class can evolve with new tests to provide more complex behaviors. But it should be as short and simple as possible. The same principle can be used with more complex outputs, by recording them to serve them back through the fake API. This is often done for third-party servers such as LDAP or SQL.

It is important to know that special care should be taken when monkey patching any built-in or third-party module. If not done properly, such an approach might leave unwanted side effects that will propagate between tests. Fortunately, many testing frameworks and tools provide proper utilities that make the patching of any code units safe and easy. In our example, we did everything manually and provided a custom `patch_smtplib()` fixture function with separated setup and teardown steps. A typical solution in `py.test` is much easier. This framework comes with a built-in monkey patch fixture that should satisfy most of our patching needs:

```python
import smtplib
from mailer import send


class FakeSMTP(object):
    def __init__(self, *args, **kw):
        # arguments are not important in our example
        pass
```

```
        def quit(self):
            pass

        def sendmail(self, *args, **kw):
            return {}


    def test_send(monkeypatch):
        monkeypatch.setattr(smtplib, 'SMTP', FakeSMTP)

        res = send(
            'john.doe@example.com',
            'john.doe@example.com',
            'topic',
            'body'
        )
        assert res == {}
```

You should know that *fakes* have real limitations. If you decide to fake an external
dependency, you might introduce bugs or unwanted behaviors the real server
wouldn't have or vice versa.

Using mocks

Mock objects are generic fake objects that can be used to isolate the tested code. They
automate the building process of the object's input and output. There is a greater use
of mock objects in statically typed languages, where monkey patching is harder, but
they are still useful in Python to shorten the code to mimic external APIs.

There are a lot of mock libraries available in Python, but the most recognized one is
`unittest.mock` and is provided in the standard library. It was created as a third-
party package and not as a part of the Python distribution but was shortly included
into the standard library as a provisional package (refer to `https://docs.python.
org/dev/glossary.html#term-provisional-api`). For Python versions older than
3.3, you will need to install it from PyPI:

`pip install Mock`

In our example, using `unittest.mock` to patch SMTP is way simpler than creating a
fake from scratch:

```
    import smtplib
    from unittest.mock import MagicMock
    from mailer import send
```

```
def test_send(monkeypatch):
    smtp_mock = MagicMock()
    smtp_mock.sendmail.return_value = {}

    monkeypatch.setattr(
        smtplib, 'SMTP', MagicMock(return_value=smtp_mock)
    )

    res = send(
        'john.doe@example.com',
        'john.doe@example.com',
        'topic',
        'body'
    )
    assert res == {}
```

The `return_value` argument of a mock object or method allows you to define what value is returned by the call. When the mock object is used, every time an attribute is called by the code, it creates a new mock object for the attribute on the fly. Thus, no exception is raised. This is the case (for instance) for the `quit` method we wrote earlier that does not need to be defined anymore.

In the preceding example, we have in fact created two mocks:

- The first one that mocks the SMTP class object and not its instance. This allows you to easily create a new object regardless of the expected __init__() method. Mocks by default return new `Mock()` objects if treated as callable. This is why we needed to provide another mock as its `return_value` keyword argument to have control on the instance interface.
- The second one that mocks the actual instance returned on the patched `smtplib.SMTP()` call. In this mock, we control the behavior of the `sendmail()` method.

In our example, we have used the monkey-patching utility available from the `py.test` framework, but `unittest.mock` provides its own patching utilities. In some situations (like patching class objects), it may be simpler and faster to use them instead of your framework-specific tools. Here is example of monkey patching with the `patch()` context manager provided by `unittest.mock` module:

```
from unittest.mock import patch
from mailer import send

def test_send():
    with patch('smtplib.SMTP') as mock:
        instance = mock.return_value
```

```
instance.sendmail.return_value = {}
res = send(
    'john.doe@example.com',
    'john.doe@example.com',
    'topic',
    'body'
)
assert res == {}
```

Testing environment and dependency compatibility

The importance of environment isolation has already been mentioned in this book many times. By isolating your execution environment on both application level (virtual environments) and system level (system virtualization), you are able to ensure that your tests run under repeatable conditions. This way, you protect yourself from rare and obscure problems caused by broken dependencies.

The best way to allow the proper isolation of a test environment is to use good continuous integration systems that support system virtualization. There are good free solutions for open source projects such as Travis CI (Linux and OS X) or AppVeyor (Windows), but if you need such a thing for testing proprietary software, it is very likely that you will need to spend some time on building such a solution by yourself on top of some existing open source CI tools (GitLab CI, Jenkins, and Buildbot).

Dependency matrix testing

Testing matrixes for open source Python projects in most cases focus only on different Python versions and rarely on different operating systems. Not doing your tests and builds on different systems is completely OK for projects that are purely Python and where there are no expected system interoperability issues. But some projects, especially when distributed as compiled Python extensions, should be definitely tested on various target operating systems. For open source projects, you may even be forced to use a few independent CI systems to provide builds for just the three most popular ones (Windows, Linux, and Mac OS X). If you are looking for a good example, you can take a look at the small pyrilla project (refer to `https://github.com/swistakm/pyrilla`) that is a simple C audio extension for Python. It uses both Travis CI and AppVeyor in order to provide compiled builds for Windows and Mac OS X and a large range of CPython versions.

But dimensions of test matrixes do not end on systems and Python versions. Packages that provide integration with other software such as caches, databases, or system services very often should be tested on various versions of integrated applications. A good tool that makes such testing easy is tox (refer to `http://tox.readthedocs.org`). It provides a simple way to configure multiple testing environments and run all tests with a single `tox` command. It is a very powerful and flexible tool but is also very easy to use. The best way to present its usage is to show you an example of a configuration file that is in fact the core of tox. Here is the `tox.ini` file from the django-userena project (refer to `https://github.com/bread-and-pepper/django-userena`):

```
[tox]
downloadcache = {toxworkdir}/cache/

envlist =
    ; py26 support was dropped in django1.7
    py26-django{15,16},
    ; py27 still has the widest django support
    py27-django{15,16,17,18,19},
    ; py32, py33 support was officially introduced in django1.5
    ; py32, py33 support was dropped in django1.9
    py32-django{15,16,17,18},
    py33-django{15,16,17,18},
    ; py34 support was officially introduced in django1.7
    py34-django{17,18,19}
    ; py35 support was officially introduced in django1.8
    py35-django{18,19}

[testenv]
usedevelop = True
deps =
    django{15,16}: south
    django{15,16}: django-guardian<1.4.0
    django15: django==1.5.12
    django16: django==1.6.11
    django17: django==1.7.11
    django18: django==1.8.7
    django19: django==1.9
    coverage: django==1.9
    coverage: coverage==4.0.3
    coverage: coveralls==1.1

basepython =
    py35: python3.5
```

```
    py34: python3.4
    py33: python3.3
    py32: python3.2
    py27: python2.7
    py26: python2.6


commands={envpython} userena/runtests/runtests.py userenaumessages
{posargs}

[testenv:coverage]
basepython = python2.7
passenv = TRAVIS TRAVIS_JOB_ID TRAVIS_BRANCH
commands=
    coverage run --source=userena userena/runtests/runtests.py
userenaumessages {posargs}
    coveralls
```

This configuration allows you to test django-userena on five different versions
of Django and six versions of Python. Not every Django version will work on
every Python version and the tox.ini file makes it relatively easy to define such
dependency constraints. In practice, the whole build matrix consists of 21 unique
environments (including a special environment for code coverage collection). It
would require tremendous effort to create each testing environment manually or
even using shell scripts.

Tox is great but its usage gets more complicated if we would like to change other
elements of the testing environment that are not plain Python dependencies. This is
a situation when we need to test under different versions of system packages and
backing services. The best way to solve this problem is again to use good continuous
integration systems that allow you to easily define matrixes of environment variables
and install system software on virtual machines. A good example of doing that
using Travis CI is provided by the ianitor project (refer to https://github.com/
ClearcodeHQ/ianitor/) that was already mentioned in *Chapter 9, Documenting Your
Project*. It is a simple utility for the Consul discovery service. The Consul project has
a very active community and many new versions of its code are released every year.
This makes it very reasonable to test against various versions of that service. This
makes sure that the ianitor project is still up to date with the latest version of that
software but also does not break compatibility with previous Consul versions. Here
is the content of the .travis.yml configuration file for Travis CI that allows you to
test against three different Consul versions and four Python interpreter versions:

```
language: python

install: pip install tox --use-mirrors
env:
```

```
matrix:
    # consul 0.4.1
    - TOX_ENV=py27      CONSUL_VERSION=0.4.1
    - TOX_ENV=py33      CONSUL_VERSION=0.4.1
    - TOX_ENV=py34      CONSUL_VERSION=0.4.1
    - TOX_ENV=py35      CONSUL_VERSION=0.4.1

    # consul 0.5.2
    - TOX_ENV=py27      CONSUL_VERSION=0.5.2
    - TOX_ENV=py33      CONSUL_VERSION=0.5.2
    - TOX_ENV=py34      CONSUL_VERSION=0.5.2
    - TOX_ENV=py35      CONSUL_VERSION=0.5.2

    # consul 0.6.4
    - TOX_ENV=py27      CONSUL_VERSION=0.6.4
    - TOX_ENV=py33      CONSUL_VERSION=0.6.4
    - TOX_ENV=py34      CONSUL_VERSION=0.6.4
    - TOX_ENV=py35      CONSUL_VERSION=0.6.4

    # coverage and style checks
    - TOX_ENV=pep8      CONSUL_VERSION=0.4.1
    - TOX_ENV=coverage CONSUL_VERSION=0.4.1

before_script:
  - wget https://releases.hashicorp.com/consul/${CONSUL_VERSION}/
consul_${CONSUL_VERSION}_linux_amd64.zip
  - unzip consul_${CONSUL_VERSION}_linux_amd64.zip
  - start-stop-daemon --start --background --exec `pwd`/consul --
agent -server -data-dir /tmp/consul -bootstrap-expect=1

script:
  - tox -e $TOX_ENV
```

The preceding example provides 14 unique test environments (including pep8 and coverage builds) for the ianitor code. This configuration also uses tox to create actual testing virtual environments on Travis VMs. This is actually a very popular approach to integrate tox with different CI systems. By moving as much of a test environment configuration as possible to tox, you are reducing the risk of locking yourself to a single vendor. Things like the installation of new services or defining system environment variables are supported by most of the Travis CI competitors, so it should be relatively easy to switch to a different service provider if there is a better product available on the market or Travis will change their pricing model for open source projects.

Document-driven development

doctests are a real advantage in Python compared to other languages. The fact that documentation can use code examples that are also runnable as tests changes the way TDD can be done. For instance, a part of the documentation can be done through `doctests` during the development cycle. This approach also ensures that the provided examples are always up to date and really working.

Building software through doctests rather than regular unit tests is called **Document-Driven Development (DDD)**. Developers explain what the code is doing in plain English while they are implementing it.

Writing a story

Writing doctests in DDD is done by building a story about how a piece of code works and should be used. The principles are described in plain English and then a few code usage examples are distributed throughout the text. A good practice is to start to write text on how the code works and then add some code examples.

To see an example of doctests in practice, let's look at the `atomisator` package (refer to `https://bitbucket.org/tarek/atomisator`). The documentation text for its `atomisator.parser` subpackage (under `packages/atomisator.parser/atomisator/parser/docs/README.txt`) is as follows:

```
==================
atomisator.parser
==================


The parser knows how to return a feed content, with
the `parse` function, available as a top-level function::

>>> from atomisator.parser import Parser

This function takes the feed url and returns an iterator
over its content. A second parameter can specify a maximum
number of entries to return. If not given, it is fixed to 10::

>>> import os
>>> res = Parser()(os.path.join(test_dir, 'sample.xml'))
>>> res
<itertools.imap ...>

Each item is a dictionary that contain the entry::
```

```
>>> entry = res.next()
>>> entry['title']
u'CSSEdit 2.0 Released'

The keys available are:

>>> keys = sorted(entry.keys())
>>> list(keys)
    ['id', 'link', 'links', 'summary', 'summary_detail', 'tags',
     'title', 'title_detail']

Dates are changed into datetime::

>>> type(entry['date'])
>>>
```

Later, the doctest will evolve to take into account new elements or the required changes. This doctest is also a good documentation for developers who want to use the package and should be changed with this usage in mind.

A common pitfall in writing tests in a document is to transform it into an unreadable piece of text. If this happens, it should not be considered as part of the documentation anymore.

That said, some developers that are working exclusively through doctests often group their doctests into two categories: the ones that are readable and usable so that they can be a part of the package documentation, and the ones that are unreadable and are just used to build and test the software.

Many developers think that doctests should be dropped for the latter in favor of regular unit tests. Others even use dedicated doctests for bug fixes.

So, the balance between doctests and regular tests is a matter of taste and is up to the team, as long as the published part of the doctests is readable.

 When DDD is used in a project, focus on the readability and decide which doctests are eligible to be a part of the published documentation.

Summary

This chapter advocated the usage of TDD and provided more information on:

- `unittest` pitfalls
- Third-party tools: `nose` and `py.test`
- How to build fakes and mocks
- Documentation-driven development

Since we already know how to build, package, and test software, in the next two chapters we will focus on ways to find performance bottlenecks and optimize your programs.

11
Optimization – General Principles and Profiling Techniques

"We should forget about small efficiencies, say about 97% of the time: premature optimization is the root of all evil."

– Donald Knuth

This chapter is about optimization and provides a set of general principles and profiling techniques. It gives the three rules of optimization every developer should be aware of and provides guidelines on optimization. Last, it focuses on how to find bottlenecks.

The three rules of optimization

Optimization has a price, no matter what the results are. When a piece of code works, it might be better (sometimes) to leave it alone than to try making it faster at all costs. There are a few rules to keep in mind when doing any kind of optimization:

- Make it work first
- Work from the user's point of view
- Keep the code readable

Make it work first

A very common mistake is to try to optimize the code while you are writing it. This is mostly pointless because the real bottlenecks are often located where you would have never thought they would be.

An application is usually composed of very complex interactions, and it is impossible to get a full picture of what is going on before it is really used.

Of course, this is not a reason to write a function or a method without trying to make it as fast as possible. You should be careful to lower its complexity as much as possible and avoid useless repetition. But the first goal is to make it work. This goal should not be hindered by optimization efforts.

For line-level code, the Python philosophy is that there's one, and preferably only one, way to do it. So, as long as you stick with a Pythonic syntax, described in *Chapter 2, Syntax Best Practices – below the Class Level,* and *Chapter 3, Syntax Best Practices – above the Class Level,* your code should be fine. Often, writing less code is better and faster than writing more code.

Don't do any of these things until you have gotten your code working and you are ready to profile:

- Start to write a global dictionary to cache data for a function
- Think about externalizing a part of the code in C or hybrid languages such as Cython
- Look for external libraries to do some basic calculation

For very specialized areas, such as scientific calculation or games, the usage of specialized libraries and externalization might be unavoidable from the beginning. On the other hand, using libraries like NumPy might ease the development of specific features and produce simpler and faster code at the end. Furthermore, you should not rewrite a function if there is a good library that does it for you.

For instance, Soya 3D, which is a game engine on top of OpenGL (see `http://home.gna.org/oomadness/en/soya3d/index.html`), uses C and Pyrex for fast matrix operations when rendering real-time 3D.

 Optimization is carried out on programs that already work.
As Kent Beck says, "Make it work, then make it right, then make it fast."

Work from the user's point of view

I have seen teams working on optimizing the startup time of an application server that worked really fine when it was already up and running. Once they finished speeding it, they promoted that work to their customers. They were a bit frustrated to notice that the customers didn't really care about it. This was because the speed-up work was not motivated by the user feedback but by the developer's point of view. The people who built the system were launching the server multiple times every day. So the startup time meant a lot to them but not to their customers.

While making a program start faster is a good thing from an absolute point of view, teams should be careful to prioritize the optimization work and ask themselves the following questions:

- Have I been asked to make it faster?
- Who finds the program slow?
- Is it really slow, or acceptable?
- How much will it cost to make it go faster and is it worth it?
- What parts need to be fast?

Remember that optimization has a cost and that the developer's point of view is meaningless to customers, unless you are writing a framework or a library and the customer is a developer too.

 Optimization is not a game. It should be done only when necessary.

Keep the code readable and maintainable

Even if Python tries to make the common code patterns the fastest, optimization work might obfuscate your code and make it really hard to read. There's a balance to keep between producing readable, and therefore maintainable, code and defacing it in order to make it faster.

When you have reached 90% of your optimization objectives and the 10% left to be done makes your code completely unreadable, it might be a good idea to stop the work there or to look for other solutions.

 Optimization should not make your code unreadable. If it happens, you should look for alternative solutions such as externalization or redesign. Look for a good compromise between readability and speed.

Optimization strategy

Let's say your program has a real speed problem you need to resolve. Do not try to guess how to make it faster. Bottlenecks are often hard to find by looking at the code, and a set of tools is needed to find the real problem.

A good optimization strategy can start with three steps:

- **Find another culprit**: Make sure a third-party server or resource is not faulty
- **Scale the hardware**: Make sure the resources are sufficient
- **Write a speed test**: Create a scenario with speed objectives

Find another culprit

Often, a performance problem occurs at production level and the customer alerts you that it is not working as it used to when the software was being tested. Performance problems might occur because the application was not planned to work in the real world with a high number of users and an increase of data size.

But if the application interacts with other applications, the first thing to do is to check if the bottlenecks are located on those interactions. For instance, a database server or an LDAP server might be responsible for extra overhead and might make everything slower.

The physical links between applications should also be considered. Maybe the network link between your application server and another server in the intranet is really slow due to a misconfiguration or congestion.

The design documentation should provide a diagram of all interactions and the nature of each link to get an overall picture of the system and offer help when trying to resolve a speed problem.

 If your application uses third-party servers of resources, every interaction should be audited to make sure the bottleneck is not located there.

Scale the hardware

When there is no more volatile memory available, the system starts to use the hard disk to store data. This is swapping.

This involves a lot of overhead and the performances drop drastically. From a user's point of view, the system is considered dead at this stage. So, it is important to scale the hardware to prevent this.

While having enough memory on a system is important, it is also important to make sure that the applications are not acting crazy and eating too much memory. For instance, if a program works on big video files that can weigh in at several hundreds of megabytes, it should not load them entirely in memory but rather work on chunks or use disk streams.

Disk usage is also important. A full partition might really slow down your application if the I/O errors are hidden in the code that tries to write repeatedly on the disk. Furthermore, even if the code only tries to write once, the hardware and OS might try to write multiple times.

Note that scaling up the hardware (vertical scaling) has some obvious limitations. You cannot fit an infinite amount of hardware to a single rack. Also, highly efficient hardware is extremely expensive (law of diminishing returns), so there is also an economical bound to this approach. From this point of view, it is always better to have the system that can be scaled by adding new computation nodes or workers (horizontal scaling). This allows you to scale out your service with commodity software that has the best performance/price ratio.

Unfortunately, designing and maintaining highly scalable distributed systems is both hard and expensive. If your system cannot be easily scaled horizontally or it is faster and cheaper to scale it vertically, it may be better to do so instead of wasting time and resources on a total redesign of your system architecture. Remember that hardware invariably tends to be faster and cheaper with time. Many products stay in this sweet spot where their scaling needs align with the trend of raising hardware performance.

Writing a speed test

When starting with optimization work, it is important to work using a workflow similar to test-driven development rather than running some manual tests continuously. A good practice is to dedicate a test module in the application where the sequence of calls that are to be optimized is written. Having this scenario will help you to track your progress while you are optimizing the application.

You can even write a few assertions where you set some speed objectives. To prevent speed regression, these tests can be left after the code has been optimized:

```
>>> def test_speed():
...     import time
...     start = time.time()
...     the_code()
...     end = time.time() - start
```

```
...     assert end < 10, \
...     "sorry this code should not take 10 seconds !"
...
```

 Measuring the execution speed depends on the power of the CPU used. But we will see in the next section how to write universal duration measures.

Finding bottlenecks

Finding bottlenecks is done by:

- Profiling CPU usage
- Profiling memory usage
- Profiling network usage

Profiling CPU usage

The first source of bottlenecks is your code. The standard library provides all the tools needed to perform code profiling. They are based on a deterministic approach.

A **deterministic profiler** measures the time spent in each function by adding a timer at the lowest level. This introduces a bit of overhead but provides a good idea on where the time is consumed. A **statistical profiler**, on the other hand, samples the instruction pointer usage and does not instrument the code. The latter is less accurate but allows running the target program at full speed.

There are two ways to profile the code:

- **Macro-profiling**: This profiles the whole program while it is being used and generates statistics
- **Micro-profiling**: This measures a precise part of the program by instrumenting it manually

Macro-profiling

Macro-profiling is done by running the application in a special mode where the interpreter is instrumented to collect statistics on the code usage. Python provides several tools for this:

- profile: This is a pure Python implementation
- cProfile: This is a C implementation that provides the same interface as that of the profile tool but has less overhead

The recommended choice for most Python programmers is cProfile due to its reduced overhead. Anyway, if you need to extend the profiler in some way, then profile will probably be a better choice because it does not use C extensions.

Both tools have the same interface and usage, so we will use only one of them to show how they work. The following is a myapp.py module with a main function that we are going to test with cProfile:

```python
import time


def medium():
    time.sleep(0.01)


def light():
    time.sleep(0.001)


def heavy():
    for i in range(100):
        light()
        medium()
        medium()
    time.sleep(2)


def main():
    for i in range(2):
        heavy()

if __name__ == '__main__':
    main()
```

The module can be called directly from the prompt and the results are summarized here:

```
$ python3 -m cProfile myapp.py
         1208 function calls in 8.243 seconds


   Ordered by: standard name


   ncalls  tottime  percall  cumtime  percall filename:lineno(function)
        2    0.001    0.000    8.243    4.121 myapp.py:13(heavy)
        1    0.000    0.000    8.243    8.243 myapp.py:2(<module>)
        1    0.000    0.000    8.243    8.243 myapp.py:21(main)
      400    0.001    0.000    4.026    0.010 myapp.py:5(medium)
      200    0.000    0.000    0.212    0.001 myapp.py:9(light)
        1    0.000    0.000    8.243    8.243 {built-in method exec}
      602    8.241    0.014    8.241    0.014 {built-in method sleep}
```

The statistics provided are a print view of a statistic object filled by the profiler. A manual invocation of the tool can be:

```
>>> import cProfile
>>> from myapp import main
>>> profiler = cProfile.Profile()
>>> profiler.runcall(main)
>>> profiler.print_stats()
         1206 function calls in 8.243 seconds


   Ordered by: standard name


   ncalls  tottime  percall  cumtime  percall file:lineno(function)
        2    0.001    0.000    8.243    4.121 myapp.py:13(heavy)
        1    0.000    0.000    8.243    8.243 myapp.py:21(main)
      400    0.001    0.000    4.026    0.010 myapp.py:5(medium)
      200    0.000    0.000    0.212    0.001 myapp.py:9(light)
      602    8.241    0.014    8.241    0.014 {built-in method sleep}
```

The statistics can also be saved in a file and then read by the `pstats` module. This module provides a class that knows how to handle profile files and gives a few helpers to play with them invocation:

```
>>> import pstats
>>> import cProfile
>>> from myapp import main
>>> cProfile.run('main()', 'myapp.stats')
>>> stats = pstats.Stats('myapp.stats')
>>> stats.total_calls
1208
>>> stats.sort_stats('time').print_stats(3)
Mon Apr  4 21:44:36 2016    myapp.stats

         1208 function calls in 8.243 seconds

   Ordered by: internal time
   List reduced from 8 to 3 due to restriction <3>

   ncalls  tottime  percall  cumtime  percall file:lineno(function)
      602    8.241    0.014    8.241    0.014 {built-in method sleep}
      400    0.001    0.000    4.025    0.010 myapp.py:5(medium)
        2    0.001    0.000    8.243    4.121 myapp.py:13(heavy)
```

From there, you can browse the code by printing out the callers and callees for each function:

```
>>> stats.print_callees('medium')
   Ordered by: internal time
   List reduced from 8 to 1 due to restriction <'medium'>

Function                  called...
                    ncalls  tottime  cumtime
myapp.py:5(medium) ->  400    4.025    4.025  {built-in method sleep}

>>> stats.print_callees('light')
   Ordered by: internal time
   List reduced from 8 to 1 due to restriction <'light'>

Function                  called...
                    ncalls  tottime  cumtime
myapp.py:9(light)  ->  200    0.212    0.212  {built-in method sleep}
```

Being able to sort the output allows working on different views to find the bottlenecks. For instance, consider the following scenarios:

- When the number of calls is really high and takes up most of the global time, the function or method is probably in a loop. Possible optimization may be done by moving this call to different scope in order to reduce number of operations

- When one function is taking very long time, a cache might be a good option, if possible

Another great way to visualize bottlenecks from profiling data is to transform them into diagrams (see *Figure 1*). **Gprof2Dot** (`https://github.com/jrfonseca/gprof2dot`) can be used to turn profiler data into a dot graph. You can download this simple script PyPI using `pip` and use it on the stats as long as Graphviz (see `http://www.graphviz.org/`) is installed in your environment:

```
$ gprof2dot.py -f pstats myapp.stats | dot -Tpng -o output.png
```

The advantage of `gprof2dot` is that it tries to be language agnostic. It is not limited to Python `profile` or `cProfile` output and can read from multiple other profiles such as Linux perf, xperf, gprof, Java HPROF, and many others.

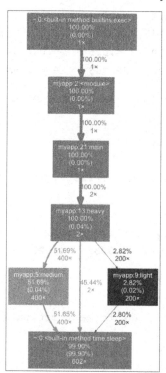

Figure 1 An example of profiling overview diagram generated with gprof2dot

Macro-profiling is a good way to detect the function that has a problem, or at least its neighborhood. When you have found it, you can jump to micro-profiling.

Micro-profiling

When the slow function is found, it is sometimes necessary to do more profiling work that tests just a part of the program. This is done by manually instrumenting a part of the code in a speed test.

For instance, the cProfile module can be used from a decorator:

```
>>> import tempfile, os, cProfile, pstats
>>> def profile(column='time', list=5):
...     def _profile(function):
...         def __profile(*args, **kw):
...             s = tempfile.mktemp()
...             profiler = cProfile.Profile()
...             profiler.runcall(function, *args, **kw)
...             profiler.dump_stats(s)
...             p = pstats.Stats(s)
...             p.sort_stats(column).print_stats(list)
...         return __profile
...     return _profile
...
>>> from myapp import main
>>> @profile('time', 6)
... def main_profiled():
...     return main()
...
>>> main_profiled()
Mon Apr  4 22:01:01 2016    /tmp/tmpvswuovz_

         1207 function calls in 8.243 seconds

   Ordered by: internal time
   List reduced from 7 to 6 due to restriction <6>
```

ncalls	tottime	percall	cumtime	percall	file:lineno(function)
602	8.241	0.014	8.241	0.014	{built-in method sleep}
400	0.001	0.000	4.026	0.010	myapp.py:5(medium)
2	0.001	0.000	8.243	4.121	myapp.py:13(heavy)
200	0.000	0.000	0.213	0.001	myapp.py:9(light)
1	0.000	0.000	8.243	8.243	myapp.py:21(main)
1	0.000	0.000	8.243	8.243	<stdin>:1(main_profiled)

```
>>> from myapp import light
>>> stats = profile()(light)
>>> stats()
Mon Apr  4 22:01:57 2016    /tmp/tmpnp_zk7dl

        3 function calls in 0.001 seconds

   Ordered by: internal time
```

ncalls	tottime	percall	cumtime	percall	file:lineno(function)
1	0.001	0.001	0.001	0.001	{built-in method sleep}
1	0.000	0.000	0.001	0.001	myapp.py:9(light)

This approach allows testing parts of the application and sharpens the statistics output. But at this stage, having a list of callees is probably not interesting, as the function has already been pointed out as the one to optimize. The only interesting information is to know how fast it is, and then enhance it.

timeit fits this need better by providing a simple way to measure the execution time of a small code snippet with the best underlying timer the host system provides (time.time or time.clock):

```
>>> from myapp import light
>>> import timeit
>>> t = timeit.Timer('main()')
>>> t.timeit(number=5)
10000000 loops, best of 3: 0.0269 usec per loop
10000000 loops, best of 3: 0.0268 usec per loop
10000000 loops, best of 3: 0.0269 usec per loop
```

```
10000000 loops, best of 3: 0.0268 usec per loop
10000000 loops, best of 3: 0.0269 usec per loop
5.6196951866149902
```

The module allows you to repeat the call and is oriented to try out isolated code snippets. This is very useful outside the application context, in a prompt, for instance, but is not really handy to use within an existing application.

A deterministic profiler will provide results depending on what the computer is doing, and so results may vary each time. Repeating the same test multiple times and making averages provides more accurate results. Furthermore, some computers have special CPU features, such as **SpeedStep**, that might change the results if the computer is idling when the test is launched (see http://en.wikipedia.org/wiki/SpeedStep). So, continually repeating the test is a good practice for small code snippets. There are also various caches to keep in mind such as DNS caches or CPU caches.

But the results of `timeit` should be used with caution. It is a very good tool to objectively compare two short snippets of code but it also allows you to easily make dangerous mistakes that will lead you to confusing conclusions. Here, for example, is the comparison of two innocent snippets of code with the `timeit` module that could make you think that string concatenation by addition is faster than the `str.join()` method:

```
$ python3 -m timeit -s 'a = map(str, range(1000))' '"".join(a)'
1000000 loops, best of 3: 0.497 usec per loop

$ python3 -m timeit -s 'a = map(str, range(1000)); s=""' 'for i in a: s
+= i'
10000000 loops, best of 3: 0.0808 usec per loop
```

From *Chapter 2, Syntax Best Practices – below the Class Level*, we know that string concatenation by addition in not a good pattern. Despite there are some minor CPython micro-optimizations designed exactly for such use case, it will eventually lead to quadratic run time. The problem lies in nuances about the `setup` argument of `timeit` (`-s` parameter in the command line) and how the range in Python 3 works. I won't discuss the details of the problem but will leave it to you as an exercise. Anyway, here is the correct way to compare string concatenation in addition with the `str.join()` idiom under Python 3:

```
$ python3 -m timeit -s 'a = [str(i) for i in range(10000)]' 's="".
join(a)'
10000 loops, best of 3: 128 usec per loop
```

```
$ python3 -m timeit -s 'a = [str(i) for i in range(10000)]' '
>s = ""
>for i in a:
>    s += i
>'
1000 loops, best of 3: 1.38 msec per loop
```

Measuring Pystones

When measuring execution time, the result depends on the computer hardware. To be able to produce a universal measure, the simplest way is to benchmark the speed of a fixed sequence of code and calculate a ratio out of it. From there, the time taken by a function can be translated to a universal value that can be compared on any computer.

 A lot of generic benchmarking tools for the measurement of computer performance are available. Surprisingly, some of them that were created many years ago are still used today. For instance, Whetstone was created in 1972, and back then it provided a computer performance analyzer in Algol 60 (see http://en.wikipedia.org/wiki/Whetstone_%28benchmark%29). It is used to measure the **Millions Of Whetstone Instructions Per Second** (**MWIPS**). A table of results for old and modern CPUs is maintained at http://freespace.virgin.net/roy.longbottom/whetstone%20results.htm.

Python provides a benchmark utility in its test package that measures the duration of a sequence of well-chosen operations. The result is a number of **pystones** per second the computer is able to perform and the time used to perform the benchmark, which is generally around one second on modern hardware:

```
>>> from test import pystone
>>> pystone.pystones()
(1.0500000000000007, 47619.047619047589)
```

The rate can be used to translate a profile duration into a number of pystones:

```
>>> from test import pystone
>>> benchtime, pystones = pystone.pystones()
>>> def seconds_to_kpystones(seconds):
...     return (pystones*seconds) / 1000
...
```

```
...
>>> seconds_to_kpystones(0.03)
1.4563106796116512
>>> seconds_to_kpystones(1)
48.543689320388381
>>> seconds_to_kpystones(2)
97.087378640776762
```

The `seconds_to_kpystones` returns the number of **kilo pystones**. This conversion can be included in your test if you want to code some speed assertions.

Having pystones will allow you to use this decorator in tests so that you can set assertions on execution times. These tests will be runnable on any computer and will allow developers to prevent speed regressions. When a part of the application has been optimized, they will be able to set its maximum execution time in tests and make sure it won't be breached by further changes. This approach is, of course, not ideal and 100% accurate, but it is at least better than hardcoding execution time assertions in raw values expressed as seconds.

Profiling memory usage

Another problem you may encounter when optimizing an application is memory consumption. If a program starts to eat so much memory that the system begins to swap, there is probably a place in your application where too many objects are created or objects that you don't intend to keep are still kept alive by some unintended reference. This is often easy to detect through classical profiling because consuming enough memory to make a system swap involves a lot of CPU work that can be detected. But sometimes it is not obvious and the memory usage has to be profiled.

How Python deals with memory

Memory usage is probably the hardest thing to profile in Python when you use the CPython implementation. While languages such as C allow you to get the memory size of any element, Python will never let you know how much a given object consumes. This is due to the dynamic nature of the language, and the fact that memory management is not directly accessible to the language user.

Some raw details of memory management were already explained in *Chapter 7, Python Extensions in Other Languages*. We already know that CPython uses reference counting to manage object allocation. This is the deterministic algorithm which ensures that object deallocation will be triggered when the reference count of the object goes to zero. Despite being deterministic, this process is not easy to track manually and to reason about in complex codebases. Also, the deallocation of objects on a reference count level does not necessarily mean that the actual process heap memory is freed by the interpreter. Depending on CPython interpreter compilation flags, system environment, or runtime context, the internal memory manager layer might decide to leave some blocks of free memory for future reallocation instead of releasing it completely.

Additional micro-optimizations in CPython implementation also make it even harder to predict actual memory usage. For instance, two variables that point to the same short string or small integer value might or might not point to the same object instance in memory.

Despite being quite scary and seemingly complex, memory management in Python is very well documented (refer to `https://docs.python.org/3/c-api/memory.html`). Note that, micro-optimizations mentioned earlier can, in most cases, be ignored when debugging memory issues. Also, reference counting is roughly based on a simple statement—if a given object is not referenced anymore, it is removed. In other words, all local references in a function are removed after the interpreter:

- Leaves the function
- Makes sure the object is not being used anymore

So, objects that remain in memory are:

- Global objects
- Objects that are still referenced in some way

Be careful with the **argument inbound outbound** edge case. If an object is created within the arguments, the argument reference will still be alive if the function returns the object. This can lead to unexpected results if it is used as a default value:

```
>>> def my_function(argument={}):  # bad practice
...     if '1' in argument:
...         argument['1'] = 2
...     argument['3'] = 4
...     return argument
...
```

```
>>> my_function()
{'3': 4}
>>> res = my_function()
>>> res['4'] = 'I am still alive!'
>>> print my_function()
{'3': 4, '4': 'I am still alive!'}
```

That is why nonmutable objects should always be used, like this:

```
>>> def my_function(argument=None):  # better practice
...     if argument is None:
...         argument = {}  # a fresh dict is created everytime
...     if '1' in argument:
...         argument['1'] = 2
...     argument['3'] = 4
...     return argument
...
>>> my_function()
{'3': 4}
>>> res = my_function()
>>> res['4'] = 'I am still alive!'
>>> print my_function()
{'3': 4}
```

Reference counting in Python is handy and frees you from the obligation of manually tracking object references of objects, and therefore you don't have to manually destroy them. Although this introduces another problem, since developers never clean up instances in memory, it might grow in an uncontrolled way if developers don't pay attention to the way they use their data structures.

The usual memory eaters are:

- Caches that grow uncontrolled
- Object factories that register instances globally and do not keep track of their usage, such as a database connector creator used on the fly every time a query is called
- Threads that are not properly finished

- Objects with a `__del__` method and involved in a cycle are also memory eaters. In older versions of Python (prior to 3.4 version), the garbage collector will not break the cycle since it cannot be sure which object should be deleted first. Hence, you will leak memory. Using this method is a bad idea in most cases.

Unfortunately, the management of reference counts must be done manually in C extensions using Python/C API with `Py_INCREF()` and `Py_DECREF()` macros. We discussed caveats of handling reference counts and reference ownership earlier in *Chapter 7, Python Extensions in Other Languages*, so you should already know that it is a pretty hard topic riddled with various pitfalls. This is the reason why most memory issues are caused by C extensions that are not written properly.

Profiling memory

Before starting to hunt down memory issues in Python, you should know that the nature of memory leaks in Python is quite special. In some of the compiled languages such as C and C++, the memory leaks are almost exclusively caused by allocated memory blocks that are no longer referenced by any pointer. If you don't have reference to memory, you cannot release it, and this very situation is called a *memory leak*. In Python, there is no low level memory management available for the user, so we rather deal with leaking references—references to objects that are not needed anymore but were not removed. This stops the interpreter from releasing resources but is not the same situation as a memory leak in C. Of course, there is always the exceptional case of C extensions, but they are a different kind of beast that need completely different tool chains and cannot be easily inspected from Python code.

So, memory issues in Python are mostly caused by unexpected or unplanned resource acquiring patterns. It happens very rarely that this is an effect of real bugs caused by the mishandling of memory allocation and deallocation routines. Such routines are available to the developer only in CPython when writing C extension with Python/C APIs and you will deal with them very rarely, if ever. Thus, most so-called memory leaks in Python are mostly caused by the overblown complexity of the software and minor interactions between its components that are really hard to track. In order to spot and locate such deficiencies of your software, you need to know how an actual memory usage looks in the program.

Getting information about how many objects are controlled by the Python interpreter and about their real size is a bit tricky. For instance, knowing how much a given object weighs in bytes would involve crawling down all its attributes, dealing with cross-references and then summing up everything. It's a pretty difficult problem if you consider the way objects tend to refer to each other. The `gc` module does not provide high-level functions for this, and it would require Python to be compiled in debug mode to have a full set of information.

Often, programmers just ask the system about the memory usage of their application after and before a given operation has been performed. But this measure is an approximation and depends a lot on how the memory is managed at system level. Using the `top` command under Linux or the Task Manager under Windows, for instance, makes it possible to detect memory problems when they are obvious. But this approach is laborious and makes it really hard to track down the faulty code block.

Fortunately, there are a few tools available to make memory snapshots and calculate the number and size of loaded objects. But let's keep in mind that Python does not release memory easily, preferring to hold on to it in case it is needed again.

For some time, one of most popular tools to use when debugging memory issues and usage in Python was Guppy-PE and its Heapy component. Unfortunately, it seems to be no longer maintained and it lacks Python 3 support. Luckily, there are some other alternatives that are Python 3 compatible to some extent:

- **Memprof** (`http://jmdana.github.io/memprof/`): It is declared to work on Python 2.6, 2.7, 3.1, 3.2, and 3.3 and some POSIX-compliant systems (Mac OS X and Linux)

- **memory_profiler** (`https://pypi.python.org/pypi/memory_profiler`): It is declared to support the same Python versions and systems as Memprof

- **Pympler** (`http://pythonhosted.org/Pympler/`): It is declared to support Python 2.5, 2.6, 2.7, 3.1, 3.2, 3.3, and 3.4 and to be OS independent

Note that the preceding information is based purely on trove classifiers used by the latest distributions of featured packages. This could easily change in the time after this book was written. Nevertheless, there is one package that currently supports the widest spectrum of Python versions and is also known to work flawlessly under Python 3.5. It is `objgraph`. Its APIs seem to be a bit clumsy and have a very limited set of functionalities. But it works, does well what it needs to and is really easy to use. Memory instrumentation is not a thing that is added to the production code permanently, so this tool does not need to be pretty. Because of its wide support of Python versions in OS independence, we will focus only on `objgraph` when discussing examples of memory profiling. The other tools mentioned in this section are also exciting pieces of software but you need to research them by yourself.

objgraph

objgraph (refer to http://mg.pov.lt/objgraph/) is a simple tool for creating diagrams of object references that should be useful when hunting memory leaks in Python. It is available on PyPI but it is not a completely standalone tool and requires Graphviz in order to create memory usage diagrams. For developer-friendly systems like Mac OS X or Linux, you can easily obtain it using your preferred system package manager. For Windows, you need to download the Graphviz installer from the project page (refer to http://www.graphviz.org/) and install it manually.

objgraph provides multiple utilities that allow you to list and print various statistics about memory usage and object counts. An example of such utilities in use is shown in the following transcript of interpreter session.

```
>>> import objgraph
>>> objgraph.show_most_common_types()
function                    1910
dict                        1003
wrapper_descriptor          989
tuple                       837
weakref                     742
method_descriptor           683
builtin_function_or_method  666
getset_descriptor           338
set                         323
member_descriptor           305
>>> objgraph.count('list')
266
>>> objgraph.typestats(objgraph.get_leaking_objects())
{'Gt': 1, 'AugLoad': 1, 'GtE': 1, 'Pow': 1, 'tuple': 2, 'AugStore': 1,
'Store': 1, 'Or': 1, 'IsNot': 1, 'RecursionError': 1, 'Div': 1, 'LShift':
1, 'Mod': 1, 'Add': 1, 'Invert': 1, 'weakref': 1, 'Not': 1, 'Sub': 1,
'In': 1, 'NotIn': 1, 'Load': 1, 'NotEq': 1, 'BitAnd': 1, 'FloorDiv':
1, 'Is': 1, 'RShift': 1, 'MatMult': 1, 'Eq': 1, 'Lt': 1, 'dict': 341,
'list': 7, 'Param': 1, 'USub': 1, 'BitOr': 1, 'BitXor': 1, 'And': 1,
'Del': 1, 'UAdd': 1, 'Mult': 1, 'LtE': 1}
```

As already said, objgraph allows you to create diagrams of memory usage patterns and cross-references that link all the objects in the given namespace. The most useful diagramming utilities of that library are objgraph.show_refs() and objgraph.show_backrefs(). They both accept reference to the object being inspected and save a diagram image to file using the Graphviz package. Examples of such graphs are presented in *Figure 2* and *Figure 3*.

Here is the code that was used to create these diagrams:

```
import objgraph


def example():
    x = []
    y = [x, [x], dict(x=x)]

    objgraph.show_refs(
        (x, y),
        filename='show_refs.png',
        refcounts=True
    )
    objgraph.show_backrefs(
        (x, y),
        filename='show_backrefs.png',
        refcounts=True
    )


if __name__ == "__main__":
    example()
```

Figure 2 shows the diagram of all references hold by x and y objects. From top to bottom and left to right it presents exactly four objects:

- `y = [x, [x], dict(x=x)]` list instance
- `dict(x=x)` dictionary instance
- `[x]` list instance
- `x = []` list instance

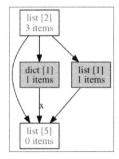

Figure 2 An example result of the show_refs() diagram from the example() function

Figure 3 shows not only references between x and y but also all the objects that hold references to these two instances. There are so-called back references and are really helpful in finding objects that stop other objects from being deallocated.

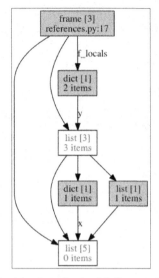

Figure 3 An example result of the show_backrefs() diagram from the example() function

In order to show how objgraph may be used in practice, let's review some practical examples. As we have already noted a few times in this book, CPython has its own garbage collector that exists independently from its reference counting method. It's not used for general purpose memory management but only to solve the problem of cyclic references. In many situations, objects may reference each other in a way that would make it impossible to remove them using simple techniques based on tracking the number of references. Here is the most simple example:

```
x = []
y = [x]
x.append(y)
```

Such a situation is visually presented in *Figure 4*. In the preceding case, even if all external references to x and y objects will be removed (for instance, by returning from local scope of a function), these two objects cannot be removed because there are still two cross-references owned by these two objects. This is the situation where Python garbage collector steps in. It can detect cyclic references to objects and trigger their deallocation if there are no other valid references to these objects outside the cycle.

Figure 4 An example diagram of cyclic references between two objects

The real problem starts when at least one of the objects in such a cycle has the custom __del__() method defined. It is a custom deallocation handler that will be called when the object's reference count finally goes to zero. It can execute any arbitrary Python code and so can also create new references to featured object. This is the reason why garbage collector prior to Python 3.4 version could not break reference cycles if at least one of the objects provided the custom __del__() method implementation. PEP 442 introduced safe object finalization to Python and became a part of the standard starting from Python 3.4. Anyway, this may still be a problem for packages that worry about backwards compatibility and target a wide spectrum of Python interpreter versions. The following snippet of code shows you the differences in behavior of cyclic garbage collector in different Python versions:

```python
import gc
import platform
import objgraph


class WithDel(list):
    """ list subclass with custom __del__ implementation """
    def __del__(self):
        pass


def main():
    x = WithDel()
    y = []
    z = []

    x.append(y)
    y.append(z)
    z.append(x)

    del x, y, z
```

```
        print("unreachable prior collection: %s" % gc.collect())
        print("unreachable after collection: %s" % len(gc.garbage))
        print("WithDel objects count:        %s" %
              objgraph.count('WithDel'))


if __name__ == "__main__":
    print("Python version: %s" % platform.python_version())
    print()
    main()
```

The output of the preceding code, when executed under Python 3.3, shows that the cyclic garbage collector in the older versions of Python cannot collect objects that have the `__del__()` method defined:

```
$ python3.3 with_del.py
Python version: 3.3.5


unreachable prior collection: 3
unreachable after collection: 1
WithDel objects count:        1
```

With a newer version of Python, the garbage collector can safely deal with finalization of objects even if they have the `__del__()` method defined:

```
$ python3.5 with_del.py
Python version: 3.5.1


unreachable prior collection: 3
unreachable after collection: 0
WithDel objects count:        0
```

Although custom finalization is no longer tricky in the latest Python releases, it still poses a problem for applications that need to work under different environments. As mentioned earlier, the `objgraph.show_refs()` and `objgraph.show_backrefs()` functions allow you to easily spot problematic class instances. For instance, we can easily modify the `main()` function to show all back references to the `WithDel` instances in order to see if we have leaking resources:

```
def main():
    x = WithDel()
    y = []
    z = []
```

```
x.append(y)
y.append(z)
z.append(x)

del x, y, z

print("unreachable prior collection: %s" % gc.collect())
print("unreachable after collection: %s" % len(gc.garbage))
print("WithDel objects count:        %s" %
      objgraph.count('WithDel'))

objgraph.show_backrefs(
    objgraph.by_type('WithDel'),
    filename='after-gc.png'
)
```

Running the preceding example under Python 3.3 will result in a diagram (see *Figure 5*), which shows that gc.collect() could not succeed in removing x, y, and z object instances. Additionally, objgraph highlights all the objects that have the custom __del__() method defined to make spotting such issues easier.

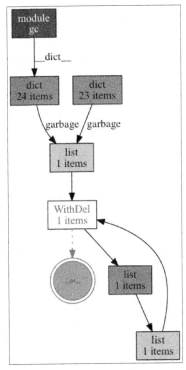

Figure 5 The diagram showing an example of cyclic references that can't be picked by the Python garbage collector prior to version 3.4

C code memory leaks

If the Python code seems perfectly fine and the memory still increases when you loop through the isolated function, the leak might be located on the C side. This happens, for instance, when a `Py_DECREF` call is missing.

The Python core code is pretty robust and tested for leaks. If you use packages that have C extensions, they might be a good place to look first. Because you will be dealing with code operating on a much lower level of abstraction than Python, you need to use completely different tools to resolve such memory issues.

Memory debugging is not easy in C, so before diving into extension internals make sure to properly diagnose the source of your problem. It is a very popular approach to isolate a suspicious package with code similar in nature to unit tests:

- Write a separate test for each API unit or functionality of an extension you are suspecting to leak memory

- Perform the test in a loop for an arbitrarily long time in isolation (one test per run)

- Observe from outside which of the tested functionalities increase memory usage over time

Using such an approach, you can isolate the faulty part of the extension and this will reduce the time required later to inspect and fix its code. This process may seem burdensome because it requires a lot of additional time and coding, but it really pays off in the long run. You can always ease your work by reusing some testing tools introduced in *Chapter 10, Test-Driven Development*. Utilities such as tox were perhaps not designed exactly for this case, but they can at least reduce the time required to run multiple tests in isolated environments.

Hopefully, you have isolated the part of the extension that is leaking memory and can finally start actual debugging. If you're lucky, a simple manual inspection of the source code may give the desired results. In many cases, the problem is as simple as adding the missing `Py_DECREF` call. Nevertheless, in most cases, our work is not that simple. In such situations, you need to bring out some bigger guns. One of the notable generic tools for fighting memory leaks in compiled code that should be in every programmer's toolbelt is **Valgrind**. It is a whole instrumentation framework for building dynamic analysis tools. Because of this, it may not be easy to learn and master, but you should definitely know the basics.

Profiling network usage

As I said earlier, an application that communicates with third-party programs such as databases, caches, web services, or an LDAP server can be slowed down when those applications are slow. This can be tracked with a regular code profiling method on the application side. But if the third-party software works fine on its own, the culprit is probably the network.

The problem might be a misconfigured hub, a low-bandwidth network link, or even a high number of traffic collisions that make computers send the same packets several times.

Here are a few elements to get you in. To find out what is going on, there are three fields to investigate at first:

- Watch the network traffic using tools such as:
    - ntop: http://www.ntop.org (Linux only)
    - wireshark: www.wireshark.org (previously named Ethereal)
- Track down unhealthy or misconfigured devices with net-snmp (http://www.net-snmp.org).
- Estimate the bandwidth between two computers using Pathrate, a statistical tool. See http://www.cc.gatech.edu/~dovrolis/bw-est/pathrate.html.

If you want to go further on network performance issues, you might also want to read *Network Performance Open Source Toolkit, Wiley,* by Richard Blum. This book exposes strategies to tune the applications that are heavily using the network and provides a tutorial to scan complex network problems.

High Performance MySQL, O'Reilly Media, by Jeremy Zawodny is also a good book to read when writing an application that uses MySQL.

Summary

In this chapter, we have seen:

- The three rules of optimization:
    - Make it work first
    - Take the user's point of view
    - Keep the code readable

- An optimization strategy based on writing a scenario with speed objectives
- How to profile CPU or memory usage and a few tips for network profiling

Now that you know how to locate your performance problems, the next chapter provides some popular and generic strategies to get rid of them.

12
Optimization – Some Powerful Techniques

Optimizing a program is not a magical process. It is done by following a simple algorithm, synthesized by Stefan Schwarzer at Europython 2006 in his original pseudocode example:

```python
def optimize():
    """Recommended optimization"""
    assert got_architecture_right(), "fix architecture"
    assert made_code_work(bugs=None), "fix bugs"
    while code_is_too_slow():
        wbn = find_worst_bottleneck(just_guess=False,
                                    profile=True)
        is_faster = try_to_optimize(wbn,
                                    run_unit_tests=True,
                                    new_bugs=None)
        if not is_faster:
            undo_last_code_change()

# By Stefan Schwarzer, Europython 2006
```

This example probably isn't the neatest and clearest one but captures pretty much all the important aspects of an organized optimization procedure. The main things we learn from it are:

- Optimization is an iterative process where not every iteration leads to better results

- The main prerequisite is code that is verified to be working properly with tests

- You should always focus on optimizing the current application bottleneck

Making your code work faster is not an easy task. In case of abstract mathematical problems, the solution of course lies in choosing the right algorithm and proper data structures. But in that case, it is very hard to provide some generic tips and tricks that can be used in any code for solving algorithmic issues. There are of course some generic methodologies for designing a new algorithm, or even meta-heuristics that can be applied to a large variety of problems but they are pretty language-agnostic and thus are rather out of scope of this book.

Anyway, some performance issues are only caused by certain code quality defects or application usage context. For instance, the speed of the application might be reduced by:

- Bad usage of basic built-in types
- Too much complexity
- Hardware resource usage patterns not matching with the execution environment
- Waiting too long for responses from third-party APIs or backing services
- Doing too much in time-critical parts of the application

More often, the solving of such performance issues does not require advanced academic knowledge but only good software craftsmanship. And a big part of craftsmanship is knowing when to use the proper tools. Fortunately, there are some well-known patterns and solutions for dealing with performance problems.

In this chapter, we will discuss some popular and reusable solutions that allow you to non-algorithmically optimize your program through:

- Reducing the complexity
- Using architectural trade offs
- Caching

Reducing the complexity

Before we dig further into optimization techniques, let's define exactly what we are going to deal with. From the chapter's introduction, we know that focusing on improving application bottlenecks is critical for successful optimization. A bottleneck is a single component that severely limits the capacity of a program or computer system. An important characteristic of every piece of code with performance issues is that it usually has only a single bottleneck. We discussed some profiling techniques in the previous chapter, so you should already be familiar with the tools required to locate and isolate such places. If your profiling results show that there are few places that need immediate improvement, then you should at first try to treat each as a separate component and optimize independently.

Of course, if there is no explicit bottleneck but your application still performs under your expectations, then you are really in a bad position. The gains of the optimization process are proportional to the performance impact of optimized bottlenecks. Optimizing every small component that does not substantially contribute to the overall execution time or resource consumption will only give you minimal benefit for all the time spent on profiling and optimization. If your application does not seem to have real bottlenecks, there is a possibility that you have missed something. Try using different profiling strategies or tools or look at it from a different perspective (memory, I/O operations, or network throughput). If that does not help, you should really consider revising your software architecture.

But if you have successfully found a single and integral component that limits your application performance, then you are really lucky. There is high chance that with only minimal code improvement, you will be able to really improve code execution time and/or resource usage. And the gain from optimization will, again, be proportional to the bottleneck size.

The first and most obvious aspect to look after when trying to improve application performance is complexity. There are many definitions of what makes a program complex and many ways to express it. Some complexity metrics can provide objective information about how the code behaves and such information can sometimes be extrapolated into performance expectations. An experienced programmer can even reliably guess how two different implementations will perform in practice knowing their complexities and realistic execution contexts.

The two popular ways to define application complexity are:

- **Cyclomatic complexity** that is very often correlated with application performance
- The Landau notation, also known as **big O notation**, that is an algorithm classification method that is very useful in objectively judging performance

From there, the optimization process may be sometimes understood as a process of reducing the complexity. This section provides simple tips for this work by simplifying loops. But first of all, let's learn how to measure complexity.

Cyclomatic complexity

Cyclomatic complexity is a metric developed by Thomas J. McCabe in 1976. Because of its author, it is very often called **McCabe's complexity**. It measures the number of linear paths through the code. All `if`, `for`, and `while` loops are counted to come up with a measure.

The code can then be categorized as follows:

Cyclomatic Complexity	What it means
1 to 10	Not complex
11 to 20	Moderately complex
21 to 50	Really complex
More than 50	Too complex

Cyclomatic complexity is rather the code quality score than a metric that objectively judges its performance. It does not replace the need for code profiling for finding performance bottlenecks. Anyway, code that has high cyclomatic complexity often tends to utilize rather complex algorithms that may not perform well with larger inputs.

Although cyclomatic complexity is not a reliable way to judge application performance, it has one very nice advantage. It is a source code metric so it can be measured with proper tools. This cannot be said about other ways of expressing complexity — the big O notation. Thanks to measurability, cyclomatic complexity may be a useful addition to profiling that gives you more information about problematic parts of the software. Complex parts of code are the first to review when considering radical code architecture redesigns.

Measuring McCabe's complexity is relatively simple in Python because it can be deduced from its Abstract Syntax Tree. Of course, you don't need to do that by yourself. A popular tool that provides cyclomatic complexity measurement for Python is `flake8` (with the `mccabe` plugin), which has already been introduced in *Chapter 4, Choosing Good Names*.

The big O notation

The most canonical method to define function complexity is the **big O notation** (see `http://en.wikipedia.org/wiki/Big_O_notation`). This metric defines how an algorithm is affected by the size of the input data. For instance, does the algorithm scale linearly with the size of the input data or quadratically?

Calculating the big O notation manually for an algorithm is the best approach to get an overview on how its performance is related with the size of the input data. Knowing the complexity of your application components gives you the ability to detect and focus on the parts that will really slow down the code.

To measure the big O notation, all constants and low-order terms are removed in order to focus on the portion that really weighs when the input data grows. The idea is to try to categorize the algorithm in one of these categories, even if it is an approximation:

Notation	Type
O(1)	Constant. Does not depend on the input data.
O(n)	Linear. Will grow as "n" grows.
O(n log n)	Quasi linear.
O(n²)	Quadratic complexity.
O(n³)	Cubic complexity.
O(n!)	Factorial complexity.

For instance, we already know from *Chapter 2, Syntax Best Practices – below the Class Level*, that a `dict` lookup has an average complexity of *O(1)*. It is considered constant regardless of how many elements are in the `dict`, whereas looking through a list of items for a particular item is *O(n)*.

Let's take another example:

```
>>> def function(n):
...     for i in range(n):
...         print(i)
...
```

In that case, the print statement will be executed *n* times. Loop speed will depend on n, so its complexity expresses using the big O notation will be *O(n)*.

If the function has conditions, the correct notation to keep is the highest one:

```
>>> def function(n):
...     if some_test:
...         print('something')
...     else:
...         for i in range(n):
...             print(i)
...
```

In this example, the function could be $O(1)$ or $O(n)$, depending on the test. But the worst case is $O(n)$, so whole function complexity is $O(n)$.

When discussing complexity expressed in big O notation, we usually review the worst case scenario. While this is the best method to define complexity when comparing two independent algorithms, it may not be the best approach in every practical situation. Many algorithms change the runtime performance depending on the statistical characteristic of input data or amortize the cost of worst case operations by doing clever tricks. This is why, in many cases, it may be better to review your implementation in terms *of average complexity* or *amortized complexity*.

For example, take a look at the operation of appending a single element to Python's `list` type instance. We know that `list` in CPython uses an array with overallocation for the internal storage instead of linked lists. In case an array is already full, appending a new element requires allocation of the new array and copying all existing elements (references) to a new area in the memory. If we look from the point of the **worst-case complexity**, it is clear that the `list.append()` method has $O(n)$ complexity. And this is a bit expensive when compared to a typical implementation of the linked list structure.

But we also know that the CPython `list` type implementation uses overallocation to mitigate the complexity of such occasional reallocation. If we evaluate the complexity over a sequence of operations, we will see that the *average complexity* of `list.append()` is $O(1)$ and this is actually a great result.

When solving problems, we often know a lot of details about our input data such as its size or statistical distribution. When optimizing the application, it is always worth using every bit of knowledge about your input data. Here, another problem of worst-case complexity starts to show up. It is intended to show the limiting behavior of the function when the input tends toward large values or infinity, rather than give a reliable performance approximation for real-life data. Asymptotic notation is great when defining the growth rate of a function but it won't give a reliable answer for the simple question: which implementation will take less time? Worst-case complexity dumps all those little details about both your implementation and data characteristic to show you how your program will behave asymptotically. It works for arbitrarily large inputs that you may not even need to consider.

For instance, let's assume that you have a problem to solve regarding data consisting of n independent elements. Let's suppose also that you know two different ways to solve this problem—*program A* and *program B*. You know that *program A* requires $100n^2$ operations to finish and *program B* requires $5n^3$ operations to give the problem a solution. Which one would you choose? When speaking about very large inputs, *program A* is of course the better choice because it behaves better asymptotically. It has $O(n^2)$ complexity compared to $O(n^3)$ complexity that characterizes *program B*.

But by solving a simple 100 n^2 > 5 n^3 inequality, we can find that *program B* will take fewer operations when n is less than 20. If we know a bit more about our input bounds, we can make slightly better decisions.

Simplifying

To reduce the complexity of code, the way data is stored is fundamental. You should pick your data structure carefully. This section provides a few examples on how the performance of simple code snippets can be improved by the proper datatypes for the job.

Searching in a list

Due to implementation details of the `list` type in Python, searching for a specific value in a list isn't a cheap operation. The complexity of the `list.index()` method is $O(n)$, where n is the number of list elements. Such linear complexity is not especially bad if you don't need to perform many element index lookups, but it can have a negative performance impact if there is a need for many such operations.

If you need fast search over a list, you can try the `bisect` module from the Python standard library. The functions in this module are mainly designed for inserting or finding insertion indexes for given values in a way that will preserve the order of the already sorted sequence. Anyway, they can be used for efficiently finding element indexes with a bisection algorithm. Here is the recipe from the official documentation of the function that finds the element index using a binary search:

```
def index(a, x):
    'Locate the leftmost value exactly equal to x'
    i = bisect_left(a, x)
    if i != len(a) and a[i] == x:
        return i
    raise ValueError
```

Note that every function from the bisect module requires a sorted sequence in order to work. If your list is not in the correct order, then sorting it is a task with at least $O(n \log n)$ complexity. This is a worse class than $O(n)$, so sorting the whole list for performing only a single search will definitely not pay off. However, if you need to perform a lot of index searches in a huge list that does not need to change often, then using a single sort operation bisect may be a very good trade off.

Also, if you already have a sorted list, you can insert new items into that list using `bisect` without needing to re-sort it.

Using a set instead of a list

When you need to build a sequence of distinct values out of a given sequence, the first algorithm that might come to your mind is:

```
>>> sequence = ['a', 'a', 'b', 'c', 'c', 'd']
>>> result = []
>>> for element in sequence:
...     if element not in result:
...         result.append(element)
...
>>> result
['a', 'b', 'c', 'd']
```

The complexity is introduced by the lookup in the `result` list with the `in` operator that has the time complexity, $O(n)$. It is then used in the loop, which costs $O(n)$. So, the overall complexity is quadratic — $O(n^2)$.

Using a `set` type for the same work will be faster because the stored values are looked up using hashes same as in the `dict` type. Also, `set` ensures the uniqueness of elements, so we don't need to do anything more but create a new set from our `sequence` object. In other words, for each value in `sequence`, the time taken to see if it is already in the `set` will be constant:

```
>>> sequence = ['a', 'a', 'b', 'c', 'c', 'd']
>>> result = set(sequence)
>>> result
set(['a', 'c', 'b', 'd'])
```

This lowers the complexity to $O(n)$, which is the complexity of the `set` object creation. The additional advantage is shorter and more explicit code.

 When you try to reduce the complexity of an algorithm, carefully consider your data structures. There are a range of built-in types, so pick the right one.

Cut the external calls, reduce the workload

A part of the complexity is introduced by calls to other functions, methods, and classes. In general, get as much of the code out of the loops as possible. This is doubly important for nested loops. Don't recalculate over and over those things that can be calculated before the loop even begins. Inner loops should be tight.

Using collections

The `collections` module provides high-performance alternatives to the built-in container types. The main types available in this module are:

- `deque`: A list-like type with extra features
- `defaultdict`: A dict-like type with a built-in default factory feature
- `namedtuple`: A tuple-like type that assigns keys for members

deque

A `deque` is an alternative implementation for lists. While a list is based on arrays, a `deque` is based on a doubly linked list. Hence, a `deque` is much faster when you need to insert something into its middle or head but much slower when you need to access an arbitrary index.

Of course, thanks to the overallocation of an internal array in the Python `list` type, not every `list.append()` call requires memory reallocation, and the average complexity of this method is *O(1)*. Still, *pops* and *appends* are generally faster when performed on linked lists instead of arrays. The situation changes dramatically when the element needs to be added on arbitrary point of sequence. Because all elements on the right of the new one need to be shifted in an array, the complexity of `list.insert()` is *O(n)*. If you need to perform a lot of pops, appends, and inserts, the `deque` in place of the list may provide substantial performance improvement. But always be sure to profile your code before switching from a `list` to the `deque`, because a few things that are fast in arrays (such as accessing arbitrary index) are extremely inefficient in linked lists.

For example, if we measure the time of appending one element and removing it from the sequence with `timeit`, the difference between `list` and `deque` may not even be noticeable:

```
$ python3 -m timeit \
> -s 'sequence=list(range(10))' \
> 'sequence.append(0); sequence.pop();'
1000000 loops, best of 3: 0.168 usec per loop

$ python3 -m timeit \
> -s 'from collections import deque; sequence=deque(range(10))' \
> 'sequence.append(0); sequence.pop();'
1000000 loops, best of 3: 0.168 usec per loop
```

But if we do similar comparison for situations when we want to add and remove the first element of the sequence, the performance difference is impressive:

```
$ python3 -m timeit \
> -s 'sequence=list(range(10))' \
> 'sequence.insert(0, 0); sequence.pop(0)'

1000000 loops, best of 3: 0.392 usec per loop
$ python3 -m timeit \
> -s 'from collections import deque; sequence=deque(range(10))' \
> 'sequence.appendleft(0); sequence.popleft()'
10000000 loops, best of 3: 0.172 usec per loop
```

And the difference is, it gets bigger when the size of the sequence grows. Here is an example of the same test performed on lists containing 10,000 elements:

```
$ python3 -m timeit \
> -s 'sequence=list(range(10000))' \
> 'sequence.insert(0, 0); sequence.pop(0)'
100000 loops, best of 3: 14 usec per loop
$ python3 -m timeit \
> -s 'from collections import deque; sequence=deque(range(10000))' \
> 'sequence.appendleft(0); sequence.popleft()'
10000000 loops, best of 3: 0.168 usec per loop
```

Thanks to efficient `append()` and `pop()` methods that work at the same speed from both ends of the sequence, `deque` makes a perfect type for implementing queues. For example, a **FIFO (First In First Out)** queue will definitely be much more efficient if implemented with a `deque` instead of `list`.

> `deque` works great when implementing queues. Anyway, starting from Python 2.6 there is a separate `queue` module in Python's standard library that provides basic implementation for FIFO, LIFO, and priority queues. If you want to utilize queues as a mechanism of interthread communication, you should really use classes from the `queue` module instead of `collections.deque`. This is because these classes provide all the necessary locking semantics. If you don't use threading and don't utilize queues as a communication mechanism, then `deque` should be enough to provide queue implementation basics.

defaultdict

The `defaultdict` type is similar to the `dict` type but adds a default factory for new keys. This avoids writing an extra test to initialize the mapping entry and is more efficient than the `dict.setdefault` method.

`defaultdict` seems just like syntactic sugar over `dict` that simply allows you to write shorter code. In fact, the fallback to a predefined value on a failed key lookup is also slightly faster than the `dict.setdefault()` method:

```
$ python3 -m timeit \
> -s 'd = {}'
> 'd.setdefault("x", None)'
10000000 loops, best of 3: 0.153 usec per loop
$ python3 -m timeit \
> -s 'from collections import defaultdict; d=defaultdict(lambda: None)' \
> 'd["x"]'
10000000 loops, best of 3: 0.0447 usec per loop
```

The difference isn't great because the computational complexity hasn't changed. The `dict.setdefault` method consist of two steps (key lookup and key set), both of which have a complexity of $O(1)$, as we have seen in the *Dictionaries* section in *Chapter 2, Syntax Best Practices – below the Class Level*. There is no way to have a complexity class lower than $O(1)$. But it is indisputably faster in some situations and it is worth knowing because every small speed improvement counts when optimizing critical code sections.

The `defaultdict` type takes a factory as a parameter and can therefore be used with built-in types or classes whose constructor does not take arguments. Here is an example from the official documentation that shows how to use `defaultdict` for counting:

```
>>> s = 'mississippi'
>>> d = defaultdict(int)
>>> for k in s:
...     d[k] += 1
...
>>> list(d.items())
[('i', 4), ('p', 2), ('s', 4), ('m', 1)]
```

namedtuple

namedtuple is a class factory that takes a type name and a list of attributes and creates a class out of it. The class can then be used to instantiate a tuple-like object and provide accessors for its elements:

```
>>> from collections import namedtuple
>>> Customer = namedtuple(
...     'Customer',
...     'firstname lastname'
... )
>>> c = Customer('Tarek', 'Ziadé')
>>> c.firstname
'Tarek'
```

It can be used to create records that are easier to write compared to a custom class that would require some boilerplate code to initialize values. On the other hand, it is based on tuple, so access to its elements by index is very fast. The generated class can be subclassed to add more operations.

The gain from using namedtuple instead of other datatypes may not be obvious at first. The main advantage is that it is way more easier to use, understand, and interpret than ordinary tuples. Tuple indexes don't carry any semantics, so it is great to access tuple elements by attributes too. However, you could get the same benefit from dictionaries that have an $O(1)$ average complexity of get/set operations.

The first advantage in terms of performance is that namedtuple is still the flavor of tuple. It means that it is immutable, so the underlying array storage is allocated exactly for the needed size. Dictionaries, on the other hand, need to use overallocation of the internal hash table to ensure low average complexity of get/set operations. So, namedtuple wins over dict in terms of memory efficiency.

The fact that namedtuple is based on a tuple may also be beneficial for performance. Its elements may be accessed by an integer index, like in two other simple sequence objects—lists and tuples. This operation is both simple and fast. In the case of dict or custom class instances (that also use dictionaries for storing attributes), the element access requires hash table lookup. It is highly optimized to ensure good performance independently from collection size, but the mentioned $O(1)$ complexity is actually only the *average complexity*. The actual, amortized worst case complexity for set/get operations in dict is $O(n)$. The real amount of work when performing such an operation at a given moment is dependent on both collection size and its history. So, in sections of code that are critical for performance, sometimes it may be wise to use lists or tuples instead of dictionaries. This is only because they are more predictable when it comes to performance.

In such a situation, `namedtuple` is a great type that combines the advantages of dictionaries and tuples:

- In sections where readability is more important, the attribute access may be preferred
- In performance-critical sections, elements may be accessed by their indexes

> Reduced complexity can be achieved by storing the data in an efficient data structure that works well with the way the algorithm will use it.
>
> That said, when the solution is not obvious, you should consider dropping and rewriting the incriminated part instead of killing the code readability for the sake of performance.
>
> Often, the Python code can be both readable and fast. So, try to find a good way to perform the work instead of trying to work around a flawed design.

Using architectural trade-offs

When your code cannot be improved any further by reducing the complexity or choosing the proper data structure, a good approach may be to consider doing some trade-offs. If we review user problems and define what is really important for them, we can relax some of the application requirements. The performance can often be improved by:

- Replacing exact solution algorithms with heuristics and approximation algorithms
- Deferring some work to delayed task queues
- Using probabilistic data structures

Using heuristics and approximation algorithms

Some algorithmic problems simply don't have *good state of the art* solutions that could run in time acceptable to the user. For example, consider a program that deals with some complex optimization problems such as **Traveling Salesman Problem** (**TSP**) or **Vehicle Routing Problem** (**VRP**). Both problems are *NP-hard* problems in combinatorial optimization. The exact algorithms for such problems that have low complexity are not known. This means that the size of the problems that can be practically solved is greatly limited. For very large inputs, it is very unlikely that it will be able to provide the exact solution in a time that would be acceptable for any user.

Fortunately, it is very probable that the user is not interested in the best possible solution but the one that is good enough and the one that can be obtained in a timely manner. So, it really makes sense to use **heuristics** or **approximation algorithms** whenever they provide an acceptable quality of results:

- Heuristics solve given problems by trading optimality, completeness, accuracy, or precision for speed. They concentrate on the speed, but it may be really hard to prove their solution quality compared to the result of exact algorithms.

- Approximation algorithms are similar in idea to heuristics, but unlike heuristics have provable solution quality and run-time bounds.

For instance, there are known good heuristics and approximation problems that can solve extremely large TSP problems within a reasonable time. They also have a high probability of producing results just 2-5% from the optimal solution.

Another good thing about heuristics is that they don't always need to be constructed from scratch for every new problem you need to solve. Their higher-level versions, called **metaheuristics**, provide strategies for solving mathematical optimization problems that are not problem-specific and can thus be applied in many situations. Some popular metaheuristic algorithms include:

- Simulated annealing
- Genetic algorithms
- Tabu search
- Ant colony optimization
- Evolutionary computation

Using task queues and delayed processing

Sometimes it's not about doing a lot but about doing things at the right time. A good example of that is sending e-mails in web applications. In that case, increased response times may not necessarily be the result of your implementation. The response time may be dominated by some third-party service, such as an e-mail server. Can you optimize your application if it just spends most of its time on waiting for other services to reply?

The answer is both: yes and no. If you don't have any control over a service that is the main contributor to your processing time and there is no other faster solution you could use, you, of course, cannot speed it up any further. You cannot simply skip in time to get the replies you are waiting for. A simple example of processing an HTTP request that results in sending an e-mail is presented in the following figure (*Figure 1*). You cannot reduce the waiting time, but you can change the way users will perceive it!

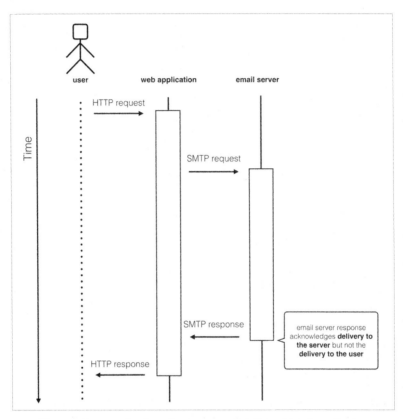

Figure 1 An example of synchronous e-mail delivery in web application

The usual pattern for such type of problems is using message/task queues. When you need to do something that may take an indefinite amount of time, just add this to the queue of work that needs to be done and immediately respond to the user whose request was accepted. Here, we come to the reason why sending e-mails is such a great example. E-mails are already task queues! If you submit a new message to the e-mail server using SMTP protocol, the successful response does not mean that your e-mail was delivered to addressee. It means that the e-mail was delivered to the e-mail server and it will try later to deliver it further.

So, if the response from the server does not guarantee that the e-mail was delivered at all, you don't need to wait for it in order to generate an HTTP response for the user. The updated flow of processing requests with the usage of the task queue is presented in the following figure:

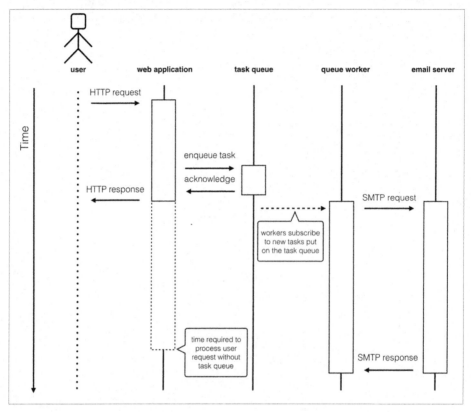

Figure 2 An example of asynchronous e-mail delivery in web application

Of course, your e-mail server may be responding blazingly fast, but you need some more time to generate the message that needs to be sent. Perhaps you are generating yearly reports in an XLS format or maybe delivering invoices in PDF files. If you use e-mail transport that is already asynchronous, then put the whole message generation task to the message processing system too. If you cannot guarantee the exact time of delivery, then you should not bother to generate your deliverables synchronously.

The proper usage of task/message queues in critical sections of the application can also give you other benefits:

- Web workers that serve HTTP requests will be relieved from additional work and processing requests faster. This means that you will be able to process more requests with the same resources and thus handle greater load.

- Message queues are generally more immune to transient failures of external services. For instance, if your database or e-mail server times out from time to time, you can always re-queue the currently processed task and retry it later.

- With a good message queue implementation, you can easily distribute the work on multiple machines. This approach may improve the scalability of some of your application components.

As you can see in *Figure 2*, adding an asynchronous task processing to your application inevitably increases the complexity of the whole system's architecture. You will need to set up some new backing services (a message queue such as RabbitMQ) and create workers that will be able to process these asynchronous jobs. Fortunately, there are some popular tools for building distributed task queues. The most popular one among Python developers is **Celery** (`http://www.celeryproject.org/`). It is a full-fledged task queue framework with support of multiple message brokers that also allows for the scheduled execution of tasks (it can replace your `cron` jobs). If you need something simpler, then RQ (`http://python-rq.org/`) might be a good alternative. It is a lot simpler than Celery and uses Redis key/value storage as its message broker (**RQ** actually stands for **Redis Queue**).

Although there are some good and battle-tested tools, you should always carefully consider your approach to the task queues. Definitely not every kind of work should be processed in queues. They are good at solving a few types of issues but also introduce a load of new problems:

- Increased complexity of system architecture
- Dealing with *more than once* deliveries
- More services to maintain and monitor
- Larger processing delays
- More difficult logging

Using probabilistic data structures

Probabilistic data structures are structures that are designed to store collections of values in a way that allows you to answer some specific questions within time or resource constraints that would not be possible with other data structures. The most important fact is that the answer is only probable to be true or is the approximation of the real value. However, the probability of the correct answer or its accuracy can be easily estimated. So, despite not always giving the correct answer, it can be still useful if we accept some level of error.

There are a lot of data structures with such probabilistic properties. Each one of them solves some specific problems, and due to theirs stochastic nature cannot be used in every situation. But to give a practical example, let's talk about one of them that is especially popular — **HyperLogLog**.

HyperLogLog (refer to `https://en.wikipedia.org/wiki/HyperLogLog`) is an algorithm that approximates the number of distinct elements in a multiset. With ordinary sets, you need to store every element, and this may be very impractical for very large datasets. HLL is distinct from the classical way of implementing sets as programming data structures. Without digging into implementation details, let's say that it only concentrates on providing an approximation of the set cardinality. Thus, real values are never stored. They cannot be retrieved, iterated, and tested for membership. HyperLogLog trades accuracy and correctness for time complexity and size in memory. For instance, the Redis implementation of HLL takes only 12k bytes with a standard error of 0.81% with no practical limit of collection size.

Using probabilistic data structures is a very interesting way of solving performance problems. In most cases, it is about trading off some accuracy or correctness for faster processing or better resource usage. But it does not always need to be that way. Probabilistic data structures are very often used in key/value storage systems to speed up key lookups. One of the popular techniques used in such systems is called approximate member query (AMQ). One interesting data structure that can be used for that purpose is Bloom filter (refer to `https://en.wikipedia.org/wiki/Bloom_filter`).

Caching

When some of your application function takes too long to compute, the useful technique to consider is caching. Caching is nothing but saving a return value for future reference. The result of a function or method that is expensive to run can be cached as long as:

- The function is deterministic and the results have the same value every time, given the same input
- The return value of the function continues to be useful and valid for some period of time (nondeterministic)

In other words, a deterministic function always returns the same result for the same set of arguments, whereas a nondeterministic one returns results that may vary in time. Such an approach usually greatly reduces the time of computation and allows you to save a lot of computer resources.

The most important requirement for any caching solution is to have a storage that allows you to retrieve saved values significantly faster than it takes to calculate them. Good candidates for caching are usually:

- Results from callables that query databases
- Results from callables that render static values, such as file content, web requests, or PDF rendering
- Results from deterministic callables that perform complex calculations
- Global mappings that keep track of values with expiration times, such as web session objects
- Results that needs to be accessed often and quickly

Another important use case for caching is saving results from third-party APIs served over the Web. This may greatly improve application performance by cutting off the network latencies but also allows you to save money if you are billed for every request to such API.

Depending on your application architecture, the cache can be implemented in many ways and with various levels of complexity. There are many ways to provide caching and complex applications can use different approaches on different levels of the application architecture stack. Sometimes a cache may be as simple as a single global data structure (usually a `dict`) kept in the process memory. In other situations, you may want to set up a dedicated caching service that will run on carefully tailored hardware. This section will provide you with basic information on the most popular caching approaches and guide you through the usual use cases and also the common pitfalls.

Deterministic caching

Deterministic functions are the easiest and safest use case for caching. Deterministic functions always return the same value if given exactly the same input, so generally you can store their result indefinitely. The only limitation is the size of storage you use for caching. The simplest way to cache such results is to put them into process memory because it is usually the fastest place to retrieve data from. Such a technique is often called **memoization**.

Memoization is very useful when optimizing recursive functions that may evaluate the same inputs multiple times. We already discussed recursive implementation for the Fibonacci sequence in *Chapter 7, Python Extensions in Other Languages*. Back then, we tried to improve the performance of our program with C and Cython. Now we will try to achieve the same goal by simpler means—with the help of caching. But before we do that, let's recall the code for the `fibonacci()` function:

```python
def fibonacci(n):
    """ Return nth Fibonacci sequence number computed recursively
    """
    if n < 2:
        return 1
    else:
        return fibonacci(n - 1) + fibonacci(n - 2)
```

As we see, `fibonacci()` is a recursive function that calls itself twice if the input value is more than two. This makes it highly inefficient. The run time complexity is $O(2^n)$ and its execution creates a very deep and vast call tree. For the large value, this function will take extremely long to execute and there is high chance of quickly exceeding the maximal recursion limit of the Python interpreter.

If you take a closer look at *Figure 3*, which presents an example call tree, you will see that it evaluates many of the intermediate results multiple times. A lot of time and resources could be saved if we could reuse some of these values.

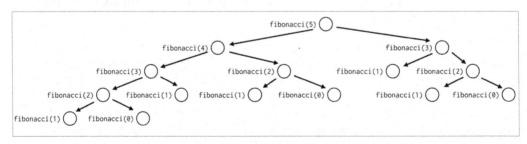

Figure 3 Call tree for fibonacci(5) execution

A simple memoization attempt would be to store results of the previous runs in a dictionary and retrieve them if they are available. Both the recursive calls in the `fibonacci()` function are contained in a single line of code:

```
return fibonacci(n - 1) + fibonacci(n - 2)
```

We know that Python evaluates instructions from left to right. This means that, in this situation, the call to the function with a higher argument value will be executed before the call to the function with a lower argument. Thanks to this, we can provide memoizaton by constructing a very simple decorator:

```python
def memoize(function):
    """ Memoize the call to single-argument function
    """
    call_cache = {}

    def memoized(argument):
        try:
            return call_cache[argument]
        except KeyError:
            return call_cache.setdefault(argument,
                                         function(argument))

    return memoized


@memoize
def fibonacci(n):
    """ Return nth Fibonacci sequence number computed recursively
    """
    if n < 2:
        return 1
    else:
        return fibonacci(n - 1) + fibonacci(n - 2)
```

We used the dictionary on the closure of the `memoize()` decorator as a simple storage from cached values. Saving and retrieving value to that data structure has an average *O(1)* complexity, so this greatly reduces the overall complexity of the memoized function. Every unique function call will be evaluated only once. The call tree of such an updated function is presented in *Figure 4*. Without going into mathematical proofs, we can visually deduce that without changing the core of the `fibonacci()` function, we reduced the complexity from the very expensive *O(2n)* to the linear *O(n)*.

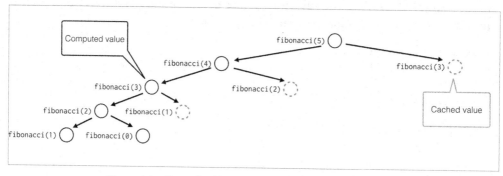

Figure 4 A call tree for fibonacci(5) execution with memoization

The implementation of our `memoize()` decorator is, of course, not perfect. It worked well for that simple example, but it definitely isn't a reusable piece of software. If you need to memoize functions with multiple arguments or want to limit the size of your cache, you need something more generic. Luckily, the Python standard library provides a very simple and reusable utility that may be used in most cases when you need to cache in memory the results of deterministic functions. It is the `lru_cache(maxsize, typed)` decorator from the `functools` module. The name comes from the LRU cache, which stands for *last recently used*. The additional parameters allow for finer control over memoization behavior:

- `maxsize`: This sets the maximum size of the cache. The `None` value means no limit at all.

- `typed`: This defines if the values of different types that compare as equal should be cached as giving the same result.

The usage of `lru_cache` in our Fibonacci sequence example would be as follows:

```
@lru_cache(None)
def fibonacci(n):
    """ Return nth Fibonacci sequence number computed recursively
    """
    if n < 2:
        return 1
    else:
        return fibonacci(n - 1) + fibonacci(n - 2)
```

Nondeterministic caching

The caching of nondeterministic functions is way more trickier that memoization. Due to the fact that every execution of such a function may give different results, it is usually impossible to use previous values for an arbitrarily long amount of time. What you need to do is to decide for how long a cached value can be considered valid. After a defined period of time passes, the stored results are considered to be stale and the cache needs to be refreshed by a new value.

Nondeterministic functions that are usually a subject of caching very often depend on some external state that is hard to track inside of your application code. Typical examples of components are:

- Relational databases and generally any type of structured data storage engine
- Third-party services accessible through network connection (web APIs)
- Filesystems

So, in other words, nondeterministic caching is used in any situation when you temporarily use precomputed results without being sure if they represent a state that is consistent with the state of other system components (usually, the backing service).

Note that such an implementation of caching is obviously a trade-off. Thus, it is somehow related to the techniques we featured in the *Using architectural trade-offs* section. If you resign from running part of your code every time and instead use the results saved in the past, you are risking using data that becomes stale or represents an inconsistent state of your system. This way, you are trading the correctness and/or completeness for speed and performance.

Of course, such caching is efficient as long as the time taken to interact with the cache is less than the time taken by the function. If it's faster to simply recalculate the value, by all means do so! That's why setting up a cache has to be done only if it's worth it; setting it up properly has a cost.

The actual things that are cached are usually the whole results of interaction with other components of your system. If you want to save time and resources when communicating with the database, it is worth to cache expensive queries. If you want to reduce the number of I/O operations, you may want to cache the content of the files that are accessed very often (configuration files, for instance).

Techniques for caching non-deterministic functions are actually very similar to those used in caching the deterministic ones. The most notable difference is that they usually require the option to invalidate cached values by their age. This means that the `lru_cache()` decorator from the `functools` module has very limited use in such situations. It should not be so hard to extend this function to provide the expiration feature, but I will leave it as an exercise for you.

Cache services

We said that nondeterministic caching can be implemented using local process memory, but actually it is rarely done that way. It's because local process memory is very limited in its utility as storage for caching in large applications.

If you run into a situation where non-deterministic caching is your preferred solution to solve performance problems, you usually need something more than that. Usually, nondeterministic caching is your *must have* solution when you need to serve data or service to multiple users at the same time. If it's true, then sooner or later you will need to ensure that users can be served concurrently. While local memory provides a way to share data between multiple threads, it may not be the best concurrency model for every application. It does not scale well, so you will eventually need to run your application as multiple processes.

If you are lucky enough, you may need to run your application on hundreds or thousands of machines. If you would like to store cached values in local memory, it means that your cache needs to be duplicated on every process that requires it. It isn't only a total waste of resources. If every process has its own cache, that is already a trade-off between speed and consistency, how can you guarantee that all caches are consistent with each other?

Consistency across subsequent request is a serious concern (especially) for web applications with distributed backends. In complex distributed systems, it is extremely hard to ensure that the user will be always consistently served by the same process hosted on the same machine. It is of course doable to some extent, but once you solve that problem, ten others will pop up.

If you are making an application that will need to serve multiple concurrent users, then the best way to handle a nondeterministic cache is to use some dedicated service for that. With tools such as Redis or Memcached, you allow all your application processes to share the same cached results. This both reduces the usage of precious computing resources and saves you from problems caused by having multiple independent and inconsistent caches.

Memcached

If you want to be serious about caching, **Memcached** is a very popular and battle-tested solution. This cache server is used by big applications such as Facebook or Wikipedia to scale their websites. Among simple caching features, it has clustering capabilities that makes it possible to set up a highly efficient distributed cache system in no time.

The tool is Unix-based but can be driven from any platform and from many languages. There are many Python clients that differ slightly from each other but the basic usage is usually the same. The simplest interaction with Memcached almost always consists of three methods:

- `set(key, value)`: This saves the value for the given key
- `get(key)`: This gets the value for the given key if it exists
- `delete(key)`: This deletes the value under the given key if it exists

Here is an example of integration with Memcached using one of the popular Python packages—pymemcached:

```
from pymemcache.client.base import Client

# setup Memcached client running under 11211 port on localhost
client = Client(('localhost', 11211))

# cache some value under some key and expire it after 10 seconds
client.set('some_key', 'some_value', expire=10)

# retrieve value for the same key
result = client.get('some_key')
```

One of the downsides of Memcached is that it is designed to store values either as strings or a binary blob, and this isn't compatible with every native Python type. Actually, it is compatible with only one—strings. This means that more complex types need to be serialized in order to be successfully stored in Memcached. A common serialization choice for simple data structures is JSON. Here is an example of using JSON serialization with pymemcached:

```
import json
from pymemcache.client.base import Client

def json_serializer(key, value):
    if type(value) == str:
        return value, 1
    return json.dumps(value), 2

def json_deserializer(key, value, flags):
    if flags == 1:
        return value
    if flags == 2:
        return json.loads(value)
    raise Exception("Unknown serialization format")
```

```
client = Client(('localhost', 11211), serializer=json_serializer,
                deserializer=json_deserializer)
client.set('key', {'a':'b', 'c':'d'})
result = client.get('key')
```

The other problem that is very common when working with every caching service that works on the key/value storage principle is how to choose key names.

For cases when you cache simple function invocations that have basic parameters, the problem is usually simple. You can convert the function name and its arguments to strings and concatenate them together. The only thing you need to care about is to make sure there are no collisions between keys created for different functions if you use cache in many parts of your application.

A more problematic case is when cached functions have complex arguments consisting of dictionaries or custom classes. In that case, you need to find a way to convert such invocation signatures to cache keys in a consistent manner.

The last problem is that Memcached, like many other caching services, does not tend to like very long key strings. Usually, the shorter the better. Long keys may either reduce performance or just not fit the hardcoded service limits. For instance, if you cache whole SQL queries, the query strings themselves are generally good unique identifiers that could be used as keys. But on the other hand, complex queries are generally too long to be stored in typical caching services such as Memcached. A common practice is to calculate the **MD5**, **SHA**, or any other hash function and use it as a cache key instead. The Python standard library has a `hashlib` module that provides implementation for few popular hash algorithms.

Remember that calculating a hash comes at a price. However, sometimes it is the only viable solution. It is also a very useful technique when dealing with complex types that need to be used when creating cache keys. One important thing to care about when using hashing functions is hash collisions. There is no hash function that guarantees that collisions will never occur, so always be sure to know the probability and mind such risks.

Summary

In this chapter, you have learned:

- How to define the complexity of the code and some approaches to reduce it
- How to improve performance using some architectural trade-offs
- What caching is and how to use it to improve application performance

The preceding methods concentrated our optimization efforts inside a single process. We tried to reduce the code complexity, choose better datatypes, or reuse old function results. If that did not help, we tried to make some trade-offs using approximations, doing less, or leaving work for later.

In the next chapter, we will discuss a few techniques for concurrency and parallel processing in Python.

13
Concurrency

Concurrency and one of its manifestations—parallel processing—is one of the broadest topics in the area of software engineering. Most of the chapters in this book also cover vast areas, and almost all of them could be big enough topics for a separate book. But the topic of concurrency by itself is so huge that it could take dozens of positions and we would still not be able to discuss all of its important aspects and models.

This is why I won't try to fool you, and from the very beginning state that we will barely touch the surface of this topic. The purpose of this chapter is to show why concurrency may be required in your application, when to use it, and what are the most important concurrency models that you may use in Python:

- Multithreading
- Multiprocessing
- Asynchronous programming

We will also discuss some of the language features, built-in modules, and third-party packages that allow you to implement these models in your code. But we won't cover them in much detail. Treat the content of this chapter as an entry point for your further research and reading. It is here to guide you through the basic ideas and help in deciding if you really need concurrency, and if so, which approach will best suit your needs.

Why concurrency?

Before we answer the question *why concurrency*, we need to ask *what is concurrency at all?*

And the answer to the second question may be surprising for some who used to think that this is a synonym for **parallel processing**. But concurrency is not the same as parallelism. Concurrency is not a matter of application implementation but only a property of a program, algorithm, or problem. And parallelism is only one of the possible approaches to problems that are concurrent.

Leslie Lamport in his *Time, Clocks, and the Ordering of Events in Distributed Systems* paper from 1976, says:

> "*Two events are concurrent if neither can causally affect the other.*"

By extrapolating events to programs, algorithms, or problems, we can say that something is concurrent if it can be fully or partially decomposed into components (units) that are order-independent. Such units may be processed independently from each other, and the order of processing does not affect the final result. This means that they can also be processed simultaneously or in parallel. If we process information this way, then we are indeed dealing with parallel processing. But this is still not obligatory.

Doing work in a distributed manner, preferably using capabilities of multicore processors or computing clusters, is a natural consequence of concurrent problems. Anyway, it does not mean that this is the only way of efficiently dealing with concurrency. There are a lot of use cases where concurrent problems can be approached in other than synchronous ways, but without the need for parallel execution.

So, once we know what concurrency really is, it is time to explain what the fuss is about. When the problem is concurrent, it gives you the opportunity to deal with it in a special, preferably more efficient, way.

We often get used to deal with problems in a classical way by performing a sequence of steps. This is how most of us think and process information — using synchronous algorithms that do one thing at a time, step by step. But this way of processing information is not well suited for solving large-scale problems or when you need to satisfy the demands of multiple users or software agents simultaneously:

- The time to process the job is limited by the performance of the single processing unit (single machine, CPU core, and so on)
- You are not able to accept and process new inputs until your program has finished processing the previous one

So generally, approaching concurrent problems concurrently is the best approach when:

- The scale of problems is so big that the only way to process them in an acceptable time or within the range of available resources is to distribute execution to multiple processing units that can handle the work in parallel

- Your application needs to maintain responsiveness (accept new inputs) even if it has not finished processing the old ones

This covers most of the situations where concurrent processing is a reasonable option. The first group of problems definitely needs the parallel processing solution so it is usually solved with multithreading and multiprocessing models. The second group does not necessarily need to be processed in parallel, so the actual solution really depends on the problem details. Note that this group also covers cases where the application needs to serve multiple clients (users or software agents) independently, without the need to wait for others to be successfully served.

The other thing worth mentioning is that the preceding two groups are not exclusive. Very often you need to maintain application responsiveness and at the same time you are not able to handle the input on a single processing unit. This is the reason why different and seemingly alternative or conflicting approaches to concurrency may often be used at the same time. This is especially common in the development of web servers where it may be necessary to use asynchronous event loops, or threads with a conjunction of multiple processes, in order to utilize all the available resources and still maintain low latencies under high load.

Multithreading

Threading is often considered to be a complex topic by developers. While this statement is totally true, Python provides high-level classes and functions that ease the usage of threading. CPython's implementation of threads comes with some inconvenient details that make them less useful than in other languages. They are still completely fine for some set problems that you may want to solve, but not for as many as in C or Java. In this section, we will discuss the limitations of multithreading in CPython, as well as the common concurrent problems where Python threads are a viable solution.

What is multithreading?

Thread is short for a thread of execution. A programmer can split his or her work into threads that run simultaneously and share the same memory context. Unless your code depends on third-party resources, multithreading will not speed it up on a single-core processor, and will even add some overhead for thread management. Multi-threading will benefit from a multiprocessor or multi-core machine and will parallelize each thread execution on each CPU core, thus making the program faster. Note that this is a general rule that should hold true for most programming languages. In Python, the performance benefit from multithreading on multicore CPUs has some limits, but we will discuss that later. For simplicity, let's assume for now that this statement is true.

The fact that the same context is shared among threads means you must protect data from concurrent access. If two threads update the same data without any protection, a race condition occurs. This is called a **race hazard**, where unexpected results may happen because of the code run by each thread making false assumptions about the state of the data.

Lock mechanisms help in protecting data, and thread programming has always been a matter of making sure that the resources are accessed by threads in a safe way. This can be quite hard and thread programming often leads to bugs that are hard to debug, since they are hard to reproduce. The worst problem occurs when, due to poor code design, two threads lock a resource and try to get the resource that the other thread has locked. They will wait for each other forever. This is called a **deadlock** and is quite hard to debug. **Reentrant locks** help a bit in this by making sure a thread doesn't get locked by attempting to lock a resource twice.

Nevertheless, when threads are used for isolated needs with tools that were built for them, they might increase the speed of the program.

Multithreading is usually supported at the system kernel level. When the machine has one single processor with a single core, the system uses a **timeslicing** mechanism. Here, the CPU switches from one thread to another so fast that there is an illusion of threads running simultaneously. This is done at the processing level as well. Parallelism without multiple processing units is obviously virtual and there is no performance gain from running multiple threads on such hardware. Anyway, sometimes it is still useful to implement code with threads even if it has to execute on a single core, and we will see a possible use case later.

Everything changes when your execution environment has multiple processors or multiple CPU cores for its disposition. Even if timeslicing is used, processes and threads are distributed among CPUs, providing the ability to run your program faster.

How Python deals with threads

Unlike some other languages, Python uses multiple kernel-level threads that can each run any of the interpreter-level threads. But the standard implementation of the language—CPython—comes with major limitation that renders threads less usable in many contexts. All threads accessing Python objects are serialized by one global lock. This is done because much of the interpreter internal structures, as well as third-party C code, are not thread-safe and need to be protected.

This mechanism is called the **Global Interpreter Lock (GIL)** and its implementation details on the Python/C API level were already discussed in the *Releasing GIL* section of *Chapter 7*, *Python Extensions in Other Languages*. The removal of GIL is a topic that occasionally appears on the python-dev e-mail list and was postulated by developers multiple times. Sadly, until this time, no one ever managed to provide a reasonable and simple solution that would allow us to get rid of this limitation. It is highly improbable that we will see any progress in this area soon. It is safer to assume that GIL will stay in CPython forever. So we need to learn how to live with it.

So what is the point of multithreading in Python?

When threads contain only pure Python code, there is little point in using threads to speed up the program since the GIL will serialize it. But remember that GIL just enforces that only one thread can execute the Python code at any time. In practice, the global interpreter lock is released on a number of blocking system calls and can be released in sections of C extensions that do not use any Python/C API functions. This means, multiple threads can do I/O operations or execute C code in certain third-party extensions in parallel.

For nonpure code blocks where external resources are used or C code is involved, multithreading is useful for waiting for a third-party resource to return results. This is because a sleeping thread that has explicitly released the GIL can stand by and wake up when the results are back. Last, whenever a program needs to provide a responsive interface, multithreading is the answer even if it uses timeslicing. The program can interact with the user while doing some heavy computing in the so-called background.

Note that GIL does not exist in every implementation of the Python language. It is a limitation of CPython, Stackless Python, and PyPy, but does not exist in Jython and IronPython (see *Chapter 1*, *Current Status of Python*). There is although some development of the GIL-free version of PyPy, but at the time of writing this book, it is still at an experimental stage and the documentation is lacking. It is based on Software Transactional Memory and is called PyPy-STM. It is really hard to say when (or if) it will be officially released as a production-ready interpreter. Everything seems to indicate that it won't happen soon.

When should threading be used?

Despite the GIL limitation, threads can be really useful in some cases. They can help in:

- Building responsive interfaces
- Delegating work
- Building multiuser applications

Building responsive interfaces

Let's say you ask your system to copy files from a folder to another through a graphical user interface. The task will possibly be pushed into the background and the interface window will be constantly refreshed by the main thread. This way you get live feedback on the progress of the whole process. You will also be able to cancel the operation. This is less irritating than a raw `cp` or `copy` shell command that does not provide any feedback until all work is finished.

A responsive interface also allows a user to work on several tasks at the same time. For instance, Gimp will let you play around with a picture while another one is being filtered, since the two tasks are independent.

When trying to achieve such responsive interfaces, a good approach is to try to push long running tasks into the background, or at least try to provide constant feedback to the user. The easiest way to achieve that is to use threads. In such a scenario, they are not intended to increase performance, but only to make sure that the user can still operate the interface even if it needs to process some data for a longer period of time.

In case such background tasks perform a lot of I/O operations, you are able to still get some benefit from multicore CPUs. Then it's a *win-win* situation.

Delegating work

If your process depends on third-party resources, threads might really speed up everything.

Let's consider the case of a function that indexes files in a folder and pushes the built indexes into a database. Depending on the type of file, the function calls a different external program. For example, one is specialized in PDFs and another one in OpenOffice files.

Instead of treating each file in a sequence, by executing the right program and then storing the result into the database, your function can set up a thread for each converter and push jobs to be done to each one of them through a queue. The overall time taken by the function will be closer to the processing time of the slowest converter than to the sum of all the work.

Converter threads can be initialized from the start and the code in charge of pushing the result into the database can also be a thread that consumes available results in the queue.

Note that such an approach is somewhat a hybrid between multithreading and multiprocessing. If you delegate the work to external processes (for example, using the `run()` function from the `subprocess` module), you are in fact doing work in multiple processes, so this has symptoms of multiprocessing. But in our scenario, we are waiting for the processing results in separate threads, so it is still mostly multithreading from the view of the Python code.

The other common use case for threads is performing multiple HTTP requests to external services. For instance, if you want to fetch multiple results from a distant web API, it could take a lot of time to do that synchronously. If you wait for every previous response before making new requests, you will spend a lot of time just waiting for the external service to respond and additional roundtrip time delays will be added to every such request. If you are communicating with an efficient service (Google Maps API, for instance), it is highly probable that it can serve most of your requests concurrently without affecting response times of separate requests. It is then reasonable to perform multiple queries in separate threads. Remember that when doing an HTTP request, most of time is spent on reading from the TCP socket. This is a blocking I/O operation, so CPython will release the GIL when performing the `recv()` C function. This allows for great improvements in your application's performance.

Multiuser applications

Threading is also used as a concurrency base for multiuser applications. For instance, a web server will push a user request into a new thread and then will become idle, waiting for new requests. Having a thread dedicated to each request simplifies a lot of work, but requires the developer to take care of locking the resources. But this is not a problem when all the shared data is pushed into a relational database that takes care of concurrency matters. So threads in a multi-user application act almost like separate independent processes. They are under the same process only to simplify their management at the application level.

For instance, a web server will be able to put all requests in a queue and wait for a thread to be available to send the work to it. Furthermore, it allows memory sharing that can boost some work and reduce the memory load. The two very popular Python WSGI-compliant webservers: **Gunicorn** (refer to `http://gunicorn.org/`) and **uWSGI** (refer to `https://uwsgi-docs.readthedocs.org`), allow you to serve HTTP requests with threaded workers in a way that generally follows this principle.

Using multithreading to enable concurrency in multiuser applications is less expensive than using multiprocessing. Separate processes cost more resources since a new interpreter needs to be loaded for each one of them. On the other hand, having too many threads is expensive too. We know that the GIL isn't such a problem for I/O extensive applications, but there is always a time where you will need to execute Python code. Since you cannot parallelize all of the application parts with bare threads, you will never be able to utilize all resources on machines with multicore CPUs and a single Python process. This is why often the optimal solution is a hybrid of multiprocessing and multithreading—multiple workers (processes) running with multiple threads. Fortunately, many of the WSGI-compliant web servers allow for such a setup.

But before you marry multithreading with multiprocessing, consider if such an approach is really worth all the cost. Such an approach uses multiprocessing for better resource utilization and additionally multithreading for more concurrency, which should be lighter than running multiple processes. But it does not need to be true. Maybe getting rid of threads and increasing the number of processes is not as expensive as you think? When choosing the best setup, you always need to do load testing of your application (see the *Load and performance testing* section in *Chapter 10, Test-Driven Development*). Also, as a side effect of using multiple threads, you get a less safe environment where shared memory creates a risk of data corruption or dreadful deadlock. Maybe a better alternative would be using some asynchronous approach with event loops, green threads, or coroutines. We will cover such solutions later in the *Asynchronous programming* section. Again, without sensible load testing and experimentation, you cannot really tell what approach will work best in your context.

An example of a threaded application

To see how Python threading works in practice, let's construct an example application that can take some benefit from implementing multithreading. We will discuss a simple problem that you may encounter from time to time in your professional practice—making multiple parallel HTTP queries. This problem was already mentioned as a common use case for multithreading.

Let's say we need to fetch data from some web service using multiple queries that cannot be batched into a single big HTTP request. As a realistic example, we will use geocoding endpoints from Google Maps API. The reasons for that choice are as follows:

- It is very popular and a well-documented service
- There is a free tier of this API that does not require any authentication keys
- There is a `python-gmaps` package available on PyPI that allows you to interact with various Google Maps API endpoints and is extremely easy to use

Geocoding means simply the transformation of address or place into coordinates. We will try to geocode a predefined list of various cities into latitude/longitude tuples and display results on the standard output with `python-gmaps`. It is as simple as shown in the following code:

```
>>> from gmaps import Geocoding
>>> api = Geocoding()
>>> geocoded = api.geocode('Warsaw')[0]
>>> print("{:>25s}, {:6.2f}, {:6.2f}".format(
...        geocoded['formatted_address'],
...        geocoded['geometry']['location']['lat'],
...        geocoded['geometry']['location']['lng'],
...    ))
Warsaw, Poland,  52.23,  21.01
```

Since our goal is to show how a multithreaded solution to concurrent problems compares to standard synchronous solution, we will start with an implementation that does not use threads at all. Here is the code of a program that loops over the list of cities, queries the Google Maps API, and displays information about their addresses and coordinates in a text-formatted table:

```
import time

from gmaps import Geocoding

api = Geocoding()


PLACES = (
    'Reykjavik', 'Vien', 'Zadar', 'Venice',
```

```
        'Wrocław', 'Bolognia', 'Berlin', 'Słubice',
        'New York', 'Dehli',
    )


def fetch_place(place):
    geocoded = api.geocode(place)[0]

    print("{:>25s}, {:6.2f}, {:6.2f}".format(
        geocoded['formatted_address'],
        geocoded['geometry']['location']['lat'],
        geocoded['geometry']['location']['lng'],
    ))


def main():
    for place in PLACES:
        fetch_place(place)

if __name__ == "__main__":
    started = time.time()
    main()
    elapsed = time.time() - started

    print()
    print("time elapsed: {:.2f}s".format(elapsed))
```

Around the execution of the main() function, we added a few statements that are intended to measure how much time it took to finish the job. On my computer, this program usually takes around 2 to 3 seconds to complete its task:

```
$ python3 synchronous.py
        Reykjavík, Iceland,  64.13,  -21.82
           Vienna, Austria,  48.21,   16.37
            Zadar, Croatia,  44.12,   15.23
             Venice, Italy,  45.44,   12.32
            Wrocław, Poland,  51.11,   17.04
            Bologna, Italy,  44.49,   11.34
           Berlin, Germany,  52.52,   13.40
            Slubice, Poland,  52.35,   14.56
           New York, NY, USA,  40.71,  -74.01
     Dehli, Gujarat, India,  21.57,   73.22


time elapsed: 2.79s
```

Every run of our script will always take a different amount of time because it mostly depends on a remote service accessible through a network connection. So there is a lot of nondeterministic factors affecting the final result. The best approach would be to make longer tests, repeat them multiple times, and also calculate some average from the measurements. But for the sake of simplicity, we won't do that. You will see later that this simplified approach is just enough for illustrational purposes.

Using one thread per item

Now it is time for improvement. We don't do a lot of processing in Python and the long execution time is caused by communication with the external service. We send an HTTP request to the server, it calculates the answer, and then we wait until the response is transferred back. There is a lot of I/O involved, so multithreading seems like a viable option. We can start all the requests at once in separate threads and then just wait until they receive data. If the service that we are communicating with is able to process our request concurrently, we should definitely see a performance improvement.

So let's start with the easiest approach. Python provides clean and easy to use abstraction over system threads with the `threading` module. The core of this standard library is the `Thread` class that represents a single thread instance. Here is a modified version of the `main()` function, which creates and starts a new thread for every place to geocode and then waits until all the threads finish:

```
from threading import Thread


def main():
    threads = []
    for place in PLACES:
        thread = Thread(target=fetch_place, args=[place])
        thread.start()
        threads.append(thread)

    while threads:
        threads.pop().join()
```

It is quick-and-dirty change that has some serious issues that we will try to address later. It approaches the problem in a bit of a frivolous way, and it is not a way to write reliable software that will serve thousands or millions of users. But hey, it works:

```
$ python3 threaded.py
          Wrocław, Poland,  51.11,   17.04
          Vienna, Austria,  48.21,   16.37
    Dehli, Gujarat, India,  21.57,   73.22
        New York, NY, USA,  40.71,  -74.01
           Bologna, Italy,  44.49,   11.34
      Reykjavík, Iceland,  64.13,  -21.82
          Zadar, Croatia,  44.12,   15.23
          Berlin, Germany,  52.52,   13.40
         Slubice, Poland,  52.35,   14.56
            Venice, Italy,  45.44,   12.32


time elapsed: 1.05s
```

So when we know that threads have a beneficial effect on our application, it is time to use them in a slightly saner way. First we need to identify the issues in the preceding code:

- We start a new thread for every parameter. Thread initialization also takes some time but this minor overhead is not the only problem. Threads also consume other resources such as memory and file descriptors. Our example input has a strictly defined number of items, what if it did not have? You definitely don't want to run an unbound number of threads that depend on the arbitrary size of data input.

- The `fetch_place()` function executed in threads calls the built-in `print()` function and in practice it is very unlikely that you would want to do that outside of the main application thread. At first, it is due to the fact how the standard output is buffered in Python. You can experience malformed output when multiple calls to this function interleave between threads. Also, the `print()` function is considered slow. If used recklessly in multiple threads, it can lead to serialization, which will undo all the benefits of multithreading.

- Last but not least, by delegating every function call to a separate thread, we make it extremely hard to control the rate at which our input is processed. Yes, we want to do the job as fast as possible, but very often external services enforce hard limits on the rate of requests from a single client that they can process. Sometimes it is reasonable to design the program in a way that enables you to throttle the rate of processing, so your application won't be blacklisted by external APIs for abusing their usage limits.

Using a thread pool

The first issue we will try to solve is the unbound limit of threads that are run by our program. A good solution would be to build a pool of threaded workers with strictly defined sizes that will handle all the parallel work and communicate with workers through some thread-safe data structure. By using this thread pool approach, we will also make it easier to solve the two other problems that we just mentioned.

So the general idea is to start some predefined number of threads that will consume the work items from a queue until it is done. When there is no other work to do, the threads will return and we will be able to exit from the program. A good candidate for our structure to be used to communicate with the workers is the `Queue` class from the built-in `queue` module. It is a FIFO (First In First Out) queue implementation that is very similar to the `deque` collection from the `collections` module and was specifically designed to handle interthread communication. Here is a modified version of the `main()` function that starts only a limited number of worker threads with a new `worker()` function as a target, and communicates with them using a thread-safe queue:

```python
from queue import Queue, Empty
from threading import Thread

THREAD_POOL_SIZE = 4


def worker(work_queue):
    while not work_queue.empty():
        try:
            item = work_queue.get(block=False)
        except Empty:
            break
        else:
            fetch_place(item)
            work_queue.task_done()
```

```
def main():
    work_queue = Queue()

    for place in PLACES:
        work_queue.put(place)

    threads = [
        Thread(target=worker, args=(work_queue,))
        for _ in range(THREAD_POOL_SIZE)
    ]

    for thread in threads:
        thread.start()

    work_queue.join()

    while threads:
        threads.pop().join()
```

The result of running a modified version of our program is similar to the previous one:

```
$ python threadpool.py
        Reykjavík, Iceland,  64.13,  -21.82
           Venice, Italy,  45.44,   12.32
          Vienna, Austria,  48.21,   16.37
           Zadar, Croatia,  44.12,   15.23
         Wrocław, Poland,  51.11,   17.04
          Bologna, Italy,  44.49,   11.34
         Slubice, Poland,  52.35,   14.56
          Berlin, Germany,  52.52,   13.40
        New York, NY, USA,  40.71,  -74.01
     Dehli, Gujarat, India,  21.57,   73.22


time elapsed: 1.20s
```

The run time will be slower than in a situation with one thread per argument, but at least now it is not possible to exhaust all the computing resources with an arbitrary long input. Also, we can tweak the THREAD_POOL_SIZE parameter a for better resource/time balance.

Using two-way queues

The other issue that we are now able to solve is the potentially problematic printing of the output in threads. It would be much better to leave such a responsibility to the main thread that started the other threads. We can handle that by providing another queue that will be responsible for collecting results from our workers. Here is the complete code that puts everything together with the main changes highlighted:

```python
import time
from queue import Queue, Empty
from threading import Thread

from gmaps import Geocoding

api = Geocoding()


PLACES = (
    'Reykjavik', 'Vien', 'Zadar', 'Venice',
    'Wrocław', 'Bolognia', 'Berlin', 'Słubice',
    'New York', 'Dehli',
)

THREAD_POOL_SIZE = 4


def fetch_place(place):
    return api.geocode(place)[0]


def present_result(geocoded):
    print("{:>25s}, {:6.2f}, {:6.2f}".format(
        geocoded['formatted_address'],
        geocoded['geometry']['location']['lat'],
        geocoded['geometry']['location']['lng'],
    ))


def worker(work_queue, results_queue):
    while not work_queue.empty():
        try:
            item = work_queue.get(block=False)
        except Empty:
            break
```

```
        else:
            results_queue.put(
                fetch_place(item)
            )
            work_queue.task_done()


def main():
    work_queue = Queue()
    results_queue = Queue()

    for place in PLACES:
        work_queue.put(place)

    threads = [
        Thread(target=worker, args=(work_queue, results_queue))
        for _ in range(THREAD_POOL_SIZE)
    ]

    for thread in threads:
        thread.start()

    work_queue.join()

    while threads:
        threads.pop().join()

    while not results_queue.empty():
        present_result(results_queue.get())


if __name__ == "__main__":
    started = time.time()
    main()
    elapsed = time.time() - started

    print()
    print("time elapsed: {:.2f}s".format(elapsed))
```

This eliminates the risk of malformed output, which we could experience if the `present_result()` function does more `print()` statements or performs some additional computation. We don't expect any performance improvement from this approach with small inputs, but in fact we also reduce the risk of thread serialization due to slow `print()` execution. Here is our final output:

```
$ python threadpool_with_results.py
        Vienna, Austria,  48.21,  16.37
    Reykjavík, Iceland,  64.13, -21.82
        Zadar, Croatia,  44.12,  15.23
         Venice, Italy,  45.44,  12.32
        Wrocław, Poland,  51.11,  17.04
        Bologna, Italy,  44.49,  11.34
        Slubice, Poland,  52.35,  14.56
       Berlin, Germany,  52.52,  13.40
     New York, NY, USA,  40.71, -74.01
 Dehli, Gujarat, India,  21.57,  73.22


time elapsed: 1.30s
```

Dealing with errors and rate limiting

The last of the issues mentioned earlier that you may experience when dealing with such problems are rate limits imposed by external service providers. In the case of the Google Maps API, at the time of writing this book, the official rate limit for free and non-authenticated requests is 10 requests per second and 2,500 requests per day. When using multiple threads, it is very easy to exhaust such a limit. The problem is even more serious due to the fact that we did not cover any failure scenarios yet, and dealing with exceptions in multithreaded Python code is a bit more complicated than usual.

The `api.geocode()` function will raise an exception when the client exceeds Google's rate and this is good news. But this exception is raised separately and will not crash the entire program. The worker thread will of course exit immediately, but the main thread will wait for all tasks stored on `work_queue` to be finished (with the `work_queue.join()` call). This means that our worker threads should gracefully handle possible exceptions and make sure that all items from the queue are processed. Without further improvement, we may end up in a situation where some of the worker threads crashed and the program will never exit.

Let's make some minor changes to our code in order to be prepared for any issues that may occur. In the case of exceptions in the worker thread, we may put an error instance in the `results_queue` queue and mark the current task as done, the same as we would do if there was no error. That way we make sure that the main thread won't lock indefinitely while waiting in `work_queue.join()`. The main thread might then inspect the results and re-raise any of the exceptions found on the results queue. Here are the improved versions of the `worker()` and `main()` functions that can deal with exceptions in a safer way:

```python
def worker(work_queue, results_queue):
    while True:
        try:
            item = work_queue.get(block=False)
        except Empty:
            break
        else:
            try:
                result = fetch_place(item)
            except Exception as err:
                results_queue.put(err)
            else:
                results_queue.put(result)
            finally:
                work_queue.task_done()


def main():
    work_queue = Queue()
    results_queue = Queue()

    for place in PLACES:
        work_queue.put(place)

    threads = [
        Thread(target=worker, args=(work_queue, results_queue))
        for _ in range(THREAD_POOL_SIZE)
    ]

    for thread in threads:
        thread.start()

    work_queue.join()
```

```
    while threads:
        threads.pop().join()

    while not results_queue.empty():
        result = results_queue.get()

        if isinstance(result, Exception):
            raise result

        present_result(result)
```

When we are ready to handle exceptions, it is time to break our code and exceed the rate limit. We can do that easily by modifying some initial conditions. Let's increase the number of places to geocode and the size of our thread pool:

```
PLACES = (
    'Reykjavik', 'Vien', 'Zadar', 'Venice',
    'Wrocław', 'Bolognia', 'Berlin', 'Słubice',
    'New York', 'Dehli',
) * 10

THREAD_POOL_SIZE = 10
```

If your execution environment is fast enough, you should get a similar error soon:

```
$ python3 threadpool_with_errors.py
        New York, NY, USA,    40.71,  -74.01
          Berlin, Germany,    52.52,   13.40
         Wrocław, Poland,    51.11,   17.04
           Zadar, Croatia,    44.12,   15.23
          Vienna, Austria,    48.21,   16.37
          Bologna, Italy,    44.49,   11.34
      Reykjavík, Iceland,    64.13,  -21.82
           Venice, Italy,    45.44,   12.32
   Dehli, Gujarat, India,    21.57,   73.22
          Slubice, Poland,    52.35,   14.56
          Vienna, Austria,    48.21,   16.37
           Zadar, Croatia,    44.12,   15.23
           Venice, Italy,    45.44,   12.32
      Reykjavík, Iceland,    64.13,  -21.82
```

```
Traceback (most recent call last):
  File "threadpool_with_errors.py", line 83, in <module>
    main()
  File "threadpool_with_errors.py", line 76, in main
    raise result
  File "threadpool_with_errors.py", line 43, in worker
    result = fetch_place(item)
  File "threadpool_with_errors.py", line 23, in fetch_place
    return api.geocode(place)[0]
  File "...\site-packages\gmaps\geocoding.py", line 37, in geocode
    return self._make_request(self.GEOCODE_URL, parameters, "results")
  File "...\site-packages\gmaps\client.py", line 89, in _make_request
    )(response)
gmaps.errors.RateLimitExceeded: {'status': 'OVER_QUERY_LIMIT', 'results':
[], 'error_message': 'You have exceeded your rate-limit for this API.',
'url': 'https://maps.googleapis.com/maps/api/geocode/json?address=Wroc%C5
%82aw&sensor=false'}
```

The preceding exception is of course not the result of faulty code. This program simply is a bit too fast for this free service. It makes too many concurrent requests, and in order to work correctly, we need to have a way to limit their rate.

Limiting the pace of work is often called throttling. There are a few packages on PyPI that allow you to limit the rate of any kind of work and are really easy to use. But we won't use any external code here. Throttling is a good opportunity to introduce some locking primitives for threading, so we will try to build a solution from scratch.

The algorithm we will use is sometimes called token bucket and is very simple:

1. There is a bucket with a predefined amount of tokens.

2. Each token responds to a single permission to process one item of work.

3. Each time the worker asks for a single or multiple tokens (permission):

     ◦   We measure how much time was spent from the last time we refilled the bucket

     ◦   If the time difference allows for it, we refill the bucket with the amount of tokens that respond to this time difference

     ◦   If the amount of stored tokens is bigger or equal to the amount requested, we decrease the number of stored tokens and return that value

     ◦   If the amount of stored tokens is less than requested, we return zero

The two important things are to always initialize the token bucket with zero tokens and never allow it to fill with more tokens that is available by its rate, expressed in tokens, as per our standard quant of time. If we don't follow these precautions, we can release the tokens in bursts that exceed the rate limit. Because in our situation the rate limit is expressed in requests per second, we don't need to deal with arbitrary quants of time. We assume that the base for our measurement is one second, so we will never store more tokens than the number of requests allowed for that quant of time. Here is an example implementation of the class that allows for throttling with a token bucket algorithm:

```
From threading import Lock

class Throttle:
    def __init__(self, rate):
        self._consume_lock = Lock()
        self.rate = rate
        self.tokens = 0
        self.last = 0

    def consume(self, amount=1):
        with self._consume_lock:
            now = time.time()

            # time measument is initialized on first
            # token request to avoid initial bursts
            if self.last == 0:
                self.last = now

            elapsed = now - self.last

            # make sure that quant of passed time is big
            # enough to add new tokens
            if int(elapsed * self.rate):
                self.tokens += int(elapsed * self.rate)
                self.last = now

            # never over-fill the bucket
            self.tokens = (
                self.rate
                if self.tokens > self.rate
                else self.tokens
            )
```

```
        # finally dispatch tokens if available
        if self.tokens >= amount:
            self.tokens -= amount
        else:
            amount = 0


        return amount
```

The usage of this class is very simple. Assume that we created only one instance of Throttle (with Throttle(10) for instance) in the main thread and passed it to every worker thread as a positional argument. Using the same data structure in different threads is safe because we guarded manipulation of its internal state with the instance of Lock class from the threading module. We can now update the worker() function implementation to wait with every item until throttle releases a new token:

```
def worker(work_queue, results_queue, throttle):
    while True:
        try:
            item = work_queue.get(block=False)
        except Empty:
            break
        else:
            while not throttle.consume():
                pass

            try:
                result = fetch_place(item)
            except Exception as err:
                results_queue.put(err)
            else:
                results_queue.put(result)
            finally:
                work_queue.task_done()
```

Multiprocessing

Let's be honest, multithreading is challenging—we have already seen that in the previous section. It's a fact that the simplest approach to the problem required only minimal effort. But dealing with threads in a sane and safe manner required a tremendous amount of code.

We had to set up thread pool and communication queues, gracefully handle exceptions from threads, and also care about thread safety when trying to provide rate limiting capability. Tens lines of code only to execute one function from an external library in parallel! And we only assume that this is production-ready because there is a promise from the external package creator that his library is thread-safe. Sounds like a high price for a solution that is practically applicable only for doing I/O bound tasks.

An alternative approach that allows you to achieve parallelism is multiprocessing. Separate Python processes that do not constrain each other with GIL allow for better resource utilization. This is especially important for applications running on multicore processors that are performing really CPU-extensive tasks. Right now this is the only built-in concurrent solution available for Python developers (using the CPython interpreter) that allows you to take benefit from multiple processor cores.

The other advantage of using multiple processes is the fact that they do not share memory context. So it is harder to corrupt data and introduce deadlocks into your application. Not sharing the memory context means that you need some additional effort to pass the data between separate processes, but fortunately there are many good ways to implement reliable interprocess communication. In fact, Python provides some primitives that make communication between processes as easy as possible between threads.

The most basic way to start new processes in any programming language is usually by **forking** the program at some point. On POSIX systems (Unix, Mac OS, and Linux) a fork is a system call exposed in Python through the `os.fork()` function, which will create a new child process. The two processes then continue the program on their own right after forking. Here is an example script that forks itself exactly once:

```python
import os

pid_list = []


def main():
    pid_list.append(os.getpid())
    child_pid = os.fork()

    if child_pid == 0:
        pid_list.append(os.getpid())
        print()
        print("CHLD: hey, I am the child process")
        print("CHLD: all the pids i know %s" % pid_list)

    else:
        pid_list.append(os.getpid())
```

```
        print()
        print("PRNT: hey, I am the parent")
        print("PRNT: the child is pid %d" % child_pid)
        print("PRNT: all the pids i know %s" % pid_list)


    if __name__ == "__main__":
        main()
```

And here is an example of running it in a terminal:

```
$ python3 forks.py


PRNT: hey, I am the parent

PRNT: the child is pid 21916

PRNT: all the pids i know [21915, 21915]


CHLD: hey, I am the child process

CHLD: all the pids i know [21915, 21916]
```

Notice how both processes have exactly the same initial state of their data before the `os.fork()` call. They both have the same PID number (process identifier) as a first value of the `pid_list` collection. Later, both states diverge and we can see that the child process added the `21916` value while the parent duplicated its `21915` PID. This is because the memory contexts of these two processes are not shared. They have the same initial conditions but cannot affect each other after the `os.fork()` call.

After the fork memory context is copied to the child, each process deals with its own address space. To communicate, processes need to work with system-wide resources or use low-level tools such as **signals**.

Unfortunately, `os.fork` is not available under Windows, where a new interpreter needs to be spawned in order to mimic the fork feature. So it needs to be different depending on the platform. The `os` module also exposes functions that allow you to spawn new processes under Windows, but eventually you will use them rarely. This is also true for `os.fork()`. Python provides great a `multiprocessing` module that creates a high-level interface for multiprocessing. The great advantage of this module is that it provides some of the abstractions that we had to code from scratch in *An example of a threaded application* section. It allows you to limit the amount of boilerplate code, so it improves application maintainability and reduces its complexity. Surprisingly, despite its name, the `multiprocessing` module also exposes a similar interface for threads, so you will probably want to use the same interface for both approaches.

The built-in multiprocessing module

multiprocessing provides a portable way to work with processes as if they were threads.

This module contains a Process class that is very similar to the Thread class, and can be used on any platform:

```
from multiprocessing import Process
import os


def work(identifier):
    print(
        'hey, i am a process {}, pid: {}'
        ''.format(identifier, os.getpid())
    )


def main():
    processes = [
        Process(target=work, args=(number,))
        for number in range(5)
    ]
    for process in processes:
        process.start()

    while processes:
        processes.pop().join()


if __name__ == "__main__":
    main()
```

The preceding script, when executed, gives the following result:

```
$ python3 processing.py
hey, i am a process 1, pid: 9196
hey, i am a process 0, pid: 8356
hey, i am a process 3, pid: 9524
hey, i am a process 2, pid: 3456
hey, i am a process 4, pid: 6576
```

Concurrency

When the processes are created, the memory is forked (on POSIX systems). The most efficient usage of processes is to let them work on their own after they have been created to avoid overhead, and check on their states from the main thread. Besides the memory state that is copied, the `Process` class also provides an extra `args` argument in its constructor so that data can be passed along.

The communication between process modules requires some additional work because their local memory is not shared by default. To simplify this, the multiprocessing module provides a few ways of communication between processes:

- Using the `multiprocessing.Queue` class, which is a near clone of `queue.Queue`, which was used earlier for communication between threads

- Using `multiprocessing.Pipe`, which is a socket-like two-way communication channel

- Using the `multiprocessing.sharedctypes` module, which allows you to create arbitrary C types (from the `ctypes` module) in a dedicated pool of memory that is shared between processes

The `multiprocessing.Queue` and `queue.Queue` classes have the same interface. The only difference is that the first is designed for use in multiple process environments, rather than with multiple threads, so it uses different internal transports and locking primitives. We already saw how to use Queue with multithreading in the *An example of a threaded application* section, so we won't do the same for multiprocessing. The usage stays exactly the same, so such an example would not bring anything new.

A more interesting pattern right now is provided by the `Pipe` class. It is a duplex (two-way) communication channel that is very similar in concept to Unix pipes. The interface of Pipe is also very similar to a simple socket from the built-in `socket` module. The difference from raw system pipes and sockets is that it allows you to send any pickable object (using the `pickle` module) instead of just raw bytes. This allows for a lot easier communication between processes because you can send almost any basic Python type:

```
from multiprocessing import Process, Pipe


class CustomClass:
    pass


def work(connection):
    while True:
        instance = connection.recv()
```

```
        if instance:
            print("CHLD: {}".format(instance))

        else:
            return


def main():
    parent_conn, child_conn = Pipe()

    child = Process(target=work, args=(child_conn,))

    for item in (
        42,
        'some string',
        {'one': 1},
        CustomClass(),
        None,
    ):
        print("PRNT: send {}:".format(item))
        parent_conn.send(item)

    child.start()
    child.join()


if __name__ == "__main__":
    main()
```

When looking at an example output of the preceding script, you will see that you can easily pass custom class instances and that they have different addresses depending on the process:

```
PRNT: send: 42
PRNT: send: some string
PRNT: send: {'one': 1}
PRNT: send: <__main__.CustomClass object at 0x101cb5b00>
PRNT: send: None
CHLD: recv: 42
CHLD: recv: some string
CHLD: recv: {'one': 1}
CHLD: recv: <__main__.CustomClass object at 0x101cba400>
```

The other way to share a state between processes is to use raw types in a shared memory pool with the classes provided in `multiprocessing.sharedctypes`. The most basic ones are `Value` and `Array`. Here is an example code from the official documentation of the `multiprocessing` module:

```
from multiprocessing import Process, Value, Array


def f(n, a):
    n.value = 3.1415927
    for i in range(len(a)):
        a[i] = -a[i]


if __name__ == '__main__':
    num = Value('d', 0.0)
    arr = Array('i', range(10))

    p = Process(target=f, args=(num, arr))
    p.start()
    p.join()

    print(num.value)
    print(arr[:])
```

And this example will print the following output:

```
3.1415927
[0, -1, -2, -3, -4, -5, -6, -7, -8, -9]
```

When working with `multiprocessing.sharedctypes`, you need to remember that you are dealing with shared memory, so to avoid the risk of data corruption you need to use locking primitives. Multiprocessing provides some of the classes available in threading, such as `Lock`, `RLock`, and `Semaphore`, to do that. The downside of classes from `sharedctypes` is that they allow you only to share the basic C types from the `ctypes` module. If you need to pass more complex structures or class instances, you need to use Queue, Pipe, or other interprocess communication channels instead. In most cases, it is reasonable to avoid types from `sharedctypes` because they increase code complexity and bring all the dangers known from multithreading.

Using process pools

Using multiple processes instead of threads adds some substantial overhead. Mostly, it increases the memory footprint because each process has its own independent memory context. This means allowing for an unbound number of child processes is even more of a problematic issue than in multithreaded applications.

The best pattern to control resource usage in applications that rely on multiprocessing for better resource utilization is to build a process pool in a similar way as described for threads in the *Using a thread pool* section.

And the best thing about the `multiprocessing` module is that it provides a ready-to-use `Pool` class that handles all the complexity of managing multiple process workers for you. This pool implementation greatly reduces the amount of boilerplate required and the number of issues related to two-way communication. You also are not required to use the `join()` method manually, as Pool can be used as the context manager (using the `with` statement). Here is one of our previous threading examples rewritten to use the `Pool` class from the `multiprocessing` module:

```python
from multiprocessing import Pool

from gmaps import Geocoding

api = Geocoding()


PLACES = (
    'Reykjavik', 'Vien', 'Zadar', 'Venice',
    'Wrocław', 'Bolognia', 'Berlin', 'Słubice',
    'New York', 'Dehli',
)

POOL_SIZE = 4


def fetch_place(place):
    return api.geocode(place)[0]


def present_result(geocoded):
    print("{:>25s}, {:6.2f}, {:6.2f}".format(
        geocoded['formatted_address'],
        geocoded['geometry']['location']['lat'],
        geocoded['geometry']['location']['lng'],
    ))
```

```
def main():
    with Pool(POOL_SIZE) as pool:
        results = pool.map(fetch_place, PLACES)

    for result in results:
        present_result(result)


if __name__ == "__main__":
    main()
```

As you can see, the code is now a lot shorter. It means that it is now easier to maintain and debug in case of issues. Actually, there are now only two lines of code that explicitly deal with multiprocessing. This is a great improvement over the situation where we had to build the processing pool from scratch. Now we don't even need to care about communication channels because they are created implicitly inside of the `Pool` implementation.

Using multiprocessing.dummy as a multithreading interface

The high-level abstractions from the `multiprocessing` module, such as the `Pool` class, are great advantages over the simple tools provided in the `threading` module. But no, it does not mean that multiprocessing is always a better approach than multithreading. There are a lot of use cases where threads may be a better solution than processes. This is especially true for situations where low latency and/or high resource efficiency is required.

But it does not mean that you need to sacrifice all the useful abstractions from the `multiprocessing` module whenever you want to use threads instead of processes. There is the `multiprocessing.dummy` module, which replicates the `multiprocessing` API but uses multiple threads instead of forking/spawning new processes.

This allows you to reduce the amount of boilerplate in your code and also make a more pluggable interface. For instance, let's take yet another look at our `main()` function from the previous examples. If we wanted to give the user control over which processing backend he wants to use (processes or threads), we could do that simply by replacing the `Pool` class:

```
from multiprocessing import Pool as ProcessPool
from multiprocessing.dummy import Pool as ThreadPool


def main(use_threads=False):
    if use_threads:
```

```
        pool_cls = ThreadPool
    else:
        pool_cls = ProcessPool

    with pool_cls(POOL_SIZE) as pool:
        results = pool.map(fetch_place, PLACES)

    for result in results:
        present_result(result)
```

Asynchronous programming

Asynchronous programming has gained a lot of traction in recent years. In Python 3.5, it finally got some syntax features that solidify concepts of asynchronous execution. But it does not mean that asynchronous programming is only possible starting from Python 3.5. A lot of libraries and frameworks were provided a lot earlier, and most of them have origins in the old versions of Python 2. There is even a whole alternate implementation of Python called Stackless (see *Chapter 1, Current Status of Python*), which concentrated on this single programming approach. Some of these solutions, such as Twisted, Tornado, or Eventlet, still have huge and active communities and are really worth knowing. Anyway, starting from Python 3.5, asynchronous programming is easier than ever before. So it is expected that its built-in asynchronous features will replace the bigger parts of older tools, or external projects will gradually transform into a kind of high-level frameworks based on Python built-ins.

When trying to explain what asynchronous programming is, the easiest way is to think about this approach as something similar to threads but without system scheduling involved. This means that an asynchronous program can concurrently process problems but its context is switched internally and not by a system scheduler.

But, of course, we don't use threads to concurrently handle the work in an asynchronous program. Most of the solutions use a different kind of concept and, depending on the implementation, it is named differently. Some example names used to describe such concurrent program entities are:

- Green threads or greenlets (greenlet, gevent, or eventlet projects)
- Coroutines (Python 3.5 native asynchronous programming)
- Tasklets (Stackless Python)

These are mainly the same concepts, but often implemented in a bit different way. For obvious reasons, in this section, we will concentrate only on coroutines that are natively supported by Python, starting from version 3.5.

Cooperative multitasking and asynchronous I/O

Cooperative multitasking is the core of asynchronous programming. In this style of computer multitasking, it's not a responsibility of the operating system to initiate a context switch (to another process or thread), but instead every process voluntarily releases control when it is idle to enable simultaneous execution of multiple programs. This is why it is called *cooperative*. All processes need to cooperate in order to multitask smoothly.

This model of multitasking was sometimes employed in operating systems, but now it is hardly ever found as a system-level solution. This is because there is a risk that one poorly designed service can easily break the whole system's stability. Thread and process scheduling with context switches managed directly by the operating system is now the dominant approach for concurrency on the system level. But cooperative multitasking is still a great concurrency tool on the application level.

When speaking about cooperative multitasking on the application level, we do not deal with threads or processes that need to release control because all the execution is contained within a single process and thread. Instead, we have multiple tasks (coroutines, tasklets, and green threads) that release control to the single function that handles the coordination of tasks. This function is usually some kind of event loop.

To avoid confusion later (due to Python terminology), from now on we will refer to such concurrent tasks as *coroutines*. The most important problem in cooperative multitasking is when to release control. In most of asynchronous applications, control is released to the scheduler or event loop on I/O operations. No matter whether a program reads data from a filesystem or communicates through a socket, such I/O operation is always related to some waiting time when the process becomes idle. The waiting time depends on the external resource, so it is a good opportunity to release control so that other coroutines can do their work until they too would need to wait.

This makes such an approach somewhat similar in behavior to how multithreading is implemented in Python. We know that GIL serializes Python threads but it is also released on every I/O operation. The main difference is that threads in Python are implemented as system-level threads, so the operating system can preempt the currently running thread and give control to another one at any point in time. In asynchronous programming, tasks are never preempted by the main event loop. This is why this style of multitasking is also called **non-preemptive multitasking**.

Of course every Python application runs on an operating system where there are other processes competing for resources. This means that the operating system always has the right to preempt the whole process and give control to another one. But when our asynchronous application is running back, it continues from the same place where it was paused when the system scheduler stepped in. This is why coroutines are still considered nonpreemptive.

Python async and await keywords

The async and await keywords are the main building blocks in Python asynchronous programming.

The async keyword used before the def statement defines a new coroutine. The execution of the coroutine function may be suspended and resumed in strictly defined circumstances. Its syntax and behavior is very similar to generators (refer to *Chapter 2, Syntax Best Practices – below the Class Level*) In fact, generators need to be used in older versions of Python in order to implement coroutines. Here is an example of a function declaration that uses the async keyword:

```
async def async_hello():
    print("hello, world!")
```

Functions defined with the async keyword are special. When called, they do not execute the code inside but instead return a coroutine object:

```
>>> async def async_hello():
...     print("hello, world!")
...
>>> async_hello()
<coroutine object async_hello at 0x1014129e8>
```

The coroutine object does not do anything until its execution is scheduled in the event loop. The asyncio module is available in order to provide the basic event loop implementation, as well as lot of other asynchronous utilities:

```
>>> import asyncio
>>> async def async_hello():
...     print("hello, world!")
...
>>> loop = asyncio.get_event_loop()
>>> loop.run_until_complete(async_hello())
hello, world!
>>> loop.close()
```

Obviously, since we have created only one simple coroutine, there is no concurrency involved in our program. In order to see something really concurrent, we need to create more tasks that will be executed by the event loop.

New tasks can be added to the loop by calling the `loop.create_task()` method or by providing another object to wait for using the `asyncio.wait()` function. We will use the latter approach and try to asynchronously print a sequence of numbers generated with the `range()` function:

```python
import asyncio

async def print_number(number):
    print(number)


if __name__ == "__main__":
    loop = asyncio.get_event_loop()

    loop.run_until_complete(
        asyncio.wait([
            print_number(number)
            for number in range(10)
        ])
    )
    loop.close()
```

The `asyncio.wait()` function accepts a list of coroutine objects and returns immediately. The result is a generator that yields objects representing future results (futures). As the name suggests, it is used to wait until all of the provided coroutines complete. The reason why it returns a generator instead of a coroutine object is backwards compatibility with previous versions of Python, which will be explained later. The result of running this script may be as follows:

```
$ python asyncprint.py
0
7
8
3
9
4
1
5
2
6
```

As we can see, the numbers are not printed in the same order as we created our coroutines. But this is exactly what we wanted to achieve.

The second important keyword added in Python 3.5 is `await`. It is used to wait for the results of coroutine or a future (explained later) and release the control over execution to the event loop. To better understand how it works, we need to review a more complex example of code.

Let's say we want to create two coroutines that will perform some simple task in a loop:

- Wait a random number of seconds
- Print some text provided as an argument and the amount of time spent in sleep

Let's start with a simple implementation that has some concurrency issues which we will later try to improve with the additional `await` usage:

```python
import time
import random
import asyncio


async def waiter(name):
    for _ in range(4):
        time_to_sleep = random.randint(1, 3) / 4
        time.sleep(time_to_sleep)
        print(
            "{} waited {} seconds"
            "".format(name, time_to_sleep)
        )


async def main():
    await asyncio.wait([waiter("foo"), waiter("bar")])


if __name__ == "__main__":
    loop = asyncio.get_event_loop()
    loop.run_until_complete(main())
    loop.close()
```

When executed in the terminal (with the `time` command to measure time), it might give the following output:

```
$ time python corowait.py
bar waited 0.25 seconds
bar waited 0.25 seconds
bar waited 0.5 seconds
bar waited 0.5 seconds
foo waited 0.75 seconds
foo waited 0.75 seconds
foo waited 0.25 seconds
foo waited 0.25 seconds


real    0m3.734s
user    0m0.153s
sys     0m0.028s
```

As we can see, both the coroutines completed their execution but not in an asynchronous manner. The reason is that they both use the `time.sleep()` function that is blocking but not releasing the control to the event loop. This would work better in a multithreaded setup, but we don't want to use threads now. So how do we fix this?

The answer is to use `asyncio.sleep()`, which is the asynchronous version of `time.sleep()` and await its result using the `await` keyword. We already used this statement in the first version of the `main()` function, but it was only to improve clarity of code. It clearly did not make our implementation more concurrent. Let's see an improved version of the `waiter()` coroutine that uses `await asyncio.sleep()`:

```python
async def waiter(name):
    for _ in range(4):
        time_to_sleep = random.randint(1, 3) / 4
        await asyncio.sleep(time_to_sleep)
        print(
            "{} waited {} seconds"
            "".format(name, time_to_sleep)
        )
```

If we run the updated script, we can see how the output of two functions interleave with each other:

```
$ time python corowait_improved.py
bar waited 0.25 seconds
foo waited 0.25 seconds
bar waited 0.25 seconds
foo waited 0.5 seconds
foo waited 0.25 seconds
bar waited 0.75 seconds
foo waited 0.25 seconds
bar waited 0.5 seconds


real    0m1.953s
user    0m0.149s
sys     0m0.026s
```

The additional advantage of this simple improvement is that the code ran faster. The overall execution time was less than the sum of all sleeping times because coroutines were cooperatively releasing control.

asyncio in older versions of Python

The `asyncio` module appeared in Python 3.4. So it is the only version of Python that has serious support for asynchronous programming before Python 3.5. Unfortunately, it looks like these two subsequent versions are just enough to introduce compatibility concerns.

Like it or not, the core of asynchronous programming in Python was introduced earlier than the syntax elements supporting this pattern. Better late than never, but this created a situation where there are two syntaxes available for working with coroutines.

Starting from Python 3.5, you can use `async` and `await`:

```
async def main():
    await asyncio.sleep(0)
```

But for Python 3.4, you need to use the `asyncio.coroutine` decorator and the `yield from` statement:

```
@asyncio.couroutine
def main():
    yield from asyncio.sleep(0)
```

The other useful fact is that the `yield from` statement was introduced in Python 3.3 and there is an `asyncio` backport available on PyPI. This means that you can use this implementation of cooperative multitasking with Python 3.3 too.

A practical example of asynchronous programming

As has already been mentioned multiple times in this chapter, asynchronous programming is a great tool for handling I/O bound operations. So it's time to build something more practical than the simple printing of sequences or asynchronous waiting.

For the sake of consistency, we will try to handle the same problem we solved with the help of multithreading and multiprocessing. So we will try to asynchronously fetch some data from external resources through the network connection. It would be great if we could use the same `python-gmaps` package as in the previous sections. Unfortunately, we can't.

The creator of `python-gmaps` was a bit lazy and took a shortcut. In order to simplify development, he chose a `requests` package as his HTTP client library of choice. Unfortunately, `requests` do not support asynchronous I/O with `async` and `await`. There are some other projects that aim to provide some concurrency to the `requests` project, but they either rely on Gevent (`grequests`, refer to https://github.com/kennethreitz/grequests) or thread/process pool execution (`requests-futures`, refer to https://github.com/ross/requests-futures). Neither of these solves our problem.

> Before you get upset that I'm scolding an innocent open source developer, calm down. The person behind the `python-gmaps` package is me. Poor selection of dependencies is one of the issues of this project. I just like to publicly criticize myself from time to time. This should be a bitter lesson for me as `python-gmaps` in its most recent version (0.3.1 at the time of writing this book) cannot be easily integrated with Python's asynchronous I/O. Anyway, this may change in the future, so nothing is lost.

Knowing the limitations of the library that was so easy to use in the previous examples, we need to build something that will fill in the gap. The Google Maps API is really simple to use, so we will build a quick-and-dirty asynchronous utility only for illustration purposes. The standard library for Python in version 3.5 still lacks a library that would make asynchronous HTTP requests as simple as calling `urllib.urlopen()`. We definitely don't want to build the whole protocol support from scratch, so we will use a little help from the `aiohttp` package available on PyPI. It's a really promising library that adds both client and server implementations for asynchronous HTTP. Here is a small module built on top of `aiohttp` that creates a single `geocode()` helper function which makes geocoding requests to the Google Maps API service:

```python
import aiohttp

session = aiohttp.ClientSession()


async def geocode(place):
    params = {
        'sensor': 'false',
        'address': place
    }
    async with session.get(
        'https://maps.googleapis.com/maps/api/geocode/json',
        params=params
    ) as response:
        result = await response.json()
        return result['results']
```

Let's assume that this code is stored in a module named `asyncgmaps`, which we are going to use later. Now we are ready to rewrite the example used when discussing multithreading and multiprocessing. Previously, we used to split the whole operation into two separate steps:

1. Perform all request to the external service in parallel using the `fetch_place()` function.

2. Display all the results in a loop using the `present_result()` function.

But because cooperative multitasking is something completely different from using multiple processes or threads, we can slightly modify our approach. Most of the issues raised in the *Using one thread per item* section are no longer our concern. Coroutines are nonpreemptive, so we can easily display results immediately after HTTP responses are awaited. This will simplify our code and make it clearer:

```python
import asyncio
# note: local module introduced earlier
from asyncgmaps import geocode, session


PLACES = (
    'Reykjavik', 'Vien', 'Zadar', 'Venice',
    'Wrocław', 'Bolognia', 'Berlin', 'Słubice',
    'New York', 'Dehli',
)


async def fetch_place(place):
    return (await geocode(place))[0]


async def present_result(result):
    geocoded = await result
    print("{:>25s}, {:6.2f}, {:6.2f}".format(
        geocoded['formatted_address'],
        geocoded['geometry']['location']['lat'],
        geocoded['geometry']['location']['lng'],
    ))


async def main():
    await asyncio.wait([
        present_result(fetch_place(place))
        for place in PLACES
    ])


if __name__ == "__main__":
    loop = asyncio.get_event_loop()
    loop.run_until_complete(main())

    # aiohttp will raise issue about unclosed
    # ClientSession so we perform cleanup manually
    loop.run_until_complete(session.close())
    loop.close()
```

Integrating nonasynchronous code with async using futures

Asynchronous programming is great, especially for backend developers interested in building scalable applications. In practice, it is one of the most important tools for building highly concurrent servers.

But the reality is painful. A lot of popular packages that deal with I/O bound problems are not meant to be used with asynchronous code. The main reasons for that are:

- Still low adoption of Python 3 and some of its advanced features
- Low understanding of various concurrency concepts among Python beginners

This means that very often migration of the existing synchronous multithreaded applications and packages is either impossible (due to architectural constraints) or too expensive. A lot of projects could benefit greatly from incorporating the asynchronous style of multitasking, but only a few of them will eventually do that.

This means that right now, you will experience a lot of difficulties when trying to build asynchronous applications from the start. In most cases, this will be something similar to the problem mentioned in the *A practical example of asynchronous programming* section — incompatible interfaces and nonasynchronous blocking of I/O operations.

Of course, you can sometimes resign from `await` when you experience such incompatibility and just fetch the required resources synchronously. But this will block every other coroutine from executing its code while you wait for the results. It technically works but also ruins all the gains of asynchronous programming. So in the end, joining asynchronous I/O with synchronous I/O is not an option. It is a kind of *all or nothing* game.

The other problem is long running CPU-bound operations. When you are performing an I/O operation, it is not a problem to release control from a coroutine. When writing/reading from a filesystem or socket, you will eventually wait, so calling using `await` is the best you can do. But what to do when you need to actually compute something and you know it will take a while? You can of course slice the problem into parts and release control every time you move the work forward a bit. But you will shortly find that this is not a good pattern. Such a thing may make the code a mess, and also does not guarantee good results. Timeslicing should be the responsibility of the interpreter or operating system.

So what to do if you have some code that makes long synchronous I/O operations that you can't or are unwilling to rewrite. Or what to do when you have to make some heavy CPU-bound operations in an application designed mostly with asynchronous I/O in mind? Well... you need to use a workaround. And by workaround I mean multithreading or multiprocessing.

This may not sound nice, but sometimes the best solution may be the one that we tried to escape from. Parallel processing of CPU-extensive tasks in Python is always done better with multiprocessing. And multithreading may deal with I/O operations equally good (fast and without lot of resource overhead) as `async` and `await`, if set-up properly and handled with care.

So sometimes when you don't know what to do, when something simply does not fit your asynchronous application, use a piece of code that will defer it to separate thread or process. You can pretend that this was a coroutine, release control to the event loop and eventually process the results when they are ready. Fortunately for us, the Python standard library provides the `concurrent.futures` module, which is also integrated with the `asyncio` module. These two modules together allow you to schedule blocking functions executed in threads or additional processes as it were asynchronous nonblocking coroutines.

Executors and futures

Before we see how to inject threads or processes into an asynchronous event loop, we will take a closer look at the `concurrent.futures` module, which will later be the main ingredient of our so-called workaround.

The most important classes in the `concurrent.futures` module are `Executor` and `Future`.

`Executor` represents a pool of resources that may process work items in parallel. This may seem very similar in purpose to classes from the `multiprocessing` module — `Pool` and `dummy.Pool` — but has a completely different interface and semantics. It is a base class not intended for instantiation and has two concrete implementations:

- `ThreadPoolExecutor`: This is the one that represents a pool of threads
- `ProcessPoolExecutor`: This is the one that represents a pool of processes

Every executor provides three methods:

- `submit(fn, *args, **kwargs)`: This schedules the `fn` function for execution on a pool of resources and returns the `Future` object representing the execution of a callable

- `map(func, *iterables, timeout=None, chunksize=1)`: This executes the `func` function over an iterable in a similar way to the `multiprocessing.Pool.map()` method

- `shutdown(wait=True)`: This shuts down the executer and frees all of its resources

The most interesting method is `submit()` because of the `Future` object it returns. It represents the asynchronous execution of a callable and only indirectly represents its result. In order to obtain the actual return value of the submitted callable, you need to call the `Future.result()` method. And if the callable is already finished, the `result()` method will not block it and will just return the function output. If it is not true, it will block it until the result is ready. Treat it like a promise of a result (actually it is the same concept as a promise in JavaScript). You don't need to unpack it immediately after receiving it (with the `result()` method), but if you try to do that it is guaranteed to eventually return something:

```
>>> def loudy_return():
...     print("processing")
...     return 42
...
>>> from concurrent.futures import ThreadPoolExecutor
>>> with ThreadPoolExecutor(1) as executor:
...     future = executor.submit(loudy_return)
...
processing
>>> future
<Future at 0x33cbf98 state=finished returned int>
>>> future.result()
42
```

If you want to use the `Executor.map()` method, it does not differ in usage from the `Pool.map()` method of the Pool class from `multiprocessing` module:

```
def main():
    with ThreadPoolExecutor(POOL_SIZE) as pool:
        results = pool.map(fetch_place, PLACES)

    for result in results:
        present_result(result)
```

Using executors in an event loop

The `Future` class instances returned by the `Executor.submit()` method is conceptually very close to the coroutines used in asynchronous programming. This is why we can use executors to make hybrid between cooperative multitasking and multiprocessing or multithreading.

The core of this workaround is the `BaseEventLoop.run_in_executor(executor, func, *args)` method of the event loop class. It allows you to schedule the execution of the `func` function in a process or thread pool represented by the `executor` argument. The most important thing about that method is that it returns a new *awaitable* (an object that can be *awaited* with the `await` statement). So thanks to this, you can execute a blocking function that is not a coroutine exactly as it were a coroutine, and it will not block no matter how long it takes to finish. It will stop only the function that is awaiting results from such a call, but the whole event loop will still keep spinning.

And a useful fact is that you don't need to even create your executor instance. If you pass `None` as an executor argument, the `ThreadPoolExecutor` class will be used with the default number of threads (for Python 3.5 it is the number of processors multiplied by 5).

So, let's assume that we did not want to rewrite the problematic part of the `python-gmaps` package that was the cause of our headache. We can easily defer the blocking call to a separate thread with the `loop.run_in_executor()` invocation while still leaving the `fetch_place()` function as an awaitable coroutine:

```
async def fetch_place(place):
    coro = loop.run_in_executor(None, api.geocode, place)
    result = await coro
    return result[0]
```

Such a solution is not as good as having a fully asynchronous library to do the job, but you know *half a loaf is better than no bread*.

Summary

It was a long journey, but we successfully struggled through the most basic approaches to concurrent programming available for Python programmers.

After explaining what concurrency really is, we jumped into action and dissected one of the typical concurrent problems with the help of multithreading. After identifying the basic deficiencies of our code and fixing them, we turned to multiprocessing to see how it would work in our case.

We found that multiple processes are much easier to use with the `multiprocessing` module than base threads with `threading`. But just after that, we have realized that we can use the same API with threads too, thanks to `multiprocessing.dummy`. So the choice between multiprocessing and multithreading is now only a matter of which solution better suits the problem and not which solution has a better interface.

And speaking about problem fit, we finally tried asynchronous programming, which should be the best solution for I/O bound applications, only to realize that we cannot completely forget about threads and processes. So we made a circle, back to the place where we started!

And this leads us to the final conclusion of this chapter. There is no silver bullet. There are some approaches that you may prefer or like more. There are some approaches that may fit better for a given set of problems, but you need to know them all in order to be successful. In realistic scenarios, you may find yourself using the whole arsenal of concurrency tools and styles in a single application and this is not uncommon.

The preceding conclusion is a great introduction to the topic of the next chapter, *Chapter 14, Useful Design Patterns*. This is because there is no single pattern that will solve all of your problems. You should know as many as possible because eventually you will end up using all of them on a daily basis.

14
Useful Design Patterns

A design pattern is a reusable, somewhat language-specific solution to a common problem in software design. The most popular book on this topic is *Design Patterns: Elements of Reusable Object-Oriented Software*, *Addison-Wesley Professional*, written by Gamma, Helm, Johnson, and Vlissides, also known as the *Gang of Four* or *GoF*. It is considered as a major writing in this area and provides a catalogue of 23 design patterns with examples in SmallTalk and C++.

While designing an application code, these patterns help in solving common problems. They ring a bell to all developers since they describe proven development paradigms. But they should be studied with the used language in mind, since some of them do not make sense in some languages or are already built-in.

This chapter describes the most useful patterns in Python or patterns that are interesting to discuss, with implementation examples. The following are the three sections that correspond to design pattern categories defined by the GoF:

- **Creational patterns**: These are patterns that are used to generate objects with specific behaviors

- **Structural patterns**: These are patterns that help in structuring the code for specific use cases

- **Behavioral patterns**: These are patterns that help in assigning responsibilities and encapsulating behaviors

Creational patterns

Creational patterns deal with object instantiation mechanism. Such a pattern might define a way as to how object instances are created or even how classes are constructed.

These are very important patterns in compiled languages such as C or C++, since it is harder to generate types on-demand at run time.

But creating new types at runtime is pretty straightforward in Python. The built-in `type` function lets you define a new type object by code:

```
>>> MyType = type('MyType', (object,), {'a': 1})
>>> ob = MyType()
>>> type(ob)
<class '__main__.MyType'>
>>> ob.a
1
>>> isinstance(ob, object)
True
```

Classes and types are built-in factories. We already dealt with the creation of new class objects and you can interact with class and object generation using metaclasses. These features are the basics for implementing the **factory** design pattern, but we won't further describe it in this section because we extensively covered the topic of class and object creation in *Chapter 3, Syntax Best Practices – above the Class Level*.

Besides factory, the only other creational design pattern from the GoF that is interesting to describe in Python is singleton.

Singleton

Singleton restricts the instantiation of a class to only a single object instance.

The singleton pattern makes sure that a given class has always only one living instance in the application. This can be used, for example, when you want to restrict a resource access to one and only one memory context in the process. For instance, a database connector class can be a singleton that deals with synchronization and manages its data in memory. It makes the assumption that no other instance is interacting with the database in the meantime.

This pattern can simplify a lot the way concurrency is handled in an application. Utilities that provide application-wide functions are often declared as singletons. For instance, in web applications, a class that is in charge of reserving a unique document ID would benefit from the singleton pattern. There should be one and only one utility doing this job.

There is a popular semi-idiom to create singletons in Python by overriding the
__new__() method of a class:

```
class Singleton:
    _instance = None

    def __new__(cls, *args, **kwargs):
        if cls._instance is None:
            cls._instance = super().__new__(cls, *args, **kwargs)

        return cls._instance
```

If you try to create multiple instances of that class and compare their IDs, you will
find that they all represent the same object:

```
>>> instance_a = Singleton()
>>> instance_b = Singleton()
>>> id(instance_a) == id(instance_b)
True
>>> instance_a == instance_b
True
```

I call this a semi-idiom because it is a really dangerous pattern. The problem starts
when you try to subclass your base singleton class and create an instance of this new
subclass if you already created an instance of the base class:

```
>>> class ConcreteClass(Singleton): pass
>>> Singleton()
<Singleton object at 0x000000000306B470>
>>> ConcreteClass()
<Singleton object at 0x000000000306B470>
```

This may become even more problematic when you notice that this behavior is
affected by an instance creation order. Depending on your class usage order, you
may or may not get the same result. Let's see what the results are if you create the
subclass instance first and after that, the instance of the base class:

```
>>> class ConcreteClass(Singleton): pass
>>> ConcreteClass()
<ConcreteClass object at 0x00000000030615F8>
>>> Singleton()
<Singleton object at 0x000000000304BCF8>
```

As you can see, the behavior is completely different and very hard to predict. In large applications, it may lead to very dangerous and hard-to-debug problems. Depending on the run time context, you may or may not use the classes that you were meant to. Because such a behavior is really hard to predict and control, the application may break because of changed import order or even user input. If your singleton is not meant to be subclassed, it may be relatively safe to implement that way. Anyway, it's a ticking bomb. Everything may blow up if someone disregards the risk in future and decides to create a subclass from your singleton object. It is safer to avoid this particular implementation and use an alternative one.

It is a lot safer to use a more advanced technique—metaclasses. By overriding the __call__() method of a metaclass, you can affect the creation of your custom classes. This allows creating a reusable singleton code:

```python
class Singleton(type):
    _instances = {}

    def __call__(cls, *args, **kwargs):
        if cls not in cls._instances:
            cls._instances[cls] = super().__call__(*args,
                                                   **kwargs)
        return cls._instances[cls]
```

By using this Singleton as a metaclass for your custom classes, you are able to get singletons that are safe to subclass and independent of instance creation order:

```python
>>> ConcreteClass() == ConcreteClass()
True
>>> ConcreteSubclass() == ConcreteSubclass()
True
>>> ConcreteClass()
<ConcreteClass object at 0x000000000307AF98>
>>> ConcreteSubclass()
<ConcreteSubclass object at 0x000000000307A3C8>
```

Another way to overcome the problem of trivial singleton implementation is to use what Alex Martelli proposed. He came out with something similar in behavior to singleton but completely different in structure. This is not a classical design pattern coming from the GoF book, but it seems to be common among Python developers. It is called **Borg** or **Monostate**.

The idea is quite simple. What really matters in the singleton pattern is not the number of living instances a class has, but rather the fact that they all share the same state at all times. So, Alex Martelli came up with a class that makes all instances of the class share the same __dict__:

```
class Borg(object):
    _state = {}

    def __new__(cls, *args, **kwargs):
        ob = super().__new__(cls, *args, **kwargs)
        ob.__dict__ = cls._state
        return ob
```

This fixes the subclassing issue but is still dependent on how the subclass code works. For instance, if __getattr__ is overridden, the pattern can be broken.

Nevertheless, singletons should not have several levels of inheritance. A class that is marked as a singleton is already specific.

That said, this pattern is considered by many developers as a heavy way to deal with uniqueness in an application. If a singleton is needed, why not use a module with functions instead, since a Python module is already singleton? The most common pattern is to define a module-level variable as an instance of a class that needs to be singleton. This way, you also don't constrain the developers to your initial design.

> The singleton factory is an *implicit* way of dealing with the uniqueness of your application. You can live without it. Unless you are working in a framework à la Java that requires such a pattern, use a module instead of a class.

Structural patterns

Structural patterns are really important in big applications. They decide how the code is organized and give developers recipes on how to interact with each part of the application.

For a long time, the most well-known implementation of many structural patterns in the Python world provided the Zope project with its **Zope Component Architecture (ZCA)**. It implements most of the patterns described in this section and provides a rich set of tools to work with them. The ZCA is intended to run not only in the Zope framework, but also in other frameworks such as Twisted. It provides an implementation of interfaces and adapters among other things.

Unfortunately (or not), Zope lost almost all of its momentum and is not as popular as it used to be. But its ZCA may still be a good reference on implementing structural patterns in Python. Baiju Muthukadan created *A Comprehensive Guide to Zope Component Architecture*. It is available both in print and freely online (refer to `http://muthukadan.net/docs/zca.html`). It was written in 2009, so it does not cover the latest versions of Python but should still be a good read because it provides a lot of rationale for some of the mentioned patterns.

Python already provides some of the popular structural patterns through its syntax. For instance, the class and function decorators can be considered a flavor of the **decorator pattern**. Also, support for creating and importing modules is an emanation of **module pattern**.

The list of common structural patterns is actually quite long. The original *Design Patterns* book featured as many as seven of them and the list was later extended by other literature. We won't discuss all of them but will focus only on the three most popular and recognized ones, which are:

- Adapter
- Proxy
- Facade

Adapter

The **Adapter** pattern allows the interface of an existing class to be used from another interface. In other words, an adapter wraps a class or an object A so that it works in a context intended for a class or an object B.

Creating adapters in Python is actually very straightforward due to how typing in this language works. The typing philosophy in Python is commonly referred to as duck-typing:

> *"If it walks like a duck and talks like a duck, then it's a duck!"*

According to this rule, if a value for a function or method is accepted, the decision should not be based on its type but rather on its interface. So, as long as the object behaves as expected, that is, has proper method signatures and attributes, its type is considered compatible. This is completely different from many statically typed languages where such a thing is rarely available.

In practice, when some code is intended to work with a given class, it is fine to feed it with objects from another class as long as they provide the methods and attributes used by the code. Of course, this assumes that the code isn't calling an `instance` to verify that the instance is of a specific class.

The adapter pattern is based on this philosophy and defines a wrapping mechanism where a class or an object is wrapped in order to make it work in a context that was not primarily intended for it. StringIO is a typical example, as it adapts the str type, so it can be used as a file type:

```
>>> from io import StringIO
>>> my_file = StringIO('some content')
>>> my_file.read()
'some content'
>>> my_file.seek(0)
>>> my_file.read(1)
's'
```

Let's take another example. A DublinCoreInfos class knows how to display the summary of some subset of Dublin Core information (see http://dublincore.org/) for a given document provided as a dict. It reads a few fields, such as the author's name or the title, and prints them. To be able to display Dublin Core for a file, it has to be adapted in the same way StringIO does. The following figure shows a UML-like diagram for such a kind of adapter pattern implementation.

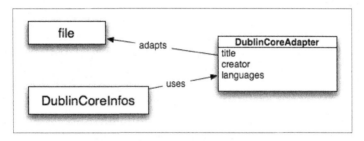

Figure 2 UML diagram for simple adapter pattern example

DublinCoreAdapter wraps a file instance and provides metadata access over it:

```
from os.path import split, splitext


class DublinCoreAdapter:
    def __init__(self, filename):
        self._filename = filename

    @property
    def title(self):
        return splitext(split(self._filename)[-1])[0]
```

```
        @property
        def languages(self):
            return ('en',)

        def __getitem__(self, item):
            return getattr(self, item, 'Unknown')


    class DublinCoreInfo(object):
        def summary(self, dc_dict):
            print('Title: %s' % dc_dict['title'])
            print('Creator: %s' % dc_dict['creator'])
            print('Languages: %s' % ', '.join(dc_dict['languages']))
```

And here is the example usage:

```
>>> adapted = DublinCoreAdapter('example.txt')
>>> infos = DublinCoreInfo()
>>> infos.summary(adapted)
Title: example
Creator: Unknown
Languages: en
```

Besides the fact that it allows substitution, the adapter pattern can also change the way developers work. Adapting an object to work in a specific context makes the assumption that the class of the object does not matter at all. What matters is that this class implements what DublinCoreInfo is waiting for and this behavior is fixed or completed by an adapter. So, the code can, somehow, simply tell whether it is compatible with objects that are implementing a specific behavior. This can be expressed by *interfaces*.

Interfaces

An **interface** is a definition of an API. It describes a list of methods and attributes a class should have to implement with the desired behavior. This description does not implement any code but just defines an explicit contract for any class that wishes to implement the interface. Any class can then implement one or several interfaces in whichever way it wants.

While Python prefers duck-typing over explicit interface definitions, it may be better to use them sometimes. For instance, explicit interface definition makes it easier for a framework to define functionalities over interfaces.

The benefit is that classes are loosely coupled, which is considered as a good practice. For example, to perform a given process, a class A does not depend on a class B, but rather on an interface I. Class B implements I, but it could be any other class.

The support for such a technique is built-in in many statically typed languages such as Java or Go. The interfaces allow the functions or methods to limit the range of acceptable parameter objects that implement a given interface, no matter what kind of class it comes from. This allows for more flexibility than restricting arguments to given types or their subclasses. It is like an explicit version of duck-typing behavior: Java uses interfaces to verify a type safety at compile time rather than use duck-typing to tie things together at run time.

Python has a completely different typing philosophy to Java, so it does not have native support for interfaces. Anyway, if you would like to have more explicit control on application interfaces, there are generally two solutions to choose from:

- Use some third-party framework that adds a notion of interfaces
- Use some of the advanced language features to build your methodology for handling interfaces.

Using zope.interface

There are a few frameworks that allow you to build explicit interfaces in Python. The most notable one is a part of the Zope project. It is the zope.interface package. Although, nowadays, Zope is not as popular as it used to be, the zope.interface package is still one of the main components of the Twisted framework.

The core class of the zope.interface package is the Interface class. It allows you to explicitly define a new interface by subclassing. Let's assume that we want to define the obligatory interface for every implementation of a rectangle:

```python
from zope.interface import Interface, Attribute


class IRectangle(Interface):
    width = Attribute("The width of rectangle")
    height = Attribute("The height of rectangle")

    def area():
        """ Return area of rectangle
        """

    def perimeter():
        """ Return perimeter of rectangle
        """
```

Some important things to remember when defining interfaces with `zope.interface` are as follows:

- The common naming convention for interfaces is to use `I` as the name suffix.
- The methods of the interface must not take the `self` parameter.
- As the interface does not provide concrete implementation, it should consist only of empty methods. You can use the `pass` statement, raise `NotImplementedError`, or provide a docstring (preferred).
- An interface can also specify the required attributes using the `Attribute` class.

When you have such a contract defined, you can then define new concrete classes that provide implementation for our `IRectangle` interface. In order to do that, you need to use the `implementer()` class decorator and implement all of the defined methods and attributes:

```python
@implementer(IRectangle)
class Square:
    """ Concrete implementation of square with rectangle interface
    """

    def __init__(self, size):
        self.size = size

    @property
    def width(self):
        return self.size

    @property
    def height(self):
        return self.size

    def area(self):
        return self.size ** 2

    def perimeter(self):
        return 4 * self.size


@implementer(IRectangle)
class Rectangle:
    """ Concrete implementation of rectangle
    """
    def __init__(self, width, height):
        self.width = width
        self.height = height
```

```
    def area(self):
        return self.width * self.height

    def perimeter(self):
        return self.width * 2 + self.height * 2
```

It is common to say that the interface defines a contract that a concrete implementation needs to fulfill. The main benefit of this design pattern is being able to verify consistency between contract and implementation before the object is being used. With the ordinary duck-typing approach, you only find inconsistencies when there is a missing attribute or method at runtime. With zope.interface, you can introspect the actual implementation using two methods from the zope.interface. verify module to find inconsistencies early on:

- verifyClass(interface, class_object): This verifies the class object for existence of methods and correctness of their signatures without looking for attributes

- verifyObject(interface, instance): This verifies the methods, their signatures, and also attributes of the actual object instance

Since we have defined our interface and two concrete implementations, let's verify their contracts in an interactive session:

```
>>> from zope.interface.verify import verifyClass, verifyObject
>>> verifyObject(IRectangle, Square(2))
True
>>> verifyClass(IRectangle, Square)
True
>>> verifyObject(IRectangle, Rectangle(2, 2))
True
>>> verifyClass(IRectangle, Rectangle)
True
```

Nothing impressive. The Rectangle and Square classes carefully follow the defined contract so there is nothing more to see than a successful verification. But what happens when we make a mistake? Let's see an example of two classes that fail to provide full IRectangle interface implementation:

```
@implementer(IRectangle)
class Point:
    def __init__(self, x, y):
        self.x = x
        self.y = y
```

```
@implementer(IRectangle)
class Circle:
    def __init__(self, radius):
        self.radius = radius

    def area(self):
        return math.pi * self.radius ** 2

    def perimeter(self):
        return 2 * math.pi * self.radius
```

The Point class does not provide any method or attribute of the IRectangle interface, so its verification will show inconsistencies already on the class level:

```
>>> verifyClass(IRectangle, Point)
```

```
Traceback (most recent call last):
  File "<stdin>", line 1, in <module>
  File "zope/interface/verify.py", line 102, in verifyClass
    return _verify(iface, candidate, tentative, vtype='c')
  File "zope/interface/verify.py", line 62, in _verify
    raise BrokenImplementation(iface, name)
zope.interface.exceptions.BrokenImplementation: An object has failed to
implement interface <InterfaceClass __main__.IRectangle>

        The perimeter attribute was not provided.
```

The Circle class is a bit more problematic. It has all the interface methods defined but breaks the contract on the instance attribute level. This is the reason why, in most cases, you need to use the verifyObject() function to completely verify the interface implementation:

```
>>> verifyObject(IRectangle, Circle(2))
```

```
Traceback (most recent call last):
  File "<stdin>", line 1, in <module>
  File "zope/interface/verify.py", line 105, in verifyObject
    return _verify(iface, candidate, tentative, vtype='o')
  File "zope/interface/verify.py", line 62, in _verify
    raise BrokenImplementation(iface, name)
```

```
zope.interface.exceptions.BrokenImplementation: An object has failed to
implement interface <InterfaceClass __main__.IRectangle>
```

> The width attribute was not provided.

Using `zope.inteface` is an interesting way to decouple your application. It allows you to enforce proper object interfaces without the need for the overblown complexity of multiple inheritance, and it also allows to catch inconsistencies early. However, the biggest downside of this approach is the requirement that you explicitly define that the given class follows some interface in order to be verified. This is especially troublesome if you need to verify instances coming from external classes of built-in libraries. `zope.interface` provides some solutions for that problem, and you can of course handle such issues on your own by using the adapter pattern, or even monkey-patching. Anyway, the simplicity of such solutions is at least arguable.

Using function annotations and abstract base classes

Design patterns are meant to make problem solving easier and not to provide you with more layers of complexity. The `zope.interface` is a great concept and may greatly fit some projects, but it is not a silver bullet. By using it, you may soon find yourself spending more time on fixing issues with incompatible interfaces for third-party classes and providing never-ending layers of adapters instead of writing the actual implementation. If you feel that way, then this is a sign that something went wrong. Fortunately, Python supports for building lightweight alternative to the interfaces. It's not a full-fledged solution like `zope.interface` or its alternatives but it generally provides more flexible applications. You may need to write a bit more code, but in the end you will have something that is more extensible, better handles external types, and may be more *future proof*.

Note that Python in its core does not have explicit notions of interfaces, and probably will never have, but has some of the features that allow you to build something that resembles the functionality of interfaces. The features are:

- **Abstract base classes (ABCs)**
- Function annotations
- Type annotations

The core of our solution is abstract base classes, so we will feature them first.

As you probably know, the direct type comparison is considered harmful and not *pythonic*. You should always avoid comparisons as follows:

```
assert type(instance) == list
```

Comparing types in functions or methods that way completely breaks the ability to pass a class subtype as an argument to the function. The slightly better approach is to use the `isinstance()` function that will take the inheritance into account:

```
assert isinstance(instance, list)
```

The additional advantage of `isinstance()` is that you can use a larger range of types to check the type compatibility. For instance, if your function expects to receive some sort of sequence as the argument, you can compare against the list of basic types:

```
assert isinstance(instance, (list, tuple, range))
```

Such a way of type compatibility checking is OK in some situations but it is still not perfect. It will work with any subclass of `list`, `tuple`, or `range`, but will fail if the user passes something that behaves exactly the same as one of these sequence types but does not inherit from any of them. For instance, let's relax our requirements and say that you want to accept any kind of iterable as an argument. What would you do? The list of basic types that are iterable is actually pretty long. You need to cover list, tuple, range, str, bytes, dict, set, generators, and a lot more. The list of applicable built-in types is long, and even if you cover all of them it will still not allow you to check against the custom class that defines the __iter__() method, but will instead inherit directly from `object`.

And this is the kind of situation where abstract base classes (ABC) are the proper solution. ABC is a class that does not need to provide a concrete implementation but instead defines a blueprint of a class that may be used to check against type compatibility. This concept is very similar to the concept of abstract classes and virtual methods known in the C++ language.

Abstract base classes are used for two purposes:

- Checking for implementation completeness
- Checking for implicit interface compatibility

So, let's assume we want to define an interface which ensures that a class has a `push()` method. We need to create a new abstract base class using a special `ABCMeta` metaclass and an `abstractmethod()` decorator from the standard `abc` module:

```
from abc import ABCMeta, abstractmethod

class Pushable(metaclass=ABCMeta):

    @abstractmethod
    def push(self, x):
        """ Push argument no matter what it means
        """
```

The `abc` module also provides an ABC base class that can be used instead of the metaclass syntax:

```
from abc import ABCMeta, abstractmethod


class Pushable(metaclass=ABCMeta):
    @abstractmethod
    def push(self, x):
        """ Push argument no matter what it means
        """
```

Once it is done, we can use that `Pushable` class as a base class for concrete implementation and it will guard us from the instantiation of objects that would have incomplete implementation. Let's define `DummyPushable`, which implements all interface methods and the `IncompletePushable` that breaks the expected contract:

```
class DummyPushable(Pushable):
    def push(self, x):
        return


class IncompletePushable(Pushable):
    pass
```

If you want to obtain the `DummyPushable` instance, there is no problem because it implements the only required `push()` method:

```
>>> DummyPushable()
<__main__.DummyPushable object at 0x10142bef0>
```

But if you try to instantiate `IncompletePushable`, you will get `TypeError` because of missing implementation of the `interface()` method:

```
>>> IncompletePushable()
Traceback (most recent call last):
  File "<stdin>", line 1, in <module>
TypeError: Can't instantiate abstract class IncompletePushable with
abstract methods push
```

The preceding approach is a great way to ensure implementation completeness of base classes but is as explicit as the zope.interface alternative. The DummyPushable instances are of course also instances of Pushable because Dummy is a subclass of Pushable. But how about other classes with the same methods but not descendants of Pushable? Let's create one and see:

```
>>> class SomethingWithPush:
...     def push(self, x):
...         pass
...
>>> isinstance(SomethingWithPush(), Pushable)
False
```

Something is still missing. The SomethingWithPush class definitely has a compatible interface but is not considered as an instance of Pushable yet. So, what is missing? The answer is the __subclasshook__(subclass) method that allows you to inject your own logic into the procedure that determines whether the object is an instance of a given class. Unfortunately, you need to provide it by yourself, as abc creators did not want to constrain the developers in overriding the whole isinstance() mechanism. We got full power over it, but we are forced to write some boilerplate code.

Although you can do whatever you want to, usually the only reasonable thing to do in the __subclasshook__() method is to follow the common pattern. The standard procedure is to check whether the set of defined methods are available somewhere in the MRO of the given class:

```
from abc import ABCMeta, abstractmethod


class Pushable(metaclass=ABCMeta):

    @abstractmethod
    def push(self, x):
        """ Push argument no matter what it means
        """

    @classmethod
    def __subclasshook__(cls, C):
        if cls is Pushable:
            if any("push" in B.__dict__ for B in C.__mro__):
                return True
        return NotImplemented
```

With the __subclasshook__() method defined that way, you can now confirm that the instances that implement the interface implicitly are also considered instances of the interface:

```
>>> class SomethingWithPush:
...       def push(self, x):
...              pass
...
>>> isinstance(SomethingWithPush(), Pushable)
True
```

Unfortunately, this approach to the verification of type compatibility and implementation completeness does not take into account the signatures of class methods. So, if the number of expected arguments is different in implementation, it will still be considered compatible. In most cases, this is not an issue, but if you need such fine-grained control over interfaces, the zope.interface package allows for that. As already said, the __subclasshook__() method does not constrain you in adding more complexity to the isinstance() function's logic to achieve a similar level of control.

The two other features that complement abstract base classes are function annotations and type hints. Function annotation is the syntax element described briefly in *Chapter 2, Syntax Best Practices – below the Class Level*. It allows you to annotate functions and their arguments with arbitrary expressions. As explained in *Chapter 2, Syntax Best Practices – below the Class Level*, this is only a feature stub that does not provide any syntactic meaning. There is no utility in the standard library that uses this feature to enforce any behavior. Anyway, you can use it as a convenient and lightweight way to inform the developer of the expected argument interface. For instance, consider this IRectangle interface rewritten from zope. interface to abstract the base class:

```
from abc import (
    ABCMeta,
    abstractmethod,
    abstractproperty
)


class IRectangle(metaclass=ABCMeta):

    @abstractproperty
    def width(self):
        return
```

```
    @abstractproperty
    def height(self):
        return

    @abstractmethod
    def area(self):
        """ Return rectangle area
        """

    @abstractmethod
    def perimeter(self):
        """ Return rectangle perimeter
        """

    @classmethod
    def __subclasshook__(cls, C):
        if cls is IRectangle:
            if all([
                any("area" in B.__dict__ for B in C.__mro__),
                any("perimeter" in B.__dict__ for B in C.__mro__),
                any("width" in B.__dict__ for B in C.__mro__),
                any("height" in B.__dict__ for B in C.__mro__),
            ]):
                return True
        return NotImplemented
```

If you have a function that works only on rectangles, let's say `draw_rectangle()`, you could annotate the interface of the expected argument as follows:

```
def draw_rectangle(rectangle: IRectange):
    ...
```

This adds nothing more than information for the developer about expected information. And even this is done through an informal contract because, as we know, bare annotations contain no syntactic meaning. However, they are accessible at runtime, so we can do something more. Here is an example implementation of a generic decorator that is able to verify interface from function annotation if it is provided using abstract base classes:

```
def ensure_interface(function):
    signature = inspect.signature(function)
    parameters = signature.parameters

    @wraps(function)
    def wrapped(*args, **kwargs):
```

```
        bound = signature.bind(*args, **kwargs)
        for name, value in bound.arguments.items():
            annotation = parameters[name].annotation

            if not isinstance(annotation, ABCMeta):
                continue

            if not isinstance(value, annotation):
                raise TypeError(
                    "{} does not implement {} interface"
                    "".format(value, annotation)
                )

        function(*args, **kwargs)

    return wrapped
```

Once it is done, we can create some concrete class that implicitly implements the IRectangle interface (without inheriting from IRectangle) and update the implementation of the draw_rectangle() function to see how the whole solution works:

```
class ImplicitRectangle:
    def __init__(self, width, height):
        self._width = width
        self._height = height

    @property
    def width(self):
        return self._width

    @property
    def height(self):
        return self._height

    def area(self):
        return self.width * self.height

    def perimeter(self):
        return self.width * 2 + self.height * 2


@ensure_interface
def draw_rectangle(rectangle: IRectangle):
    print(
```

```
            "{} x {} rectangle drawing"
            "".format(rectangle.width, rectangle.height)
    )
```

If we feed the `draw_rectangle()` function with an incompatible object, it will now raise `TypeError` with a meaningful explanation:

```
>>> draw_rectangle('foo')
Traceback (most recent call last):
  File "<input>", line 1, in <module>
  File "<input>", line 101, in wrapped
TypeError: foo does not implement <class 'IRectangle'> interface
```

But if we use `ImplicitRectangle` or anything else that resembles the `IRectangle` interface, the function executes as it should:

```
>>> draw_rectangle(ImplicitRectangle(2, 10))
2 x 10 rectangle drawing
```

Our example implementation of `ensure_interface()` is based on the `typechecked()` decorator from the `typeannotations` project that tries to provide run-time checking capabilities (refer to https://github.com/ceronman/typeannotations). Its source code might give you some interesting ideas about how to process type annotations to ensure run-time interface checking.

The last feature that can be used to complement this interface pattern landscape are type hints. Type hints are described in detail by PEP 484 and were added to the language quite recently. They are exposed in the new `typing` module and are available from Python 3.5. Type hints are built on top of function annotations and reuse this slightly forgotten syntax feature of Python 3. They are intended to guide type hinting and check for various *yet-to-come* Python type checkers. The `typing` module and PEP 484 document aim to provide a standard hierarchy of types and classes that should be used for describing type annotations.

Still, type hints do not seem to be something revolutionary because this feature does not come with any type checker built-in into the standard library. If you want to use type checking or enforce strict interface compatibility in your code, you need to create your own tool because there is none worth recommendation yet. This is why we won't dig into details of PEP 484. Anyway, type hints and the documents describing them are worth mentioning because if some extraordinary solution emerges in the field of type checking in Python, it is highly probable that it will be based on PEP 484.

Using collections.abc

Abstract base classes are like small building blocks for creating a higher level of abstraction. They allow you to implement really usable interfaces but are very generic and designed to handle lot more than this single design pattern. You can unleash your creativity and do magical things but building something generic and really usable may require a lot of work. Work that may never pay off.

This is why custom abstract base classes are not used so often. Despite that, the `collections.abc` module provides a lot of predefined ABCs that allow to verify interface compatibility of many basic Python types. With base classes provided in this module, you can check, for example, whether a given object is callable, mapping, or if it supports iteration. Using them with the `isinstance()` function is way better than comparing them against the base python types. You should definitely know how to use these base classes even if you don't want to define your own custom interfaces with `ABCMeta`.

The most common abstract base classes from `collections.abc` that you will use from time to time are:

- `Container`: This interface means that the object supports the `in` operator and implements the `__contains__()` method
- `Iterable`: This interface means that the object supports the iteration and implements the `__iter__()` method
- `Callable`: This interface means that it can be called like a function and implements the `__call__()` method
- `Hashable`: This interface means that the object is hashable (can be included in sets and as key in dictionaries) and implements the `__hash__` method
- `Sized`: This interface means that the object has size (can be a subject of the `len()` function) and implements the `__len__()` method

A full list of the available abstract base classes from the `collections.abc` module is available in the official Python documentation (refer to `https://docs.python.org/3/library/collections.abc.html`).

Proxy

Proxy provides indirect access to an expensive or a distant resource. A **Proxy** is between a **Client** and a **Subject**, as shown in the following figure:

It is intended to optimize Subject accesses if they are expensive. For instance, the `memoize()` and `lru_cache()` decorators described in *Chapter 12, Optimization – Some Powerful Techniques,* can be considered as proxies.

A proxy can also be used to provide smart access to a subject. For instance, big video files can be wrapped into proxies to avoid loading them into memory when the user just asks for their titles.

An example is given by the `urllib.request` module. `urlopen` is a proxy for the content located at a remote URL. When it is created, headers can be retrieved independently from the content itself without the need to read the rest of the response:

```
>>> class Url(object):
...     def __init__(self, location):
...         self._url = urlopen(location)
...     def headers(self):
...         return dict(self._url.headers.items())
...     def get(self):
...         return self._url.read()
...
>>> python_org = Url('http://python.org')
>>> python_org.headers().keys()
dict_keys(['Accept-Ranges', 'Via', 'Age', 'Public-Key-Pins', 'X-Clacks-
Overhead', 'X-Cache-Hits', 'X-Cache', 'Content-Type', 'Content-Length',
'Vary', 'X-Served-By', 'Strict-Transport-Security', 'Server', 'Date',
'Connection', 'X-Frame-Options'])
```

This can be used to decide whether the page has been changed before getting its body to update a local copy, by looking at the `last-modified` header. Let's take an example with a big file:

```
>>> ubuntu_iso = Url('http://ubuntu.mirrors.proxad.net/hardy/ubuntu-8.04-
desktop-i386.iso')
>>> ubuntu_iso.headers()['Last-Modified']
'Wed, 23 Apr 2008 01:03:34 GMT'
```

Another use case of proxies is **data uniqueness**.

For example, let's consider a website that presents the same document in several locations. Extra fields specific to each location are appended to the document, such as a hit counter and a few permission settings. A proxy can be used in that case to deal with location-specific matters and also to point to the original document instead of copying it. So, a given document can have many proxies, and if its content changes, all locations will benefit from it without having to deal with version synchronization.

Generally speaking, proxy pattern is useful for implementing a local handle of something that may live somewhere else to:

- Make the process faster
- Avoid external resource access
- Reduce memory load
- Ensure data uniqueness

Facade

Facade provides high-level, simpler access to a subsystem.

A facade is nothing but a shortcut to use a functionality of the application, without having to deal with the underlying complexity of a subsystem. This can be done, for instance, by providing high-level functions at the package level.

Facade is usually done on existing systems, where a package's frequent usage is synthesized in high-level functions. Usually, no classes are needed to provide such a pattern and simple functions in the __init__.py module are sufficient.

A good example of project that provides a big facade over complicated and complex interfaces is the requests package (refer to http://docs.python-requests.org/). It really simplifies the madness of dealing with HTTP requests and responses in Python by providing a clean API that is easily readable to developers. It is actually even advertised as *HTTP for humans*. Such ease of use always comes at some price but eventual tradeoffs and additional overhead does not scare most people from using the Requests project as their HTTP tool of choice. In the end, it allows us to finish projects faster and a developer's time is usually more expensive than hardware.

 Facade simplifies the usage of your packages. Facades are usually added after a few iterations with usage feedback.

Behavioral patterns

Behavioral patterns are intended to simplify the interactions between classes by structuring the processes of their interaction.

This section provides three examples of popular behavioral patterns that you may want to consider when writing Python code:

- Observer
- Visitor
- Template

Observer

The **observer** pattern is used to notify a list of objects about a state change of the observed component.

Observer allows adding features in an application in a pluggable way by de-coupling the new functionality from the existing code base. An event framework is a typical implementation of the observer pattern and is described in the figure that follows. Every time an event occurs, all observers for this event are notified with the subject that has triggered this event.

An event is created when something happens. In graphical user interface applications, event-driven programming (see `http://en.wikipedia.org/wiki/Event-driven_programming`) is often used to link the code to user actions. For instance, a function can be linked to the `MouseMove` event so it is called every time the mouse moves over the window.

In case of GUI application, de-coupling the code from the window management internals simplifies the work a lot. Functions are written separately and then registered as event observers. This approach exists from the earliest versions of Microsoft's MFC framework (see `http://en.wikipedia.org/wiki/Microsoft_Foundation_Class_Library`) and in all GUI development tools such as Qt or GTK. Many frameworks use the notion of *signals*, but they are simply another manifestation of the observer pattern.

The code can also generate events. For instance, in an application that stores documents in a database, `DocumentCreated`, `DocumentModified`, and `DocumentDeleted` can be three events provided by the code. A new feature that works on documents can register itself as an observer to get notified every time a document is created, modified, or deleted and do the appropriate work. A document indexer could be added that way in an application. Of course, this requires that all the code in charge of creating, modifying, or deleting documents is triggering events. But this is rather easier than adding indexing hooks all over the application code base! A popular web framework that follows this pattern is Django with its mechanism of signals.

An `Event` class can be implemented for the registration of observers in Python by working at the class level:

```python
class Event:
    _observers = []

    def __init__(self, subject):
        self.subject = subject

    @classmethod
    def register(cls, observer):
        if observer not in cls._observers:
            cls._observers.append(observer)

    @classmethod
    def unregister(cls, observer):
        if observer in cls._observers:
            cls._observers.remove(observer)

    @classmethod
    def notify(cls, subject):
        event = cls(subject)
        for observer in cls._observers:
            observer(event)
```

The idea is that observers register themselves using the `Event` class method and get notified with `Event` instances that carry the subject that triggered them. Here is an example of the concrete `Event` subclass with some observers subscribed to its notifications:

```python
class WriteEvent(Event):
    def __repr__(self):
        return 'WriteEvent'
```

```
def log(event):
    print(
        '{!r} was fired with subject "{}"'
        ''.format(event, event.subject)
    )


class AnotherObserver(object):
    def __call__(self, event):
        print(
            "{!r} trigerred {}'s action"
            "".format(event, self.__class__.__name__)
        )


WriteEvent.register(log)
WriteEvent.register(AnotherObserver())
```

And here is an example result of firing the event with the `WriteEvent.notify()` method:

```
>>> WriteEvent.notify("something happened")
WriteEvent was fired with subject "something happened"
WriteEvent trigerred AnotherObserver's action
```

This implementation is simple and serves only as illustrational purposes. To make it fully functional, it could be enhanced by:

- Allowing the developer to change the order or events
- Making the event object hold more information than just the subject

De-coupling your code is fun and the observer is the right pattern to do it. It componentizes your application and makes it more extensible. If you want to use an existing tool, try **Blinker** (refer to `https://pythonhosted.org/blinker/`). It provides fast and simple object-to-object and broadcast signaling for Python objects.

Visitor

Visitor helps in separating algorithms from data structures and has a similar goal to that of the observer pattern. It allows extending the functionalities of a given class without changing its code. But the visitor goes a bit further by defining a class that is responsible for holding data and pushes the algorithms to other classes called `Visitors`. Each visitor is specialized in one algorithm and can apply it on the data.

This behavior is quite similar to the MVC paradigm (refer to http://en.wikipedia. org/wiki/Model-view-controller), where documents are passive containers pushed to views through controllers, or where models contain data that is altered by a controller.

Visitor pattern is implemented by providing an entry point in the data class that can be visited by all kinds of visitors. A generic description is a `Visitable` class that accepts `Visitor` instances and calls them, as shown in the following figure:

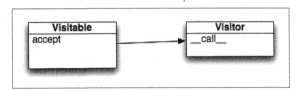

The `Visitable` class decides how it calls the `Visitor` class, for instance, by deciding which method is called. For example, a visitor in charge of printing built-in type content can implement the `visit_TYPENAME()` methods, and each of these types can call the given method in its `accept()` method:

```python
class VisitableList(list):
    def accept(self, visitor):
        visitor.visit_list(self)


class VisitableDict(dict):
    def accept(self, visitor):
        visitor.visit_dict(self)


class Printer(object):
    def visit_list(self, instance):
        print('list content: {}'.format(instance))

    def visit_dict(self, instance):
        print('dict keys: {}'.format(
            ', '.join(instance.keys()))
        )
```

This is done as shown in the following example:

```
>>> visitable_list = VisitableList([1, 2, 5])
>>> visitable_list.accept(Printer())
list content: [1, 2, 5]
>>> visitable_dict = VisitableDict({'one': 1, 'two': 2, 'three': 3})
>>> visitable_dict.accept(Printer())
dict keys: two, one, three
```

But this pattern means that each visited class needs to have an `accept` method to be visited, which is quite painful.

Since Python allows code introspection, a better idea is to automatically link visitors and visited classes:

```
>>> def visit(visited, visitor):
...     cls = visited.__class__.__name__
...     method_name = 'visit_%s' % cls
...     method = getattr(visitor, method_name, None)
...     if isinstance(method, Callable):
...         method(visited)
...     else:
...         raise AttributeError(
...             "No suitable '{}' method in visitor"
...             "".format(method_name)
...         )
...
>>> visit([1,2,3], Printer())
list content: [1, 2, 3]
>>> visit({'one': 1, 'two': 2, 'three': 3}, Printer())
dict keys: two, one, three
>>> visit((1, 2, 3), Printer())
Traceback (most recent call last):
  File "<input>", line 1, in <module>
  File "<input>", line 10, in visit
AttributeError: No suitable 'visit_tuple' method in visitor
```

This pattern is used in this way in the `ast` module, for instance, by the `NodeVisitor` class that calls the visitor with each node of the compiled code tree. This is because Python doesn't have a match operator like Haskell.

Another example is a directory walker that calls Visitor methods depending on the file extension:

```
>>> def visit(directory, visitor):
...     for root, dirs, files in os.walk(directory):
...         for file in files:
...             # foo.txt → .txt
...             ext = os.path.splitext(file)[-1][1:]
...             if hasattr(visitor, ext):
...                 getattr(visitor, ext)(file)
...
>>> class FileReader(object):
...     def pdf(self, filename):
...         print('processing: {}'.format(filename))
...
>>> walker = visit('/Users/tarek/Desktop', FileReader())
processing slides.pdf
processing shol123.pdf
```

If your application has data structures that are visited by more than one algorithm, the Visitor pattern will help in separating concerns. It is better for a data container to focus only on providing access to data and holding them, and nothing else.

Template

Template helps in designing a generic algorithm by defining abstract steps which are implemented in subclasses. This pattern uses the **Liskov substitution principle**, which is defined by Wikipedia as:

> *"If S is a subtype of T, then objects of type T in a program may be replaced with objects of type S without altering any of the desirable properties of that program."*

In other words, an abstract class can define how an algorithm works through steps that are implemented in concrete classes. The abstract class can also give a basic or partial implementation of the algorithm and let developers override its parts. For instance, some methods of the `Queue` class in the `queue` module can be overridden to make its behavior vary.

Let's implement an example, as shown in the figure that follows.

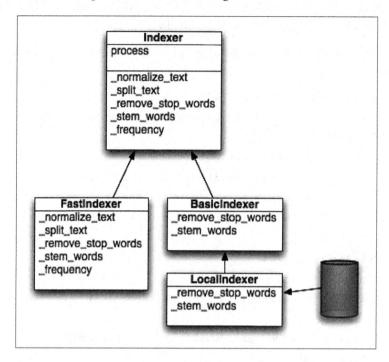

`Indexer` is an indexer class that processes a text in five steps, which are common steps no matter what indexing technique is used:

- Text normalization
- Text split
- Stop words removal
- Stem words
- Frequency

An `Indexer` provides partial implementation for the process algorithm but requires `_remove_stop_words` and `_stem_words` to be implemented in a subclass. `BasicIndexer` implements the strict minimum, while `LocalIndex` uses a stop word file and a stem words database. `FastIndexer` implements all steps and could be based on a fast indexer such as **Xapian** or **Lucene**.

A toy implementation can be:

```python
from collections import Counter

class Indexer:
    def process(self, text):
        text = self._normalize_text(text)
        words = self._split_text(text)
        words = self._remove_stop_words(words)
        stemmed_words = self._stem_words(words)

        return self._frequency(stemmed_words)

    def _normalize_text(self, text):
        return text.lower().strip()

    def _split_text(self, text):
        return text.split()

    def _remove_stop_words(self, words):
        raise NotImplementedError

    def _stem_words(self, words):
        raise NotImplementedError

    def _frequency(self, words):
        return Counter(words)
```

From there, a `BasicIndexer` implementation can be:

```python
class BasicIndexer(Indexer):
    _stop_words = {'he', 'she', 'is', 'and', 'or', 'the'}

    def _remove_stop_words(self, words):
        return (
            word for word in words
            if word not in self._stop_words
        )

    def _stem_words(self, words):
        return (
            (
                len(word) > 3 and
```

```
            word.rstrip('aeiouy') or
            word
        )
        for word in words
    )
```

And, like always, here is an example usage for the preceding example code:

```
>>> indexer = BasicIndexer()
>>> indexer.process("Just like Johnny Flynn said\nThe breath I've taken
and the one I must to go on")
Counter({"i'v": 1, 'johnn': 1, 'breath': 1, 'to': 1, 'said': 1, 'go': 1,
'flynn': 1, 'taken': 1, 'on': 1, 'must': 1, 'just': 1, 'one': 1, 'i': 1,
'lik': 1})
```

Template should be considered for an algorithm that may vary and can be expressed into isolated substeps. This is probably the most used pattern in Python and does not always needs to be implemented via subclassing. For instance, a lot of built-in Python functions that deal with algorithmic problems accept arguments that allow you to delegate part of the implementation to external implementation. For instance, the sorted() function allows for an optional key keyword argument that is later used by a sorting algorithm. This is also the same for min() and max() functions that find minimum and maximum values in the given collection.

Summary

Design patterns are reusable, somewhat language-specific solutions to common problems in software design. They are a part of the culture of all developers, no matter what language they use.

So, using implementation examples for the most used patterns for a given language is a great way to document that. Both on the Web and in other books, you will easily find implementation for every design pattern mentioned in GoF books. This is why we concentrated only on patterns that are the most common and popular in the context of the Python language.

Index

D

data descriptor 93
data uniqueness 488
deadlock 424
decorator pattern 472
decorators
  about 56, 57
  as class 58
  as functions 58
  implementations 57, 58
  introspection preserving 60, 61
  parametrizing 59, 60
  syntax 57, 58
defaultdict 403
delayed processing
  using 406-409
demand-side platforms (DSP) 229
dependency compatibility 358
dependency matrix testing 358-361
deque 401, 402
descriptor protocol 92
design patterns
  about 467
  behavioral patterns 490
  creational patterns 467
  structural patterns 471
deterministic caching 412-414
deterministic profiler 370
development mode 162
devpi
  URL 197
dictionaries
  about 45, 46
  implementation details 47
  weaknesses and alternatives 48
distributed systems
  about 268, 269
  distributed strategies 270
Distributed VCS (DVCS) 268
Django REST Framework
  URL 113
django-userena project
  URL 359
doctest
  about 337, 339
  URL 333

doctest module
  reference link 128
documentation
  building 308
  portfolio, building 308, 309
documentation portfolio 308
Document-Driven Development (DDD)
  about 362
  story, writing 362, 363
document landscape 308
Domain Specific Language (DSL) 102
Dublin Core information
  reference link 473
Dylan programming language
  URL 83
dynamic libraries, without extensions
  ctypes 255
  interfacing 255

E

Elasticsearch 220
Epydoc
  reference link 314
eval() 117, 118
event-driven programming
  reference link 490
exec
  about 117
  URL 117
executors
  and futures 462, 463
  using, in event loop 464
extensions
  custom datatypes, creating 230
  Cython 248
  existing code written in different languages,
    integrating 229
  performance, improving in critical code
    sections 228, 229
  pure C extensions 231-233
  third-party dynamic libraries,
    integrating 230
  using 228
  writing 230, 231
extra commands 153
eXtreme Programming (XP) 277

function annotations, using 479-484
zope.interface, using 475-478
interpreter directive 175
IOPS (Input Output Operations Per Second) 222
IPython
about 30
URL 30
ironclad
URL 15
IronPython
about 14, 15
URL 14
isolation 207, 208
iterators 51, 52

J

Jenkins
about 282-286
advantages 284
reference link 282
Jython
about 14
URL 14

K

Kibana 221
kilo pystones 379

L

landscape, building
about 316
consumer's layout 318-320
producer's layout 317
lazily loaded modules 7
linearization 83
Liskov substitution principle 495
lists
about 40
comprehensions 42, 43
external calls, cutting 400
implementation details 41
other idioms 43, 44
searching in 399
set, using instead 400

workload, reducing 400
load tests 332
logrotate 220
Logstash 220

M

macro-profiling 371-375
MacroPy project
URL 119
MD5 418
memcached 416-418
memoizing
URL 64
memory_profiler
URL 383
memory usage, bottlenecks
C code memory 390
memory, profiling 382, 383
memory, usage 379-382
objgraph 384-389
profiling 379
Memprof
URL 383
metaclasses
new Python 3 syntax 112-114
pitfalls 115, 116
syntax 109-112
usage 115
metaheuristics 406
meta hooks 120
metaprogramming
about 102
class decorators 103-105
methods 103
metaclasses 108
Method Resolution Order (MRO) 82
MFC framework
reference link 490
micro-profiling 375-377
Millions Of Whetstone Instructions Per Second (MWIPS)
URL 378
mixedCase 132
mocks
using 356, 357

conventions and practices 207
Filesystem Hierarchy Standard 207
isolation 207, 208
processes, reloading 211, 212
process supervision tools, using 208-210
reverse HTTP proxies, using 210, 211
rules 189
URL 189
type annotations
reference link 486

U

unittest
about 333-335
alternatives 340
pitfalls 339, 340
URL 333
unit tests 331
usage, portfolio
about 310
module helper 311-314
recipe 311
tutorial 311-313
user acceptance tests 330
uWSGI
reference link 428

V

Vagrant
using, for virtual development
environments 26, 27
Valgrind 390
variables
arguments 134
classes 135
constants 128
functions 131
methods 132
modules 135
naming 129, 130
packages 135

private controversy 132, 133
private variable 130, 131
properties 134
public variable 130
special methods 134
usage 129, 130
Vehicle Routing Problem (VRP) 405
venv
about 23
URL 23
version control systems (VCS)
about 265
centralized systems 266-268
centralized version control systems 271
distributed systems 268
Git flow 272-276
GitHub flow 272-276
Git, using 271
virtualenv 21-23
virtualization
versus containerization 28
visitor pattern 492-495

W

wireshark
URL 391
worst-case complexity 398

X

XML-RPC protocol
URL 62

Y

yield statement 53-56

Z

Zope Component Architecture (ZCA)
about 471
reference link 472

CPSIA information can be obtained
at www.ICGtesting.com
Printed in the USA
FSOW03n2343201216
28754FS